THE HERMENEUTIC TRADITION

SUNY series, Intersections:
Philosophy and Critical Theory

Rodolphe Gasché and Mark C. Taylor, Editors

The Hermeneutic Tradition

From Ast to Ricoeur

Edited by

Gayle L. Ormiston and Alan D. Schrift

STATE UNIVERSITY OF NEW YORK PRESS

Published by
State University of New York Press, Albany

©1990   State University of New York

For information, address State University of New York
Press, State University Plaza, Albany NY   12246

Library of Congress Cataloging-in-Publication Data

The Hermeneutic tradition : from Ast to Ricoeur / edited by Gayle L.
   Ormiston and Alan D. Schrift.
       p.   cm.—(SUNY series, intersections. Philosophy and
   critical theory)
     Bibliography: p.
     Includes index.
     ISBN 0-7914-0136-7. —ISBN 0-7914-0137-5 (pbk.)
     1. Hermeneutics.   I. Ormiston, Gayle L., 1951-   .   II. Schrift,
   Alan D., 1955-   .   III. Series: Intersections (Albany, N.Y.)
   BD241.H355   1990
   121'.68—dc 19   89-4173
                                                                            CIP

10 9 8 7 6 5 4 3 2 1

Contents

Preface

There are certain unavoidable risks incurred in any attempt to catalogue a tradition. When this project began, we hoped to present certain canonical statements on hermeneutics from the nineteenth and twentieth centuries with certain current perspectives on the "practices" of interpretation theory that stand both within and apart from what might be called the "classical hermeneutical tradition." In the process of deciding which representative texts to include, we realized that the breadth and depth of such an endeavor made impractical the binding of these diverse interpretive perspectives within one volume. Faced with eliminating or abridging certain selections, or dividing the project into two books that would reflect our "original intention" to juxtapose both familiar and contemporary voices within the tradition, the choice was clear. Because of our commitment to presenting relatively complete expressions that display both recognized and unexpected continuities, we divided the material in terms of the marked differences between the authors' interpretations of interpretive practices. We believe *The Hermeneutic Tradition: From Ast to Ricoeur* can stand alone. But we hope the connections with its companion, *Transforming the Hermeneutic Context: From Nietzsche to Nancy*, will be as apparent to the reader as they have been to its editors throughout the life of the project.

There are many individuals and institutions without whose assistance the completion of this project would not have been possible. For their encouragement and valuable support, we wish to thank our families, friends, and colleagues. Special thanks are due to Eric Blondel, Fred Dallmayr, Rodolphe Gasché, David E. Linge, Jean-Luc Nancy, Richard Palmer, Paul Ricoeur, John Sallis, and Calvin O. Schrag. For their time and expertise in generously contributing their translations, we thank George H. Leiner, John B. Thompson, and Dora Van Vranken. Further, we would like to acknowledge the financial, secretarial, and computer services support provided by the University of Colorado at Colorado Springs, Grinnell College, Denison University, Purdue University, and the University of California at Riverside. Additional major funding was supplied to Gayle L. Ormiston by the University of Colorado's Committee on Research and Creative Works and the President's Fund for the Humanities, and to Alan D. Schrift by the American Council of Learned Societies Fellowship for Modern Society and

Values and the Grinnell College Grant Board. And for their valuable assistance during the preparation of the final manuscript, we thank Carola Sautter, Dana Foote, and Susan Zorn.

    Finally, above all we would like to express our individual and joint appreciation and thanks to Lynn and Jill for their unwavering support during the several years it took to complete our work.

                                        G. L. O. and A. D. S.

Acknowledgments

We gratefully acknowledge the kind permission of the following publishers, authors, and translators to reprint, and in some cases translate, the works included in this volume.

D. Reidel Publishing, Jan Wojcik, and Roland Haas, for permission to reprint Friedrich D. E. Schleiermacher, "The Aphorisms on Hermeneutics from 1805, and 1809–10," originally published in *Cultural Hermeneutics* 4, no. 4 (1977): 367–90.

The Johns Hopkins University Press, Jan Wojcik, and Roland Haas, for permission to reprint Friedrich D.E. Schleiermacher, "*The Hermeneutics*: Outline of the 1819 Lectures," originally published in *New Literary History*, 10, no.1 (Autumn 1978): 1–16.

The Johns Hopkins University Press, for permission to reprint Wilhelm Dilthey, "The Rise of Hermeneutics," originally published in *New Literary History* 3, no. 2 (Winter 1972): 230–44.

Harper and Row, Publishers, Inc., for permission to reprint Martin Heidegger, *Being and Time*, translated by John Macquarrie and Edward Robinson, pages 182–210. Copyright © 1962 by SCM Press, Ltd.

The University of California Press and David E. Linge, for kind permission to reprint Hans-Georg Gadamer, "The Universality of the Hermeneutical Problem," originally published in Hans-Georg Gadamer, *Philosophical Hermeneutics*, translated by David E. Linge, pages 3–17. Copyright © by the University of California Press, 1977.

Associated Book Publishers (incorporating Routledge and Kegan Paul), for permission to reprint Emilio Betti, "Hermeneutics as the General Methodology of the *Geisteswissenschaften*," originally published in *Contemporary Hermeneutics: Hermeneutics as method, philosophy and critique*, edited and translated by Josef Bleicher, pages 51–94. Copyright © by Routledge and Kegan Paul, 1980.

Crossroad/Continuum Publishing Corporation, for permission to reprint the "Introduction" and "Foreword to the Second Edition" of Hans-Georg Gadamer, *Truth and Method*, translated by John Cumming and Garrett Barden, pages xi–xxvi. English translation copyright © by Sheed and Ward, Ltd. 1975.

The University of Notre Dame Press and Fred R. Dallmayr, for kind permission to reprint Jürgen Habermas, "A Review of Gadamer's *Truth and Method*," English translation by Fred R. Dallmayr and Thomas A. McCarthy first reprinted in *Understanding and Social Inquiry*, edited by Fred R. Dallmayr and Thomas A. McCarthy, pages 335–63. Copyright © by the University of Notre Dame Press, 1977.

Associated Book Publishers (incorporating Routledge and Kegan Paul), for permission to reprint Jürgen Habermas, "The Hermeneutic Claim to Universality," originally published in *Contemporary Hermeneutics: Hermeneutics as method, philosophy, and critique*, edited and translated by Josef Bleicher, pages 181–212. Copyright © by Routledge and Kegan Paul, 1980.

Suhrkamp Verlag and Hans-Georg Gadamer, for permission to translate and publish Hans-Georg Gadamer, "Replik," originally published in *Hermeneutik und Ideologiekritik*, pages 283–317. Copyright © by Suhrkamp Verlag Frankfurt am Main, 1971.

Cambridge University Press and John B. Thompson, for permission to reprint Paul Ricoeur, "Hermeneutics and the Critique of Ideology," originally published in *Hermeneutics and the Human Sciences*, edited and translated by John B. Thompson, pages 63–100. Copyright © by Cambridge University Press, 1981.

Editors' Introduction

Gayle L. Ormiston and Alan D. Schrift

I know not what to say to it; but experience makes it manifest, that so many interpretations dissipate the truth, and break it . . . Who will not say that glosses augment doubts and ignorance, since there is no book to be found, either human or divine, which the world busies itself about, whereof the difficulties are cleared by interpretation. The hundredth commentator passes it on to the next, still more knotty and perplexed than he found it. When were we ever agreed among ourselves: "this book has enough; there is now no more to be said about it?" . . . do we find any end to the need of interpreting? is there, for all that, any progress or advancement toward peace, or do we stand in need of any fewer advocates and judges? . . . There is more ado to interpret interpretations than to interpret things; and more books upon books than upon any other subject; we do nothing but comment upon one another. Every place swarms with commentaries . . . Is it not the common and final end of all studies? Our opinions are grafted upon one another; the first serves as a stock to the second, the second to the third, and so forth . . .

—Michel de Montaigne, *Essays*[1]

The "Experience" of Interpretation:
"there are only interpretations . . ."

Montaigne's comments on interpretation, cited here, appear in an essay entitled "Of Experience." In this essay, Montaigne begins with an allusion to Aristotle's famous dictum: "All men by nature desire to know."[2] Montaigne writes: "There is no desire more natural than that of knowledge. We try all ways that can lead us to it; where reason is wanting, we therein employ experience."[3] What follows this paraphrase is a *gloss*; it is an interpretation of the thought that opens Aristotle's *Metaphysics*, introducing the single, very complex theme which, momentarily, orders Montaigne's musings. In short, the gloss "interprets" Aristotle while it simultaneously

1

"interprets" *itself*, inserting itself into the Aristotelian text and tradition. Beyond offering an exegesis of the thought that organizes Montaigne's commentary, in a provisional fashion, there is a rewriting, indeed a reformulation, of a thought which eclipses the epistemological and metaphysical tradition that binds Montaigne.

By way of a *commentary* that turns away from itself, toward a different text, *and* that turns in on itself, Montaigne articulates a line of inquiry inextricably inscribed in a certain epistemological and metaphysical tradition of Western thought. Montaigne's text, then, announces a sentiment that has come to regulate and provide a refuge for a particular current in contemporary philosophical analysis: "there are only interpretations of interpretations." The name given to this inquiry, and the line(s) of thought it has produced, is *"hermeneutics."* It is the purpose of the selections collected in this volume, under the title *The Hermeneutic Tradition: From Ast to Ricoeur*, to trace certain *paths* traversed within selected discourse(s) and tradition(s) of hermeneutics in the nineteenth and twentieth centuries. To be sure, like Montaigne's *Essays*, each of the selections presented in this volume can be seen as an interpretation of interpretations, announcing once again—rethinking and rewriting—hermeneutics and its fundamental motifs.[4]

*
* *

Where reason, in its different forms and capacities, takes into account the resemblance and similitude among ideas and objects, Montaigne claims that the conclusions which can be drawn from these comparisons are always "unsure" and incomplete. "There is no quality so universal in this image of things, as diversity and variety."[5] Resemblance and similitude simultaneously betray and employ difference(s). As such, dissimilitude, difference, and dissimulation intrude upon all of our works, judgments, and pronouncements. "Resemblance does not so much make one, as difference makes another. Nature has obliged herself to make nothing other, that was not unlike."[6]

What promise does this condition hold for those analyses interested in explicating the "nature" of knowledge? If knowledge claims are "grounded" in the otherness of that point where resemblance and difference converge, the "nature" of knowledge can be neither certain nor uncertain. As a consequence, the authority as well as the legitimacy of epistemological claims, and those metaphysical and ontological claims made regarding the "nature" of understanding, and our understanding of nature, must be suspended. The only recourse we have, the only "law" to which we can turn to adjudicate the differences and legitimate our assertions, is *interpretation*—to comment upon, to analyze the announcements, the discourses, the texts offered in behalf and in support of various theoretical and practical positions.

Resemblance, difference, and similitude converge in acts of interpretation; through individual *acts* of interpreting, our sensibilities are challenged, our expectations are confirmed or subverted. Thus, whatever claims to truth are advanced, even about the concept "truth" itself, the authority and the significance—the "truth"—of these claims is dispersed, placed in circulation through a proliferation of interpretations. "We exchange one word for another, and often for one less understood."[7] And so, Montaigne asks, is this not our common experience, in the end, in all fields of study?

In the idiom of contemporary, Western philosophical discourse, the exchange of "one word for another" is an analogue for the substitution of one interpretation for another. To invoke two technical terms taken from the grammatology of Jacques Derrida, we might say it is the "supplementation" or "reinscription" of interpretation by interpretation:[8] that is to say, it is the grafting of one text to others, the "sharing" or "multiplication" of voices in dialogue, as identified by Jean-Luc Nancy.[9] In fact, Montaigne's gloss offers an apt description of the context in which, and the conditions out of which, today, one encounters the question of interpretation in philosophy, literary criticism, film studies, art criticism, the theories of "natural" and "social" science, jurisprudence, psychoanalysis, feminist theory, theology, and other fields. If "there are only interpretations . . . of interpretations," then the systematic pursuit of "truth"— "truth" as the *object* of inquiry—or the search for axiological, epistemological, and metaphysical foundations, will never be brought to completion. Is this not *a* central consequence of the hermeneutical circle, or, at the very least, of the chain of discourses and interpretations which identify and determine the "hermeneutical circle"?[10] The search after truth, as it were, is deferred, diverted, caught in a network of contextually bound and generated commentaries. Here we begin to see how the proposition that "there are only interpretations of interpretations" is intertwined with and conditioned by certain classical problems. In particular, one may consider the question of reference, especially as it emanates from what Hegel calls the desire for *absolute knowledge*.

The problem of reference arises in this context for the following reasons. The desire for absolute knowledge is the desire to make present the fundamental unity or ground of knowledge and understanding through the unveiling of *self-evident* first principles and truths. But there is a more significant presumption which involves reference and signification. The ideal object of this desire—"truth," metaphysical "first principles" of "self" and "God," the Kantian "thing in-itself," or Husserlian transcendental conditions—is presumed to stand outside or independent of the linguistic framework, the interpretive context in which it is *"re-presented."* Here interpretation—"hermeneutics," more appropriately—intervenes; it must come to terms with certain questions regarding the status of its *object*, the representation of that object, and the relation(s) between our commentaries, "interpretations," and the object *itself*.

Does interpretation lead or extend beyond itself? Does it refer to an "external" world, a specific field of objects that stands outside the linkage of interpretations? Is there a necessary connection assumed between interpretation and its object, a "text" or *the* ("intended") meaning of a text? Does interpretation exhaust itself in its attempt to reveal *its* object? Does it exhaust its object in this attempt? In the language of semiology, we might ask, analogously, if there is a necessary connection assumed between signifier and signified.[11] If interpretation *is* connected to the world in varying ways, what conditions make this connection possible? Is language not the medium for making such links and references? If so, is language anything other than a system of signs, coherent and systematic marks for representation and communication? What would allow for any kind of reference outside the system? Or is language to be understood as an open-ended system of signs and traces that refer only to other signs and traces ad infinitum? Does not the determination of referential conditions and possibilities itself introduce the question of interpretation? Is this determination not an interpretive intervention?

As these questions indicate, interpretation, hermeneutics, and the attendant claim that "there are only interpretations . . . " are not merely conditioned by the desire for absolute knowledge and the problem of reference. The act of interpreting—always and already bound to a chain of interpretations, which is not to say a predetermined meaning or set of possible meanings—stands in complicity with the desire for absolute knowledge: interpretation works on behalf of absolute knowledge *and* it struggles to free itself from the all-encompassing framework of the desire for absolute knowledge. Interpretation, or what Montaigne calls "the need to interpret," mediates, and, in effect, is mediated by this desire. As a consequence of this complicity, the act of interpreting, especially if comprehended as an act of *creating connections*, reintroduces the question of unity and harmony, that is to say, *totality*. Creating connections could be understood in accordance to Wilhelm Dilthey's notion of *Zusammenhang*,[12] as well as Julia Kristeva's reformulation of the (Aristotelian and) Stoic conception of interpretation, where "to interpret" means "to make a connection."[13] It reformulates, it translates, if you will, the question of the unity of knowledge and understanding into question*s* concerning the unity of sign and signified, of word and object, the harmony of language and reality, of thought and reality, of thought and action. Given this set of conditions, we might answer Montaigne's question "Do we find any end to the need of interpreting?" by asking "How could we find an end to this need when interpretation disguises itself in so many ways, when interpretation masks itself and its desire for absolute knowledge in the drive toward satiety?" How could we find an end to this need to interpret when, apparently, by its very production and introduction, interpretation defers and transforms its object, and the path it follows (or blazes) in its desire to reveal its object? Is this not a condition which perpetuates the need to interpret?

"Like everything metaphysical," writes Ludwig Wittgenstein in *Zettel*, "the harmony between thought and reality is to be found in the grammar of the language."[14] Like Montaigne's gloss on the Aristotelian metaphysical text and tradition, Wittgenstein's remark points directly to a general issue emanating from the question of interpretation: the congruence and compatibility of discourse (language, interpretation) and the "meaning" of human-being, thereby raising the question of understanding the discourse of others. If, in general, the condition of discourse is one where we are unable to thwart the need to interpret, then it should come as no surprise that finally, today, "after two thousand years" of submission to the axiom "the Word became flesh,"[15] we are coming to recognize the far-reaching implications in having "achieved a discourse on discourse, an interpretation of interpretation."[16] And yet, to recognize this achievement is to acknowledge our quandary: the word, propositions, words on words, interpretations mediate and betray our understanding, our acts, the experience of interpretation.[17]

With the recognition of this condition, what fascinates the imagination, and what provokes the critical skills and sensibilities of our discourse today, is the *difference* of interpretation, that is to say, the conflict(s) that arises in and through the attempts to offer a commentary on another text, discourse, or analysis. However, one might ask: "What hangs on this difference—the difference of interpretation?" Here the difference, the conflict, the incommensurability of interpretation(s) (or Wittgensteinian "language-games") demonstrates, ironically, how the proposition "there are only interpretations . . . " cannot be granted the status of law, cannot be taken as a first principle nor as the last word. Stated otherwise: interpretation cannot be taken for granted; meaning is not a given with interpretation; its path(s) must be determined.[18] The proposition is, itself, an announcement of the conditions which make interpretation possible as the interpretation of interpretation. It subverts its own claim to "truth." But this is only one concern among many, and the fascination with interpretation theory or hermeneutics does not end here, nor is it to be limited to the issues addressed in this discussion.

Today, one can imagine a contemporary Montaigne asking whether there is a book, any text, that presents *the* word, *another* gospel, a "new" testament regarding a particular subject matter or thematic complex. Is there a text, today, that espouses a certain critical perspective or theory, about which one could say it has offered the last word, about which one could assert that a consensus has been reached? At the very least, can one agree with its proclamation about how to reach consensus in order to resolve certain philosophical and political dilemmas? Is there a philosophical or political position, for example, taken toward specific questions which would bring one to the point of claiming that "there is now no more to be said about it"? By advancing any one of these claims, would we not do so both in opposition to the desire for absolute knowledge *and* in its name, both against the desire of *philo-sophia and* in its name as well?

The themes and questions identified in this all-too-provisional-and-all-too-brief exegesis of Montaigne's text are announced, suspended from a specific historical epoch and cultural and intellectual context. The issues and questions posed in Montaigne's essay, as they relate to the question of interpretation, have been translated into a foreign context and idiom, and displaced and rewritten for a purpose completely different from what may have given rise to their expression in Montaigne's *Essays*. In this regard, the displacement and translation of "Montaigne"—the proper name, the text, the questions, the interpretations, and so forth—illustrate some of the *consequences* engendered by the proposition that "there are only interpretations . . . of interpretations." "We come to what is tangible and conceivably practical," writes Charles Sanders Peirce, as the "ground" for the determination of meaning(s). Is this not what hangs on the difference of interpretation, or the *differance* of interpretation, to reiterate Derrida's neologism? Groundings? Foundations? Privileged sources? The practice of interpretation, or "active interpretation," is this ground. It provides its *own* condition of possibility, but one which always shifts under one's feet, and one which is fissured and fails to secure certainty. "[T]here is no distinction of meaning so fine as to consist in anything but a possible difference of practice."[19]

Like Montaigne's gloss of Aristotle, the reading of Montaigne's text is a reading between the lines, the insertion of disparate, different assumptions and interests between the lines of another text. If "there are only interpretations . . . ," then each gloss, each reading, becomes a textual intervention and provocation. Such a reading withdraws the "unity" of a text—here the totality of Montaigne's "thought"; it is always and already working toward other purposes, already attempting to achieve other ends. Like Montaigne's gloss, the reading of Montaigne's text, as it relates to the conditions surrounding the question of interpretation in a particular tradition of contemporary Western thought, is always selective, fragmentary, and incomplete, while remaining constitutive of its object and itself. As Michel Foucault remarks, an interpretation "always has to interpret itself . . . [it] cannot fail to return to itself."[20] This is the "experience" of interpretation to which Montaigne refers: interpretation finds itself always positioned, as it comments on other "texts," to comment on itself endlessly, "always correcting itself."[21] This is the "life of interpretation,"[22] and this "experience," this practice, this "life," constituting the complex domain of hermeneutics, is the subject for the essays included in this volume.

To advance the proposition that "there are only interpretations of interpretations," or to focus, however provisionally, on the "life of interpretation," then, is to survey one site, among many, in the field of hermeneutics whereby the question of interpretation (both as a problematic and as the subject of an interrogation) can be isolated. It is not an attempt to reduce the question of interpretation or hermeneutics to any one specific theme or set of issues. It is, however, to take account of the heterogeneity of the so-called "hermeneutic tradition."

Moreover, to advance this proposition, to provide this focus, is not an attempt to perpetuate or to give primacy of place to an aloof or disengaged academic debate (though one cannot prohibit this as a possible consequence). At the most rudimentary level of comprehension, interpretation— the exchange of words for words, what others might call "dialogue"—is concerned with the "world," "reality," the historical, cultural, political, economic, technological context or setting into which it is inserted, and against which it is asserted. Interpretation does not release or disengage us from the world. To the contrary, it is through interpretation that we engage the world, our surroundings; through the act of interpretation the world becomes what it *is*, a "text."[23] Interpretation sets the stage for engagement: we draw the world closer to us through words and language. As with any text, we represent its heterogeneity to ourselves and others; we demonstrate our comprehension of this world through words and language; we articulate our needs and desires, our joys and disappointments, our questions and insights, on the basis of interpretation(s).[24] On the basis of this kind of engagement, these interpretive interventions, we seek and determine, again provisionally, the rules which regulate our actions. But, if our interpretive interventions and provocations lead in these directions, do they not already engage certain assumptions regarding basic categories of

thought, and their attendant dichotomies—categories that regulate our efforts to comprehend action and discourse? Is the determination of these
presumed categories not itself an *issue* of interpretation?

Furthermore, to advance the proposition that "there are only interpretations . . . ," to insist upon the "experience" of interpretation as a transitory point of focus, is one way to bring into relief a complex set of issues
which traverses the history of hermeneutics. The concern with interpreting
the words or speech of an other, for example, in light of the duplicitous
character of language, is given one of its earliest treatments by Plato's
Socrates in the *Cratylus*. Hermes, as his *name* indicates (herald and messenger of other gods, the god of science and cunning, the protector of
boundaries, or so the story goes), is an interpreter, "or messenger, or thief,
or liar, or bargainer; all that sort of thing has a great deal to do with language." (408a–b).[25] Hermes is represented as a "contriver of tales or
speeches." That "speech signifies all things, and is always turning them
round and round" (408c), as Socrates announces somewhat ironically, has
little to do with Hermes himself. What is important, in this context, is not
that Hermes is responsible for the duplicitous character of language and
interpretation, except that he "invented language and speech." It is more to
the point to note that if Hermes is responsible, it is because he "invents"
through the *use* of language. Throughout the dialogues of Plato, as Jean-
Luc Nancy points out through his reading of *Ion*,[26] it is "the word" which
mediates the experience of "all things." *Use* creates, ordering the linguistic
field which it engages and the interpretive boundaries of that field. Thus, it
is the self-production, the self-effacement of language, in this case the dialogue, which twists and turns words through their use, that determines (1)
how one understands the ideas and objects one encounters, (2) *what* one
understands *about* these ideas and objects, and (3) *that* understanding is
possible. Linguistic meaning is determined in and through the dialogue,
itself the scene or stage on which the experience of interpretation is played
out.[27]

The experience of interpretation, as Montaigne's text insinuates,
founds itself on the recognition that language, in a general and systematic
fashion, and individual acts of interpretation, in particular, generate the
conditions and limits of and for the possibility of understanding. As already
noted, Plato's dialogues—specifically, the *Cratylus* and *Ion*—take into account this feature of interpretation and understanding. In a concomitant
fashion, Aristotle's *Peri hermēneias* (*De Interpretatione*, *On Interpretation*),
a text which by *name* alone, if not by content, has become the ostensible
source for many of the themes and questions addressed in the discourse of
hermeneutics, argues for the "linguistic" determination of meaning.[28]

On Interpretation is one of six treatises included in Aristotle's *Organon*. The *Organon*, in general, deals with issues of logic: the principles of argumentation and the techniques of proof or demonstration. Within this domain, *On Interpretation* holds an *intermediary* position among the first three of the six treaties; its subject—*hermēneia*, interpretation—mediates the concerns of *Categories*, which precedes it in the *Organon*, and the *Prior Analytics*, which follows it. Where the *Categories* articulates the classical notion of Substance (chapter 5), the differentiation of substance according to the categories of objects of thought (chapter 4), and uncombined simple terms (chapter 2), the subject of *On Interpretation* is the combination of terms in propositions, the relation of terms, and how any understanding of propositions includes the expression of "truth" or "falsity" (4 17a 1–8). The *Prior Analytics*, then, is concerned with the derivation of inference based upon a set or combination of propositions that, in the end, is expressive of the relation between thought and what it predicates (1 24b 5–20).

The subject of *On Interpretation* is decidedly linguistic, even though at the outset its problematic overlaps with that of *De Anima* (*On the Soul*) (1 16a 7–8). But for Aristotle's purposes, *hermēneia* is to be separated from rhetoric and poetry. *On Interpretation* analyzes the character of propositions: a proposition is a sentence that expresses something true or false about the world. According to Aristotle, "propositions correspond with facts" (9 19a 33–34). Other kinds of sentences or statements, such as, a prayer (4 17a 4), poetry, and a question and an answer (*Poetics* 19 1456b 8–10), are subsumed by the study of rhetoric or poetics.

All propositions, according to Aristotle, simple or complex, indicate a fact or facts, by way of universal and particular affirmation or negation. Propositions are significant because they are presentations of either "mental experience" or "spoken words," depending on whether they are expressed as spoken words or written words. "Spoken words are the symbols [representations] of mental experience and written words are the symbols [representations] of spoken words" (*On Interpretation* 1 16a 3–4). Thus, every proposition has meaning because it is the function of the *combination* and *disjunction* of symbols. As Socrates' depiction of Hermes' "invention" of language points out, meaning is created by use, by "the limitation of convention" (2 16a 19–29). A noun or a name, a sentence or a proposition, has meaning, or is part of meaningful discourse, because it *represents, expresses* something about some-thing. The connections, the relations that exist between the symbol and that which it represents, between spoken words and mental experience, between written words and spoken words, are not natural, but the products of "convention."[29]

In the idiom of Montaigne's discourse on interpretation, we can see how Aristotle's concern with understanding propositions, which are themselves "symbols," "representations," "interpretations" of facts, and as such "correspond" with facts, can be comprehended according to another proposition, "there are only interpretations . . . " The proposition makes an announcement; it announces the experience, the life of interpretation, through the interpretation of the other.

*

* *

The point here is not to gloss over the differences that distinguish the ancient texts of Plato and Aristotle from each other and the texts of Montaigne, or for that matter any of the texts selected for this volume. Indeed, if there is one moment in the experience or life of interpretation which we would hope to celebrate and to embrace, it is the *difference/différance* of interpretation (reading, writing, understanding) that makes possible the continued reiteration of terms, ideas, and concepts from one philosophical epoch to another. We are situated within certain historically and linguistically different contexts, and the repetition of terms, ideas, and concepts entails the transformation of their force and significance. As the epigraph from Montaigne notes, "Our opinions [interpretations] are grafted upon one another; the first serves as a stock to the second, the second to the third, and so forth." When we reinscribe these hermeneutic motifs, when we trace the paths blazed in their formulation, we interpret, we translate, these motifs according to a different set of desires and interests. And yet, "Whatever and however we may try to think, we think within the sphere of tradition."[30] This interpretive transformation involves the displacement of old concepts; it involves leaping, as Wittgenstein says, "from one level of thought to another."[31] The task, then, is to record the difference(s)/ *différance* of interpretation, the experience of interpretation, not by blurring the conflicts and confrontations but by affirming the differences and points of divergence and appropriation as making possible a preliminary articulation of the proposition "there are only interpretations . . . of interpretations."

Toward this end, we have divided the selections included in this collection into two parts: I. The Hermeneutic Legend, and II. Hermeneutics and Critical Theory: Dialogues on Methodology. Part I includes selections from the nineteenth and twentieth centuries that help to identify the tradition of hermeneutics according to a definite line of thought and style of discourse. In effect, the selections from Friedrich Ast, Friedrich Schleiermacher, Wilhelm Dilthey, and Martin Heidegger create the "historical" background against which the issues and themes pursued in part II will be configured.[32]

Part II brings together certain post-Heideggerian lines of debate that surround the hermeneutic project inaugurated in Hans-Georg Gadamer's *Truth and Method*. Assembled in this section are selections by Gadamer, Emilio Betti, Jürgen Habermas, and Paul Ricoeur that address two intertwining points of contention: (1) the "universality" and methodology of the hermeneutic project, as it is stated in Gadamer's philosophical hermeneutics, and the "objective status" of interpretation argued for by Betti, as it pertains to the Diltheyan notion of *Geisteswissenschaften*; and (2) how the hermeneutic claim of "universality" contends with or accommodates the critique of ideology, as articulated by Habermas. In terms of their historical and philosophical import, the debates contained in part II are germinal. They incorporate and cast anew certain fundamental concerns expressed in the writings of Ast, Schleiermacher, Dilthey, and Heidegger. The textual exchanges between Gadamer and Betti, Gadamer and Habermas, and Ricoeur and Gadamer and Habermas can be cast not only against the historical context of the selections that appear in part I. These texts demonstrate once more, in a different context, in their respective ways, the force of Montaigne's remark regarding the experience of interpretation. Part I focuses on the historical and conceptual foundations, broadly construed, for modern hermeneutics. Part II offers a concentrated look at the leitmotifs of post-Heideggerian hermeneutics, isolated by their articulation in several "dialogues" and "debates" regarding hermeneutical method and universality, and the objectivity and critical force of interpretation.

Part I: The Hermeneutic Legend

The modern use of the term "hermeneutics" can be traced to the work of Friedrich Schleiermacher and Wilhelm Dilthey. In general, Schleiermacher is credited with taking the first steps toward establishing a *general* hermeneutic methodology in contrast to a variety of *regional* hermeneutic approaches. Prior to Schleiermacher, the task of textual interpretation was thought to require different methods as determined by the type of text to be interpreted. Thus, legal texts gave rise to a juridical hermeneutic, sacred scripture to a biblical hermeneutic, literary texts to a philological hermeneutic, and so on. Friedrich Ast's work in philology, along with the writings of Friedrich August Wolf, exemplifies the sort of regional hermeneutics that provides the foundations for Schleiermacher's speculations on a "general hermeneutic."

The first selection in part I is by Friedrich Ast, whose *Basic Elements of Grammar, Hermeneutics, and Criticism* (1808) is cited by Schleiermacher for asserting the basic principles of the hermeneutic circle.[33] According to Ast, the aim of philology is to comprehend the spirit (*Geist*) of antiquity as transmitted through literary texts. To achieve this goal, a knowledge of the language ("Grammar") is necessary. In addition, we require principles for understanding antiquity and explaining its written works. Hermeneutics will supply these principles, and Ast offers a three-part framework for understanding ancient authors and their works: (1) historical understanding of the content of their works; (2) grammatical understanding of their language and style; and (3) spiritual understanding of the total *Geist* of the individual and their age (section 74). With this third form of understanding, one recognizes the significance of Ast's contributions to hermeneutics.

In his discussion of spiritual understanding, Ast identifies the circular structure of understanding. Because of what Ast terms the "original unity of all being" (section 72), which we call "spirit," understanding must be forged in the context of a dialectical relation between part and whole: "the basic principle of all understanding and knowledge is to find in the particular the spirit of the whole, and to comprehend the particular through the whole" (section 76). Through this circular framework, hermeneutics seeks to extract and to illuminate the inner meaning and spirit of the text through its own internal development. As such, the elucidation of the internal textual meaning must take into account the work's relation to the historical epoch in which it appears.

The threefold conception of understanding leads Ast to distinguish between three corresponding forms of explication (*Erklärung*): (1) the hermeneutics of the letter (section 83); (2) the hermeneutics of meaning (section 84); and (3) the hermeneutics of the spirit (sections 85ff.). The hermeneutics of the letter involves an explanation of the particular words (grammatical understanding), subject matter (historical understanding), and, in general, a knowledge of the grammar and history of antiquity. The hermeneutics of meaning explains a particular meaning intended by the author with reference to the historical context in which the author's works first appeared. As such, this hermeneutic requires a knowledge of literary history as well as knowledge of the author's life. It is the task of the hermeneutics of meaning to explain, for example, why a passage from Aristotle's *Politics* might bear a very different meaning from the "same words" which might have appeared in Plato's *Republic*. The hermeneutics of textual spirit explains the textual passage in terms of the "one idea" that guides the text as a whole. Great art is unified, Ast says, around a foundational, controlling idea (*Grundidee*) (section 88), and an understanding of this idea will expose its presence in every aspect of the work. Lesser works exhibit a lesser unity, but, nevertheless, it is the task of spiritual hermeneutics to seek out the guiding idea in the case of literary writers, the *intuition* (*Anschauung*) in the case of empirical-historical writers, the *concept* (*Begriff*) in the case of logical-philosophical writers (section 85).

Expressed in the Romantic language of Herder and Hegel, and open to charges of idealism and psychologism, Ast's deliberations set the stage for the development of contemporary hermeneutics. With this inaugural articulation of (1) the hermeneutic circle (sections 75–76), (2) the dialectic of understanding and explication (section 77), (3) understanding as reproduction (section 80), and (4) the importance of literary history (section 84) and genre criticism (section 91), Ast provides the background for Schleiermacher to pursue the development of a *general* hermeneutics.

With Schleiermacher, hermeneutics addresses, for the first time, the phenomenon of understanding itself. In the first aphorism from 1805, Schleiermacher indicates his departure from Johann August Ernesti's (and Ast's) inclusion of explication within the scope of hermeneutics, conceived as the art of understanding. Schleiermacher's project of a "general hermeneutics," as announced in the opening sentence of his 1819 lecture on hermeneutics, seeks to uncover the interpretive techniques which operate universally within understanding. To make hermeneutics an art requires methodological formalization, and his early writings, as the selections included here reveal, oscillate between the exhortational and the programmatic.[34] On the one hand, we have his pleas to bring the tools of philology, biblical hermeneutics, and juristics together to create a universal art of understanding based on more or less formalized rules. On the other hand, we have his distinction between grammatical interpretation (with several "*canones*," including the hermeneutic circle: "the meaning of every word in a given passage must be determined in relation to its coexistence with the words surrounding it")[35] and technical interpretation. Because discourse is composed of two "elements"—the whole of language and the mind of the thinker—the art of understanding must grasp their interaction (pp. 86–7). Thus, this art will proceed by working out the dialectic between a grammatical interpretation, which lays out (*legt aus*) the objective rules for understanding a language in terms of its original audience, and a technical interpretation, which suggests ways to apprehend the thoughts of the author.

Whereas Schleiermacher's focus on language (p. 66) was to be his lasting contribution, his own hermeneutic theory subordinates the understanding of language to the goal of understanding as the reconstruction of an author's mental life. His hermeneutics, thus, takes on what some regard to be an overtly "psychologistic" tone: the goal of hermeneutics is to understand the "original" meaning of a text, "to understand the discourse just as well as and even better than its creator." (p. 93)[36] This goal will be attained through a psychological reconstruction of the author; the interpreter must project oneself "inside" the author and re-construct the original imposition of a univocal sense (p. 81). Conceived in this way, hermeneutics is bound by a basic limitation: the author's intended meaning must guide the interpretation, the sole aim of which is to appropriate this original authorial intent.[37]

Wilhelm Dilthey follows Schleiermacher's call for a general hermeneutic method. Like Schleiermacher, Dilthey sees hermeneutics as the "methodology of the understanding of recorded expressions."[38] But he is critical of Schleiermacher for limiting hermeneutics to the analysis of "understanding as a reexperiencing or reconstruction in its vital relationship to the process of literary production itself" (p. 110). Dilthey regards hermeneutics as having a broader epistemological application than that acknowledged by Schleiermacher, and he attempts to broaden the scope of hermeneutic methodology to facilitate the acquisition of knowledge of *all* aspects of mental (*geistige*) life. The aim of hermeneutics is to concern itself with all objects in which human life is expressed. So, Dilthey writes, in addition to the "philological procedures" delineated in Schleiermacher's work, hermeneutics has

> a further purpose behind such theorizing, indeed its *main* purpose: to preserve the general validity of interpretation against the inroads of romantic caprice and skeptical subjectivity, and to give a theoretical justification for such validity, upon which all the certainty of historical knowledge is founded. Seen in the context of the theory of knowledge, of logic, and the methodology of the human studies, the theory of interpretation becomes an essential connecting link between philosophy and the historical disciplines, an essential component in the foundation of the human studies themselves (p. 114).

In this remark, we see Dilthey's central task: as a response to the anti-Hegelian positivism of his day, Dilthey's hermeneutic method will provide a philosophical foundation for the human sciences (*Geisteswissenschaften*) that will be as secure as the foundation provided by the scientific method for natural sciences (*Naturwissenschaften*). To do so requires a definitive answer to the question "How is historical knowledge possible?" For Dilthey, the possibility of historical knowledge raises the question of how the knowing subject comes to know *objectively* that which has been subjectively created. Dilthey's answer to this question involves the process of understanding: although the facts of nature can be explained, facts concerning human life, both social and psychological, need to be understood. Dilthey's formulation of hermeneutic methodology is introduced in terms of the relation between lived experience, expression, and understanding. In lived experience (*Erlebnis*), human beings express themselves in meaningful ways and the task of the historical observer is to understand these experiences. What is expressed in lived experience is *Geist*, and, thus, expression (*Ausdruck*) is, strictly speaking, the objectification of the human mind or spirit. As the succession of these objectifications, history will be understood when "the individual processes which combine in the creation of this system can be sorted out and it can be shown what part each of them plays, both in the construction of the historical course of events in the mind-constructed world and in the discovery of its systematic nature."[39]

Understanding is, for Dilthey, the process in which one mind reconstructs the mental objectifications of another. It is "a rediscovery of the I in the Thou: the mind rediscovers itself at ever higher levels of complex involvement: this identity of the mind in the I and the Thou, in every subject of a community, in every system of a culture and finally, in the totality of mind and universal history, makes successful cooperation between different processes in the human studies possible."[40] Where Schleiermacher construed this reconstructive process in psychological terms, as the reproduction of the psychic state of the author, Dilthey directs understanding toward the reconstruction of the historical product, whether it is an event or an object. In emphasizing the objects or events produced by the mind rather than the mind per se, Dilthey avoids the problems of psychologism that have been associated with Schleiermacher's hermeneutics. He also makes it necessary to expand the perimeter(s) of the hermeneutic circle, for now the parts, in terms of which the whole is to be understood, must include a range of phenomena (historical background, social customs, cultural and political institutions, and so forth) ignored by Schleiermacher.

With the writings of Martin Heidegger a fundamental shift in the approach to and discourse of hermeneutics takes place. To overcome the epistemological limitations and methodological prohibitions which emerge in the works of Schleiermacher and Dilthey, Heidegger turns hermeneutic analysis toward the question of Being. Hermeneutics is no longer directed toward discovering the epistemological foundations of the human sciences, or the methodological principles which lead to objective knowledge in the *Geisteswissenschaften*. Instead, emphasis is placed on the disclosure of the ontological conditions which underlie such knowledge or claims to knowledge. As a methodology for the human sciences, Heidegger views the hermeneutic projects of Schleiermacher and Dilthey as derivative of hermeneutics' primordial signification, "through which the authentic meaning of Being, and also those basic structures of Being which Dasein itself possesses, are *made known* to Dasein's understanding of Being."[41] The hermeneutic of Dasein, "as an analytic of *existence*," is thus, for Heidegger, the point of departure for philosophy conceived as "universal phenomenological ontology.''[42] In other words, the first step on the way to fundamental ontology, as the uncovering of the meaning of Being, will be a hermeneutic inquiry into the structures of Being implicated in the activities of understanding and interpretation.

Understanding is revealed as one of our primordial ways of being-in-the-world. As understanding, Dasein projects its Being upon possibilities. Interpretation (*Auslegung*), as a possibility of understanding, is the working out, the laying out (*legt aus*) of possibilities projected by understanding. Interpretation is the articulation of what is projected in the understanding; it discloses what is already understood. To comprehend the relation between understanding and interpretation (the hermeneutic circle), we need to explicate the fore-structures of understanding, the as-structure of interpretation, and meaning as an existentiale of Dasein. As the laying out of what is already understood, interpretation takes place within the totality of our involvements with the world: that is to say, interpretation, as the articulation of understanding, involves seeing something *as* something. Even though this articulation may not be expressed, we do not perceive pure sense-data. We do not first perceive redness, roundness, glossiness and then, subsequently, impose the interpretation "apple." In one move, we appropriate the apple *as* red, *as* glossy, and so forth. All perception is always already interpretation, which is to say that interpretation is never a presuppositionless apprehension of what is presented to us. Rather, interpretation functions as the disclosive articulation of what we already understand through the fore-structures of understanding.

According to Heidegger, interpretation is always founded on a fore-having (*Vorhabe*), a fore-sight (*Vorsicht*), and a fore-conception (*Vorgriff*). By fore-having, Heidegger refers to the totality of involvements with Being that we already have and that we bring with us to each interpretive act. Fore-sight refers to the point of view that we have in advance of appropriation, the perspective we bring to the interpretive act. Fore-conception designates the conceptual reservoir that we hold in advance and bring to the interpretive act. To try to make this more concrete, consider the following example: your task is to interpret a short story by Kafka. Your fore-having would be your knowledge of language, your involvement with literature, and so on. Your fore-sight might include your understanding of literary genre, your political ideology, and so on. Your fore-conception might be your familiarity with other works by Kafka, your general conception of Kafka as a writer, and so on. Each fore-structure would play a part in the way you interpret the story. Thus, Heidegger claims that although we like to appeal to what "stands there" when we offer an interpretation, "one finds that 'what stands there' in the first instance is nothing other than the obvious undiscussed assumption of the person who does the interpreting'' (p. 123).

Meaning (*Sinn*), then, is articulated in the interpretive disclosure of understanding. Meaning is articulated when something becomes intelligible *as* something; deriving its structure from the fore-structures of understanding, meaning is disclosed as the interpretation lays bare that which makes possible what has been projected—the Being of the there—Dasein. Dasein alone has meaning, for meaning is an existentiale of Dasein rather than a property imposed on things. Only Dasein can be meaningful or meaningless, filled with meaning or without meaning. In other words, meaning is not an epistemological category—it is part of the ontological structure of Dasein which emerges as Dasein comes to articulate the as-structure of its Being *as* understanding.

Heidegger summarizes these points in his discussion of Dasein's structure as ontologically circular with respect to understanding, interpretation, and meaning. Dasein articulates meaning in the form of an interpretation. This interpretation is always grounded in a prior understanding, which is itself constituted by the fore-structures. Thus, what can be contributed to understanding by interpretation has already been understood. The circle, Heidegger claims, is not a vicious one. The point is not to avoid the circle but to recognize one's involvement in the circle already, thus revealing the way the fore-structures work in their genuine apprehension of Dasein's possibilities in relation to the things themselves which Dasein confronts.

The primordial status of understanding and interpretation in the analytic of *Being and Time* leads Heidegger to conclude that assertion (*Aussage*) is a derivative mode of interpretation. Assertion, like interpretation, is grounded in discourse (*Rede*) as the articulation of intelligibility. But assertions, by which Heidegger means predicative statements of the forms ''S is p'' (his example is ''The hammer is heavy''), are derivative because although, like interpretations, they are grounded in the fore-structures of understanding, they, unlike interpretations, leave these fore-structures unarticulated. As ''a pointing-out which gives something a definite character and which communicates'' (p. 129), assertion modifies the as-structure. For Heidegger, then, there is a difference between the ''existential-hermeneutic as'' of interpretation and the ''apophantic as'' of assertion. The ''hermeneutic as'' interprets something *as* something in the context of the totality of involvements which constitute the ''world,'' whereas the ''apophantic as'' indicates a particular property of an object as present-at-hand and ready for use. Assertion lets an entity to be seen from itself as having a definite property which can be communicated, and, as such, it is derivative of the "hermeneutic as" of interpretation, which allows an entity to be seen *as something* in its totality of involvements.

Part II: Hermeneutics and Critical Theory: Dialogues on Methodology

Although Heidegger stopped speaking of his project as "hermeneutical" shortly after the publication of *Being and Time*, the importance and influence of (his) situating hermeneutics within ontology rather than within epistemology should not be underestimated. In fact, many points of contention within hermeneutics involve debates regarding the placement of hermeneutics in one or the other of these realms of discourse. The readings that constitute part II chronicle certain post-Heideggerian debates that surround the hermeneutic project inaugurated by Hans-Georg Gadamer's *Truth and Method*.

Gadamer's "philosophical hermeneutics" elaborates Heidegger's phenomenological approach to hermeneutics by developing the Heideggerian insight into the "linguisticality" (*Sprachlichkeit*) of understanding. For Gadamer, "language is the universal medium in which understanding itself is realized and the mode or realization of language is interpretation."[43] Like Heidegger, Gadamer rejects limiting the scope of hermeneutical inquiry to problems "proper to the methodology of the human sciences" (p. 198). Hermeneutics is conceived as the study of "the phenomenon of understanding and of the correct interpretation of what has been understood." Insofar as all understanding is mediated by language, the task of hermeneutics is seen as a descriptive ontological analysis of the linguistically mediated dialogue between the tradition and the reflective appropriation of it.[44] Thus, Gadamer concludes that "language constitutes the hermeneutical event proper not as language, whether as grammar or as lexicon, but in the coming into language of that which has been said in the tradition: an event that is at once assimilation and interpretation."[45] Within language Gadamer locates a "universal ontological structure" insofar as language is a central point where "I" and world "manifest their original unity." For Gadamerian hermeneutical reflection, the universal ontological significance of linguisticality cannot be overestimated: "Being that can be understood is language."[46]

Gadamer's articulation of the universal scope of hermeneutics has led to several significant "dialogues" that incorporate and recast the fundamental concerns announced and analyzed by Ast, Schleiermacher, Dilthey, and Heidegger. From a historical perspective, the first of these dialogues took place between Gadamer and Emilio Betti, the Italian jurist and legal historian whose *Teoria generale della interpretazione* appeared in 1955.

Betti's response to Gadamer's philosophical hermeneutics centers on questions concerning the "objective" status of interpretation. Following the appearance of *Truth and Method*, Betti objected to Gadamer's rejection of method on the grounds that such a lack of methodology threatens the objective standing and standards of interpretation.

Betti returns to the Diltheyan notion of mental objectifications and meaningful forms to identify interpretation as a triadic process in which the interpreter (subject) apprehends the object—the meaningful form as an objectification of mind—in a way that reproduces the original creative activity of the author. Betti explicates four canons that will guide the interpreter in the task of objectively reproducing the original meaning. First and foremost is the "canon of the hermeneutical autonomy of the object." According to Betti, for the object to be regarded as autonomous means that it "should be judged in relation to the standards immanent in the original intention: the intention, that is, which the created forms should correspond to from the point of view of the author and his formative impulse in the course of the creative process" . . . (p. 164).

The second canon Betti calls "the canon of the coherence of meaning" or the "principle of totality." According to this canon, there is an internal relationship between the individual parts of a speech or text and between these parts and the whole. In this canon, Betti formulates his version of the circularity of understanding: "the meaning of the whole has to be derived from its individual elements, and an individual element has to be understood by reference to the comprehensive, penetrating whole of which it is a part" (p. 165). Third is the "canon of the actuality of understanding," by which Betti acknowledges that the interpreter, in the process of reconstructing the author's creative process and intended meaning, will necessarily appropriate these processes and this meaning in terms of his or her own subjectivity. Fourth is the "canon of the hermeneutical correspondence of meaning" or "meaning-adequacy in understanding," which encourages the interpreter to bring his or her own subjectivity into the "closest harmony with the stimulation" received from the interpreted object: that is to say, while recognizing that the interpreter will understand things in terms of his or her own experiences, every effort must be made to control one's "prejudices" and to subordinate one's experiences to the meaningfulness that the interpreted object seeks to communicate.

In arguing for the essential autonomy of the object to be interpreted, Betti criticizes Gadamer's dialogical approach for inserting the subject into the hermeneutical circle. Such an introduction, in his view, inevitably leads to both subjectivism and relativism, with the consequence that hermeneutics is unable to adjudicate between correct and incorrect interpretations.[47] For Betti, Gadamer's subjectivist position

tends toward the confounding of interpretation and meaning-inference
[*Sinngebung*] and the removing of the canon of the autonomy of the
object, with the consequence of putting into doubt the objectivity of
the results of interpretive procedures in all the human sciences. It is
my opinion that it is our duty as guardians and practitioners of the
study of history to protect this kind of objectivity and to provide evidence of the epistemological condition of its possibility. . . . The obvious difficulty with the hermeneutical method proposed by Gadamer
seems to lie, for me, in that it enables a substantive agreement between text and reader—i.e., between the apparently easily accessible
meaning of a text and the subjective conception of the reader—to be
formed without, however, guaranteeing the correctness of understanding; for that it would be necessary that the understanding arrived at
corresponded fully to the meaning underlying the text as an objectivation of the mind. Only then would the objectivity of the result be
guaranteed on the basis of a reliable process of interpretation (pp.
177–78, pp. 182–83).

Betti concludes that Gadamer concerns himself with a *quaestio facti*, that of
"ascertaining what actually happens in the activity of thought apparent in
interpretation." Against this purely descriptive concern, Betti claims that
the proper task of hermeneutics is to provide a solution to the *quaestio
juris*, "i.e., what one should aim for in the task of interpretation, what
methods to use and what guidelines to follow in the correct execution of
this task" (p. 187).

Gadamer's reply to Betti's objections operates on two levels. On the
one hand, he distinguishes the goal of his theory from Betti's goal of working out a methodology for a general theory of interpretation. Gadamer conceives his project as descriptive and "philosophical" rather than prescrip-
tive and methodological. He wants (1) to discover what is common to all
modes of understanding and (2) to put to this the Kantian transcendental
questions: What are the conditions of such understanding? and How is understanding possible? In other words, his response reaffirms the ontological
dimension of hermeneutics: understanding is the primordial way of Being
human, not a task that, once methodologically purified, will lead to truth.

The second line of Gadamer's reply concerns Betti's charge of subjectivism. Gadamer responds that the validity of this charge depends on its
being posed within a dualistic framework. Only if understanding is construed, as it is apparently by Betti, as the project of a subject confronting
an alien object, is the activity of understanding a "subjective behavior." If
one construes understanding dialogically and dialectically, as a process of
question and answer (what Gadamer calls the "hermeneutical *Urphä-*

nomen'') (p. 153), then one realizes that ''understanding belongs to the being of that which is understood'' (p. 205). Both the hermeneutical ''subject'' and ''object'' unfold in history, and hermeneutical awareness will be a consciousness that is effected by history, *wirkungsgeschichtliche Bewusstsein*.

In addition to this objectivist critique of Gadamer's alleged subjectivism and relativism, we find Gadamer accused of dogmatism in his debate with Jürgen Habermas. Habermas emphasizes the critical function of interpretive understanding, and he objects both to Gadamer's claim regarding the universality of hermeneutics and to what he sees as Gadamer's uncritical acceptance of tradition.

The foundation of Habermas's response lies in his view of language. Language must be grasped as an effective ideological tool. On this basis, he objects to Gadamer's notion of prejudice, his view of the relation between tradition and authority, and ultimately his claim of hermeneutic universality. Habermas accepts the hermeneutic insight Gadamer takes from Heidegger, that understanding is anticipatory, that is, that what we understand is framed by the structure of our prejudices (*Vorurteile*). But he thinks that Gadamer takes the unavoidability of the fore-structures as a legitimation of prejudices. Habermas, on the other hand, believes that this fore-structuration should emerge as an object for *critical* appropriation. According to Habermas, Gadamer acquiesces to the authority of tradition because he believes that authority need not be authoritarian. For Habermas, this attitude amounts to a denial of critical reflection. Critical reflection, the critique of ideology, is essential to hermeneutic understanding because, as Habermas argues, ''language is *also* a medium of domination and social power; it serves to legitimate relations or organized force'' (p. 239).

The ideological dimension of language as the transmitter of tradition leads Habermas to challenge Gadamer's hermeneutic claim to universality. Habermas's analysis of psychoanalytic depth hermeneutics leads him to the conclusion that certain forms of communication are ''systematically distorted.'' According to Habermas, Gadamer's claim to universality is grounded in the ontological priority of the linguistic tradition, and this claim can be defended only if the consensus forming the linguistic tradition ''has been achieved without compulsion or distortion'' (p. 266). Insofar as historical as well as psychoanalytic analysis reveals the possibility of repressive forces that ''deform the intersubjectivity of agreement as such and systematically distort everyday communication,'' Habermas argues that a ''critically enlightened hermeneutic'' must differentiate between insight and delusion, and incorporate within itself the ''meta-hermeneutic awareness of the conditions for the possibility of systematically distorted communication'' (p. 267). He concludes that Gadamer's philosophical hermeneutics, to the extent that it lacks this *critical*, *meta*-hermeneutic awareness, cannot provide a universal account of understanding because it cannot account for the understanding gained through ideology-critique.

In Gadamer's reply to his critics, once again he restates his objection to the view of hermeneutics as an interpretive technique—that is to say, the *technē hermēneutikē*, a technique for special purposes.[48] Although hermeneutics at one point in its recent history, with Schleiermacher, was understood as a technical doctrine which sought to ground interpretation on a number of rules and procedural canons, *philosophical hermeneutics* seeks a "critical reflective knowledge" of the interpretive experience. The goal of philosophical hermeneutics is, thus, not wisdom (*epistēmē* or *theōria*) but practical wisdom (*phronēsis*), understanding drawn from hermeneutical praxis.

Here Gadamer responds directly to Habermas's charges of dogmatism, conservatism, and blind obedience to the tradition, and, in so doing, he raises an important question regarding Habermas's own hermeneutic praxis. Gadamer refuses to accept Habermas and Apel's charge that philosophical hermeneutics entails a *passive* acceptance of the tradition. Although we are obliged to open ourselves to the tradition in our effort to understand, we are not obliged to blindly accept its teachings and customs. Gadamer continues to maintain that our relation to tradition is based not on obedience but on the recognition of its superiority.[49] Gadamer confesses to some amazement that his critics see in him a privileging of contemporary prejudices and a subservience to the past. Instead, he claims, philosophical hermeneutics requires "critical discrimination" of one's own prejudices and the prejudices of others. This will be the basis on which the "connection with tradition" is to be established and understood. To Habermas's charge of dogmatism, Gadamer replies that Habermas's claims that authority is always authoritarian and that emancipation will come through critical reflection appear dogmatic (see pp. 236–37 and Gadamer, pp. 288, 290). Furthermore, Gadamer questions Habermas's attempt to privilege the psychoanalytic situation as a communicative model for social dialogue. According to Gadamer, it is ironic that Habermas charges him with a conservative acquiescence to the authority of tradition, when Habermas appears blind to the dogmatism that pervades the doctor-patient relationship. Because of the unequal distribution of power within the analytic encounter, and because the patient willingly submits himself or herself to the authority of the physician and the dogmatism of technique, the psychoanalytic model fails both as a model for social dialogue and as an example of hermeneutic universality.

More than anyone, Paul Ricoeur has tried to work out an account of hermeneutics that reconciles and ameliorates the conflict, the differences, between Gadamer's philosophical hermeneutics and Habermas's critique of ideology. Ricoeur directs his own project toward answering the following question: "Is it possible to formulate a hermeneutics which would render justice to the critique of ideology, which would show the necessity of the latter at the very heart of its own concerns?" (p. 298). In effecting a successful rapprochement of hermeneutics and the critique of ideology, Ricoeur seeks neither to conflate the two positions nor to synthesize them into some more universal "super-system." Instead he tries to demonstrate what Heidegger might have called the "belonging-together" of hermeneutics and ideology-critique by eliminating the "deceptive antinomies" that separate them.

In the first part of his essay, "Hermeneutics and the Critique of Ideology," Ricoeur offers a summary of Gadamer's and Habermas's positions. Here he identifies four basic issues which differentiate the two. (1) Where Gadamer rehabilitates the concept of prejudice from philosophical Romanticism and links it to authority and tradition by means of Heidegger's hermeneutical fore-structures, Habermas develops the concept of interest which he appropriates from the Frankfurt School Marxists, aligning it with the Ideal of the Enlightenment. (2) Where Gadamer focuses on the human sciences' attempt to overcome distantiation (*Verfremdung*) from the tradition, Habermas is concerned with the critical social sciences and the emancipatory possibilities of critical reflection on institutional reifications. (3) Further, Gadamer takes "misunderstanding" as the inner obstacle to understanding, whereas Habermas focuses on ideology, understood as the "systematic distortion of communication by the hidden exercise of force" (p. 313). (4) Finally, where Gadamer sees the task of hermeneutics as arriving at a prior understanding—"the dialogue which we are"—which misunderstanding presupposes, Habermas looks forward to a notion of "an unrestricted and unconstrained communication" which will serve as a regulative ideal.

In the second part of his essay, Ricoeur attempts to show that there is in each of these disagreements a "zone of intersection" which the two views share. To show the "critical" dimension internal to hermeneutics, Ricoeur recalls that Heidegger's initial hermeneutical gesture was critical: the destruction of metaphysics which would proceed by means of a critique of the onto-theo-logical prejudices of the Western tradition. However, Gadamer's own hermeneutic emphasis on the overcoming of distantiation prevents him from recognizing this critical move. According to Ricoeur, a return to the hermeneutic question of the text, although not refuting Gadamerian hermeneutics, critically supplements its emphasis on the dialogue with tradition by marking a place for critique *within* hermeneutics.[50] Thus, whereas distantiation was a fault which the dialogue with tradition sought to overcome, Ricoeur's focus on the text views it as a positive element which makes interpretation possible. Distantiation is implied by writing as a fixation of discourse, and this fixation makes the autonomy of the text possible, especially with respect to its author, its historical context, and its original audience. This "emancipation of the text constitutes the most fundamental condition for the recognition of a critical instance at the heart of interpretation" (p. 325).

In similar fashion, a textual hermeneutic will appeal to the insights of semiological and structural analysis, thus overcoming the "ruinous dichotomy, inherited from Dilthey, between 'explanation' and 'understanding'." Placing discourse under the category of work, a category which pertains to praxis, allows for the intervention of critique inasmuch as "discourse as a work 'takes hold' in structures calling for a description and an explanation that mediate 'understanding' " (pp. 325–26). A hermeneutics of texts turns to the critique of ideology in two additional ways. First, as a text opens up a world as a fictional redescription of present conditions, it opens itself up as a possibility for a "critique of the real." Second, to the extent that the hermeneutics of the text sees, as its primary concern, the unfolding of a world in front of the text, rather than the discovery of the subjective intentions of the author behind the text, the relation of this world to the subjectivity of the reader is transformed. Exposing oneself to the world that the text puts forward makes possible "a critique of the illusions of the subject" (p. 327). Although the hermeneutics of tradition closes this possibility by prematurely introjecting the concept of appropriation against alienating distantiation, Ricoeur's acknowledgment of the positive potential of distantiation can allow the "critique of false consciousness" to become an integral and acute part of hermeneutics.

Turning to Habermas, Ricoeur first notes that Habermas's theory of interests (technical, practical, emancipatory) is grounded in an analysis similar to Heidegger's existential analytic of the fore-structure of understanding. On the basis of this analytic, Ricoeur draws the preliminary conclusion that Habermas's theory of interests is dependent upon hermeneutics—specifically, a hermeneutics of finitude. Looking next at the critical social sciences' motif of emancipation, Ricoeur notes that the model of emancipation that underlies Habermas's discussion of psychoanalysis is strikingly similar to the hermeneutic overcoming of distantiation: both take as their goal successful communication without distortion. If the critique of ideology seeks emancipation as the absence of communicative distortions, is this interest distinct from the hermeneutic goal of understanding? More importantly, Ricoeur argues, distortions can be criticized only in the name of a consensus, an ideal which is exemplified, "and one of the very few places of exemplification of the ideal of communication is precisely our capacity to overcome cultural distance in the interpretation of works received from the past" (p. 330).

To awaken communicative action and political responsibility will necessitate a "creative renewal of our cultural heritage" because this preceding consensus provides the only real basis for our future freedom as an unrestricted and unrestrained communicative community. On the one hand, according to Ricoeur, this opposition marks the basic disagreement between hermeneutics' "ontology of prior understanding" and the critique of ideology's "eschatology of freedom." But on the other hand, this is a false antinomy, because there is no necessity in choosing between "reminiscence and hope," between "the recollection of tradition and the anticipation of freedom" (p. 332). Insofar as hermeneutics and the critique of ideology each privilege their respective claims to universality, Ricoeur suggests a return to the notion of regional hermeneutics that would account for the two theories speaking from different places. But ultimately he strives "to show that each can recognize the other's claim to universality in a way which marks the place of one in the structure of the other" (p. 299).

Even though Ricoeur's attempt to identify a zone where the differences between Gadamer's philosophical hermeneutics and Habermas's ideology-critique converge is not intended to invoke a universal "supersystem," it recalls, at its outset and at its termination, the spirit of the Hegelian *Aufhebung*. Ricoeur's rapprochement of the hermeneutics of ontology and the ideological critique of critical theory constitutes a threefold reclamation. (1) The call for a return to a *regional* hermeneutics sublates the differences: that is to say, the differences in perspectives are preserved in alterity, yet they are affirmed through the synthesis of opposition. Despite their differences, and perhaps because of their differences—because the antinomies these differences indicate are "false" according to Ricoeur—both Gadamer's and Habermas's claims regarding the universality of their respective projects are legitimate. As far as Ricoeur is concerned, hermeneutics and the critique of ideology are complements of one another.

(2) Thematic unity is constituted in these differences. The question which Ricoeur posed at the outset was "How can we conceive and articulate a hermeneutics that accommodates the critique of ideology and takes into account the ideological character of language?" The only way to resolve this question is to preserve the hermeneutical circle, to synthesize its different articulations, as found in Ast, Schleiermacher, Dilthey, Heidegger, and Gadamer, to elevate it to a "higher," more comprehensive level of understanding. In this recovery of the hermeneutic circle, the individual theoretical perspectives of Gadamer and Habermas are to be maintained in their opposition to one another. But their hermeneutic significance is to be understood as "parts" of a more encompassing dialogue, the perimeters of which can be comprehended only in terms of the parts, their alterity, the conflict of interpretations. Thus, (3) Ricoeur is able to preserve the Heideg-

gerian tradition of a "destructive" hermeneutics of ontology alongside the "grand narratives"[51] of Gadamer's dialogical hermeneutics of tradition and Habermas's critical reflection on the ideological function of language.

Continuities and Differences Within the Life of Interpretation: The Postmodernity of Interpretation

If the selections included here can be said to stress, in their respective ways, the themes of (textual) unity, universality, and legitimacy, then the fragments and essays included in *Transforming the Hermeneutic Context: From Nietzsche to Nancy* suspend these themes. The universality of the "ontology of prior understanding" and the legitimacy of ideology-critique, for example, assume particular goals, ends which are informed by privileged categories and rules. The selections contained in *Transforming the Hermeneutic Context*, in general, emphasize *the act* of interpretation, *the performative* character of interpretation, where the performance is not governed or regulated by a set of preestablished, prosaic principles or categories. Instead, the questions of communication, understanding, interpretation, and representation are used, radicalized in an elliptical fashion, as Hamacher suggests in his reading of Schleiermacher,[52] to show how the principles or categories thought to regulate "interpretation" are put forward, set forth in the act(s) of communication (dialogue), the *event(s)* of interpretation, the production of representation. Unity, universality, and legitimation are fictive consequences of interpretation, sent forth in the multiplication of interpretive strategies and devices. In this way, the hermeneutic legend is transfigured, the hermeneutical context transformed. Displacement and fragmentation, rather than the unity and harmony of either a generalized or regionalized "hermeneutics," prefigures the discourse on interpretation.

The selections and essays contained in *Transforming the Hermeneutic Context* provide "readings" which not only reinscribe certain basic hermeneutic themes, but as such effect a dissemination, a scattering of themes across a field of diverse perspectives and orientations. It includes selections and essays from Friedrich Nietzsche, Michel Foucault, Eric Blondel, Julia Kristeva, Jacques Derrida, Manfred Frank, Werner Hamacher, and Jean-Luc Nancy. In spite of the eclectic character of their assays, in their respective ways, these writers share certain concerns—concerns that traverse the history of hermeneutics—with the writers brought together in *The Hermeneutic Tradition*: questions surrounding the character and goals of interpretation; the effects of interpretive intervention; the representation, multiplication, and articulation of alternate voices in philosophical, political, and poetic exchange; and the desire to expose and, perhaps, to work up against the "limits" of language imposed by traditional conceptions of interpretation and understanding, all the while remaining painfully aware that limits are established through use.

To borrow an image that plays a central role in Jean-Luc Nancy's "Sharing Voices," it seems appropriate to say that the "authors" represented in *Transforming the Hermeneutic Context* are analogues, though no more nor less so than the "authors" included in parts I and II of this book, of the Greek rhapsodes described in Plato's *Ion*. Just as the rhapsode is an interpreter of a poet, who is an interpreter—*creator*, "inventor"—of the myths regarding the Gods, the authors represented in *Transforming the Hermeneutic Context* are interpreters of the words, declarations, and writings that constitute the "hermeneutic tradition." Each provides a theatrical interpretation of some question or theme already articulated or inscribed within the tradition of hermeneutics. Each offers an "inspired" performance, an announcement of some theme or question issued by the hermeneutic tradition—if not the "thought" and words of a "poet." In this regard, these authors—indeed all of us—are tethered to the tradition, as the iron rings in *Ion* are linked to one another by a magnetic force. The force of magnetism "passes through the rings, which are able to act (*poiein*) in their turn like the magnet, and attract other rings."[53] And yet, as Nancy notes, even though this constitutes " 'a very long series of rings suspended from one another' " (*Ion* 533 c), the rings, the voices, the interpretations of interpretation, are not "chained" to one another. They are "suspended from one another." In this way, they remain "*unchained* (in every manner one can imagine it), and they hold together."[54]

The *suspension* of hermeneutic themes, then, is also a fragmentation of the hermeneutic legend. It entails the displacement of those themes, those points of connections, and the transformation of what, in effect, can be called the "hermeneutic context"—the conditions and settings of and for the life of interpretation. Further, suspension of the hermeneutic question, that is, of those familiar interpretations of "interpretation," in the writings of Nietzsche, Foucault, Blondel, Kristeva, Derrida, Frank, Hamacher, and Nancy sets the stage for *exploring* what we call the "postmodernity" of interpretation.

We do not intend for the selections contained in *Transforming the Hermeneutic Context*, specifically, to be associated or identified with the contemporary movement known as "postmodernism." Nor do we intend to offer these selections as so-called postmodern theories of interpretations and, in doing so, oppose them to the selections contained in *The Hermeneutic Tradition*. There is an overwhelming number of art forms (architecture, film, dance, painting), and theories of literary criticism, historiography, and psychoanalysis, as well as philosophical perspectives,

which at once fall under the rubric of "postmodernism." By drawing attention to the "postmodernity" of interpretation, we wish only to erect mark-
ers that indicate what others have called a "condition,"[55] an "occasion,"[56]
an "awareness,"[57] or even a "turn" or "sensibility."[58] Referring to "postmodernity," we wish to mark out what seems to be the nascent condition of
interpretation, whether one is concerned with issues of method, objectivity,
ideology-critique, or the dissemination of interpretation through interpretation. To refer to the "postmodernity" of interpretation is to refer to the
possibilities of hermeneutics, the possibilities of histories and traditions,
the possibilities of interpretation. As such, these possibilities, this condition, is "always already there"—that is to say, it is always and already a
current issue, never limited in its effects to a specific historical moment.
Passing from hand to hand, as it were, the word, "interpretation" always
circulates—suspending, fragmenting, decentering, but always transforming
its object and subject in the experience of interpretation. The postmodernity
of interpretation, then, indicates the ever-present possibilities of otherness,
the difference(s) of sign and its object, of interpretation and the text that
mark the life of interpretation.

Notes

1. Michel de Montaigne, *Essays*, translated by Charles Cotton and edited by
W. Carew Hazlitt (New York: A. L. Burt, Publisher, 1892). Book II, chapter XLIV,
pp. 563–64, 565–66.

2. Aristotle, *Metaphysics*, 980a, *The Basic Works of Aristotle*, edited by Richard McKeon (New York: Random House, 1941). For the sake of comparison, Montaigne's text should be juxtaposed to Aristotle's. The complete first paragraph of the
Metaphysics reads as follows: "All men by nature desire to know. An indication of
this is the delight we take in our senses; for even apart from their usefulness they
are loved for themselves; and above all others the sense of sight. For not only with
a view to action, but even when we are not going to do anything, we prefer seeing
(one might say) to everything else. The reason is that this, most of all the senses,
makes us know and brings to light many differences between things."

3. Montaigne, *Essays*, II, XLIV, p. 561.

4. The attempt to trace certain paths within selected discourses and traditions
of hermeneutics in the nineteenth and twentieth centuries is continued in *Transforming the Hermeneutic Context: From Nietzsche to Nancy*, edited by Gayle L. Ormiston and Alan D. Schrift (Albany: State University of New York Press, 1990).
Transforming the Hermeneutic Context provides selections associated with certain
currents in contemporary philosophy and literary criticism, especially those

"schools" that have come to be known by the names "poststructuralism," "semiotic analysis," "reader-response" criticism, and "deconstructionist" criticism. With both *The Hermeneutic Tradition* and *Transforming the Hermeneutic Context* we hope to demonstrate certain thematic linkages between the allegedly nontraditional practices of interpretation represented in *Transforming the Hermeneutic Context* and the supposed "tradition" of hermeneutics reflected in this volume. Subsequent reference to selections included in *Transforming the Hermeneutic Context* will be cited by the abbreviation THC and page numbers.

5. Montaigne, *Essays*, II, XLIV, p. 561.

6. *Ibid.*

7. *Ibid.*

8. Jacques Derrida, *Of Grammatology*, translated by Gayatri Chakravorty Spivak (Baltimore, Md.: Johns Hopkins University Press, 1974). See especially part II, chapter 4: "From/Of the Supplement to the Source: The Theory of Writing," especially pp. 275–95 and pp. 303–4.

9. Jean-Luc Nancy, "Sharing Voices," THC, pp. 211–59. The French title of Nancy's text is *Le partage des voix* (Paris: Éditions Galilée, 1982). The ambiguity of *partage* should not be overlooked: its field of designation covers sharing, multiplying, distributing, differentiating, as well as fate, destiny, and determination. Moreover, *voix* is simultaneously the singular "voice" and the plural "voices." As Montaigne's comments indicate, interpretation is the interpretation(s) of interpretation(s): in this regard, as Nancy notes, politically and poetically we each share and multiply our voice(s) with the voice(s) of others—we each have a stake in determining the path(s) of our dialogues.

10. To be sure, the "hermeneutical circle" has been the locus of hermeneutical discourse, but this does not signify consensus regarding the character and function of the "circle." The differences in "interpreting" the hermeneutical circle are clearly indicated in general by each of the selections contained in parts I and II. More recent discussions, valuations and revaluations of this primary hermeneutical theme will be found in THC, especially the selections by Eric Blondel, Julia Kristeva, Manfred Frank, Werner Hamacher, and Jean-Luc Nancy.

11. Although not an issue foreign to the developments of either field, the relational mapping that can be drawn between the discourse of semiology (and Peircean semeiotic) and hermeneutics remains uncharted for the most part. However, this is not to say that this problem has not been discussed. Ricoeur has addressed the intersection of semiology and hermeneutics in many of his texts; see, for example, *The Conflict of Interpretations*, edited by Don Ihde (Evanston, Ill.: Northwestern University Press, 1974), and *The Rule of Metaphor: Multi-Disciplinary Studies of the Creation of Meaning in Language*, translated by Robert Czerny et al. (Toronto: University of Toronto Press, 1977). In *Truth and Method*, Gadamer is critical of what he calls the "instrumental theory of signs"; *Truth and Method*, trans-

lated by Garrett Barden and John Cumming (New York: Seabury Press, 1977); see pp. 87, 134, and 377ff.

The problem receives direct comment and analysis from Nietzsche, Foucault, Blondel, and Kristeva in THC. The lines of contention are distinct in each case. As an example, on the one hand, Michel Foucault claims that "*hermeneutics and semiology are two ferocious enemies*" and that their differences must always be recalled (THC, p. 67). On the other hand, Julia Kristeva writes that "the birth of interpretation [and hermeneutics] is considered the birth of semiology, since the semiological sciences relate a sign (an event-sign) to a signified in order to *act* accordingly," that is, "to interpret" or "to make connections," "consistently, consequently" (THC, p. 90).

12. See Wilhelm Dilthey, *Plan der Fortsetzung zum Aufbau der geschichtlichen Welt in den Geisteswissenschaften* and *Ideen über eine beschreibende und zergliedernde Psychologie, Gesammelte Schriften*, volumes 7 and 5 (Stuttgart: B. G. Teubner, 1958). *Zusammenhang* has a variety of meanings, given the context of Dilthey's text. In some instances it covers "connection," "interrelation," "internal structure," "coherence," "system." He writes in the *Plan der Fortsetzung* that "We understand *Zusammenhang. Zusammenhang* and understanding correspond to each other" (p. 257). And in the *Ideen* we find the following statement: "Life exists everywhere only as *Zusammenhang*" (p. 144). Cf. Wilhelm Dilthey, *Descriptive Psychology and Historical Understanding*, translated by Richard M. Zaner and Kenneth L. Heiges (The Hague: Nijhoff, 1977), p. 28.

13. Julia Kristeva, "Psychoanalysis and the Polis," THC; see p. 90.

14. Ludwig Wittgenstein, *Zettel*, translated by G. E. M. Anscombe (Berkeley: University of California Press, 1967), section 55.

15. Kristeva, "Psychoanalysis and the Polis," THC, p. 99.

16. *Ibid*.

17. See, for example, Martin Heidegger's formulation of this problem as it is articulated in *On the Way to Language*, translated by Peter Hertz and Joan Stambaugh (New York: Harper and Row, 1971) and *Identity and Difference*, translated by Joan Stambaugh (New York: Harper and Row, 1969). In a very simple, direct, and historically (metaphysically) bound manner, Heidegger identifies the difficulty which faces "interpretation," especially in *Identity and Difference*. First, he asserts that the withdrawal, the "step back," from metaphysics would remain "unaccomplished, and the path which it opens and points out would remain untrod." Why? Because the challenge to thought in this regard, the challenge of withdrawing from metaphysics, "lies in language." He continues:

Our Western languages are languages of metaphysical thinking, each in its own way. It must remain an open question whether the nature of Western languages is in itself marked with the exclusive brand of metaphysics, and thus marked permanently by onto-theo-logic, or whether these languages offer other possibilities of utterance . . . The little word "is," which speaks everywhere in our language, and tells of Being even where It does not appear expressly, contains the whole destiny of Being [*das ganze Geschick des Seins*] (p. 73).

There is an interesting point of comparison to be found in Aristotle's *Peri hermēneias*. In a section which deals explicitly with the "little word 'is'," (3 16b 19–25), Aristotle claims that even though verbs are "substantial and have significance" they do so because the one who expresses them "fixes" the attention of the hearer. But verbs do not bear any "existential import" in and of themselves—and, for Aristotle, this is especially true for the verb "to be." Something must be added—a subject and a predicate. "To be," "being," and "is" indicate nothing by themselves, but *can only imply copulation, a possible or potential connection with the world*. Moreover, in Aristotle's eyes, to form a conception of the "copula" apart from the terms coupled or conjoined is impossible. (In anticipation, cf. Manfred Frank, "The Interpretation of a Text," THC, pp. 145–76, and Werner Hamacher, "Hermeneutic Ellipses: Writing the Hermeneutical Circle in Schleiermacher," THC, pp. 178–210.)

The point here is this: if "is" carries and contains the "*whole* destiny of Being," if "is" refers to "Being" even where "It does not appear expressly," and if "our Western languages" or "language" in general carries the mark of metaphysics, it is not because language, in and of itself, whatever "It" may be, has an inherent metaphysical or onto-theo-logical orientation. It is because language *is used* toward the realization of certain metaphysical and onto-theo-logical ends. So, for Heidegger to claim that "is" contains "the whole destiny of Being," he must note that it is the *use* of the copula, as Aristotle indicates, what can be termed its "iterative structure," which allows it to refer to "Being" in any capacity whatsoever.

In "Sending: On Representation," Jacques Derrida examines the "possibility" of a "step back" from metaphysics (THC, pp. 107–18). In order to "step back" from metaphysics and onto-theo-logy, there must be a different use of language, one which accepts and affirms the "iterative structure" of language as its condition for *use* and *articulation*. To "step back," as Derrida points out, one would have to withdraw from the "metaphysical/onto-theo-logical" representational use of language. In "Sending: On Representation," Derrida concerns himself with just that possibility.

18. Cf. Ludwig Wittgenstein, *Philosophical Grammar*, edited by Rush Rhees and translated by Anthony Kenny (Berkeley: University of California Press, 1974). According to Wittgenstein's notes, which constitute this text, nothing has, already, a specific interpretation. In other words, there are no predetermined interpretations of images, pictures, signs, and so forth. Rather, Wittgenstein claims that "what gives an image an interpretation is the *path* on which it lies" (section 99).

19. Charles Sanders Peirce, *Collected Papers*, edited by Charles Hartshorne and Paul Weiss (Cambridge, Mass.: Harvard University Press, 1931–35), 5.400.

20. Michel Foucault, "Nietzsche, Freud, Marx," THC, pp. 59–67.

21. *Ibid.*

22. *Ibid.*

23. For Eric Blondel, the interplay between semiology and interpretation, that is, *metaphor*, as articulated in Nietzsche's texts, indicates anew in what ways "being" is, "life" is, "existence" is what it is. Language is not only the means of expressing our understanding, but through this articulation the world is allowed "to be." Cf. Eric Blondel, "Nietzsche's Style of Affirmation: The Metaphors of Genealogy," in *Nietzsche as Affirmative Thinker*, edited by Yirmiyahu Yovel (Dordrecht: Martinus Nijhoff, 1986), pp. 132–46; "Nietzsche: Life as Metaphor," in *The New Nietzsche: Contemporary Styles of Interpretation*, edited by David B. Allison (Cambridge, Mass.: MIT Press, 1987), pp. 150–75; and "Interpreting Texts With and Without Nietzsche," THC, pp. 69–88.

24. E. D. Hirsch, well known for his defense of a hermeneutic approach that privileges the author's intention in the determination of the meaning of a text, strikes an interesting note in this regard in his most recent text, *Cultural Literacy: What Every American Needs to Know* (Boston: Houghton Mifflin Company, 1987), p. 48: "All continuing experience is partial and fragmented . . . Our cognitive life takes place through a small window of attention that is framed by short-term memory. We use past knowledge to interpret this window of experience, to place momentary fragments within larger wholes that give them a function and a place . . . In our minds these transitory fragments can acquire meaning only by being placed within larger, not presently visible wholes that are based on past knowledge." One should not be misled here. Beyond its present context and use, Hirsch's remark must be examined in terms of the purposes for which he makes this claim, that is, the realignment of "national" educational goals with the realization of a "cultural" *telos*.

25. David Hoy begins his discussion in *The Critical Circle* by citing the same passage from the *Cratylus*: "Words . . . have the power to reveal, but they also conceal, speech can signify all things, but it also turns things this way and that." On the basis of this acknowledgment, and with the recognition that today Hermes is absent, Hoy claims that "the modern age needs hermeneutics"; it needs an understanding of "the methodology of interpretation of texts." See *The Critical Circle: Literature, History, and Philosophical Hermeneutics* (Berkeley: University of California Press, 1978), p. 1.

26. Nancy, "Sharing Voices," THC, p. 237.

27. Cf. Martin Heidegger, "A Dialogue on Language between a Japanese and an Inquirer," *On the Way to Language*, translated by Peter Hertz (New York: Harper and Row, 1971); Gadamer, *Truth and Method*, especially part III, p. 364ff and 402–4; and Nancy, "Sharing Voices," THC, pp. 230–48.

28. Aristotle, *On Interpretation*, translated by E. M. Edghill, in *The Basic Works of Aristotle*, edited by Richard McKeon. Aristotle's text is taken as a symbol for the historical importance of hermeneutics. Today, very little use is made of this

short text. To paraphrase Aristotle, one might say that *On Interpretation* is a significant text in the history of hermeneutics by its *name* alone because it has become a symbol for the questions and concerns which dominate current discourse in this field. In other words, for a name to have meaning it must become a symbol, and a symbol has meaning only because it is bound to the "conventions" of a linguistic system. Today, hermeneutics provides the necessary system of conventions.

29. Cf. Ricoeur, *The Conflict of Interpretations*, p. 4.

30. Heidegger, *Identity and Difference*, p. 41.

31. Wittgenstein, *Philosophical Grammar*, section 99.

32. The selections from Ast, Schleiermacher, Dilthey, and Heidegger, included in part I of this text, also create the "historical" background against which the issues and themes pursued in THC will be configured.

33. Cf. Friedrich D. E. Schleiermacher, *Hermeneutics: The Handwritten Manuscripts*, edited by Heinz Kimmerle, translated by James Duke and Jack Forstman (Missoula, Mont.: Scholars Press, 1977), p. 195ff; and "Hermeneutics," section 78, pp. 45–6, below. Subsequent references to the selections included in this volume will appear parenthetically in the text.

34. As the recent editions of Schleiermacher's collected works show, his mature writings are far more programmatic, and his final works are guided by an architechtonic approach. See, for example, Schleiermacher's *Dialektik*, edited by Andras Arndt (Hamburg: Meiner, 1986), *Hermeneutik und Kritik*, edited by Manfred Frank (Frankfurt: Suhrkamp, 1977), and *Kritische Gesamtausgabe*, edited by Hans-Joachim Birkner et al. (Berlin: Walter de Gruyter, 1980).

35. Schleiermacher, *Hermeneutics: The Handwritten Manuscripts*, p. 127.

36. The question of Schleiermacher's "psychologism" is discussed in detail by Manfred Frank in "The Interpretation of a Text," THC, pp. 158–70, and by Werner Hamacher in "Hermeneutic Ellipsis: Writing the Hermeneutical Circle in Schleiermacher," THC, pp. 191–205.

37. The privileging of authorial intent, retrieved in part II by Betti, is challenged by the readings of Schleiermacher offered by Frank and Hamacher in THC.

38. Wilhelm Dilthey, *Selected Writings*, edited, translated, and introduced by H. P. Rickman (Cambridge: Cambridge University Press, 1976), p. 261.

39. *Ibid.*, p. 207.

40. *Ibid.*, p. 208.

41. Martin Heidegger, *Being and Time*, translated by John Macquarrie and Edward Robinson (New York: Harper and Row, 1962), p. 62.

42. *Ibid.*, p. 487.

43. Gadamer, *Truth and Method*, p. 350.

44. See Hans-Georg Gadamer, *Philosophical Hermeneutics*, translated and edited by David E. Linge (Berkeley: University of California Press, 1976), p. 28; see also *Truth and Method*, p. 263.

45. Gadamer, *Truth and Method*, p. 421.

46. *Ibid.*, pp. 431–32.

47. E. D. Hirsch follows Betti in this critique of Gadamer's alleged subjectivism and relativism, as we can see in the following explication of the goal of interpretation: "The interpreter's primary task is to reproduce in himself the author's 'logic,' his attitudes, his cultural givens, in short, his world. Even though the process of verification is highly complex and difficult, the ultimate verificative principle is very simple—the imaginative reconstruction of the speaking subject." See E. D. Hirsch, *Validity in Interpretation* (New Haven, Conn.: Yale University Press, 1967), p. 242.

As the title of Hirsch's work indicates, the task of hermeneutics is to achieve *validity* in interpretation. "The activity of interpretation can lay claim to intellectual respectability only if its results can lay claim to validity" (p. 164). To be valid, an interpretation must reproduce the "determinate meaning" of the object being interpreted and, in Hirsch's view, the only meaning which will satisfy this condition of determinacy is the author's intended meaning. "On purely practical grounds, therefore, it is preferable to agree that the meaning of a text is the author's meaning" (p. 24).

48. Ricoeur concurs with Gadamer, and Heidegger, on this point. In *The Conflict of Interpretations*, Ricoeur notes that even for Aristotle, in the *Peri hermēneias*, "hermeneutics involves the general problem of comprehension" (p. 4). See also Nancy's discussion of the difference between interpretation as a "technique" and as a "divine gift" in his reading of Plato's *Ion*, "Sharing Voices," THC, pp. 237–48.

49. Gadamer, *Truth and Method*, pp. 248–49.

50. Even though Ricoeur returns to the textual origins of hermeneutics found in Schleiermacher's philology and Dilthey's emphasis on historical inscriptions, he acknowledges that Gadamer's own hermeneutics addresses the question of "being towards the text." See, for example, Gadamer's "Reply to My Critics," p. 292, below. However, he claims that Gadamer does not sufficiently appreciate the hermeneutic importance of textuality.

51. The phrase "grand narrative" is taken from Jean-François Lyotard's analysis of legitimation as it appears in *The Postmodern Condition: A Report on Knowledge,* translated by Geoff Bennington and Brian Massumi (Minneapolis: University of Minnesota Press, 1984); see p. 31ff. The phrase is used in this context to indicate another way of comprehending the claims to universality made by Gadamer and Habermas on behalf of their respective theoretical perspectives.

52. Hamacher, "Hermeneutic Ellipses: Writing the Hermeneutical Circle in Schleiermacher," THC, p. 200.

53. Nancy, "Sharing Voices," THC, p. 234.

54. *Ibid.*

55. Cf. Lyotard, *The Postmodern Condition*, pp. 79–81. Consider Lyotard's "working" definition of the "postmodern": "A work can become modern only if it is first postmodern. Postmodernism thus understood is not modernism at its end but in the nascent state, and this state is constant." And again: "The postmodern would be that which, *in the modern*, puts forward the unpresentable in presentation itself; that which denies itself the solace of good forms, the consensus of a taste which would make it possible to share collectively the nostalgia for the unattainable."

56. Cf. William V. Spanos, *Repetitions: The Postmodern Occasion in Literature and Culture* (Baton Rouge and London: Louisiana State University Press, 1987); see chapter 5, "Postmodern Literature and Its Occasion: Retrieving the Preterite Middle," pp. 189–276. Regarding the occasion of postmodernism, Spanos writes: "The measure of postmodern occasion form is, in other words, the differential measure of diaspora: not the inseminating Patriarchal Word that establishes a dynastic relationship between the temporal words, but of the disseminating words of contemporary man's [*sic*] orphanage, not of the One but of the many, not of Unity but of dispersal, not of Identity but of ontological difference" (p. 234).

57. Cf. Mark C. Taylor, editor, *Deconstruction in Context* (Chicago: University of Chicago Press, 1986), p. 34. "Postmodern awareness is born of the recognition that the past that was never present eternally returns as the future that never arrives to displace all contemporaneity and defer forever the presence of the modern."

58. Cf. Ihab Hassan, *The Postmodern Turn: Essays in Postmodern Theory and Culture* (Columbus: Ohio State University Press, 1987). It is interesting that in his review of specific themes found in Nietzsche's texts that can be associated with a "postmodern sensibility," Hassan lists "hermeneutics" along with the following: "the decenterment of man," "the vitality of the new," "the demystification of reason," "the refusal of unity," "the empty subject," "the liminality of language," "thinking in fictions," "the denial of origins," "the energetics of value," "ludic arts, the metaphysics of play," and "the collapse of being and becoming, a new ontology"; see pp. 46–51.

Part I

The Hermeneutic Legend

1

Hermeneutics*

Friedrich Ast

69.

All action has its own manner or method which proceeds from its own essence; every activity of life has its own principles, without whose guidance it will lose itself in indeterminate directions. These principles become all the more urgent when we move from our own spiritual [*geistig*][1] and physical world into a foreign one, where no familiar spirit [*Genius*] is guiding our uncertain steps, or is giving direction to our undefined effort. If we are to construct these principles ourselves, we shall apprehend the alien phenomena, understand the world of the unfamiliar spirit and surmise their deeper meaning only gradually and with difficulty.

To the mind [*Geist*] there is nothing foreign *as such*, since it constitutes the higher, infinite unity, the center of all life, that is unbounded by any periphery. Would it be otherwise possible for us to become capable of comprehending the strangest, hitherto most unfamiliar perceptions, sensations, and ideas, if that which exists and can become were not originally comprised in the spirit, and evolving from it, just as the One infinite light refracts into a thousand colors which issue from one source, all being merely different representations of the One, refracted into the temporal, and all dissolving again into that One? For the notion that things enter the mind from outside, through images, through sense impressions or whatever other non-elucidating explanations have been devised, is a self-annulling and long-abandoned conception. Being cannot transform itself into knowledge, or the corporeal into spirit, without being akin to or fundamentally one with it.

All life is spirit and without the spirit there is no life, no being, not even a sensory world; for the physical objects that appear to the mechanically perceiving intelligence as inert, lifeless and material, are to the more deeply inquiring person only apparently dead beings [*Geister*], extinguished in the product, petrified in their physical existence; he is familiar with their power and knows that being, which was originally life, can also never cease to be alive, and that it will express its life-force the moment a congenial power should stimulate the fluctuations of its life-forces [*Lebensgeister*].

70.

In general, all understanding and comprehension of not only a foreign world but also of an "other" is altogether impossible without the original unity and equality of everything spiritual [*Geistige*] and without the original unity of all objects within the spirit. For how can the One affect the other, the latter absorb the influence of the former, if they are not related to each other and the one is able to approximate the other, to fashion itself in its likeness or, conversely, the other to shape itself in a similar way? Thus we would understand neither antiquity in general nor a work of art or text, if our spirit were not, in itself and fundamentally, one with the spirit of antiquity, so that it is able to comprehend this spirit which is alien to it only temporally and relatively. For it is only the temporal and external (upbringing, education [*Bildung*], circumstances) that postulate a difference of the spirit. If we disregard the temporal and external as accidental differences in relation to the pure spirit, then all spirits are alike. And this, precisely, is the objective of *philological* education: the cleansing of the spirit from the temporal, accidental, and subjective, and the imparting of that originality and universality which is essential for the higher and purer human beings, for *humanitarianism*, that he may comprehend the True, the Good, and the Beautiful in all its form and representations, however alien, transforming it into his own nature [*Wesen*], thus becoming again One with the original, purely human spirit from which he departed owing to the limitations of his time, his education and his circumstances.

This is not a mere idea, as it might appear to those who contrast the actual as reality and only truth with the ideal, without considering that there is only One true and original life, which is neither ideal nor real, because both emerge from it as only *temporal* opposites, and that it is the idea which approximates this original life most closely and is therefore the abundance of all reality itself; but higher history (not mere fact-compiling history) manifests this convincingly. In the same way, namely, in which humanity is basically One, it had also been once temporally one in the most magnificent profusion and purity of its life-forces: in the Oriental world, which was mythical and religious only because it did not yet know the temporal polarity of the real and ideal form [*Bildung*].

For Paganism and Christianity are in the Indian world, for example, still One: God is at once the fullness or totality (Pantheismos) and the unity

(Theismos) of all life. Only after the disintegration of Orientalism did the individual elements of its nature reveal themselves temporally (as periods of human development): here is the beginning of the actual so-called history, the temporally and successively evolving life of mankind. The two poles of history are the Greek and Christian worlds, both of which emerged, however, from one center, Orientalism, and are striving by virtue of their original unity for reunion in our own world. The triumph of *our* development will then be the consciously created harmony of the poetic (the plastic or Greek) and the religious (the musical or Christian) life of mankind [*Menschenbildung*]. Thus everything emerged from One Spirit and everything is striving to return again to the One Spirit. Without the knowledge of this original unity which fled from itself (separating itself temporally) and is seeking itself again, we are not only incapable of understanding antiquity but also of knowing anything at all of history and of human development.

71.

All interpretation and explication of a foreign work, composed in a foreign form (language), presupposes understanding not only of a particular part, but also of the totality of this foreign world, which, in turn, presupposes the understanding of the original unity of the spirit. For through this unity, we are enabled not only to form an idea of the totality of the foreign world, but also to comprehend each individual phenomenon truthfully and correctly, i.e., in the spirit of the whole.

Hermeneutics or *exegesis* (ἑρμηνευτιχή ἐξηγητιχή also ἱστοριχή called *enarratio auctorum* by Quintillian, *De Institutione Oratoria Libri Duodecim* I. 9, 1.) presupposes hence the *understanding* of antiquity in all its external and internal elements, and bases upon it the *explication* of the written works of antiquity. For only one who has understood completely both its content and form (language and representation) can explain a work, develop its meaning and describe its internal as well as external connection to other works or to antiquity as a whole.

72.

The understanding of the works of antiquity is based upon their content and form. For everything has a certain content or subject matter and a corresponding form that expresses and reveals it. The content is that which has been shaped, and the form, the expression of its shaping.

As infinitely as antiquity in itself is formed in its entire artistic and scientific, public, and particular life, so infinitely varied is also the content of its work. Hence the understanding of the works of antiquity in terms of their content presupposes knowledge, in the widest sense of the word, of the ancient arts and sciences and archeology.

Form in the written works of antiquity is the *language*, it being the expression of the spirit. The understanding of the works of antiquity consequently presupposes also knowledge of the old languages. Content (subject-matter) and form are originally one: for everything that is formed is originally a self-forming, the form being the external expression of this self-forming, and what is originally One, a life forming itself, separates, after the self-forming has become the formed into the inner (content or subject matter) and the outer (form). The original unity of all being we call *spirit*. Hence the spirit is the vantage point at which all creation begins, to which everything that is created [*Gebildet*] must be retraced, if it is to be comprehended not in its mere appearance, but rather in its essence and truthfulness. Just as the subject matter and form emanated from the spirit, so they must both be retraced to it; only then will we recognize what they were originally and in themselves, and how they were formed.

73.

We will comprehend the whole of antiquity's life through the forms in which it represents itself only after we have inquired into the original oneness of the whole, the spirit, as the focal point from which emanated all phenomena of the internal and external life. Without this higher unity, the whole would disintegrate into a dark and lifeless mass of atomistic fragments, of which none would have a connection with the other, and thus none would have sense or meaning. The idea that antiquity, viewed as a special epoch in mankind's development [*Menschenbildung*], represents poetry or the external, free and beautifully formed life of humanity, may then best describe the spirit of antiquity in general. If we are thus able to trace back everything, even by recognizing the inner connection with the spirit of the whole, then we will truly comprehend every single work of antiquity not only in its appearance, but also in its spirit (its higher relationship and tendency).

But the spirit of antiquity assumes in every individual again a specific form, though not in its essence—for it is One spirit that is present in all—but in direction and form. The understanding of the text of antiquity requires therefore not only the comprehension of the ancient spirit as such, but also especially the recognition of the author's unique spirit, in order to examine not merely how the spirit expressed itself in an author's work in *this* content and in *this* form in order to reveal itself in *its* shaping, but also to see how an author's particular spirit is itself again only a revelation of the higher, universal spirit of the ancient world.

74.

Accordingly, the understanding of the ancient authors is threefold: (1) *historical*, in reference to the content of their works, which is either artistic, scientific, or antiquarian in the broadest sense of the word; (2) *grammatical*, in regard to their form or language and their delivery; (3) *spiritual* [*geistig*] in reference to the spirit of the individual author and of antiquity as a whole.

The third or *spiritual* understanding is the true and higher one, in which the historical and grammatical merge into one life. Historical understanding recognizes *what* the spirit formed, the grammatical *how* it formed it, and the spiritual understanding traces the *what* and the *how*, the subject matter and the form, back to their original, harmonious life in the spirit. For even the public life of antiquity, which the historical writer, for example, perceived and represented as a given, was initially a product of the universal spirit of antiquity. And the historical or antiquarian writer reproduces in himself what is already produced, by comprehending it with his spirit, according to his view and tendency. In other words, in the historical and antiquarian texts of antiquity, the content is a freely reconstructed reproduction, while in the artistic and scientific works, it is a spontaneous and voluntary creation [*Gebildetes*], produced autonomously by the spirit of the poet or thinker.

75.

The basic principle of all understanding and knowledge is to find in the particular the spirit of the whole, and to comprehend the particular through the whole; the former is the analytical, the latter, the synthetic method of cognition. However, both are posited only with and through each other. Just as the whole cannot be thought of apart from the particular as its member, so the particular cannot be viewed apart from the whole as the sphere in which it lives. Thus neither precedes the other because both condition each other reciprocally, and constitute a harmonious life. Similarly, the spirit of collective antiquity also cannot truly be comprehended unless we grasp it in its particular manifestations in the works of the authors of antiquity.

If we are able then to recognize the spirit of antiquity only through its manifestations in the works of its authors, and yet these themselves presuppose in turn the cognition of the universal spirit, how is it possible to understand the particular when it presupposes knowledge of the whole, while we can understand always only successively and are unable to comprehend the whole simultaneously? The circle, namely that I understand a, b, c, etc.

only through A, but this A itself again only through a, b, c, etc., cannot be broken if both A and a, b, c, etc. are seen as opposites that mutually condition and presuppose each other, and if A does not just emerge from a, b, c, etc., and is not generated by them, but does, rather, precede and permeate them all in the same manner, so that a, b, c are nothing but the individual representations of the one A. In A are contained then a, b, c in their original manner. These parts themselves are the individual developments of the one A; each contains A already in a particular mode, and I will not need first to go through the infinite succession of particulars in order to find their unity.

Only in this manner is it possible that I will comprehend the particular through the whole and, conversely, the whole through the particular; for both are simultaneously given in all their particularity. Together with a is also posited A, for the former is only a manifestation of the latter, i.e., the whole is posited simultaneously with the particular. And the further I progress in the comprehension of the particular, passing through the line a, b, c, etc., the more evident and alive the spirit becomes to me, the more does the idea of the whole unfold which already arose in me with the first link in the series. For the spirit is nowhere a composite of individual parts, but an original, simple, undivided essence. It is as simple, whole, and undivided in every particular as it is undivided in itself, i.e., every individual part is only a unique, manifested form of the One spirit; the particular does not produce then the spirit or idea, creating it through synthesis, but rather it stimulates and arouses the idea.

76.

Consequently, all authors of antiquity, but especially those whose works are the free product of the spirit, represent that One spirit, but each according to his own way, by his era, his individuality, his education, and the external circumstances of life. The idea and spirit of all antiquity is mediated to us through every particular poet and author of antiquity. But we understand the author fully only when we comprehend the spirit of all antiquity, which manifests itself in the author in union with his own individual spirit.

The cognition of the latter includes insight into the particular spirit of the age in which the author lived, into the individual spirit of the author himself, as well as knowledge of the education and of the external circumstances which influenced his development.

Pindar, for example, is with regard to subject matter, form, and spirit, a truly ancient poet. Hence his poetry reveals to us in these three respects the spirit of all antiquity. The athletic contests which he celebrates, the pictorial, native, and pure form of his representation, the spirit of his hymns, burning with patriotism, pride of contest, and heroic virtue, evoke in us the glorified image of a truly classical world in which man not only cultivated within himself noble sentiments and praiseworthy aspirations, but moreover delighted in great deeds for the fatherland and its gods. For the prize in the contests was not only an honorary decoration of the winner and of his fatherland, but also a glorification of the god in whose honor the games were celebrated. This is the general connection that Pindar's poems have to the spirit of antiquity as a whole. In and of themselves, however, they reveal his spirit in a unique way, for not only does the spirit of antiquity speak in them, but also the spirit of the author. This gives rise to the questions: In which age did Pindar live? What was his particular spirit [*Genius*]? How did he develop [*bilden*] and in what circumstances did he live? It is necessary to answer all these questions as completely as possible if we want to sketch a true and live picture of the spirit and character of Pindar's poetry. This is what *understanding* a poet of antiquity means.

77.

The development of understanding and its exposition is called *explication*. Explication, of course, presupposes understanding, and is based on it. For only what has been truly grasped and comprehended, i.e., understood, can be communicated and made clear to others.

Understanding contains two elements: comprehension of the particular and summation of the particular into the totality of One perception, feeling, or idea, i.e., the dissecting of its elements or characteristics and the joining of the dissected parts into the unity of the perception of the concept. Hence explication is also based upon the development of the particular or individual and the summary of the particular into a unity. Understanding and explication are accordingly *cognition* and *comprehension*.

78.

The above mentioned circle applies here also, namely, in that the particular can be understood only through the whole, and conversely, the whole, only through the particular, and in that the perception or concept precedes cognition of the particular, even though perception and concept seem to develop only through these. Here too, as above, this circle can be resolved only by acknowledging the original unity of the particular and the general as the true life of both. Then the spirit of the whole is contained in every single element, and the further the development of the particular progresses, the clearer and livelier the idea of the whole becomes. Here too, the spirit does not generate itself through the connection of the particular, but lives already and originally in the particular, wherefore the particular is indeed the manifestation of the spirit in its totality.

79.

In the explication of a work or of a particular part, the idea of the whole is not generated by the combination of all its individual parts, but is rather evoked in the person who is capable of comprehending the idea in the first place with the comprehension of the first particular, and becomes ever clearer and livelier, the further the explication of the particular progresses. The first comprehension of the idea of the whole through the particular is conjecture, i.e., as yet still indefinite and undeveloped fore-knowledge of the spirit, which turns into vivid and clear cognition through growing comprehension of the particular. Upon exploration of the sphere of the particular, the idea, which was still conjecture at the point of first comprehension, emerges now as a clear and conscious unity of the manifold presented in the individual. Understanding and explication are complete.

80.

Thus the understanding and explication of a work is a true reproduction or recreation [Nachbilden] of that which is already formed. For every creation begins with a mythical, still concealed starting point, from which, as factors of that creation, develop the elements of life. They are the actually forming, mutually limiting forces which become united into One whole through the process of reciprocal interpenetration. The idea, still undeveloped at the beginning, yet giving to the life-factors their direction, is represented completely and objectively in the created product. The aim of all creation is consequently the manifestation of the spirit, the harmonious forming of the external (the elements that separated from the original unity) and the inner (spiritual [geistig]) life. The beginning of creation is unity; the creation itself is multiplicity (the contrast of the elements); the completion of the creation or the created [Gebildete] is the permeation of the unity and multiplicity, i.e., totality.

81.

Consequently, not only the whole of a work, but also its specific parts and even its single passages, can be understood and explained only in the following manner: that as one comprehends the first particular, one is comprehending also the spirit and idea of the whole. Next, one explains the single parts and elements to gain an insight into the individual nature of the whole. Upon the cognition of all the particulars, the next step is to summarize everything into a unity which, with the cognition of all the elements, is now a clear, conscious, and in all its particulars, a live one.

The explication of a Horation ode, for example, will proceed from the originating point of the poet's production. In it, the idea of the whole is already intimated, as surely as the starting point of the poetic creation itself originated in the inspired idea of the whole. Having been given its first direction at the starting point, the idea of the whole evolves through all elements throughout the poem; and the explication must comprehend these single moments, each in its individual life, until the circle of the developing elements is complete, until the whole, made up of parts, flows back into the idea in which the production originated; until the manifold life, having evolved into many individual parts, becomes one again with the original unity, which the first represented moment of the production only intimated, and the unity, at first only indefinite, emerges as a vivid, living harmony.

Every individual passage emanates also from one perception or idea. The representation and development of this idea is the multiplicity of its life; its completion is the harmony of the unity from which this multiple life unfolds, and with the multiplicity, the real life. Every passage which is complete in itself can serve as proof and example.

82.

The particular presupposes the idea of the whole, the spirit, which shapes itself throughout the whole scheme of particulars into vivid life, returning finally into itself again. With this returning of the spirit into its original being [*Wesen*], the circle of explication is closed. Every particular, then, intimates the spirit, because it emanated from it and is permeated by it. Consequently, every particularity contains also its own life, because it reveals the spirit in a unique way. In itself, in its merely external, empirical life, the unique is the *letter*; taken in its inner being, in its significance and relationship to the spirit of the whole, which represents itself in a unique mode, it is the *meaning*; the consummate comprehension of the letter and the meaning in their harmonious unity is the *spirit*. The *letter* is the body or cloak of the spirit, through which the invisible spirit enters into the outer, visible life. *Meaning* is the harbinger and interpreter of the spirit; the *spirit* itself is true life.

For every passage that needs explication, one must first ask *what* the letter is stating; secondly, *how* it is stating it, what meaning the statement has, what significance it occupies in the text; thirdly, what the idea of the whole or of the spirit is, as that unity from which the letter emanated and into which it seeks to return. Without the meaning, the letter is dead and unintelligible. To be sure, the meaning without the spirit is in itself intelligible, but it has an individual or atomistic meaning which has no basis and no purpose without the spirit. For only through the spirit do we come to perceive the *why*, the *where-from*, and *whereto* of every object.

The *letter*, *meaning*, and *spirit* are therefore the three elements of explication. The hermeneutics of the letter is the explication of the word and subject matter of the particular; the hermeneutics of meaning [*Sinn*] is the explication of its significance [*Bedeutung*] in connection with the given passage; and the hermeneutics of the spirit is the explication of its higher relation to the idea of the whole in which the particular dissolves into the unity of the whole.

83.

The *explication* of the *word* and *subject matter* presupposes knowledge of language and archeology, in other words, grammatical and historical knowledge of antiquity. With regard to language, the various stages of its development must be determined as well as its different forms and dialects, for every writer writes in the language of his age and in the dialect of *his* people. *Homer's* language differs from the language of later epic and lyric poets, dramatists, etc., not only with respect to its genius but also with respect to its outer and formal development. Every particular passage and every word in it must be specifically understood if a meaning is to emerge. Wherever the meaning of words that are unknown or employed in an unusual or metaphorical way is not immediately clear, these words must be investigated with regard to their etymology, analogy, and various usage during different periods by different authors, in order to establish the meaning which corresponds to the meaning of the passage and the spirit (i.e., to the genius and the tendency) of the whole. The explication of the subject matter presupposes knowledge of antiquity as such, and especially of that subject which the author in question treated. In fact, we must investigate the level of development occupied at that time by the art, science, etc., chosen by a given author for the object of his representation, how antiquity in general, and particularly the author in question, viewed these disciplines, so that we do not confer upon an earlier author the achievements of a later development and knowledge, or conversely, attribute to him ideas and views that were older and as yet undeveloped.

84.

The explication of the *meaning* is based on the insight into the spirit [*Genius*] and tendency of antiquity as such and of the particular author who is the subject of the explication. For without having surmised or recognized the spirit of antiquity, it is impossible truly to comprehend the meaning of even a single passage. If the modern sentimental or logical mind [*Geist*] does not rise to pure perception of the life and spirit of antiquity, it will easily run the risk of understanding and interpreting falsely, not only the Greek or Roman work as a whole, but also its individual passages.

The meaning of a work and of a particular passage is deduced from the spirit and tendency of the author. Only the interpreter who has comprehended these and familiarized himself with these is in the position to understand every passage in the spirit of its author and to reveal its correct meaning. A passage by Plato, for example, will often have a different meaning from one almost similar in meaning and words by Aristotle. For what is in the former, concrete perception and free life, is in the latter frequently only logical concept and national reflection. But if we look at a single work on its own, then the meaning of every particular passage and every word is determined by its relationship to the other most closely related words and passages and to the work as a whole. Consequently, not only one and the same word, but also individual, similar passages, carry in a different context, different meanings. But, in order to grasp the meaning of the whole on which the understanding of the part depends, one must have explored the spirit, the intention, the time and conditions of the public and private life in which the work in question was written. The history of literature, of the individual education, of the life of the author, is therefore necessary for the understanding of every particular work.

It is necessary, furthermore, to distinguish between the simple and the allegorical meaning. In passages that are doubtful, that meaning is generally the most correct which corresponds most closely to the spirit of antiquity and especially to the spirit, the tendency, and character of the author.

85.

Explication of the *spirit* of a text or of an individual passage means the exposition of the idea which the author had in mind or was unconsciously guided by. For the idea is the higher, living unity from which all life evolves, and to which it returns again spiritually transfigured. The elements of the idea are the multiplicity, the perceptual, developed life, and the unity as the form of multiplicity or of life, i.e., perception and concept. The harmonious interpenetration of the two produces the idea. Now in many authors, the idea as such does not emerge, but only its elements, either the perception or the concept: perception in the case of empirical, historical writers; the mere concept in the logical philosophical ones. Only in the case of the truly artistic or philosophical authors is everything developed from the idea and is everything striving back to it, so that not only the whole of a text, but also the individual passages, have their life in the idea.

The idea, as the original unity (the spirit) of the perception and the concept, is superior to both, i.e., it is elevated above finitude; for the finite, which is either multiplicity (real life) or unity (form and concept of life), is posed only with the perception and the concept. These, however, pass from the idea into the temporal (evolving into opposites). Through the idea, everything is therefore being related to the original, the infinite; in it, the finite dissolves into the spiritual sublimity. Likewise, it is also the spirit of things which connects them with the higher world from which they passed into the temporal and finite, untying the fetters of the earthly and transfiguring it to a free life.

86.

In the empirical and logical writers, the explication of the spirit is primarily the development of the perception or the concept from which they set out. Every perception and every concept points to an idea, for both are only separate sundered elements of the idea. The perception of human life, for example, which the historian Herodotus adopted as that world view which he constantly kept before him while narrating his history, is apprehended as mere perception, empirical and without any higher, spiritual significance, notwithstanding the fact that it elevates itself to the religious view of a Nemesis punishing the presumptuous. What is the source of this perception? we ask rightfully, for everything finite presupposes as such a higher base. It originates in the life of things themselves, in whose sole contemplation the historian resided. But where does the law of finite objects originate, so that they have their determined limits, annulling and destroying themselves whenever they want to go beyond the limits that nature set for them? Only the idea of finitude itself explains this law to me, as well as that perception from which Herodotus proceeded.

Other historians base their history on a concept, for example, on the concept of national independence, of a judicial system that mankind seeks to realize in history; or, as pragmatists, they want to instruct the reader on certain subjects via the historical narrative, viewing history as being of the greatest public benefit, etc. What is the origin of these concepts? What are they? They are only fragmented elements of the idea of history. Like every idea, the idea of history is in itself complete and independent. But the elements, be they perceptions or concepts, that emanated from the harmonious unity in the idea, do not have an independent life, for they are determined by and founded in the idea. Hence, every perception and every concept as such is finite and limited and presupposes a higher base. The logical philosopher lives entirely in the concept, likewise leading to the idea, because every concept is founded in the idea.

87.

Through the explanation of the spirit, we are then raising ourselves above both the letter and the meaning of the letter to the original life from which both issued, namely to the idea which either stood as such clearly before the author's inner eye, or—where he failed to raise himself to the clarity of life—took the form of perception or concept.

The explication of the spirit is, however, twofold: an inner and an outer, or a subjective and an objective one. The inner or subjective explication of the spirit operates within the given sphere, in that it traces the idea from which the author set out. It develops from the idea the tendency and character of the work and reconstructs the idea itself in the particular parts of the text, so that it demonstrates the basic unity from which the whole issued, how the unity developed into multiplicity, and how, by virtue of the harmony of the whole, multiplicity interpenetrated with unity into one life again. In other words, explication demonstrates the relationship among the individual parts in a work, how each part is formed in itself, and how each part seeks to return into the unity of the whole (how it relates to the whole). In the same manner does the explication of the spirit of a particular passage, of its subject matter, and of its literal sense and meaning, relate to the idea that the author had in mind, to the spirit of his view, formation and representation. Thus too, unclear passages which express a different verbal sense and even a different meaning can only be comprehended and interpreted correctly through clear cognition of the spirit of a text (its idea and tendency).

88.

The outer or objective explication of the spirit goes beyond the given sphere of the idea represented in a work. It does so partly by demonstrating its connection to other ideas related to it, and its relation to the basic idea from which all others emanated; partly by appreciating and evaluating, from its more elevated perspective, the spirit exhibited in the text both with regard to its content, its tendency, etc., and relationship to the form of the representation.

Thus, for example, the spirit of a Platonic dialogue can be grasped and explicated correctly only if we relate the idea of every single dialogue to related ideas in other dialogues; if, in other words, we compare the similar dialogues with each other according to their spirit, tracing them back finally to the fundamental idea of Plato's writings and philosophy, in order to determine their relationship to the foundational idea. My relating one idea to other kindred ideas in the same kind of texts explains to me the individual conclusiveness of the idea represented. For one idea weaves through all dialogues, constituting the soul of the Platonic dialogues, but in every individual text, it appears in a different representation, viewed from a different perspective. This peculiarity presupposes other peculiarities. For if in one dialogue Plato treats and represents an idea only practically, this then points to a theoretical or dialectical treatment of that idea in another dialogue. Hence two such dialogues stand in the closest reciprocal relationship. However, both also point to other dialogues in which the same idea is represented, not in its division into the dialectical and practical view, but rather in its original life, etc. The relating of the idea in the individual dialogue, as well as in the most closely related dialogues, to the One focal point of all ideas, discloses the highest principle, in which the idea represented in the individual dialogues has not only its final proof, but also its true life.

89.

The evaluation and appreciation of the spirit of a work, for example, of one of Plato's dialogues, presupposes the most comprehensive and accurate knowledge possible, not only of Plato's genius, but also of antiquity and especially of philosophy and art. For I am able to evaluate the philosophical and artistic level of a given text by Plato in relation to the Platonic genius only if I have grasped and comprehended as completely as possible the genius of Plato's philosophy and art. However, only my knowledge of the philosophical and artistic spirit of the classical world will enable me to appreciate not only every single one of Plato's works, but also all of his works, in light of the spirit of antiquity, and to determine their relationship to the art and philosophy of similar works of antiquity. Both modes of evaluation, the one in regard to the genius of an author, and the other in regard to the spirit of antiquity, refer either to the content—the represented idea— or to the form—the representation of the idea.

90.

The evaluation of the content and form in reference to the genius of an author is, however, only relative, for with regard to the genius of one author a text can be most perfect, yet compared to the genius of another, highly imperfect. For example, judged according to the spirit of the ordinary Socratic, several of the smaller dialogues attributed to Plato are excellent with regard to their content, ideas, ethical principles, the beautiful view of life, etc., as well as with regard to their form—the vivid, dramatic, often mimic representation, the passion of the delivery, the naturalness and immediacy of dialogue, etc. However, when evaluated in the light of Plato's genius, these same dialogues would perhaps have to be lowered to the lowest rank of Plato's texts, because they exhibit neither the elevated life in the idea and the intellectual striving for the infinite, nor the highly gifted power of representation and the absolute imagination.

91.

The evaluation of the spirit of a text with reference to the genius of a people and an age is merely a national one. For the works of an Ionian poet or thinker will have to be judged differently from those of an Italian or Attic author. What may perhaps be excellent for an Ionian author will be of slight or of no significance for an Italian or Attic author, and vice versa. The Ionian author perhaps already accomplishes the highest objective within his sphere when, through the free, liberated life of the spirit, he penetrates the realism native to him and elevates the perception at least to the level of the concept. Conversely, the Italian—or Pythagorean—educated author may have achieved the highest in his sphere if he succeeded in shaping the idea into a concrete representation, i.e., rejoined the concept to the perception. Thus we admire in the Ionian author the ideal formation, in the Italian, the realistic; in the Attic, however, the unity of the real and ideal, i.e., the immediately represented (dramatic, dialogical) life of the idea.

As an *Ionian* poet, *Homer* is thus the most accomplished poet, and *Pindar* is so as a *Doric* lyric poet, but neither is the most accomplished poet as such, for in each, only one of the essential elements of perfect form [*Bildung*] prevails. As an Ionian poet, Homer excels over Pindar in his vivid, objective representation, as much as Pindar, conversely, outshines Homer with his deep, inner life of the spirit and soul. If, moreover, we compare the Greek nation as a whole with other peoples, this estimation also proves to be merely a national one. For example, as a Roman lyric poet, Horace is the most accomplished poet, but he is not one in general, for if included in the ranks of the Greek lyric poets, he would command perhaps only third place.

92.

There is yet still a higher appreciation of the spirit of a text than the merely relative and national one. Viewed in itself, this evaluation is the highest because it does not proceed from a particular, limited point of view, but is rather an absolute one. For it speaks no longer of individuality and nationality, but of the True, the Beautiful, and the Good, as such. The True, as such, is the point of view of philosophical and scientific texts, the Beautiful, as such, is the principle by which works of art are judged, and the Good, as such, is the spirit of life that encompasses both.

If, for example, we evaluate a Platonic text relatively and individually, we are then relating its spirit to Plato's genius; if we evaluate it nationally, the spirit of antiquity becomes the criterion of our evaluation. However, if we wish to appreciate it absolutely, then we must rise above the merely relative and national standpoint to the highest, absolute one. We will first ask how the idea represented by Plato corresponds to Truth itself. Does it approximate or depart from the absolute idea of truth? Secondly, to what extent are the Platonic dialogues works of art? How do they represent the idea of the Beautiful, as such? Does the Beautiful emerge from them purely and serenely, or is it confined by any one thing (the subject matter, the purpose, the manner, etc.)? Thirdly, what is the soul, the heart of the Platonic dialogues? Is it the inner life, the Good transfigured in them, its virtue unblemished and aspiring to sacredness, or do they bear too visibly the imprints of their age, of their national character, etc.? For Plato is one of the few writers who are at once thinkers, artists and transfigured spirits, for whom the unconditional appreciation is threefold. In contrast, most others are only thinkers or artists or witty writers.

93.

However, only that person who is capable of such a consummate appreciation as is necessary for perfect understanding, as well as for the complete explication of the author's spirit, is able to rise above the author himself, through the idea of the True, the Beautiful, and the Good, as such. And if philosophy alone is the one chosen to live in the bliss of these ideas, then also, only the *philosophically trained philologist* will be capable of rising from the temporal grounds of the grammatical and historical interpretation to the ethereal heights of the spiritual, consummate interpretation and appreciation.

Translated by Dora Van Vranken

Notes

* Friedrich Ast, *Grundlinien der Grammatik, Hermeneutik und Kritik* (Landshut, 1808), pp. 165–212.—ED.

1. In deference to the sentiment and philological-hermeneutical vantage point of Friedrich Ast's time, as well as Ast's own voice and thought-structure, I consciously opted for a close, faithful translation of the original text, even while mindful of the need to render it into idiomatic English. The wish to adhere to the text as closely as possible also prompted my decision to retain Ast's frequently extremely long and labyrinthal sentences whenever they appeared reasonably comprehensible, but when, as in a few cases, they did not, I broke them down into two or more units. Occasional additions and/or omissions of one or more words seemed advisable in order to achieve both a clearer understanding of the text and a smoother reading as well as to complete a thought or sentence that seemed otherwise incomplete. Beyond this, I resisted the temptation to edit, to eliminate frequent repetitions and unneeded modifications. Finally, in observation of Ast's practice, and as an aid to comprehension, I adhered to the example of the original text by capitalizing consistently the term "One" (*Ein*) even where used as a modifier. Ast appears to denote with *Ein* the notion of unity and common origin.

Five German terms that appear with various frequency in the text and occupy varying degrees of importance in Ast's thoughts invite some commentary on their usage and meaning: *Geist, Genius, Wesen, Bildung, Anschauung*. In some instances and contexts, their translation into a corresponding English term can be rendered only imperfectly (e.g., *geistig*: "spiritual"), and in a few others, their precise meaning cannot be determined with absolute certainty (e.g., *Genius*: "spirit," "genius"). Where this is the case, and where textual context suggests a different term in English (e.g., *Geister*: "being"), the German term is cited in brackets. The primary meaning that these terms carry in this text are as follows: *Geist*: "spirit"; *Genius*: "spirit"; *Wesen*: "nature," "essence"; *Bildung*: "shaping," "forming"; *Anschauung*: "perception," "view." Both the following commentary on these terms and the inclusion of the German term in the text should facilitate the reader's understanding. Where important, attention is also given to the corresponding verb— and adjective—forms of the five terms.

Geist (-er): As the reader is probably aware, there is no single word in English that fully expresses the range and nuances of meaning inherent in the German term *Geist*. While it can be rendered in English with "spirit," "intelligence," "mind," "soul," "essence," "imagination," "genius," "esprit," and others, it may also simultaneously suggest a combination of these nuances. In Ast's text, *Geist* is used often with the meaning that it carries in the familiar term *Zeitgeist*. Ast's reference to the *Geist* of an author or artist, of a literary or art work, of a people or nation, of a culture, age or period is translated best with "spirit"— "spirit" signifying in these instances, also a unique quality, perspective or character. Ast's other reference to *Geist* is to the abstract philosophical notion of a "universal spirit," i.e., "intelligence," "mind," "essence" or "life-force." The adjective and adjective noun (*geistig, Geistige*) do not carry the religious connotations of "spiritual," but correspond rather to the above meanings of *Geist*. In some contexts they may also denote "cultural."

Genius: Certain expressions existing in the English language today, for example, "the genius of a language," demonstrate a usage of the word "genius" parallel to the usage of *Genius* in 18th century Germany, a tradition to which Ast was heir.

Genius denoted "spirit," i.e., "life-force," but also mental "disposition," "tendency," "uniqueness." The association of *Genius* with extraordinary creative talent appears to date from a later stage. However, while the text offers a number of examples of Ast's use of *Genius* as a synonym for *Geist*, it also contains examples where *Genius* may be intended to denote creative genius. For this reason, and in order to set it off from *Geist*, the German term is cited in the translation when rendered both with "spirit" and with "genius."

Wesen: *Wesen* is used to denote the "essential nature," "fundamental property," "characteristic," "quality," "attribute," or "feature" of an object, idea, living organism, etc. This term can also be translated variously with "nature," "essence," "character," "being," or "property." Ast, for instance, describes unity or oneness (*Einheit*) as the nature, i.e., essence (*Wesen*) of the spirit (*Geist*). *Wesen* is also used to designate the real or essential aspect of something, as opposed to its appearance, and to refer to the meaning-content of an idea or concept. Correspondingly, the adjectives *wesenhaft* and *wesentlich* signify "real," "substantial," "characteristic." *Wesentlich* may also signify "essential" or "vital."

Bildung: Ast uses this term in three different ways: (l) "forming," "shaping," "creating," or "composition," (2) "development," (3) "education." In reference to a literary or artistic product, *Bildung* denotes "forming," "shaping," "creating," "producing" as well as "composition," "organization," "formation." Broader in its meaning than the corresponding English term "education," *Bildung* denotes, in addition to "education," the development or formation of the total human personality through formal education and/or more general cultural influences. "*Bildung*" also signifies "development" in the larger sense of the development of mankind or of the human spirit and mind. True to its concrete root-word, *Bild* (image, picture), the term *Bildung* still carried in Ast's time the centuries-old notion of "development" as "shaping in the image of," a notion which the related word *Entwicklung* (development) does not contain. The meaning of the verb *bilden* parallels that of the noun. The adjective *bildlich* means "graphic," "pictorial."

Anschauung: In its most common usage, *Anschauung* signifies "view," "attitude." The strong visual connotation of *Anschauung* comes into full play in philosophical and aesthetic contexts. Inherent in its meaning is a blend of the highest intellectual reflection (contemplation) with concrete visual perception. In a philosophical context, *Anschauung* is rendered by the English words "apperception," "reflective cognition," "intuition" or "perception"; in an aesthetic context with reference to an author or artist, it denotes her/his "intuition" or "perception." Applied to the reader and viewer, *Anschauung* denotes "perception" or "comprehension." The verb *anschauen* ("to look at," "to perceive") carries the same kind of meaning as the noun in philosophical and aesthetic-critical contexts. The adjective *anschaulich* signifies "concrete," "graphic," "vivid," "perceptual."—TRANS.

2

The Aphorisms on Hermeneutics
from 1805 and 1809/10*

Friedrich D. E. Schleiermacher

The Aphorisms of 1805

Only what Ernesti calls *subtilitas intelligendi* [exactness of understanding] belongs to hermeneutics; as soon as the *subtilitas explicandi* [exactness of explication] becomes more than the articulation [Lit: "outer sphere"] of understanding, it becomes itself an object for hermeneutics and belongs to the art of presentation. Hermeneutics has to do with the correct use of commentaries: not their composition.

The first part of his *subtilitas intelligendi* is the precise determination [*Analyse*] of what is to be understood: sizing up the task; others are analysis [*Lösung*] and choosing the right tools [*Hülfsmittel*].

N.I. There are two contradictory guidelines to understanding: consider everything as self evident until encountering a contradiction or nonsense; consider everything construed as equally important. Following the second guideline, understanding is an endless process.

N.I. of the 1st. Difficulties in understanding the place of individual elements in a text do not only occur when reading foreign language texts, nor have they only to do with "becoming arrested by the meaning of a

single word'' as Ernesti has it. They arise when one fails to grasp the
whole sense, being beguiled by some particular.

Ernesti's distinctions in his paragraph four do not agree with those in
paragraph five.

N.I. Grammatical interpretation is 'objective', technical interpretation 'subjective'. The first assesses the manner of construction as a simple
delimitation of meaning; the second as suggestive of meaning. They cannot
always be used in perfect harmony as this presupposes that the author used
language absolutely correctly, and that the interpreter understood it perfectly. The art of hermeneutics is to know where one should give way to the
other.

The principles of language usage such as the use of parallelisms
(see Morus, p. 16) although not merely axiomatic are still quite easy to
demonstrate.
N. 2nd. An important prerequisite for interpretation is that one must
be willing to leave one's own consciousness [*Gesinnung*] and to enter the
author's. For a negative example see Morus p. 18. In his exposition of Ro-
mans 14:23 he deliberately obscures the sense of the word πᾶν—'all' [In
the sentence "All that is not from faith is sin."], because he takes the strict
moral idea in the text to be merely a stylistic flourish. [Morus interprets the
phrase to mean: 'If one doesn't act out of conviction, one can easily go
astray'.]

N. 1st. Every word has basically one meaning, even particles; only
by understanding the basic meaning of a word can one go on to understand
its use in a trope [Lit: "its multiplicity of meaning"].

N. 1st. When one sticks to viewing the task of hermeneutics as strict understanding, then the thoughts that arise in the process will not be handled as if they were hard facts, but rather as data to be ruminated upon. Thus one could avoid all the specious arguments about the different layers of meaning in a text.

N. 1st. As Ernesti articulated it, the sense [*Sinn*] can be nothing other than the ever closer approximation of the meaning [*Bedeutung*], a particular meaning to be drawn from among general possibilities [*allgemeinen Sphäre*].

N.I. One must attempt to become the general reader for whom the work was intended [*unmittelbare Leser*], in order to understand allusions and to catch the precise drift of similes.

N. 2nd. Categorizing an author's output into works, studies, and casual writings is useful for hermeneutics; it helps facilitate the reader's communication [*Verhältnisse*] with the writer.

N. 2nd. One great difficulty is to determine which only apparent thoughts are to be viewed as signs. For example, amplifications or hyperboles are only signs of inner impressions; and inspired rhetoric [*Einfälle*] is often only signs of a state of mind. Often only the outward form of a thought is presented; its whole material only suggested by the means of presentation.

N. 2nd. Construing the author is quite different from construing a text according to its subdivisions.

N. 1st. A casual method contents itself with gaining a hazy impression of individual parts set all against a vaguely perceived unity.

N. 1st. Barbarisms in word-definitions arise from a defective knowledge of one's own word-sphere or of a foreign language. Moral terms are prone to this misuse, such as the Greek for 'righteousness': δικαιοσύνη.

N. 1st. I should consider the effect polemics often has on the use of vaguely definable words such as 'mysticism', often giving them an unfortunate nuance.

N.I. Clarifying the art of hermeneutics requires narrowing the concept of what Ernesti thought it was while broadening its application. It has to do with confronting the difficulties that arise out of the treatment [for example, ambiguity in the relationship between parts of a work], and that arise simply from the difficulty of the subject matter treated. There is first of all an understanding that both writer and reader could share. Second, there is an understanding peculiar to the writer as the reader reconstructs it; third, there is an understanding peculiar to the reader which even the author could respect as a special and extraneous meaning.

N. 2nd. The third type of understanding mentioned actually should be called accommodation. It does not belong to general hermeneutics, but is appropriate to discursive or casual writings and polemics.

N. 2nd. The second type mentioned could belong either to general hermeneutics or to a particular hermeneutics.

N. 2nd. Investigating the central idea or the unity comprising all the parts, or the individuality of a text, belongs to general hermeneutics. Investigating the possible multiplicity of meanings a text could have on a psychological or personal level belongs to various particular hermeneutics.

N.I. My introduction should also contain something about the applicability of the principles of general hermeneutics to interpreting the sacred texts.

N. 2nd. Another difficulty in interpretation is determining whether an author intended a work to be an organic whole or an inorganic fragment. Compare the works of Tieck and Schlegel in this regard. The difficulty occurs equally in the first and second parts of interpretation: grammatical analysis, intentional assessment. Another difficulty is catching the significance of the euphony of either the metrics or the emphasis which an author can draw from the form of a word, e.g., the Platonic use of the word heaven: οὐρανόζ.

N.I. My introduction should consider the effects on biblical interpretation of the doctrine of inspiration held by the exegetes. Consider what of hermeneutics is inconsistent with Catholic interpretation, how it is more universally Christian.

N. 1st. A significant use of emphasis should be expected only in texts of the high style; in interpreting texts of the low style one must expect ahead of time not to encounter any.

N. 1st. The deeper in the elements [*Elemente*], the more unresearched the language remains. [Paraphrase: 'The more purely formal or purely personal language is, the less accessible it is'.][1]

N. 1st. A mistaken understanding of a trope can arise from reading it too literally: *facies rosea, planta serpens scandens* [a rosy face, stem creeping, ascending].

N. 1st. One must cultivate a *simulitudo intelligibilis*—a knack for understanding similitude—because all godly qualities can only be expressed in tropes.

N. 1st. It is foolish to mistake an idiomatic use for a trope: 'snow white' is simply an idiom for white.

N. 1st. Sometimes the basic meaning for a word will change in time, so that a meaning originally integral [*organische*] to a work will be lost and an unintegral meaning read in its place. For that reason one must never lose sight of etymological history (like Spalding did),[2] since one could quite often mistake unintegral meanings for eternal and unchanging ones.

N. 1st. In later periods compounds that originally were without sense have been made from simple words that became inorganic, for example, *Befug-niss* [authority].

N. 1st. Even in the most ordinary tropes there is originally something extraordinary at the root: for example, the original sense of 'to not come over the threshhold'. One must therefore attend closely to the period when a word is used and to the particular meaning it is given then.

———————

N. 2nd. There are mystical tropes which are by their very natures as inexhaustible as light and knowledge. Here the context in which they appear [*Behandlung*] alone must determine how they are meant.

———————

N. 2nd. Different styles require different methods of exposition; but neither the *lex narratio* nor dogma provide legitimate criteria. [See Morus, p. 282ff.]

———————

N. 1st. History can provide an excellent principle of explanation for allegory. Yet Morus' mistaken interpretation of the prophecy about how Peter was to be killed [in John 21:18–19] shows that even this method can become akin to using 'old patches on new clothing'. [The reference to 'history' can simply be a disguised version of allegorical interpretation—where one text is used to enlighten another without regard to the intentions underlying each.—TRANS.]

———————

N. 1st. If one miscalculates the original meaning of an expression in a text, one could wind up blaming an author for ambiguity unjustly, as Heindorf[3] did Plato's use of the terms: εὖ πράττειν and ὄ, τι μαθών.

———————

N. 1st and 2nd. The emphasis a word or phrase or trope had when it was written (*Emphasis temporaria*) is not necessarily apparent in reading a text—it can be ascertained only by reconstructing the mood of the author. One could compare Morus' understanding of *audivi* and *urbs*. [See Morus pp. 323–325, 321.]

———————

N. 1st. On the other hand the phrase *vir summus* [the best man] when not referring to a specific person can be a kind of emphasis used to bring a forgotten word back to honor. [See Morus, p. 324.]

N. 1st. A misunderstanding can arise over the simplest things. Kant, for example, did not understand how to use the indirect speech of submissive servants, a whole class of words, and thus he was not acquainted with a whole realm of expression.[4] Pseudo-words are a sign of the modern times.

N. 1st. One cannot understand one epoch of a language without understanding its whole history and nature, and also not without knowing the language in general.

N.I. One cannot understand something spoken without having the most general knowledge of the language, and at the same time, an understanding of what is personally intended and uniquely expressed.

N. 2nd. I should consider how speaking is actually a diffusion: it brings about on behalf of language a metamorphosis of intensive thought into extensive understanding.

N.I. If all speaking were a living reconstruction there would be no need for hermeneutics, only for a critique of art.

N. 1st. One can notice the various strata of conceptions and preconceptions [*Anschauungsweise*] in a language. Just as the devil sowed weeds among the wheat.

N. 1st. A definition can only be derived from within the whole inter-related structure of definitions in the language itself.

N. 1st. Ellipses are signs of a developing life. One no longer has the time to waste. But there is a characteristic difference in German between the elliptical speech of every day [many sentences, shortened], and the business style [few sentences, complicated].

N. 1st. If one views everything articulated as emanating from the core of language, then all personal value disappears from the expression. Only a true artist of language is then thought to be capable of individualizing the language anew.

N.I. Previous methods of hermeneutics proceed with what is considered to be common sense understanding [*von der Landläufigkeit des Verstehens*]; they require no art [of assessment or judgment] until they stumble against what appears to be nonsense. Thus all their rules appear as arbitrary, virtually expedient, and unsystematic. They consist often of specific reactions to previous mistakes in exposition, as for example, when one interpreter might try to explain isolated passages with a rare reference to the intention [*Zwecke*] of the author.

N.I. A more comprehensive method appears at first to contain a contradiction because one approaches the subjective meaning of a work only by means of an exact understanding. It is only in this way that one can begin to strike a balance between the demands of two apparently opposing periods. The same holds true when one is mastering a language.

If one understands everything articulated as emanating from the core of the artist, then all the contemporaneity of the language disappears, excepting in as much as the artist himself grasps it and determines it in his consciousness.

Christianity made language. It was a magnified linguistic spirit from the beginning and still is. It was providential that it could not fasten itself to hellenistic truth.

Hermeneutics is the reverse of grammar and more.

I should consider how the technical [subjective] meaning of a work can be deduced from the sphere of words and the rules binding them together, so that afterwards one may presuppose it; as well as how one can use established subjective meanings as a reference for understanding new ones.

I should consider the similarity of the process of establishing facts and expanding on them used in textual exposition and juristic exposition. One could point out in both the differences between the exposition [*Auslegen*] and inference [*Einlegen*].

Language provides hermeneutics all its assumptions and presumptions, and all one's objective or subjective assumptions are to be tested against language.

Interpretations of Schlegel's poetry often provide examples of how easily one can come to a wholly inadequate, superficial understanding.

The synecdoche is itself a figure. The connection between things that it implies is usually assumed to be that of a logical extension [*contento pro continuo*]; whereas the separation [between figure and field] ought to be distinguished much more explicitly. Only by considering it as a part standing for a whole [*pars pro toto*] will one catch its exact significance [*Anschauung*].

———

As one can understand humans in light of moral law, so one can understand language from the principles of human development [*Bildungsgesetz*].

———

One must continually refer complications to simplicity, multiplicity to unity.

———

I should speak about the tension between language-usage and grammatical rules. The proper arbitration between them is a respectful usage.

———

So-called synonyms often proceed from quite different perceptions—hill and mountain, valley and ravine.

———

All concepts proceed from contrasts. Perception becomes absorbed in inflection.

———

I should seek out an example of how a figurative meaning has evolved into a literal [*eigentliche*] meaning. The same thing happens with leaders.

The depth of the language is revealed in the identity of the expression for the real and the ideal perception.

One must consider what can be learned from the fact that a word can be synonymous with another while at the same time having a plurality of meanings of its own—to understand the nature of words.

In the case of ambiguous references, the more grammatical and correct an author is the more one can rely on distinguishing the most natural and precise meaning. This is difficult to do with the New Testament, as in the phrase from Galatians 1:6: ἀπὸ τοῦ χαλέσαντος ὑμᾶς ἐν χάριτι Χριστοῦ ['from him who called you to the grace of Christ'].

One can have a facile understanding of the phrase:μετατίθεσθαι ἀπὸ τοῦ χαλέσ[αντος] ['deserting him who called you'] but one does not understand it completely if one does not grasp the original meaning.

Galatians 1:10 provides an example of a sudden shift in meaning from one concept of a word to another: ἀνθρώπους πείθω ἢ τὸν θεόν ['Do I put my confidence in men or God?'].

From being conversant with flesh and blood, Paul derived a graphic style with which to examine sensuality.

Figurative meanings are only those which derive from a definite picture, a subjective meaning which has become objective.

Every child learns how words mean through hermeneutics.

Grammatical interpretation provides the groundwork for determining the whole sense of individual parts; it is of course dependent on there being

an original unity of meaning in the work to begin with. The contrary assertion that there is a plurality of meanings runs into danger only if the process
of technical interpretation is confused with that of the grammatical.

One can say that Paul was the only writer who made use of the
wealth of Greek subjunctives, indubitably because he was a dialectician.

The main ideas (*Genetiva consequenti*) are never contained in the dependent genitive clause, especially when the main clause qualifies another.

A systematic approach [*Das* ἐν διὰ δυοῖν: lit. 'one through two'] requires substantiating the ideas. One can only recognize and criticize an erroneous meaning if one has found the definite reference clearly expressed.

I should take the opportunity to discuss whether a language becomes
more complete as it becomes more expressive. The history of the Greek
language would provide an example.

The question about 'infinite meaning', as it is posed in relation to
God as the author, is for technical interpretation to resolve. What is meant
by the 'mystical meaning' is another matter which has nothing to do with
the close examination of the language.

On proper and improper meanings. In the phrases '*tela solis*' [darts of
the sun] and '*comae arborum*' [tresses of the trees], '*telum*' does not
mean ray nor does '*coma*' mean leaf [as Morus has it, p. 42]. The proper
meaning is not just the object referred to, but the manner in which it is

expressed. Often it has to do with a fresh perception enlivening a familiar expression. Often the opposite is true; consider the conventional ways love and flowers are often described. In other cases an object can represent a perspective *par excellence*. Language has a varied capacity for representation.

With one and the same example, Morus claims that syntax is a determining factor of meaning [p. 42] and a source of ambiguity [p. 46].

The phrase πίστις ἀγαθή in Titus 2:10 ['good faith'] is not typically Greek. The Latin *fides vox media* is often the equivalent of πίστιζ, but not here [contrary to Morus, p. 43].

In Greek there are words which can have both a theoretical and a practical reference, such as δόχει and ἔοιχεν ['it seems']; therefore they can only describe a general tendency [*Grad*]. πίστιζ is such a word. In German on the other hand the contrast between the practical and the theoretical predominates. (Marginal note: what Morus says on p. 45 is correct for the construction.)

History is only a tool of exposition for that which is described as having already happened; that is to say, not for anything like a regulation about fasting (Morus p. 43; Luke 5:35), which can be much better understood without reference to history.

The opinion that a sentence exists as subject, predicate, and copula proceeds from an assumption that words have objective and logical meanings; consequently, in this view, the predicate is only an abstract thing. This view encourages the use of verbs with copulae and as participles. The question about the value of the use of copulae can be kept open only if one does not see them as necessarily linked with verbs. In each language the copula becomes more frequent as it progressively destroys the original integrity of verbs.

In the process of determining the specific meaning from the general meaning of a discourse, one must first attend to its formal elements, which determine how all the parts fit together.

There are two methods of determination: isolating an element from its place in the whole context and drawing out the theme underlying the immediate, literal meaning [*unmittelbaren*].

The formal elements of a discourse, especially particles, are themselves, in turn, determined by the subject matter [*das materielle*]. As connectives, particles can form transitions from one subject to another.

The Greeks have characteristic particles for organizing the flow of the discourse; they work far better than our punctuation.

The original particles can have either an objective or a subjective sense. This is a borderline area for technical interpretation.

One can understand too much or too little of both the content and the nuance [*Grad*].

Careful examination of particles can help one detect interpolated sentences, either by indicating where the original text breaks off, or how the original sense was tampered with.

The Harris-Wolf theory of the Greek verb is greatly deficient;[5] it handles it too abstractly and conceptually and not enough as something living. It originates with the dialectical Stoics. It also doesn't completely solve the task of grammatical understanding and doesn't completely account for inflection.

The theory of the absolute and the conditional which are applied to the new languages can hardly be correct; it merely amounts to a magnification of the verb by means of the auxiliary verb.

Many anomalies in Greek metrics originate from the epic development of the language. Its restraints on the language are usually so appropriate that everything seems expressed in the indicative quite objectively.

If subject and predicate balance each other distinctly they form a phrase.

Correctly understanding the immensity of the significance of the holy is in no way incompatible with the hermeneutical narrowing of focus.

There are examples in which it quite deceptively appears as if the meanings of a word gradually increased and expanded. But this is of course only an illusion.

Consider, following up on Morus [pp. 42, 46] the unmediated structure as forming the limits of the enquiry [petere aliquem] and the point of departure [ab aliquo].

In reference to the technical narrowing of focus one must seek out the main points. These are, however, often found in a writer only by accident.

———————

Consider to what extent a number of writers can be viewed as one: what would be the hermeneutical conception of the 'school'. In philosophy discovering the variations which develop within a school can run parallel to gaining an explanation of it.

———————

Parallels can provide a secondary form of determination [validation], help one proceed from individual ideas to general ones, and elucidate literal meanings by figurative ones.

———————

Especially where one finds a figure in an apparently parallel passage, one should not remain content with a vague notion of the similarity, but rather, should attend closely to the nature of the expression.

———————

One must know people in order to understand discourse, while one learns about people from their discourse.

———————

Consider how the general rules of composition[6] become modified through the specific character of the writer, and all the experiences which preceded the discourse. (Marginal note: is the modification an expansion or a restriction?)

———————

An individual style of composition can either be free and arbitrary in intimate or casual discourse, or disciplined by form when bound up in artistic discourse. The opposite holding true is naturally not difficult to imagine, but in this course lies ruin.

The announcement of the subject matter and the general form of a work inspires an anticipation, which is of course not closed like that of a schematic diagram. It is predicated on the subjective [qualities of the work].

There is something that one anticipates as soon as the author manifests a presence, even before one might know what the subject is; this is the subjective [quality of a work].

Authors in which one finds everything that one anticipated and nothing more are the absolutely logical, unpersonal ones, but rather bad. The productive spirit always brings out something unexpected.

The poets who are supposed to be the most subjective are the most difficult of the ancients to interpret technically. They speak individually from among the epic and gnomic masses.

The contrast between free and formal composition corresponds to that between the technical and conventional word usage.

The question of whether the composition is passive or active depends on whether the language is found to describe [assimilated or pre-existing] concepts or [the author's personal] views.

It is commonly asserted that style is an arbitrary use of language. A persistent peculiarity of expression which exceeds even the diversities that the genres tolerate has not an inner source, but rather a habitual one; springs not from individuality but rather from a blind personality; should not be called style but rather mannerism.

A unified composition manifests its variety within the various genres. The first step is organizing parts into a whole, the final is developing language to suit the purpose of the composition. Note: Instead of saying 'composition' [*Combination*] it would be better to use the term 'arrangement' [*Aufstellung*]. Usually interpretation doesn't consider the arrangement, but begins with considering the language use.

Ignoring the restrictions genre provides often results in illusionary, ungrounded observations about individual language use.

Taking a statement out of its contexts in the representation [*Nachahmung*] often makes it seem flowery ormannered. Flowery expressions are products of an imitative inability to grasp the individuality of a thing.

Even if one does not appreciate the individuality of style, recognizing the segmentation of the whole can still be the basis for a technical interpretation of the unique [qualities of a work]; the general order of the composition itself manifests these qualities.

The customary attribution of static genres to ancient writings is based for the most part on the opinions of priestly interpreters and on Plato's distinctions between tragedy and comedy. [See *The Symposium*, 223 d.]

One must consider as of primary importance the effect that the contemporary speaking style might have had on the particular style of the association of ideas and on the understanding of the listener—even on texts such as the New Testament. The meaning cannot be otherwise than as the original audience understood it. See Th. F. Stange in *Jenaische Allgemeine Literatur-Zeitung* [1805], no. 183, for his interpretation of Matthew 8:20.

The task of distinguishing the original narrative from interpolated opinion in historical texts belongs to the sphere of technical interpretation, in as much as the author himself should have been aware of the difference.

The peculiar qualities of the language are revealed in the manner in which the character of the discourse is changed. This is determined by reference to the genre. It is impossible to express anything individualistically through using a standard form in a strictly conventional manner.

The use of individual words and manners of speech has its basis more in the culture where the language is spoken than in the individuality of the writer, such as, say, Plato or Xenophon.

Hugo Grotius calls parallel passages *conjuncta origine et loco* ['connected in origin and place'].[7]

When taking up grammatical interpretation again, I should say another word about the interaction between grammar and hermeneutics. It should be stressed that every individual is developed through his language, and that therefore every understanding of an individual discourse requires a substantial understanding of language; the same principle operates in both.

Every understanding of a given discourse is based somewhat on an earlier understanding of both kinds—a previous knowledge of humanity, and a previous knowledge of the subject matter. (Marginal note: Similarly one can consider a text as part of the study of the writer or of the subject matter.)

Every understanding of a single passage is conditioned through an understanding of the whole.

Whoever would try to understand a subject should begin at the beginning—with discovering where the peculiar qualities of the subject matter can be seen to emerge from the general.

What is said above is a universal canon of purely historical study, as well as a rule for all those who desire to be understood. Both have roots in common ground. Where this is lacking there is need for auxiliary material, such as an introduction to the New Testament.

The 'whole' is originally understood as genre—even new genres can only be developed from ever larger spheres, finally from life itself.

The standard meaning [*Einheit*] of a word is a model [*Schema*], a shiftable perspective. One should not confuse the initial use of a word with its subsequent meaning [*Bedeutung*]. Just as the word is affected by the inflections of the surrounding language, so also is its meaning. One especially shies away from pinning down the meaning of very important things.

As to the direction to take in uncertainty—the less one is certain of the meaning the more strictly one must adhere to the given usage.

In learning our mother tongue we follow a natural progress of relating whole and particular areas of language. We should do the same in learning foreign languages, often using dictionaries as substitutes for patient instructors and correctors of our speech. Mastering the ambiguous is just as essential as mastering the exact.

Even before one begins the grammatical operation the process of distinguishing the parts from the whole has already begun. Novices often mistakingly neglect this, possibly because of doubts over unusual meanings.

But whence does this determination begin? First with the material element of the language: what is the fundamental relationship of the words, the substantial components of the sentence? Parse the extended sentence into its parts; discover the way the apposition of subject and predicate condition each other. Everything is determined by the formula which seems to account for how it all fits together.

The potential meaning of the subject is delimited according to its role in the theme, of the predicate according to how the subject subordinates it.

The two sides of technical hermeneutics also oscillate. The more it depends on a complete understanding of the whole thought, the less it can provide immediate aid for resolving difficulties in grammatical interpretation, and vice versa. When this division becomes impossible to make, then all aid comes from the knowledge of the train of thought. (Marginal note: Consider the significance of the task, the *cyclic relationship* of the technical and the grammatical. Style in the highest sense of the term is synonymous with essential meaning [Lit: The unity reduces to style in the highest sense]. Imitation is the highest form of knowledge. Both universality and particularity sustain each other.)

Prospecting for the uniqueness of style belongs to technical interpretation; determining the unified meaning of the words belongs to grammatical.

The author finds himself on the one hand in the grip of the theme—the objective side of his task—and on the other, free to do with it what he wants—the subjective side.

When the word is free it is usually called popular, if it caters to the popular taste for exotic foreign subjects, or lyrical if it is written to please the self.

Just as one side is the opposite of grammar, so the other is the opposite of composition [*Composition*].

The interpreter gets at the essential meaning by examining individualistic use of forms; he gets at the particularity of the text by examining the individualistic exploration of a chain of thought.

Just as the elements of composition merge the thoughts into the sphere of expression and just as the elements of expression, the words, merge into the sphere of composition, one can say with assurance that every work proceeds to build its own terminology.

[The Aphorisms of 1810]

Friday, the 2nd of March. An overview gives one a grasp of the particular way the language is used. (1) The material element 'lies' [implicit] to the same extent that the discourse remains theoretical. (Marginal note: In certain special cases the particular language use does not correspond to what appears to a general overview.) (2) The formal particularity of a work looms large to the extent that the tension between objectivity and subjectivity sharpens. Lesser tension makes for greater uniformity, to the extent say, that a text complies with Aristotelian definitions of the lyric or epic. Greater tension opens up a philosophical or historical divergence from the norm.

Of course an overview can be mistaken; there is room here for error. One must attend carefully to the parenthetical opinions that qualify the ostensible theme.

Friday, the 9th of March. Object: a theoretical principle derived from the subjective.

Saturday, the 10th of March. An objective understanding touches only the material side of the writer's consciousness. Assessing the intention behind a chain of thought is the required preparation for assessing the objective element of a composition; this must be considered an abiding principle. Assessing the subjective element is bound up with the exposition. The first task here is elaborating all the possible meanings. The true meaning gradually emerges as the objective becomes clear. (a) Negatively one needs caution, demonstrations of the necessity of the interpretation; (b) positively, a study of the milieu from which the work emerges. (Approaches to the construction of the individual unity and of the chain of thought mutually condition each other, and therefore should proceed simultaneously. Concerning individual unity: I should consider what to do when nothing seems to emerge; or when it lacks a certain charm; or when it emerges only from facile exposition, or from a difficult exposition.)—Both approaches are conditioned by the nature of the genre; whether it be obscure or accessible, leaving either too little or too much to the imagination; whether it can be grasped only at great length or by common sense; whether it be popular or subjective with an obscure purpose, or an obvious one. (Both divisions are not to be confused; every element of the latter can very well appear to be an element of the former.) The genre of a work is also affected by whether it was intended for a general audience or a specialized one—but a work for a specialized audience is not to be confused with a neglected work.

Work can also become popular when the writer discovers new insights which can be made palatable.

———————

Nothing can be decided on the basis of neologisms.

———————

What can be an objective element in one presentation can be subjective in another. Therefore the material handling of the subjective follows on the objective. This is the case especially with words with particularly divergent meanings. When these are misunderstood it is the fault of mannerism.

———————

Rhythmic idiosyncrasies that are difficult to sustain are almost always unique characteristics.

———————

Saturday, the 17th of March. The particular language usage of individual writers is to be found in the subjective element. But often what one will take to be the particular language will actually derive from the age or the writer's class, something difficult to detect when there is only one representation of it. After a while one gets a knack for assessing the particular, but even then one will come across difficult texts. There must be something general in the subjective to correspond to the objective word use. Whatever is discernible as rhythmic is only the relationship of rhythms to each other. Difficulties and defiance of the rules can break down into word games or syntactical inconsistency.

Friday, the 23rd. (1) By combining the objective and subjective elements one projects oneself into the author [*man sich dadurch in den Schriftsteller 'hinein' bildet*]. I should speak about (2) knowing the author better than he himself does—having an (a) enhanced understanding, or (b) a critical one; about (3) the difference between obscure and clear, objective and subjective motives; (4) the relationship of the special hermeneutics to the general, (a) the different connections between both types, (b) the difference they make in interpreting the Scripture, (c) the difficulties of the scientific form.

Examples for the Hermeneutics[8]

From Plato's *Republic*, II, 366a:

ἀλλ' ὦ φίλε, ψήσει λογιζόμενος, αἱ τελεταὶ α ὖ μέγα δύνανται χαὶ οἱ λύσιοι θεοί, ὡς αἱ μέγισται πόλεις λέγουσι, χαὶ οἱ θεῶν παῖδες ποιηταὶ χαὶ προφῆται τῶν θεῶν γενόμενοι οἵ ταῦτα οὕτως ἔχειν μηνύουσιν.

[But our friend will say, the rites of the dead and the absolving deities can do much, as the greatest cities assert, and the sons of the gods, who became the poets and prophets of the gods, reveal that this is the truth.]

From Goethe's *Claudine von Villa Bella*, V 389, f.:

Dass wenig vieles sei schafft nur die Lust herbei. [That little may be much creates a sense of longing.]

From Plato's *Republic*, III, 388b:

μηδὲ ἄλλα χλαίοντα, [. . .] ὅσα χαὶ οἵα ἐχεῖνος ἐποίησε.

[Not lamenting . . . in the manner and measure as the poet said.]

(I should consider Wolf's misunderstanding of whether the subject had been altered or not.)[9]

Ibid. 388b:

ὅταν τις ἐφιῆ ἰσχυρῶ γέλωτι, ἰσχυρὰν χαὶ μεταβολὴν ζητεῖ τὸ τοιοῦτον.

[When one abandons oneself to violent laughter, one does violence to one self.]

(This provides an example of an undetermined thought. Without a parallel passage it would be impossible to understand.)

Translated by Roland Haas and Jan Wojcik

Translators' Notes

* Friedrich D. E. Schleiermacher, "Die Aphorismen von 1805 und 1809/10" in *Hermeneutik*, ed. Heinz Kimmerle (Heidelberg, 1974). Schleiermacher copied his first aphorisms in 1805 as he began to lecture on hermeneutics for the first time. In 1809 he sketched in the margins of the original notebook ideas he planned to expand upon in a more comprehensive study. He marks each with an indication where it will fit, in either the general introduction, or the first or second part of the projected study—*Der erste Entwurf von 1809/10*, and later *Die Kompendienartige Darstellung von 1819*. [See the translation of *The Hermeneutics*: "Outline of the 1819 Lectures," pp. 85–100—ED.]. We render his marks with an N for note, I for introduction, 1st and 2nd for the first and second part. We indicate where the group of aphorisms added to the notebook in 1810 begin.

The special task in translating the aphorisms is to give them coherent English sense without distorting too much the sense of the elliptical, crabbed original. Schleiermacher often sketches ideas rather than expresses them. Some of the aphorisms are comments or criticisms he jots down while reading other theorists, especially: Johann August Ernesti, *Institutio Interpretis Novi Testamenti* (Leipzig, 1761); and Samuel F. Nath. Morus, *Super hermeneutica Novi Testamenti acroases academicae*, ed. Eichstaedt (Leipzig, 1797). In general we consult these works and Kimmerle's notes and Schleiermacher's later writings only sparingly to clarify obscurities, hoping to present the seeds of his thought in close to its original form.

1. In his later work Schleiermacher uses *Elemente* to refer to the formal and personal coordinates of meaning, something like the later distinction between *langue* and *parole*

2. G. L. Spalding, *Vorrede zu Platonis Dialogi quatuor*, ed. L. F. Heindorf (Berlin, 1802), pp. v–viii, esp. vi.

3. *Platonis Dialogi selecti*, ed. L. F. Heindorf, Bd. 1 (Berlin, 1802), p. 102; Bd. 2 (Berlin, 1805), p. 208.

4. According to Kimmerle, Schleiermacher here refers to Kant's decision not to write on religious topics after Friedrich Wilhelm II condemned *Die Religion innerhalb der Grenzen der Blossen Vernunft*, until after Friedrich Wilhelm died. Kant refused to write with circumspection.

5. S. Jacob Harris, *Hermes oder philosophische Untersuchung über die Allgemeine Grammatik*, trans. Chr. G. Ewerbeck, after the notes and edition of F. A. Wolf, Vol. I (Halle, 1788), p. 143ff.; Kimmerle cites an English edition of 1751.

6. In this aphorism and in the dozen or so to follow, Schleiermacher uses the word *Combination* to refer to the product of the individual writer's work with his language; the word stresses his notion that a text has input from two sources: the resistant stuff of language, the shaping energy of the mind. We translate the word 'composition' as well as his word *Composition* [noted in the text] because, stress

aside, that is his meaning, and the literal translation 'combination' would sound too much like jargon.

7. Reference untraced: Kimmerle.

8. The following entries come from a note Kimmerle found with the manuscript of the Aphorisms. Apparently, he says, they date from this time.

9. Plato, *Republik*, 10 Volumes, trans. F. A. Wolf, Vol. 1 (Altona,1799), p. 129f.

3

The Hermeneutics: Outline of the 1819 Lectures[1]

Friedrich D. E. Schleiermacher

1. Hermeneutics as the art of understanding does not yet exist in general; rather, only various specialized hermeneutics exist.

1. [We speak of] only the art of understanding, not the exposition of the understanding.[2] The latter would only be a specialized part of the art of speaking and writing that could only be dependent on the general principles of hermeneutics.

2. This refers as well to difficult points in foreign-language texts. In reading them, one more often presumes familiarity with the subject matter and the language. When one is familiar with both, the distinction between them becomes difficult to make because one has perhaps not understood properly the more apparent. Only an artistic understanding consistently grasps the discourse [*Reden*] of a text [*Schrift*].[3]

3. Usually one supposes that one could rely on a healthy knowledge of human nature for formulating the general principles of interpretation. But then there is the danger that one would also tend to rely on a healthy feeling about the exceptional qualities of a text in determining what they meant.

2. It is very difficult to determine the exact nature of a general hermeneutics.

1. For a long time it was handled as a supplement to logic, but as one had to give up all logical tenets in its practice, this had to cease. The philosopher has no inclination to establish a theory about hermeneutics because he believes that it is more important to be understood than to understand.

2. Philology has made positive contributions throughout history. But its method of hermeneutics is simply to aggregate observations.

3. [Hermeneutics is] the art of relating discourse [*Reden*] and understanding [*Verstehen*] to each other; discourse, however, being on the outer sphere of thought, requires that one must think of hermeneutics as an art, and thus as philosophical.

   1. Thus the art of exposition depends on their [the arts of discourse and understanding—ED.] composition. They are mutually dependent to the point that where discourse is without art, so is the understanding of it.

   4. Discourse is the mediation of shareable thought. As a result both rhetoric and hermeneutics share a common relationship to the dialectic.

   1. Discourse is of course also a mediation of thought among individuals. Thought becomes complete only through interior discourse, and in this respect discourse could be considered manifested thought. But where the thinker thinks original thoughts, he himself requires the act of discourse to transform them into expressions that afterwards require exposition [*Auslegung*].

   2. The unity of hermeneutics and rhetoric results from the fact that every act of understanding is the obverse of an act of discourse, in that one must come to grasp the thought which was at the base of the discourse.

   3. The dependence of both on the dialectic results from the fact that all development of knowledge is dependent on both discourse and understanding.

   5. As every discourse has a two-part reference, to the whole language and to the entire thought of its creator, so all understanding of speech consists of two elements [*Momenten*]—understanding the speech as it derives from the language and as it derives from the mind of the thinker.[4]

   1. Every speech derives from a given language. One can also turn this around and say that originally and continuously language only comes into being through discourse; at any rate, communication presupposes the accessibility of the language, that is, a shared knowledge of the same. When something comes between unmediated discourse and communication, the art of discourse begins, for one must take into consideration the possibility that the listener might find something strange in someone else's use of language.

   2. Every discourse depends on earlier thought. One can also turn this around, of course, but in relation to communication it remains true, since the art of understanding only has to do with progressive thinking.

   3. It follows that every person is on one hand a locus in which a given language is formed after an individual fashion and, on the other, a speaker who is only able to be understood within the totality of the lan-

guage. In the same way, he is also a constantly developing spirit, while his discourse remains an object within the context of other intellection.

6. Understanding is only an interaction of these two elements.

1. Discourse can only be understood as a fact of the spirit if it is understood as a characteristic of the language, because the innateness of the language modifies the spirit.

2. It can also only be understood as a modification of the language if it is understood as a fact of the spirit, because all influences of individuals on the language are manifested through discourse.

7. Both stand completely equal, and one could only with injustice claim that the grammatical interpretation is the inferior and the psychological the superior.

1. The psychological is the superior only if one views language as the means by which the individual communicates his thoughts; the grammatical is then merely a cleaning away of temporary difficulties.

2. The grammatical is the superior if one views language as stipulating the thinking of all individuals and the individual's discourse only as a locus at which the language manifests itself.

3. Only by means of such a reciprocity could one find both to be completely similar.

8. The essential hermeneutical task is to handle every part in such a way that the handling of the other parts will produce no change in the results, or, in other words, every part must be handled as a discrete unit with equal respect paid to all other parts.

1. This reciprocity is important even if one part predominates over the other according to what was said in paragraph six.

2. But each is only complete if it makes the other redundant and contributes to construing the other, because indeed language [*Sprache*] can only be learned inasmuch as its discourse [*Reden*] can be understood; and in the same way, the inner cohesion of humanity can only be understood as it manifests itself externally through its discourse.

9. Exposition [*Auslegung*] is an art.

1. Every part stands by itself. Every composition is a finite certainty out of the infinite uncertainty. Language is an infinite because every element can be determined in a specific manner only through the other elements. And this is also true for the psychological part[5] because every perspective of an individual is infinite, and the outside influences on people

extend into the disappearing horizon. A composition composed of such elements cannot be defined by rules, which carry with them the security of their application.

2. Should the grammatical part be considered by itself, one would need in some cases a complete knowledge of the language, or, in others, a complete knowledge of the person. As neither can ever be complete, one must go from one to the other, and it is not possible to give any rules as to how this should be done.

10. The successful performance of the art depends on a linguistic talent and a talent for assessing individual human nature.

1. By the first point we do not mean the facility for learning foreign languages—the difference between the mother tongue and a foreign language does not come into consideration here for the time being; rather, a sense for the contemporaneity of a language, for analogy, difference, etc. One could mean by this that rhetoric and hermeneutics must always be together. Just as hermeneutics requires other talents, so also does rhetoric, if not always the same ones. The linguistic talent, at any rate, is shared, even if the hermeneutical method develops it differently than the rhetorical method does.

2. The knowledge of human nature is here the superior of those subjective elements in the development of discourse.[6] No less importantly, hermeneutics and artistic human presentation are always together. But a great number of hermeneutical mistakes are based on the deficiency of linguistic talent, or in its faulty application.

3. Inasmuch as these talents are generally given by nature, so hermeneutics is a commonsense endeavor. In as much as a person is missing one talent, he is crippled, and the other talents can only serve to help him adjudicate about that which all together would have permitted him to know directly.

11. Not all discourse is on an equal footing for exposition. Certain discourses have no value for it, others an absolute value; the majority lie between these two points.

1. Something of no value might excite no interest as an entity, but would still be important in the language as a reiteration which language requires for the preservation of its continuity. But that which repeats only already available things is worth nothing in itself. Like talking about the weather. Alone, this is not an absolute nothing, only minimal. For it developed itself in the same way as significant things.

2. When the grammatical aspect predominates in a work, even the most imaginative, we call it classical. When the psychological aspect

predominates, we call it original. And, of course, one part could absolutely dominate the other only if the author was an absolute genius.[7]

3. To be classical, a work must be more than transitory; it must determine subsequent production. No less so the original. And even the best work cannot be free from influence.

12. When both aspects of interpretation—the analysis of the grammatical and the psychological part of a text—are used equally throughout, they are nevertheless always used in different proportions.

1. This follows from the fact that something of grammatical insignificance does not necessarily have to be of psychological insignificance, and vice versa; and insignificancy in one does not imply insignificancy in the other.

2. A minimum of psychological interpretation is needed with a predominately objective subject. [To this belongs] pure history, especially of specific individuals, as comprehensive studies tend more to draw on subjective conclusions; also epics, commercial discussions which want to become history, and strictly didactic writings of every kind. The interpreter's subjectivity should not enter the exposition; rather, it should be affected by the exposition. A minimum of grammatical [interpretation] accompanies a maximum of psychological [interpretation] in the exposition of personal letters, especially when they transmit didactic advice or historical information. (Lyrics or polemics too?)

13. There is no other diversity in the methods of exposition aside from those cited above.

1. As an example, we can take the wonderful perspective which comes from the argument over the historical exposition of the New Testament, based on the question whether there are special modes of interpretation reserved for it alone. In this debate the assertion of the historical school is the only correct one, that the New Testament authors are products of their ages. The only danger in their reasoning is their tendency to overlook the power of Christianity to create new concepts and forms of expression; they tend to explain everything in light of available concepts and forms. To correct the historical style of interpretation one has to resist this one-sidedness. Correct interpretation requires a relationship of the grammatical and psychological interpretation, since new concepts can arise out of new emotional experiences.

2. One would also err if one thought of a historical interpretation as simply a retrospective view of the textual events. One must keep in mind that what was written was often written in a different day and age from the one in which the interpreter lives; it is the primary task of inter-

pretation not to understand an ancient text in view of modern thinking, but to rediscover the original relationship between the writer and his audience.

3. The Allegorical Interpretation. First of all, it is not an interpretation of an allegory, where the only purpose is to understand the figurative meaning without reference to whether there is truth at the base of it or not. Examples of allegories would be the parable of the sower, or the story of the rich man. Rather, allegorical interpretation begins with a presupposition that the meaning is lacking in the immediate context, and so one needs to supply a figurative one. With this supposition one is unsatisfied with the general principle that every speech can have only one grammatical meaning. The dissatisfaction arises, perhaps, from the correct assessment that an allusion in a text does point to a second meaning; one who does not comprehend it could completely follow the whole context, but would still be missing one meaning situated within the discourse. The danger is that one could find an allusion which is not situated within the discourse. Then one would dissect the discourse improperly. The test for a proper allusion is this: to see whether it seems entwined as one of the contextual ideas within the main line of thought, to assess whether the explicit thoughts inspire the implicit. But the contextual ideas are not therewith to be considered merely individual and insignificant. Rather, just as the whole world is made up of many men, each idea contributes to its whole sense, even if it appears only as its dark shadow.

There is, after all, a parallelism in many various lines of thought, so that something could inspire something else; for example, there is parallelism between the physical and ethical, and between the musical and the visual arts. One should be careful, however, to detect whether there are any indications for the figurative expressions one seems to detect. The allegorical interpretations which have been made without such indication, especially in traditional interpretations of Homer and the Bible, all depend on a special assumption. This is that the books of Homer and the Old Testament are special compendiums, the Old Testament above all, which contains all wisdom in some form or another. Along with this, both of them have appeared to have a mystical content compounded of sententious philosophy on the one hand and history on the other.

With myths, however, no technical interpretation is possible, since one cannot focus on an individual text and alternatively compare the literal and the figurative meaning. There is certainly a different situation regarding the New Testament which leads to two kinds of blunders. First, its association with the Old Testament encourages the use of the same methods often associated with Old Testament interpretation. Second, the New Testament interpreters tend more than their Old Testament counterparts to view the Holy Spirit as the book's author. But the Holy Spirit cannot be thought of as a temporally contingent and characteristic consciousness. From this false view springs the inclination to find everything foreshadowed everywhere. Common sense, or precise instructions on how texts should be read, can protect texts from this inclination, but isolated passages which seem to be unmeaningful in themselves seem to encourage it.

4. Here the question occasionally intrudes upon us, whether the holy books of the Holy Spirit must be handled differently than others. We must not be concerned with dogmatic decisions about inspiration, since they themselves derive from interpretation. We must not distinguish between the preaching and the writing of the apostles, since their future church had to be built on the preaching. And it follows from this that we must not believe that the whole of Christianity directly developed from the writings, since they are all aimed at specific communities and could also not have been understood by subsequent readers if they had not been understood by the original audience. Each community simply sought out the specific characteristics of the Jesus story according to its own given particular focus on the many details. Therefore, we must expose it to the same method and consider that even if the authors were no more than dead tools, still the Holy Spirit could only have spoken through them as they themselves would have spoken.

5. The most dangerous deviation from this principle is encouraged by the cabalistic style of exposition which directs its endeavors to find everything in everything. Only their interpretive endeavors which respect the diversity which results from the various relationships of both constructed parts can rightfully be called exposition.

14. The difference between artful and crude exposition has nothing to do with whether the work is familiar or strange, or with the discourse or the text, but solely with whether one wants to understand certain things exactly or not.

1. If it were only foreign and old texts that needed the art, the original readers would not have needed it, and the art would then depend on the differences between them and us. This difference must first be resolved, of course, through a knowledge of language and history; the exposition begins only after a successful identification of the text's original meaning. The difference between interpreting an old foreign text and a local contemporary one is only that with the old text the process of discovering its relevance to its milieu cannot completely precede the identification of its meaning; rather, both must be integrated from the beginning.

2. The text [*Schrift*] is not always the focus of attention either. Otherwise the art would only become necessary through the difference be-

tween text and discourse, that is to say, by the absence of the living voice and by the inaccessibility of other personal influences. These things, however, require exposition themselves, while they always remain somewhat nebulous. A living voice can certainly facilitate understanding a great deal, but even the writer must take into consideration that writing is not the same as speaking. If it were, then the art of exposition would be superfluous, which is, of course, not the case. Consequently, the need for exposition depends on the difference between written and spoken discourse, when the latter does not accompany the former.[8]

   3. Thus, when discourse and text behave so that no other difference remains between them save the one indicated, it follows that the artfully correct exposition has no other goal than that which we have in hearing every common spoken discourse.

15. The careless practice of the art results from the fact that understanding is pursued in the light of a negative goal: that misunderstanding should be avoided.

   1. Careless interpretation tends to limit its understanding to obtaining certain easy-to-attain goals.

   2. But even it must avail itself of the art in difficult cases; and thus hermeneutics can even arise from the artless practice. But since it only sees difficulties as isolated problems, it becomes an aggregate of observations. And for the same reason tends to consider itself a specialized hermeneutics because it brings special methods to the solving of difficult problems. This is how the theological, the juristic, and the philological methods originated, and what they consider to be their special purposes.

   3. The basis for their view is the peculiarity of their special languages and the peculiar manner in which their speakers communicate to their hearers.

16. Strict interpretation begins with misunderstanding and searches out a precise understanding.

   1. This results from its beginning with an assumption about what the meaning is that properly should only be discovered in the way the language and intention present it.

   2. Careless interpretation distinguishes only the [predetermined] sense from the manner of expression, which in fact depend on each other for their mutual identity, the determination of which is the minimum requirement for avoiding artless practice.[9]

17. Two things should be avoided: qualitatively misunderstanding the content, and quantitatively misunderstanding nuance.

1. Examined objectively, qualitative misunderstanding is mistaking the place of a part of a discourse in the language with that of another one, as, for example, the confusion of the meaning of a word with that of another. The qualitative misunderstanding is subjective, the mistaking of the meaning of an expression, when one gives the same thing a different meaning than the speaker gave to it in his sphere.

2. Quantitative misunderstanding arises from a subjective response to the value of the elaboration a speaker gives to a part of the text, or by analogy from an objective response to a part taken out of context.

3. The quantitative, which is normally taken little into account, always leads to the qualitative.

4. These negative expressions cover all interpretive operations. But one could not develop the rules from their negativity alone; rather, one must develop them positively, with a constant eye on the negative.

5. One must also distinguish the difference between passive and active misunderstanding. The latter is timidity which, however it might be the consequence of a bias that nothing can appear certain unless it is very obvious, can still entertain very false assumptions.

18. The art can only develop its rules from a positive formula, and this is the historical and the divinatory [prophetic], objective and subjective reconstruction [*Nachkonstruieren*] of the given discourse.

1. Objective historical reconstruction considers how the discourse behaves in the totality of the language, and considers a text's self-contained knowledge as a product of the language. Objective divinatory reconstruction assesses how the discourse itself developed the language. Without both of these, one cannot avoid qualitative and quantitative misunderstanding.

2. Subjective historical reconstruction considers a discourse as a product of the soul; subjective divinatory reconstruction assesses how the process of writing affects the writer's inner thoughts. Without both, just as was the case above, misunderstanding is once again unavoidable.

3. The task is this, to understand the discourse just as well and even better than its creator. Since we have no unmediated knowledge of that which is within him, we must first seek to become conscious of much which he could have remained unconscious of, unless he had become self-reflectingly his own reader. For objective reconstruction he has no more data than we do.

4. Posed in this manner, the task is an infinite one, because there is an infinity of the past and the future that we wish to see in the moment of discourse. Hence, this art is just as capable of inspiration as any other. In fact, a text has no meaning unless it can give rise to this inspira-

tion. However, the decision on how far one wishes to pursue an approach must be, in any case, determined practically, and actually is a question for a specialized hermeneutics and not for a general one.

19. One must first equate oneself with the author by objective and subjective reconstruction before applying the art.

1. With objective reconstruction one proceeds through a knowledge of the language as the author used it. It must be more exact than even the original readers possessed, who themselves had to put themselves in the place of the author. With subjective reconstruction one proceeds through the knowledge of the author's inner and outer life.

2. But both can only be completely secured through a similarly complete exposition. For only from a reading of all of an author's works can one become familiar with his vocabulary, his character, and his circumstances.

20. The vocabulary and the history of the period in which an author works constitute the whole within which his texts must be understood with all their peculiarities.

1.This complete knowledge is contained within an apparent circle, so that every extraordinary thing can only be understood in the context of the general of which it is a part, and vice versa. And all knowledge can only be scientific to the extent that it is complete.

2. This circle makes possible an identification with the author, and thus it follows that, first, the more complete knowledge we possess, the better bolstered we are for exposition, and, second, no material for exposition can be understood in isolation; rather, every reading makes us better suited for understanding by enriching our previous knowledge. We can only be satisfied with immediate understanding when dealing with the meaningless.

21. If the knowledge of the particular vocabulary can only be amassed during the exposition through lexical help and through individual observation, there can exist no self-sufficient exposition.

1. Only an independent knowledge of the actual life of a language gives one a source independent of the exposition for the knowledge of the vocabulary. For this reason we have only an incomplete understanding of what Greek and Latin words mean. Hence, the first lexical task in such cases is to consider the whole literature as a context for understanding the individual linguistic item. These complementary tasks balance each other through the exposition itself, contributing to an artful exposition.

2. Under the term *vocabulary* I subsume the dialect, period, and the mode—prose or poetry.

3. Even first impressions should be based on lexical meaning, for spontaneous interpretation can only rest on prior knowledge [*Vorkenntnisse*], but even all decisions about the language in dictionaries and in explanatory notes proceed from special and other perhaps unreliable expositions.

4. In the area of the New Testament, one can say with certainty that the unreliability and arbitrariness of the exposition rests largely on this fault. This is because contrasting analogies always develop from individual observations. For example, the development of New Testament vocabulary is rooted in classical antiquity and developed through Macedonian Greek through its use by the profane Jewish writers and by Josephus and Philo, by the deuterocanonical writers, and by the writers of the Septuagint, who flavored their Greek with Hebrewisms.

22. Even if the necessary knowledge of history comes only from prolegomena, there can still exist no self-sufficient exposition.

1. Such prolegomena are the sort of critical helps it is the duty of a publisher who desires to be a mediator to use. But they must depend on a knowledge of the whole literary circle a work belongs to, and the whole development of an author himself. Thus they are themselves dependent on exposition, and so are all reckonings whose beginnings are not determined by a specific goal. The exact expositor must, however, gradually glean everything from the sources themselves, and it is because of this that his task can only progress from easy to more difficult. But the dependency becomes most injurious if one brings in such notes in the prolegomena that actually could only be derived from the interpreted work itself.

2. The New Testament has given birth to a special discipline: the writing of the introduction. This is not an actual organic component of the theological discipline; but it is a practical expedient, partly for the beginner, partly for the master, since it is easier to bring together all of the relevant examinations in one place. But the expositor should always contribute to it so as to augment and relate the great mass of evidence.

23. An individual element can only be understood in light of its place in the whole text; and therefore, a cursory reading for an overview of the whole must precede the exact exposition.

1. Understanding appears to go in endless circles, for a preliminary understanding of even the individuals themselves comes from a general knowledge of the language.

2. Synopses that the author gives himself are too dry to engage even the technical aspect of interpretation, and with summaries like those publishers authorize for prefaces one comes under the influence of their interpretations.

3. The aim is to find the main idea in light of which the others must be measured, and this goes as well for the technical aspect—to find the main procedure from which the others can more easily be found. It is similarly indispensable for grammatical interpretation, which is obvious from the various forms of misunderstanding it often raises.

4. One can omit it easier when dealing with the unmeaningful, and although with difficult works it appears to be less helpful, it is actually all the more indispensable. A general summary is characteristically the least help in understanding difficult writers.

Should the exposition be done partially, one would eventually have to connect both aspects in the execution of the interpretation, but in theory one must divide and handle each specially, even if afterwards one must endeavor to develop each so completely that the other becomes indispensable, or, what is more important, so that its result coincides with the first. The grammatical interpretation leads the way.

Part Two
The Technical Interpretation

1. The common beginning for both the technical and the grammatical interpretation is the general overview which grasps the unity of the work and the main features of the composition. The unity of the work, the theme, will be viewed here as the writer's motivating principle, and the foundation of the composition as his peculiar nature as it is manifested in each motif.

The unity of the work derives from the manner in which the grammatical constructions available in the language are composed or connected. The author sets a verbal object in motion as communication. The difference between popular and scientific works is that the author of the former arranges the subject according to his peculiar style, which mirrors itself in his ordering. Because each author has minor conceptions each of which is determined by his peculiarities, one can recognize them from among analogous omissions and anomalous inclusions.

I perceive the author as he functions in the language: partly bringing forth new things by his use of language, partly retaining qualities of language which he repeats and transmits. In the same way, from a knowledge of an area of speech, I can perceive the author's language as its product and see how he operates under its aegis. Both methods are the same process begun from different starting points.

2. The ultimate goal of the technical [psychological] exposition is nothing other than to perceive the consequences of the beginning: that is to say, to consider the work as it is formed by its parts, and to perceive every part in light of the work's overall subject as its motivation; this is also to say that the form is seen to be shaped by the subject matter.

When I have looked at everything individually, there is nothing left over to understand. It is also obvious in itself that the apparent contrast between understanding the individual parts and understanding the whole disappears when every part receives the same treatment as the whole. But the goal [of good interpretation] is only achieved in the continuity of both perspectives. Even when much is only to be understood grammatically, it is not understood fully unless one can make an intrinsic analysis which never loses sight of the genesis of the work.

3. The goal of good interpretation is to understand the style completely. We are accustomed to understanding style as the handling of language. We presume that thought and language intertwine throughout, and the specific manner with which one understands the subject requires an understanding of the arrangement of words: i.e., the handling of language.

The peculiarity of an individual conception results from what is missing or added to a conventional conception. Whatever peculiarity results from imitation or habit results in a bad style.

4. Good interpretation can only be approximated. We are, considering all advances in hermeneutical theory, still far from making it a perfect art, as the perennial fights over the writings of Homer and over the comparative merits of the three tragic writers show.

No individual inspection of a work ever exhausts its meaning; interpretation can always be rectified. Even the best is only an approximation of the meaning. Because interpretation so seldom succeeds, and because even the superior critic is open to criticism, we can see that we are still far from the goal of making hermeneutics a perfect art.

5. Before beginning the technical exposition, we must know the manner in which the subject occurred to the originator, and how he acquired his language, and anything else one can learn about his mannerisms.

First, one must consider the prior development of the genre of the work at the time when it was written; second, one must consider the use made of the genre typically in the place where the writer worked and in adjacent areas; finally, no exact understanding of the development and usage is possible without a knowledge of the related contemporary literature and especially the works the author might have used as a model. Such a cohesive study is indispensable.

The third goal raises very troublesome problems. We could say that the interpretive process as a whole is only as easy as this step is to take. But because even this step requires a judgment which can also be anticipated in the previous steps, it is possible that one might be able to omit it. Biographies of the author were originally annexed to their works for this purpose; nowadays this connection is overlooked. The best sort of prolegomena attends to the first two points.

With these contextualizations [*Vorkenntnissen*] in hand one can gain an excellent perception of the essential characteristic of a work upon a first reading.

6. The whole task requires the use of two methods, the divinatory and the comparative, which, however, as they constantly refer back to each other, must not be separated.

Using the divinatory, one seeks to understand the writer intimately [*unmittelbar*] to the point that one transforms oneself into the other. Using the comparative, one seeks to understand a work as a characteristic type, viewing the work, in other words, in light of others like it. The one is the feminine force in the knowledge of human nature; the other is the masculine.

Both refer back to each other. The first depends on the fact that every person has a susceptibility to intuiting others, in addition to his sharing many human characteristics. This itself appears to depend on the fact that everyone shares certain universal traits; divination consequently is inspired as the reader compares himself with the author.

But how does the comparative come to subsume the subject under a general type? Obviously, either by comparing, which could go on infinitely, or by divination.

Neither may be separated from the other, because divination receives its security first from an affirmative comparison, without which it might become outlandish. But the comparative of itself cannot yield a unity. The general and specific must permeate each other, and this can only happen by means of divination.

7. The idea of the work, by which the author's fundamental purpose [*Wille*] reveals itself, can only be understood in terms of the convergence of the basic material [*stoff*] and the field of its developments [*Wirkungskreise*].

The basic material by itself stipulates no set manner of execution. As a rule it is easy enough to determine, even if it is not exactly specified; but for all that, one can be mistaken. One finds the purpose of the work most precisely in its peculiar or characteristic development of its material. Often the characteristic motif has only a limited influence on certain sections of a work, but nonetheless shapes the character of the work by its influence on others. The interpretive knack is to somehow intuit the meaning while being cautiously aware of how the intuition in some ways predetermines the process of validating it.

Translated by Jan Wojcik and Roland Haas

Translators' Notes

1. Translation of "III: Die Kompendienartige Darstellung von 1819" in Heinz Kimmerle's edition of Schleiermacher's *Hermeneutik* (Heidelberg, 1974). "The Outline of the 1819 Lectures" contains Schleiermacher's most systematic development of the theory among the several works editorially subsumed under the title of his *Hermeneutik*. "The Aphorisms of 1805 and 1809/10," "The Rough Draft of 1809/10," "The Draft of the Second Part of 1832," "The Separate Exposition of the Second Part of 1829," and "The Marginal Notes of 1832/33" are drafts and glosses. The frequently cited "Academic Discourse of 1829" is discursive. The principles of the "Outline" underlie them all.

The "Outline" consists of an "Introduction," "First Part: The Grammatical Exposition," and "Second Part: The Technical [or Psychological] Interpretation." The headings are somewhat misleading. The "Introduction" gives a systematic exposition of principles for analyzing the language and the psychological manifestations of a literary text. The "First Part" elaborates the principles for the analysis of language; the "Second Part" extends the "Introduction" in describing how the two parts of interpretation work together in the "divination" of a text. (See Leo Spitzer's discussion of divination, in Leo Spitzer, *Linguistics and Literary History* [Princeton, 1967], n. 10, pp. 33–35.) We limit our translation to the "Introduction" and the "Second Part" which comprise the heart of Schleiermacher's hermeneutical principles. We have referred to the marginal notes Schleiermacher added to the manuscript in 1828 only when they clarified ambiguities in the text.

The special difficulty in translating the "Outline" is rendering Schleiermacher's elliptical notes into complete English sentences without distortion. We indicate our especially venturesome liberties.

2. Schleiermacher here distinguishes the immediate understanding [*Verstehen*] of a text from any spoken or written exposition [*Darlegung*] of the understanding. Care must be taken lest his term for rhetorical exposition [*Darlegung*] be confused with his term for discursive understanding [*Auslegung*] (see 9).

3. Discourse [*Reden*] is Schleiermacher's term for the discursive sense of a text, shaped by the particular language the author uses to express his inner thoughts (see 4–6). Here he makes a distinction between the literal meaning of a text [*Schrift*] and the discursive meaning [*Reden*] that is most obvious when one reads a somewhat unfamiliar foreign language (see 14.2).

4. Literally: as a "fact" in the mind of the speaker.

5. The terms *psychological* and *technical* interchangeably refer to what Schleiermacher calls the second part of interpretation: recognizing the presence of the author within the language of the text. (See "Part Two: The Technical Interpretation.")

6. Literally: the knowledge of human nature is here superior to the subjective elements in the combination of thoughts.

7. Literally: the identity of both of only absolute, the genius.

8. Schleiermacher again makes a distinction between the literal sense of a text [*Schrift*] and its discursive sense [*Rede*], the latter being less accessible when the atmosphere in which the author lived and breathed is past (see 1.2). "The living voice" seems to be the resonance of the idiomatic spoken language of the author's day as it affects his writing style. Artful exposition becomes the art of catching the resonance and nuance of the underlying discursive sense of a text with the same grasp one can have of a conversation with an intimate speaking one's own idiom.

9. Paraphrase: artful interpretation begins with a hunch about a text's meaning which it continuously corrects and refines; careless interpretation begins with a prejudice about a text's meaning which it forces the text to support.

4

The Rise of Hermeneutics*

Wilhelm Dilthey

I have elsewhere[1] discussed the representation of individuation in art and particularly in poetry. We have now to deal with the problem of the *scientific* knowledge of individuals and indeed the principal forms of singular existence in general. Is such knowledge possible, and what means are at our disposal to attain it?

It is a problem of the greatest significance. Action everywhere presupposes our understanding of other people; much of our happiness as human beings derives from our re-experiencing [*Nachfühlen*] of alien states of mind; the entire science of philology and of history is based on the presupposition that such recomprehension [*Nachverständnis*] of individual existence can be raised to objective validity. The historical consciousness constructed on this basis has enabled modern man to hold the entire past of humanity present within himself: across the limits of his own time he peers into vanished cultures, appropriating their energies and taking pleasure in their charm, with a consequent increase in his own happiness. And if systematically organized human studies [*Geisteswissenschaften*] are able to go on to derive more general laws and more inclusive relationships from this objective apprehension of individual life, nonetheless the preliminary operations of understanding and interpretation form the basis. Thus, these disciplines, like history itself, depend for their methodological certainty upon whether or not the understanding of individual existence may be raised to general validity. So at the threshold of human studies we encounter a problem specific to them alone and quite distinct from anything involved in the apprehension of nature.

Human studies have indeed the advantage over the natural sciences that their object is not sensory appearance as such, no mere reflection of reality within consciousness, but is rather first and foremost an inner reality, a coherence experienced from within. Yet the very way in which this reality is experienced within us raises the gravest difficulties as to its objective apprehension. It is not the purpose of the present essay to deal with those difficulties. Moreover, any inner experiencing, through which I become aware of my own disposition, can never by itself bring me to a consciousness of my own individuality. I experience the latter only through a comparison of myself with other people; at that point alone I become aware of what distinguishes me from others, and Goethe was only too right when he said that this most crucial of all our experiences is also one of the most difficult, and that our insight into the extent, nature, and limits of our powers remains at best incomplete. But the existence of other people is given us only from the outside, in sensory events, gestures, words, and actions. Only through a process of reconstruction [*Nachbildung*] do we complete this sense perception, which initially takes the form of isolated signs. We are thus obliged to translate everything—the raw material, the structure, the most individual traits of such a completion—out of our own sense of life. Thus the problem is: how can one quite individually structured consciousness bring an alien individuality of a completely different type to objective knowledge through such reconstruction? What kind of process is this, in appearance so different from the other modes of objective knowledge?

Understanding [*Verstehen*] is what we call this process by which an inside is conferred on a complex of external sensory signs. Such is ordinary usage; and that precise psychological terminology which we so desperately need can come into being only if such carefully defined, clear and usefully delimited expressions are respected by all writers to the same degree. The understanding of nature—*Interpretatio naturae*—is a metaphor. Yet even the intuition of our own inner reality can only be loosely termed a form of Understanding. To be sure, I say: "I can't understand how I could have acted thus," and even, "I don't understand myself anymore." Yet what I mean by this is that an expression of my own being in the external world now comes before me as that of a stranger and that I am unable to interpret it, or alternatively that I suddenly find myself in a mood which I look upon as something alien to me. We must therefore call Understanding that process by which we intuit, behind the sign given to our senses, that psychic reality of which it is the expression.

Such understanding ranges from the comprehension of the babblings of children to *Hamlet* or the *Critique of Pure Reason*. From stones and marble, musical notes, gestures, words and letters, from actions, economic decrees and constitutions, the same human spirit addresses us and demands interpretation. Indeed, the process of understanding, insofar as it is determined by common conditions and epistemological instruments, must everywhere present the same characteristics. It is thus unified in its essential features. If, for instance, I wish to understand Leonardo, my interpretation of his actions, paintings, sketches and writing works together as a single homogeneous and unified process.

Yet understanding has various degrees. These are determined first of all by interest. If our interest is limited, so also is our understanding. How impatiently do we listen to many arguments, merely extracting the point that happens to be important to us practically, without any interest in the inner life of the speaker, while at other times we passionately attempt to seize the innermost reality of a speaker through his every expression, his every word. Yet even the most attentive concentration can develop into an orderly and systematic procedure—one by which a measurable degree of objectivity can be reached—only where the expression of life has been fixed, so that we can return to it again and again. Such *orderly and systematic understanding of fixed and relatively permanent expressions of life is what we call exegesis or interpretation.*[2] In this sense there is also an art of exegesis whose objects are statues or paintings, and Friedrich August Wolf called for a hermeneutic specifically designed for archeology. Welcker agreed with the need for such a hermeneutic, and Preller tried to work it out. Yet Preller himself had already pointed out that such interpretation of mute works is everywhere dependent on literature itself for its elucidation.

That is indeed the immeasurable significance of literature for our understanding of spiritual life and of history, for only in speech does the inner life of man find its fullest and most exhaustive, most objectively comprehensible expression. That is why the art of understanding centers on the exegesis or *interpretation of those residues of human reality preserved in written form.*

The exegesis of such residues, along with the critical procedures inseparable from it, constituted the point of departure for *philology.* Philology is in its essence a *personal skill and virtuosity in the scrutiny of written memorials.* Other types of interpretation of monuments or historically transmitted actions can prosper only in association with philology and its findings. For we can always make mistakes about the motivation of the principal actors in history; they themselves can indeed spread misconceptions about their own motives. But the work of a great poet or innovator, or a religious genius or a genuine philosopher, can never be anything but the true expression of his spiritual life; in that human community delivered from all falsehood, such a work is ever true and unlike every other type of expression registered in signs; it is susceptible of complete and objective interpretation; indeed, it is only in the light of such works that we begin to understand the other contemporary artistic monuments and historical actions.

Such an art of interpretation has developed as gradually and as methodically and slowly as the experimental investigation of nature itself. It originated in the individual virtuosity of the philologist of genius, where it continues to flourish. Thus its tradition is predominantly handed down through personal contact with the great practitioners of exegesis or with their works. Yet every art is conducted according to *rules*. The latter teach us how to overcome difficulties. They bequeath the results of the practice of others. Hence there develops very early out of the practice of exegesis an *exposition* of its *rules*. And from conflict about these rules, from the struggles of various tendencies in the interpretation of fundamental works and the subsequent need to establish a basis for such rules, the science of hermeneutics itself came into being. The latter is the *theoretical basis for the exegesis of written monuments*.

Since hermeneutics derives the possibility of universally valid interpretation from analyzing Understanding in general, it ultimately aims at a solution to that *more general problem* with which the present essay began. The analysis of Understanding takes its place beside the analysis of inner experience, and both demonstrate the *possibility and the limits of the validity* of human studies in general, to the extent that these disciplines are governed by the way psychic facts originally come before us.

I would now like to demonstrate this orderly evolution through the history of hermeneutics: how philological virtuosity developed out of the need for deep and universally valid understanding, whence a promulgation of rules, and the ordering of those rules towards a goal conditioned by the state of knowledge in the period in question, until finally an adequate foundation for the codification of rules was discovered in the analysis of Understanding itself.

I

In Greece systematic exegesis (*hermēneía*) of the poets developed out of the requirements of the educational system. In the age of the Greek enlightenment, the interpretation and criticism of Homer and other poets was a favorite intellectual pastime wherever Greek was spoken. A more solid foundation arose when exegesis came in contact with rhetoric among the Sophists and in the schools of rhetors. For rhetoric encompassed the general principles of literary composition insofar as they pertained to eloquence. Aristotle, the great classifier and dissector of the organic world, of the state, and of literary productions, taught in his *Rhetoric* how to divide a literary whole into its parts, how to distinguish the various stylistic tropes, how to judge the effects of rhythm, periods, metaphor. *The Rhetorica ad Alexandrinum* expresses these fundamental definitions of rhetorically effective elements in yet simpler form, under the headings of Example, Argument, Maxim, Irony, Metaphor and Antithesis. And the Aristotelian *Poetics* took as its express subject matter the inner and outer form and the affective elements of poetry. These are deduced from poetry's substantive or final purpose and from its varieties.

The art of interpretation and its codification took a second important step forward with Alexandrian philology. The literary heritage of Greece was brought together in libraries, editions were prepared, and critical results were inscribed therein through an ingenious system of critical notation. Spurious works were removed, and inventories of the remaining collections made. Henceforth philology existed as the art of textual verification based on intimate linguistic knowledge, higher criticism, exegesis, and evaluation. It was one of the last and most characteristic creations of the Greek spirit, for from Homer onward joy in human discourse had been one of its mightiest impulses. And the great Alexandrian philologists began to grow aware of the rules inherent in their intuitive practice. Aristarchus consciously followed the principle of determining Homeric usage in as strict and thoroughgoing a fashion as possible and basing his elucidations and textual determinations upon it. Hipparchus deliberately grounded objective interpretation upon literary and historical research, by discovering the sources of the *Phaenomena* of Aratus and interpreting that poem on the basis of that research. Unauthentic poems were recognized among those traditionally attributed to Hesiod; a great number of verses were excised from Homer's epics and the last book of the *Iliad*; and, even more unanimously, a part of the penultimate and the last book of the *Odyssey* were found to be of more recent origin; all of these findings were made possible through the virtuoso use of the principle of analogy. According to that principle, for a given work, a canon of usage, intellectual content, inner conformity and esthetic value was established, allowing everything that contradicted this canon to be excised. The practice of such an ethico-esthetic canon by Zenodotus and Aristarchus may be quite clearly deduced from the basic principle of Athetesis derived from them: *"dia to aprepes"* ["because it is unfitting"], or in other words, *"si quid heroum vel deorum gravitatem minus decere videbatur"* ["if something seemed to be less suitable to the dignity of heroes or gods"]. Aristarchus also appealed to the authority of Aristotle.

This methodological awareness of the proper methods for interpretation was strengthened in the Alexandrian school by their hostility to the philology of Pergamum. A contest of hermeneutic tendencies which has world-historical significance! For it returned again in a new form in Christian theology, and two great and historical views on poets and religious writers were founded on it.

From the Stoics, Crates of Mallos introduced the principle of allegorical interpretation into the Pergaminian philology. The lasting influence of this interpretative method came first and foremost from its ability to resolve the contradictions between inherited religious texts and later, more abstract and purely philosophical world-views. Hence its need for the interpreters of

the Vedas, or of Homer, of the Bible and the Koran—an art as indispensable as it was futile. Yet this activity was nonetheless based on a profound
insight into literary and religious productivity. Homer was a seer, and the
contradiction in him between profound insights and sensually crude imagery
can only be explained by apprehending the imagery simply as the instrument of literary representation. And when this relationship was conceived
as a deliberate shrouding of pneumatic meanings in images, the allegorical
method came into being.

II

If I am not mistaken, the same opposition returns in a new form in
the struggle between the theological schools of Alexandria and Antioch. A
common principle of both was naturally that an inner relationship of prophecy and fulfillment links the Old to the New Testament. Such a relationship
had indeed been implied by the use of prophecy and prototype in the New
Testament itself. Now insofar as the Christian church developed on the basis of such a presupposition, it became involved in a complicated struggle
with its adversaries with respect to the interpretation of Holy Scripture.
Against the Jews the Church used allegorical interpretation to introduce the
theology of the Logos backwards into the Old Testament; but on the other
hand it had to defend itself against too thoroughgoing an application of allegorical interpretation by the Gnostics. Following in the footsteps of Philo,
both Justin and Irenaeus tried to develop rules for the limits and proper
application of the allegorical method. Tertullian adopted their strategy in
his own struggle against the Jews and the Gnostics and at the same time
worked out fruitful rules for a better kind of interpretive procedure, to
which he did not always remain true. The most consistent working out of
the opposed tendencies came in the Greek Church. Theodorus of Antioch
saw in the *Song of Songs* nothing but an epithalamium. He understood *Job*
as nothing more than the literary reworking of a traditional story that actually happened. He dismissed the titles of the Psalms and denied any application to Christ in a considerable portion of the messianic prophecies. He
did not accept a double meaning in the texts themselves, but only some
more spiritual relationship among the various events involved. On the other
side, Philo, Clement, and Origen were distinguishing pneumatic and literal
meaning within the text itself.

There now took place yet another step forward in the development
from interpretative practice towards that hermeneutic science which gives
practice a scientific formulation, and from this struggle emerged the first
fully worked out hermeneutical theories which have come down to us.
There already existed in Philo's tradition *kanones* and *nomoi tes allegorias*

which were applied to the Old Testament and served as the conscious basis for its interpretation. This is the context in which Origen, in the fourth book of his *Peri Archon*, and St. Augustine, in the third book of his *De Doctrina Christiana*, worked out a systematically argued hermeneutic theory. In refutation of it, the school of Antioch presented two works which have unfortunately been lost: the *Tis diaphora theorias kai allegorias* of Diodorus, and the *De Allegoria et Historia contra Origenem* of Theodorus.

III

Interpretation and its codification entered a new state with the Renaissance. Henceforth people were separated by their language, living conditions, and nationality from classical and Christian antiquity. Interpretation thus became even more than in ancient Rome a matter of translating an alien spiritual life through the study of grammar, monuments and history. And in many cases this new philology, learning, and criticism had to work with mere second-hand reports and with fragments. So it had to be creative and constructive in a new way. From this period, a considerable hermeneutic literature survives. It is divided into two currents, since classical and biblical writings were the two greatest forces which men of that time sought to appropriate. The classical and philological codification was known by the term *ars critica*. Such works, including those of Scoppius, Clericus, and the unfinished one of Valesius, always included a hermeneutic doctrine in their opening sections. Countless essays and prefaces gave instruction *de interpretatione*. But the ultimate codification of hermeneutics stems rather from biblical interpretation. The first important work of this kind, and perhaps the most profound, was the *Clavis* of Flacius (1567).

Here for the first time the essential rules for interpretation which had already been worked out were connected with a systematic doctrine, and this was done under the postulate that a universally valid comprehension was to be reached through the orderly and systematic application of such rules. Flacius came to this systematic view, which thenceforth dominated hermeneutics, through his experiences with the struggles of the sixteenth century. He had to fight on two fronts. Both the Anabaptists and post-reformation Catholics were insisting on the obscurity of Holy Scripture. In opposing these positions, Flacius leaned predominately on Calvin's exegesis, in which there was a constant movement from interpretation to its theological bases. The most urgent mission of a Lutheran scholar of that day was to refute the Catholic doctrine of Tradition, which had been just newly formulated. The claim of Tradition to govern the interpretation of scripture could be upheld against the Protestant principle of the Bible's supremacy only by denying that a valid interpretation could be worked out on the basis of scripture alone. The Council of Trent, which met from 1545–1563, dealt with this problem beginning with its fourth session. The first authorized promulgation of its decrees then took place in 1564. In 1581, somewhat after the appearance of Flacius' works, the most characteristic representative of Tridentine Catholicism, Bellarmin, mounted the most astute attack on the comprehensibility of the Bible in a polemic work, in which he sought to prove the need of completing scriptural interpretation with tradition. In connection with these conflicts, Flacius undertook to prove the possibility of universally valid interpretation through hermeneutics. And in his attempt to do justice to this problem he became conscious of the techniques for its solution in a way that no earlier hermeneutics had done.

If the exegete comes up against difficulties in his text, he overcomes them by referring to the context provided by the actual lived experience of Christianity. If we now translate this concept out of its dogmatic mode of thought into our own, the hermeneutic value of religious experience becomes an individual instance of a more general principle, according to which every interpretive procedure contains as a factor exegesis from the objective [*sachlichen*] context. Alongside this religious principle of interpretation there exist other, more properly rational ones. The first of these is grammatical interpretation. But besides this, Flacius understands the meaning of a psychological or technical principle of interpretation as well, according to which individual passages are to be interpreted in the light of the intent and form of the whole. And for the first time, applying this technical principle, he methodically draws on rhetorical judgment as to the inner coherence of a literary work, its form, and its most effective elements. The reworking of Aristotelian rhetoric by Melanchthon preceded him in this. Flacius is fully conscious of having thus applied, for the sake of an unambiguous determination of individual passages, a criterion inherent in the work's context, its purpose, its proportion, and in the coherence of its separate parts. He evaluates such a hermeneutic criterion from the point of view of method in general: "And indeed the individual parts of a whole everywhere draw their comprehensibility from their relationship to that whole and to the other parts." He searches for such inner form in the very style and individual elements of the work, and drafts what is for this period a most sensitive characterization of the Pauline and Johannine styles. It was indeed progress, even if it remained within the limits of the rhetorical viewpoint. For Melanchthon and Flacius, each written work is composed according to rules, and is afterwards understood according to rules. It is a kind of logical automaton, clothed with style, images, and figures.

The formal deficiencies in the work of Flacius were overcome in the hermeneutics of Baumgarten. But in the latter a second great theological-hermeneutical tendency began to make its presence felt. Through Baumgarten's *Nachrichten von Seiner Hallischen Bibliothek*, those English freethinkers and scholars who examined the Bible in the light of anthropology began to take their place beside the Dutch exegetes in the German cultural realm. Semler and Michaelis were influenced by their contact with Baumgarten and took part in his work. Michaelis was the first to apply a unified historical view of language, history, nature, and law to an interpretation of the Old Testament. Semler, the predecessor of the great Christian Baur, demolished the unity of the New Testament canon, set up the requirement that each individual section be understood in its own local context, reunited them once again into that new unity which was implicit in the living and historical conception of an initial struggle in the Church between Judaizing Christians and those following a more liberal dispensation, and then, in his propaedeutic to theological hermeneutics, peremptorily derived hermeneutic science as a whole from two basic elements: interpretation based on linguistic usage and on historical circumstances. At this point the liberation of exegesis from dogma was complete; the grammatico-historical school was founded. The sensitive and careful mind of Ernesti then provided the classic text for this new hermeneutics in his *Interpres*. It was still being read as late as Schleiermacher, who developed his own hermeneutics from it. To be sure, even these gains were made within certain fixed limits. In the hands of these exegetes the form and the intellectual content of all the writings of a given century resolved themselves into the same leading threads of locally and temporally conditioned ideas. In this pragmatic conception of history, human nature, ever self-identical in its religious and ethical formation, is limited by place and time in a merely external fashion. Such a conception is non-historical.

Up to this point, classical and biblical hermeneutics developed side by side. But shouldn't they have been understood as applications of some more general mode of interpretation? Wolf's disciple Meier took this step in his essay on the general art of exegesis, published in 1757. He defined the idea of his science in as general a way as possible, as that science which was to draft the rules to be observed in any interpretation of signs. But the book only proves, once again, that one cannot found a new science on the basis of architectonics and symmetry. That way only ends up constructing blind windows through which no one can see. An effective hermeneutics could only develop in a mind where a virtuoso practice of philological interpretation was united with a genuine capacity for philosophical thought. Such a one was Schleiermacher.

IV

The intellectual environment in which he worked: Winckelmann's interpretation of works or art; Herder's congenial empathy with the inner soul of other peoples and ages; the new philology which developed from this new esthetic attitude, that of Heyne, of Friedrich August Wolf and his disciples, among whom [was] Heindorf, who worked on Plato studies in the closest communion with Schleiermacher himself—all of this was united in him with the characteristic approach of German transcendental philosophy, which sought, behind the contents of consciousness, for some creative power that, working unconsciously but in unified fashion, brought the entire form of the world into being within us. Out of the conjunction of these two moments, the art of interpretation specific to Schleiermacher as well as the definitive foundation of a scientific hermeneutics was developed.

Until then hermeneutics had been at best a system of rules whose parts, the individual rules themselves, were held together by the aim of giving an interpretation of general validity. Hermeneutics had been able to distinguish the various functions—grammatical, historical, estheticorhetorical, and material [sachlich]—which worked together in the interpretative act. And, after centuries of philological virtuosity, it had become conscious of the rules according to which such functions had to operate. Schleiermacher now sought for an analysis of the understanding that lay behind these rules, or in other words for a formulation of the goal of the activity as a whole, and from such a formulation he derived the possibility of valid interpretation in general, along with its conceptual instruments, limits and rules. He was, however, only able to analyze Understanding as a re-experiencing or reconstruction in its vital relationship to the process of literary production itself. In the living apprehension of the creative process by which a literary work comes into being, he saw the basic condition for grasping the other procedure, which understands the whole of the work out of the individual letters, and the spiritual tendencies of its creator out of that whole. In order to solve the problem thus posed, however, he needed a new psychological and historical mode of awareness. We have traced the opposition in question here from that earliest connection which arose between Greek interpretation and the productive rhetoric associated with a determinate literary genre. Yet the apprehension of the two kinds of procedures had always been formulated in logical and rhetorical terms. The categories under which they were formulated were always the mechanical ones of logical relationship and logical order, and then a covering of this logical product with style and figure and image. Now, however, wholly new ideas were applied to the understanding of the literary product. Now, a unified and creative power, unconscious of its own shaping force, is seen as receiving the first impulses towards the creation of the work and as forming them. Receptivity and autonomous shaping are indistinguishable in this force. Such a power is individualized to the very fingertips, to the separate words themselves. Its highest expression is the outer and inner form of the literary work. And now this work carries an insatiable need to complete its own individuality through contemplation by other individualities. Understanding and Interpretation are thus instinct and active in life itself, and they reach their fulfillment in the systematic exegesis of vital works interanimated by the spirit of their creator. Such was the form which this new mode of thought took in Schleiermacher's mind.

Schleiermacher's great sketch for a general hermeneutics was, however, further influenced by the fact that his contemporaries, and he himself, had developed the new psychological and historical modes of thought into a new philological art of interpretation. With Schiller and Wilhelm von Humboldt, with the Schlegel brothers, the German spirit had turned its attention from literary production to a comprehension of the historical world. It was a movement of great breadth; Boeckh, Dissen, Welcker, Hegel, Ranke and Savigny were all influenced by it. Friedrich Schlegel became Schleiermacher's mentor in philology. The concepts developed by the former in his brilliant essays on Greek poetry, Goethe and Boccaccio, were those of the inner form of a work, of the evolution of a given writer and of Literature as a systematic whole. And behind such individual achievements of an intuitive philology there lay for Schlegel the plan for a science of criticism, an *ars critica*, which would be based on a theory of a productive literary power. How close this plan is to Schleiermacher's hermeneutics and criticism!

And from Schlegel also came the plan for a translation of Plato. Here the techniques of the new interpretation were worked out which were then applied by Boeckh and Dissen to Pindar. Plato must be understood as a philosophical artist. The goal of the interpretation is the unity between the character of Platonic philosophizing and the artistic form of Plato's works. Philosophy is here actual life, life intermingled with conversation, and its literary representation is only a way of setting it down for further reference. So it had to be dialogue, and a dialogue of such a carefully constructed kind that it forced its readers to re-create the living transactions between the thoughts. Yet at the same time, in the strict unity of Platonic thought, each dialogue must be a continuation of something earlier, must prepare something to come, and thus spin out the threads of the various parts of the philosophy. When one follows the relationships of the various dialogues to each other, there comes into view an overall structure which reveals Plato's innermost intentions. According to Schleiermacher, a genuine understanding of Plato can only be achieved through the apprehension of this systematically constructed whole. The chronological succession of the various works, although often coinciding with this logical structure, is of less moment. Boeckh was later to remark in his review article that this masterful study made Plato available to philological science for the first time.

In Schleiermacher such philological virtuosity was uniquely joined with a philosophical disposition of genius. For he had been formed by transcendental philosophy, which provided the first adequate conceptual instruments for the general apprehension and solution of the problem of hermeneutics. Out of this the general science and doctrine of exegesis emerged.

Schleiermacher worked out a first draft in the autumn of 1804, upon a reading of Ernesti's *Interpres*, as an opening lecture for his course on exegesis at Halle. We possess this hermeneutic in very fragmentary form only.[3] A student of Schleiermacher's from the period in Halle, Boeckh, gave form to this version of the theory in the splendid lectures on the subject in his *Enzyklopädie*.

I now outline those points in Schleiermacher's hermeneutics which seem to me crucial for further development.

All exegesis of written works is only the systematic working out of that general process of Understanding which stretches throughout our lives and is exercised upon every type of speech or writing. The analysis of Understanding is therefore the groundwork for the codification of exegesis. The latter can be realized, however, only by analyzing the production of literary works. Only upon this relationship between Understanding and literary productivity can that ensemble of rules be founded which will determine the means and limits of exegesis.

The possibility of generally valid interpretation can be derived from the nature of Understanding. In Understanding, the individuality of the exegete and that of the author are not opposed to each other like two incomparable facts. Rather, both have been formed upon the substratum of a general human nature, and it is this which makes possible the communion of people with each other in speech. Here the relatively formalistic terminology of Schleiermacher can be further elucidated psychologically. Individual differences are not in the last analysis determined by qualitative differences between people, but rather through a difference in the degree of development of their spiritual processes. Now inasmuch as the exegete tentatively projects his own sense of life into another historical milieu, he is able within that perspective, to strengthen and emphasize certain spiritual processes in himself and to minimize others, thus making possible within himself a re-experiencing of an alien form of life.

If we now examine the logical side of this process closely, we see it as the recognition of a holistic interrelatedness formed on the basis of only partly determined or defined individual signs, under the constant participatory influence of previous grammatical, logical, and historical knowledge. In present-day local terminology, therefore, this logical aspect of Understanding involves both the inductive application of general truths to particular cases, and a process of comparison or analogy. The next step would be the definition of the particular forms taken by such logical operations and their interaction.

It is at this point that the central difficulty in all exegetical practice makes itself felt. The whole of a work is to be understood from the individual words and their connections with each other, and yet the full comprehension of the individual part already presupposes comprehension of the whole. This circle is then reduplicated in the relationship between the individual work itself and the spiritual tendencies of its creator, and it returns again in the relationship between the work and its literary genre. Schleiermacher resolved this difficulty practically in the most elegant way in his preface to Plato's *Republic*, and I find many other examples of the same procedure in the manuscripts for his exegetical lectures. (He would begin with a review of the various divisions, which may be compared to a first rapid reading; then he would slowly block out the broad outlines of the whole, and illuminate the various difficulties, pausing reflectively at all those spots which afforded special insight into the form. Only then did the actual interpretation begin.) Theoretically we here reach the limits of all exegesis, which is able to realize its task only up to a certain point. For all understanding remains partial and can never be terminated. *Individuum est ineffabile.*

He denounced the separation of the interpretative act into the grammatical, historical, esthetic, and material modes, which had become traditional in Schleiermacher's day. These distinctions only reflect the fact that grammatical, historical, esthetic and material knowledge must be there if there is to be interpretation, and that they are able to influence it at every moment. But interpretation itself can only be resolved into the two aspects [grammatical and psychological—TRANS.] of the process of apprehending a spiritual act in linguistic signs. Grammatical exegesis works its way up through the text from individual connections to those larger relationships that dominate the whole. Psychological exegesis begins by a projection into the creative inner process, and proceeds onward to the outer and inner forms of the work, and beyond that to an intuition of its unity with the other works in the spiritual stance of its creator.

This is the place where Schleiermacher masterfully lays down the rules for the art of exegesis. His doctrine of inner and outer form is basic, and there are particularly profound observations about a general theory of literary production from which an organon for literary history can be inferred.

The ultimate goal of the hermeneutic process is to understand an author better than he understood himself. This is an idea which is the necessary consequence of the doctrine of unconscious creation.

V

Let us conclude. *Understanding* can attain general validity only in relationship to written documents. Even if hermeneutics should make interpretation conscious of its modes of procedure and of its justification, F. A. Wolf would be right not to deem the usefulness of such a theoretical discipline as very great in comparison with its living practice. But above and beyond its practical merit for the business of interpretation, there seems to me to be a further purpose behind such theorizing, indeed its *main* purpose: to preserve the general validity of interpretation against the inroads of romantic caprice and skeptical subjectivity, and to give a theoretical justification for such validity, upon which all the certainty of historical knowledge is founded. Seen in the context of the theory of knowledge, of logic, and the methodology of the human studies, the theory of interpretation becomes an essential connecting link between philosophy and the historical disciplines, an essential component in the foundation of the human studies themselves.

Translated by Fredric Jameson

Notes

*Wilhelm Dilthey, "Die Entstehung der Hermeneutik," *Gesammelte Schriften*, Vol. V (Stuttgart: B. G. Teubner; Göttingen: Vandenhoeck und Ruprecht, 1964), pp. 317–331—ED.

1. In "Die Kunst als erste Darstellung der menschlich-geschichtlichen Welt in ihrer Individuation," *Gesammelte Schriften*, V (Stuttgart, 1957), 273–303 —TRANS.

2. Throughout this translation, *Auslegung* is rendered as "exegesis" and *Interpretation* is rendered as "interpretation."

3. The fragment to which Dilthey refers is most likely Schleiermacher's notes collected as "The Aphorisms of 1805" reprinted above pp. 57–84—ED.

5

*Being and Time**

Martin Heidegger

---

31. Being-there as Understanding

State-of-mind is *one* of the existential structures in which the Being of the 'there' maintains itself. Equiprimordial with it in constituting this Being is *understanding*. A state-of-mind always has its understanding, even if it merely keeps it suppressed. Understanding always has its mood. If we Interpret understanding as a fundamental *existentiale*, this indicates that this phenomenon is conceived as a basic mode of Dasein's *Being*. On the other hand, 'understanding' in the sense of *one* possible kind of cognizing among others (as distinguished, for instance, from 'explaining'), must, like explaining, be Interpreted as an existential derivative of that primary understanding which is one of the constituents of the Being of the "there" in general.

We have, after all, already come up against this primordial understanding in our previous investigations, though we did not allow it to be included explicitly in the theme under discussion. To say that in existing, Dasein is its "there", is equivalent to saying that the world is 'there'; its *Being-there* is Being-in. And the latter is likewise 'there', as that for the sake of which Dasein is. In the "for-the-sake-of-which", existing Being-in-the-world is disclosed as such, and this disclosedness we have called "understanding".[i] In the understanding of the "for-the-sake-of-which", the significance which is grounded therein, is disclosed along with it. The disclosedness of understanding, as the disclosedness of the "for-the-sake-of-which" and of significance equiprimordially, pertains to the entirety of Being-in-the-world. Significance is that on the basis of which the world is disclosed as such. To say that the "for-the-sake-of-which" *and* significance are both disclosed in Dasein, means that Dasein is that entity which, as Being-in-the-world, is an issue for itself.

When we are talking ontically we sometimes use the expression 'understanding something' with the signification of 'being able to manage something', 'being a match for it', 'being competent to do something'.[1] In understanding, as an *existentiale*, that which we have such competence over is not a "what", but Being as existing. The kind of Being which Dasein has, as potentiality-for-Being, lies existentially in understanding. Dasein is not something present-at-hand which possesses its competence for something by way of an extra; it is primarily Being-possible. Dasein is in every case what it can be, and in the way in which it is its possibility. The Being-possible which is essential for Dasein, pertains to the ways of its solicitude for Others and of its concern with the 'world', as we have characterized them; and in all these, and always, it pertains to Dasein's potentiality-for-Being towards itself, for the sake of itself. The Being-possible which Dasein is existentially in every case, is to be sharply distinguished both from empty logical possibility and from the contingency of something present-at-hand, so far as with the present-at-hand this or that can 'come to pass'.[2] As a modal category of presence-at-hand, possibility signifies what is *not yet* actual and what is *not at any time* necessary. It characterizes the *merely* possible. Ontologically it is on a lower level than actuality and necessity. On the other hand, possibility as an *existentiale* is the most primordial and ultimate positive way in which Dasein is characterized ontologically. As with existentiality in general, we can, in the first instance, only prepare for the problem of possibility. The phenomenal basis for seeing it at all is provided by the understanding as a disclosive potentiality-for-Being.

Possibility, as an *existentiale*, does not signify a free-floating potentiality-for-Being in the sense of the 'liberty of indifference' (*libertas indifferentiae*). In every case Dasein, as essentially having a state-of-mind, has already got itself into definite possibilities. As the potentiality-for-Being which it *is*, it has let such possibilities pass by; it is constantly waiving the possibilities of its Being, or else it seizes upon them and makes mistakes.[3] But this means that Dasein is Being-possible which has been delivered over to itself—*thrown possibility* through and through. Dasein is the possibility of Being-free *for* its ownmost potentiality-for-Being. Its Being-possible is transparent to itself in different possible ways and degrees.

Understanding is the Being of such potentiality-for-Being, which is never something still outstanding as not yet present-at-hand, but which, as something which is essentially never present-at-hand, '*is*' with the Being of Dasein, in the sense of existence. Dasein is such that in every case it has understood (or alternatively, not understood) that it is to be thus or thus. As such understanding it 'knows' *what* it is capable of—that is, what its potentiality-for-Being is capable of.[4] This 'knowing' does not first arise from an immanent self-perception, but belongs to the Being of the "there", which is essentially understanding. And only *because* Dasein, in understanding, is its "there", *can* it go astray and fail to recognize itself. And in so far as understanding is *accompanied by* state-of-mind and as such is existentially surrendered to thrownness, Dasein has in every case already gone astray and failed to recognize itself. In its potentiality-for-Being it is therefore delivered over to the possibility of first finding itself again in its possibilities.

Understanding is the existential Being of Dasein's own potentiality-for-Being; and it is so in such a way that this Being discloses in itself what its Being is capable of.[5] We must grasp the structure of this *existentiale* more precisely.

As a disclosure, understanding always pertains to the whole basic state of Being-in-the-world. As a potentiality-for-Being, any Being-in is a potentiality-for-Being-in-the-world. Not only is the world, *qua* world, disclosed as possible significance, but when that which is within-the-world is itself freed, this entity is freed for *its own* possibilities. That which is ready-to-hand is discovered as such in its service*ability,* its us*ability,* and its det-riment*ality.* The totality of involvements is revealed as the categorial whole of a *possible* interconnection of the ready-to-hand. But even the 'unity' of the manifold present-at-hand, of Nature, can be discovered only if a *possibility* of it has been disclosed. Is it accidental that the question about the *Being* of Nature aims at the 'conditions of its *possibility*'? On what is such an inquiry based? When confronted with this inquiry, we cannot leave aside the question: *why* are entities which are not of the character of Dasein understood in their Being, if they are disclosed in accordance with the conditions of their possibility? Kant presupposes something of the sort, perhaps rightly. But this presupposition itself is something that cannot be left without demonstrating how it is justified.

Why does the understanding—whatever may be the essential dimensions of that which can be disclosed in it—always press forward into possibilities? It is because the understanding has in itself the existential structure which we call "*projection*".[6] With equal primordiality the understanding projects Dasein's Being both upon its "for-the-sake-of-which" and upon significance, as the worldhood of its current world. The character of understanding as projection is constitutive for Being-in-the-world with regard to the disclosedness of its existentially constitutive state-of-Being by which the factical potentiality-for-Being gets its leeway [*Spielraum*]. And as thrown, Dasein is thrown into the kind of Being which we call "projecting". Projecting has nothing to do with comporting oneself towards a plan that has been thought out, and in accordance with which Dasein arranges its Being. On the contrary, any Dasein has, as Dasein, already projected itself; and as long as it is, it is projecting. As long as it is, Dasein always has understood itself and always will understand itself in terms of possibilities. Furthermore, the character of understanding as projection is such that the understanding does not grasp thematically that upon which it projects— that is to say, possibilities. Grasping it in such a manner would take away from what is projected its very character as a possibility, and would reduce it to the given contents which we have in mind; whereas projection, in throwing, throws before itself the possibility as possibility, and lets it *be* as such.[7] As projecting, understanding is the kind of Being of Dasein in which it *is* its possibilities as possibilities.

Because of the kind of Being which is constituted by the *existentiale* of projection, Dasein is constantly 'more' than it factually is, supposing that one might want to make an inventory of it as something-at-hand and list the contents of its Being, and supposing that one were able to do so. But Dasein is never more than it factically is, for to its facticity its potentiality-for-Being belongs essentially. Yet as Being-possible, moreover, Dasein is never anything less; that is to say, it *is* existentially that which, in its potentiality-for-Being, it is *not yet*. Only because the Being of the "there" receives its Constitution through understanding and through the character of understanding as projection, only because it *is* what it becomes (or alternatively, does not become), can it say to itself 'Become what you are', and say this with understanding.

Projection always pertains to the full disclosedness of Being-in-the-world; as potentiality-for-Being, understanding has itself possibilities, which are sketched out beforehand within the range of what is essentially disclosable in it. Understanding *can* devote itself primarily to the disclosedness of the world; that is, Dasein can, proximally and for the most part, understand itself in terms of its world. Or else understanding throws itself primarily into the "for-the-sake-of-which"; that is, Dasein exists as itself. Understanding is either authentic, arising out of one's own Self as such, or inauthentic. The 'in-' of "inauthentic" does not mean that Dasein cuts itself off from its Self and understands 'only' the world. The world belongs to Being-one's-Self as Being-in-the-world. On the other hand, authentic understanding, no less than that which is inauthentic, *can* be either genuine or not genuine. As potentiality-for-Being, understanding is altogether permeated with possibility. When one is diverted into [*Sichverlegen in*] one of these basic possibilities of understanding, the other is not laid aside [*legt . . . nicht ab*]. *Because understanding, in every case, pertains rather to Dasein's full disclosedness as Being-in-the-world, this diversion of the understanding is an existential modification of projection as a whole.* In understanding the world, Being-in is always understood along with it, while understanding of existence as such is always an understanding of the world.

As factical Dasein, any Dasein has already diverted its potentiality-for-Being into a possibility of understanding.

In its projective character, understanding goes to make up existentially what we call Dasein's "*sight*" [*Sicht*]. With the disclosedness of the "there", this sight is existentially [*existenzial seiende*]; and Dasein *is* this sight equiprimordially in each of those basic ways of its Being which we have already noted: as the circumspection [*Umsicht*] of concern, as the considerateness [*Rücksicht*] of solicitude, and as that sight which is directed upon Being as such [*Sicht auf das Sein als solches*], for the sake of which any Dasein is as it is. The sight which is related primarily and on the whole to existence we call "*transparency*" [*Durchsichtigkeit*]. We choose this term to designate 'knowledge of the Self'[8] in a sense which is well understood, so as to indicate that here it is not a matter of perceptually tracking down and inspecting a point called the "Self", but rather one of seizing upon the full disclosedness of Being-in-the-world *throughout all* the constitutive items which are essential to it, and doing so with understanding. In existing, entities sight 'themselves' [*sichtet "sich"*] only in so far as they have become transparent to themselves with equal primordiality in those items which are constitutive for their existence: their Being-alongside the world and their Being-with Others.

On the other hand, Dasein's opaqueness [*Undurchsichtigkeit*] is not rooted primarily and solely in 'egocentric' self-deceptions; it is rooted just as much in lack of acquaintance with the world.

We must, to be sure, guard against a misunderstanding of the expression 'sight'. It corresponds to the "clearedness" [*Gelichtetheit*] which we took as characterizing the disclosedness of the "there". 'Seeing' does not mean just perceiving with the bodily eyes, but neither does it mean pure nonsensory awareness of something present-at-hand in its presence-at-hand. In giving an existential signification to "sight", we have merely drawn upon the peculiar feature of seeing, that it lets entities which are accessible to it be encountered unconcealedly in themselves. Of course, every 'sense' does this within that domain of discovery which is genuinely its own. But from the beginning onwards the tradition of philosophy has been oriented primarily towards 'seeing' as a way of access to entities *and to Being*. To keep the connection with this tradition, we may formalize "sight" and "seeing" enough to obtain therewith a universal term for characterizing any access to entities or to Being, as access in general.

By showing how all sight is grounded primarily in understanding (the circumspection of concern is understanding as *common sense* [*Verständigkeit*]), we have deprived pure intuition [*Anschauen*] of its priority, which corresponds noetically to the priority of the present-at-hand in traditional ontology. 'Intuition' and 'thinking' are both derivatives of understanding, and already rather remote ones. Even the phenomenological 'intuition of essences' ["*Wesensschau*"] is grounded on existential understanding. We can decide about this kind of seeing only if we have obtained explicit conceptions of Being and of the structure of Being, such as only phenomena in the phenomenological sense can become.

The disclosedness of the "there" in understanding is itself a way of Dasein's potentiality-for-Being. In the way in which its Being is projected both upon the "for-the-sake-of-which" and upon significance (the world), there lies the disclosedness of Being in general. Understanding of Being has already been taken for granted in projecting upon possibilities. In projection, Being is understood, though not ontologically conceived. An entity whose kind of Being is the essential projection of Being-in-the-world has understanding of Being, and has this as constitutive for its Being. What was posited dogmatically at an earlier stage[ii] now gets exhibited in terms of the Constitution of the Being in which Dasein as understanding is its "there". The existential meaning of this understanding of Being cannot be satisfactorily clarified within the limits of this investigation except on the basis of the Temporal Interpretation of Being.

As *existentialia*, states-of-mind and understanding characterize the primordial disclosedness of Being-in-the-world. By way of having a mood, Dasein 'sees' possibilities, in terms of which it is. In the projective disclosure of such possibilities, it already has a mood in every case. The projection of its ownmost potentiality-for-Being has been delivered over to the Fact of its thrownness into the "there". Has not Dasein's Being become more enigmatical now that we have explicated the existential constitution of the Being of the "there" in the sense of thrown projection? It has indeed. We must first let the full enigmatical character of this Being emerge, even if all we can do is to come to a genuine breakdown over its 'solution', and to formulate anew the question about the Being of thrown projective Being-in-the-world.

But in the first instance, even if we are just to bring into view the everyday kind of Being in which there is understanding with a state-of-mind, and if we are to do so in a way which is phenomenally adequate to the full disclosedness of the "there", we must work out these *existentialia* concretely.[9]

32. Understanding and Interpretation[10]

As understanding, Dasein projects its Being upon possibilities. This *Being-towards-possibilities* which understands is itself a potentiality-for-Being, and it is so because of the way these possibilities, as disclosed, exert their counter-thrust [*Rückschlag*] upon Dasein. The projecting of the understanding has its own possibility—that of developing itself [*sich auszu-bilden*]. This development of the understanding we call "interpretation".[11]

In it the understanding appropriates understandingly that which is understood by it. In interpretation, understanding does not become something different. It becomes itself. Such interpretation is grounded existentially in understanding; the latter does not arise from the former. Nor is interpretation the acquiring of information about what is understood; it is rather the working-out of possibilities projected in understanding. In accordance with the trend of these preparatory analyses of everyday Dasein, we shall pursue the phenomenon of interpretation in understanding the world—that is, in inauthentic understanding, and indeed in the mode of its genuineness.

In terms of the significance which is disclosed in understanding the world, concernful Being-alongside the ready-to-hand gives itself to understand whatever involvement that which is encountered can have.[12] To say that "circumspection discovers" means that the 'world' which has already been understood comes to be interpreted. The ready-to-hand comes *explicitly* into the sight which understands. All preparing, putting to rights, repairing, improving, rounding-out, are accomplished in the following way: we take apart[13] in its "in-order-to" that which is circumspectively ready-to-hand, and we concern ourselves with it in accordance with what becomes visible through this process. That which has been circumspectively taken apart with regard to its "in-order-to", and taken apart as such—that which is *explicitly* understood—has the structure of *something as something*. The circumspective question as to what this particular thing that is ready-to-hand may be, receives the circumspectively interpretative answer that it is for such and such a purpose [*es ist zum . . .*]. If we tell what it is for [*des Wozu*], we are not simply designating something; but that which is designated is understood *as* that *as* which we are to take the thing in question. That which is disclosed in understanding—that which is understood—is already accessible in such a way that its 'as which' can be made to stand out explicitly. The 'as' makes up the structure of the explicitness of something that is understood. It constitutes the interpretation. In dealing with what is environmentally ready-to-hand by interpreting it circumspectively, we 'see' it *as* a table, a door, a carriage, or a bridge; but what we have thus interpreted [*Ausgelegte*] need not necessarily be also taken apart [*auseinander zu legen*] by making an assertion which definitely characterizes it. Any mere pre-predicative seeing of the ready-to-hand is, in itself, something which already understands and interprets. But does not the absence of such an 'as' make up the mereness of any pure perception of something? Whenever we see with this kind of sight, we already do so understandingly and interpretatively. In the mere encountering of something, it is understood in terms of a totality of involvements; and such seeing hides in itself the explicitness of the assignment-relations (of the "in-order-to") which belong to that totality. That which is understood gets Articulated when the entity to be understood is brought close interpretatively by taking as our clue the 'something as something'; and this Articulation lies *before* [*liegt vor*] our making any thematic assertion about it. In such an assertion the 'as' does not turn up for the first time; it just gets expressed for the first time, and this is possible only in that it lies before us as something expressible.[14] The fact that when we look at something, the explicitness of assertion can be absent, does not justify our denying that there is any Articulative interpretation in such mere seeing, and hence that there is any as-structure in it. When we have to do with anything, the mere seeing of the Things which are closest to us bears in itself the structure of interpretation, and in so primordial a manner that just to grasp something *free*, as it were, *of the* "*as*", requires a certain readjustment. When we merely stare at something, our just-having-it-before-us lies before us *as a failure to understand it any more*. This grasping which is free of the "as", is a privation of the kind of seeing in which one *merely* understands. It is not more primordial than that kind of seeing, but is derived from it. If the 'as' is ontically unexpressed, this must not seduce us into overlooking it as a constitutive state for understanding, existential and *a priori*.

But if we never perceive equipment that is ready-to-hand without already understanding and interpreting it, and if such perception lets us circumspectively encounter something as something, does this not mean that in the first instance we have experienced something purely present-at-hand, and then taken it *as* a door, *as* a house? This would be a misunderstanding of the specific way in which interpretation functions as disclosure. In interpreting, we do not, so to speak, throw a 'signification' over some naked thing which is present-at-hand, we do not stick a value on it; but when something within-the-world is encountered as such, the thing in question already has an involvement which is disclosed in our understanding of the world, and this involvement is one which gets laid out by the interpretation.[15]

The ready-to-hand is always understood in terms of a totality of involvements. This totality need not be grasped explicitly by a thematic interpretation. Even if it has undergone such an interpretation, it recedes into an understanding which does not stand out from the background. And this is the very mode in which it is the essential foundation for everyday circumspective interpretation. In every case this interpretation is grounded in *something we have in advance*—in a *fore-having*.[16] As the appropriation of understanding, the interpretation operates in Being towards a totality of involvements which is already understood—a Being which understands. When something is understood but is still veiled, it becomes unveiled by an act of appropriation, and this is always done under the guidance of a point of view, which fixes that with regard to which what is understood is to be interpreted. In every case interpretation is grounded in *something we see in advance*—in a *fore-sight*. This fore-sight 'takes the first cut' out of what has been taken into our fore-having, and it does so with a view to a definite way in which this can be interpreted.[17] Anything understood which is held in our fore-having and towards which we set our sights 'foresightedly', becomes conceptualizable through the interpretation. In such an interpretation, the way in which the entity we are interpreting is to be conceived can be drawn from the entity itself, or the interpretation can force the entity into concepts to which it is opposed in its manner of Being. In either case, the interpretation has already decided for a definite way of conceiving it, either with finality or with reservations; it is grounded in *something we grasp in advance*—in a *fore-conception*.

Whenever something is interpreted as something, the interpretation will be founded essentially upon fore-having, fore-sight, and fore-conception. An interpretation is never a presuppositionless apprehending of something presented to us.[18] If, when one is engaged in a particular concrete kind of interpretation, in the sense of exact textual Interpretation, one likes to appeal [*beruft*] to what 'stands there', then one finds that what 'stands there' in the first instance is nothing other than the obvious undiscussed assumption [*Vormeinung*] of the person who does the interpreting. In an interpretative approach there lies such an assumption, as that which has been 'taken for granted' ["*gesetzt*"] with the interpretation as such— that is to say, as that which has been presented in our fore-having, our fore-sight, and our fore-conception.

How are we to conceive the character of this 'fore'? Have we done so if we say formally that this is something '*a priori*'? Why does understanding, which we have designated as a fundamental *existentiale* of Dasein, have this structure as its own? Anything interpreted, as something interpreted, has the 'as'-structure as its own; and how is this related to the 'fore' structure? The phenomenon of the 'as'-structure is manifestly not to be dissolved or broken up 'into pieces'. But is a primordial analytic for it thus ruled out? Are we to concede that such phenomena are 'ultimates'? Then there would still remain the question, "why?" Or do the fore-structure of understanding and the as-structure of interpretation show an existential-ontological connection with the phenomenon of projection? And does this phenomenon point back to a primordial state of Dasein's Being?

Before we answer these questions, for which the preparation up till now has been far from sufficient, we must investigate whether what has become visible as the fore-structure of understanding and the as-structure of interpretation, does not itself already present us with a unitary phenomenon—one of which copious use is made in philosophical problematics, though what is used so universally falls short of the primordiality of ontological explication.

In the projecting of the understanding, entities are disclosed in their possibility. The character of the possibility corresponds, on each occasion, with the kind of Being of the entity which is understood. Entities within-the-world generally are projected upon the world—that is, upon a whole of significance, to whose reference-relations concern, as Being-in-the-world, has been tied up in advance. When entities within-the-world are discovered along with the Being of Dasein—that is, when they have come to be understood—we say that they have *meaning [Sinn]*. But that which is understood, taken strictly, is not the meaning but the entity, or alternatively, Being. Meaning is that wherein the intelligibility *[Verständlichkeit]* of something maintains itself. That which can be Articulated in a disclosure by which we understand, we call "meaning". The *concept of meaning* embraces the formal existential framework of what necessarily belongs to that which an understanding interpretation Articulates. *Meaning is the "upon-which" of a projection in terms of which something becomes intelligible as something; it gets its structure from a fore-having, a fore-sight, and a fore-conception.*[19] In so far as understanding and interpretation make up the existential state of Being of the "there", "meaning" must be conceived as the formal-existential framework of the disclosedness which belongs to understanding. Meaning is an *existentiale* of Dasein, not a property attaching to entities, lying 'behind' them, or floating somewhere as an 'intermediate domain'. Dasein only 'has' meaning, so far as the disclosedness of Being-in-the-world can be 'filled in' by the entities discoverable in that disclosedness.[20] *Hence only Dasein can be meaningful [sinnvoll] or meaningless [sinnlos].* That is to say, its own Being and the entities disclosed with its Being can be appropriated in understanding, or can remain relegated to non-understanding.

This Interpretation of the concept of 'meaning' is one which is ontologico-existential in principle; if we adhere to it, then all entities whose kind of Being is of a character other than Dasein's must be conceived as *unmeaning [unsinniges]*, essentially devoid of any meaning at all. Here 'un-meaning' does not signify that we are saying anything about the value of such entities, but it gives expression to an ontological characteristic. *And only that which is unmeaning can be absurd [widersinnig].* The present-at-hand, as Dasein encounters it, can, as it were, assault Dasein's Being; natural events, for instance, can break in upon us and destroy us.

And if we are inquiring about the meaning of Being, our investigation does not then become a "deep" one *[tiefsinnig]*, nor does it puzzle out what stands behind Being. It asks about Being itself in so far as Being enters into the intelligibility of Dasein. The meaning of Being can never be contrasted with entities, or with Being as the 'ground' which gives entities support; for a 'ground' becomes accessible only as meaning, even if it is itself the abyss of meaninglessness.[21]

As the disclosedness of the "there", understanding always pertains to the whole of Being-in-the-world. In every understanding of the world, existence is understood with it, and *vice versa*. All interpretation, moreover, operates in the fore-structure, which we have already characterized. Any interpretation which is to contribute understanding, must already have understood what is to be interpreted. This is a fact that has always been remarked, even if only in the area of derivative ways of understanding and interpretation, such as philological Interpretation. The latter belongs within the range of scientific knowledge. Such knowledge demands the rigour of a demonstration to provide grounds for it. In a scientific proof, we may not presuppose what it is our task to provide grounds for. But if interpretation must in any case already operate in that which is understood, and if it must draw its nurture from this, how is it to bring any scientific results to maturity without moving in a circle, especially if, moreover, the understanding which is presupposed still operates within our common information about man and the world? Yet according to the most elementary rules of logic, this *circle* is a *circulus vitiosus*. If that be so, however, the business of historiological interpretation is excluded *a priori* from the domain of rigorous knowledge. In so far as the Fact of this circle in understanding is not eliminated, historiology must then be resigned to less rigorous possibilities of knowing. Historiology is permitted to compensate for this defect to some extent through the 'spiritual signification' of its 'objects'. But even in the opinion of the historian himself, it would admittedly be more ideal if the circle could be avoided and if there remained the hope of creating some time a historiology which would be as independent of the standpoint of the observer as our knowledge of Nature is supposed to be.

But if we see this circle as a vicious one and look out for ways of avoiding it, even if we just 'sense' it as an inevitable imperfection, then the act of understanding has been misunderstood from the ground up. The assimilation of understanding and interpretation to a definite ideal of knowledge is not the issue here. Such an ideal is itself only a subspecies of understanding—a subspecies which has strayed into the legitimate task of grasping the present-at-hand in its essential unintelligibility [*Unverständlichkeit*]. If the basic conditions which make interpretation possible are to be fulfilled, this must rather be done by not failing to recognize beforehand the essential conditions under which it can be performed. What is decisive is not to get out of the circle but to come into it in the right way. This circle of understanding is not an orbit in which any random kind of knowledge may move; it is the expression of the existential *fore-structure* of Dasein itself. It is not to be reduced to the level of a vicious circle, or even of a circle which is merely tolerated. In the circle is hidden a positive possibility of the most primordial kind of knowing. To be sure, we genuinely take hold of this possibility only when, in our interpretation, we have understood that our first, last, and constant task is never to allow our fore-having, fore-sight, and fore-conception to be presented to us by fancies and popular conceptions, but rather to make the scientific theme secure by working out these fore-structures in terms of the things themselves. Because understanding, in accordance with its existential meaning, is Dasein's own potentiality-for-Being, the ontological presuppositions of historiological knowledge transcend in principle the idea of rigour held in the most exact sciences. Mathematics is not more rigorous than historiology, but only narrower, because the existential foundations relevant for it lie within a narrower range.

The 'circle' in understanding belongs to the structure of meaning, and the latter phenomenon is rooted in the existential constitution of Dasein— that is, in the understanding which interprets. An entity for which, as Being-in-the-world, its Being is itself an issue, has, ontologically, a circular structure. If, however, we note that 'circularity' belongs ontologically to a kind of Being which is present-at-hand (namely, to subsistence [*Bestand*]), we must altogether avoid using this phenomenon to characterize anything like Dasein ontologically.

33. Assertion as a Derivative Mode of Interpretation

All interpretation is grounded on understanding. That which has been articulated[22] as such in interpretation and sketched out beforehand in the understanding in general as something articulable, is the meaning. In so far as assertion ('judgment')[23] is grounded on understanding and presents us with a derivative form in which an interpretation has been carried out, it *too* 'has' a meaning. Yet this meaning cannot be defined as something which occurs 'in' ["*an*"] a judgment along with the judging itself. In our present context, we shall give an explicit analysis of assertion, and this analysis will serve several purposes.

For one thing, it can be demonstrated, by considering assertion, in what ways the structure of the 'as', which is constitutive for understanding and interpretation, can be modified. When this has been done, both understanding and interpretation will be brought more sharply into view. For another thing, the analysis of assertion has a special position in the problematic of fundamental ontology, because in the decisive period when ancient ontology was beginning, the λόγος functioned as the only clue for obtaining access to that which authentically is [*zum eigentlich Seienden*], and for defining the Being of such entities. Finally assertion has been accepted from ancient times as the primary and authentic 'locus' of *truth*. The phenomenon of truth is so thoroughly coupled with the problem of Being that our investigation, as it proceeds further, will necessarily come up against the problem of truth; and it already lies within the dimensions of that problem, though not explicitly. The analysis of assertion will at the same time prepare the way for this latter problematic.

In what follows, we give three significations to the term *"assertion"*. These are drawn from the phenomenon which is thus designated, they are connected among themselves, and in their unity they encompass the full structure of assertion.

1. The primary signification of "assertion" is *"pointing out"* [*Aufzeigen*]. In this we adhere to the primordial meaning of λόγος as ἀπόφανσις—letting an entity be seen from itself. In the assertion, 'The hammer is too heavy', what is discovered for sight is not a 'meaning', but an entity in the way that is ready-to-hand. Even if this entity is not close enough to be grasped and 'seen', the pointing-out has in view the entity itself and not, let us say, a mere "representation" [*Vorstellung*] of it— neither something 'merely represented' nor the psychical condition in which the person who makes the assertion "represents" it.

2. "Assertion" means no less than *"predication"*. We 'assert' a 'predicate' of a 'subject', and the 'subject' is *given a definite character* [*bestimmt*] by the 'predicate'. In this signification of "assertion", that which is put forward in the assertion [*Das Ausgesagte*] is not the predicate, but 'the hammer itself'. On the other hand, that which does the asserting [*Das Aussagende*] (in other words, that which gives something a definite character) lies in the 'too heavy'. That which is put forward in the assertion in the second signification of "assertion" (that which is given a definite character, as such) has undergone a narrowing of content as compared with what is put forward in the assertion in the first signification of this term. Every predication is what it is, only as a pointing-out. The second signification of "assertion" has its foundation in the first. Within this pointing-out, the elements which are Articulated in predication—the subject and predicate—arise. It is not by giving something a definite character that we first discover that which shows itself—the hammer—as such; but when we give it such a character, our seeing gets *restricted* to it in the first instance, so that by this explicit *restriction*[24] of our view, that which is already manifest may be made *explicitly* manifest in its definite character. In giving something a definite character, we must, in the first instance, take a step back when confronted with that which is already manifest—the hammer

that is too heavy. In 'setting down the subject', we dim entities down to focus in 'that hammer there', so that by thus dimming them down we may let that which is manifest be seen *in* its own definite character as a character that can be determined.[25] Setting down the subject, setting down the predicate, and setting down the two together, are thoroughly 'apophantical' in the strict sense of the word.

3. "Assertion" means "*communication*" [*Mitteilung*], speaking forth [*Heraussage*]. As communication, it is directly related to "assertion" in the first and second significations. It is letting someone see with us what we have pointed out by way of giving it a definite character. Letting someone see with us shares with [*teilt . . . mit*] the Other that entity which has been pointed out in its definite character. That which is 'shared' is our *Being towards* what has been pointed out—a Being in which we see it in common. One must keep in mind that this Being-towards is Being-in-the-world, and that from out of this very world what has been pointed out gets encountered. Any assertion, as a communication understood in this existential manner, must have been expressed.[26] As something communicated, that which has been put forward in the assertion is something that Others can 'share' with the person making the assertion, even though the entity which he has pointed out and to which he has given a definite character is not close enough for them to grasp and see it. That which is put forward in the assertion is something which can be passed along in 'further retelling'. There is a widening of the range of that mutual sharing which sees. But at the same time, what has been pointed out may become veiled again in this further retelling, although even the kind of knowing which arises in such hearsay (whether knowledge that something is the case [*Wissen*] or merely an acquaintance with something [*Kennen*]) always has the entity itself in view and does not 'give assent' to some 'valid meaning' which has been passed around. Even hearsay is a Being-in-the-world, and a Being towards what is heard.

There is prevalent today a theory of 'judgment' which is oriented to the phenomenon of 'validity'.[27] We shall not give an extensive discussion of it here. It will be sufficient to allude to the very questionable character of this phenomenon of 'validity', though since the time of Lotze people have been fond of passing this off as a 'primal phenomenon' which cannot be traced back any further. The fact that it can play this role is due only to its ontologically unclarified character. The 'problematic' which has established itself round this idolized word is no less opaque. In the first place, validity is viewed as the '*form*' *of actuality* which goes with the content of the judgment, in so far as that content remains unchanged as opposed to the changeable 'psychical' process of judgment. Considering how the status of the question of Being in general has been characterized in the introduction to this treatise, we would scarcely venture to expect that 'validity' as 'ideal Being' is distinguished by special ontological clarity. In the second place, ''validity'' means at the same time the validity of the meaning of the judgment, which is valid of the 'Object' it has in view; and thus it attains the signification of an *'Objectively valid character'* and of Objectivity in general. In the third place, the meaning which is thus 'valid' *of* an entity, and which is valid 'timelessly' in itself, is said to be 'valid' also in the sense of being valid *for* everyone who judges rationally. ''Validity'' now means a *bindingness*, or 'universally valid' character.[28] Even if one were to advocate a 'critical' epistemological theory, according to which the subject does not 'really' 'come out' to the Object, then this valid character, as the validity of an Object (Objectivity), is grounded upon that stock of true(!) meaning which is itself valid. The three significations of 'being valid' which we have set forth—the way of Being of the ideal, Objectivity, and bindingness—not only are opaque in themselves but constantly get confused with one another. Methodological fore-sight demands that we do not choose such unstable concepts as a clue to Interpretation. We make no advance restriction upon the concept of ''meaning'' which would confine it to signifying the 'content of judgment', but we understand it as the existential phenomenon already characterized, in which the formal framework of what can be disclosed in understanding and Articulated in interpretation becomes visible.

If we bring together the three significations of 'assertion' which we have analysed, and get a unitary view of the full phenomenon, then we may define ''*assertion*'' as ''*a pointing-out which gives something a definite character and which communicates*''. It remains to ask with what justification we have taken assertion as a mode of interpretation at all. If it is something of this sort, then the essential structures of interpretation must recur in it. The pointing-out which assertion does is performed on the basis of what has already been disclosed in understanding or discovered circumspectively. Assertion is not a free-floating kind of behaviour which, in its own right, might be capable of disclosing entities in general in a primary way: on the contrary it always maintains itself on the basis of Being-in-the-world. What we have shown earlier[iii] in relation to knowing the world, holds just as well as assertion. Any assertion requires a fore-having of whatever has been disclosed; and this is what it points out by way of giving something a definite character. Furthermore, in any approach when one gives something a definite character, one is already taking a look directionally at what is to be put forward in the assertion. When an entity which has been presented is given a definite character, the function of giving it such a character is taken over by that with regard to which we set our sights to-

wards the entity.[29] Thus any assertion requires a fore-sight; in this the predicate which we are to assign [*zuzuweisende*] and make stand out, gets
loosened, so to speak, from its unexpressed inclusion in the entity itself. To
any assertion as a communication which gives something a definite character there belongs, moreover, an Articulation of what is pointed out, and this
Articulation is in accordance with significations. Such an assertion will operate with a definite way of conceiving: "The hammer is heavy", "Heaviness belongs to the hammer", "The hammer has the property of
heaviness". When an assertion is made, some fore-conception is always
implied; but it remains for the most part inconspicuous, because the language already hides in itself a developed way of conceiving. Like any interpretation whatever, assertion necessarily has a fore-having, a fore-sight,
and a fore-conception as its existential foundations.

But to what extent does it become a *derivative* mode of interpretation? What has been modified in it? We can point out the modification if
we stick to certain limiting cases of assertion which function in logic as
normal cases and as examples of the 'simplest' assertion-phenomena. Prior
to all analysis, logic has already understood 'logically' what it takes as a
theme under the heading of the "categorical statement"—for instance,
'The hammer is heavy'. The unexplained presupposition is that the 'meaning' of this sentence is to be taken as: "This Thing—a hammer—has the
property of heaviness". In concernful circumspection there are no such assertions 'at first'. But such circumspection has of course its specific ways
of interpreting, and these, as compared with the 'theoretical judgment' just
mentioned, may take some such form as 'The hammer is too heavy', or
rather just 'Too heavy!', 'Hand me the other hammer!' Interpretation is
carried out primordially not in a theoretical statement but in an action of
circumspective concern—laying aside the unsuitable tool, or exchanging it,
'without wasting words'. From the fact that words are absent, it may not be
concluded that interpretation is absent. On the other hand, the kind of interpretation which is circumspectively *expressed* is not necessarily already
an assertion in the sense we have defined. *By what existential-ontological
modifications does assertion arise from circumspective interpretation?*

The entity which is held in our fore-having—for instance, the hammer—is proximally ready-to-hand as equipment. If this entity becomes the
'object' of an assertion, then as soon as we begin this assertion, there is
already a change-over in the fore-having. Something *ready-to-hand with
which* we have to do or perform something, turns into something '*about
which*' the assertion that points it out is made. Our fore-sight is aimed at
something present-at-hand in what is ready-to-hand. Both *by* and *for* this
way of looking at it [*Hin-sicht*], the ready-to-hand becomes veiled as ready-
to-hand. Within this discovering of presence-at-hand, which is at the same

time a covering-up of readiness-to-hand, something present-at-hand which we encounter is given a definite character in its Being-present-at-hand-in-such-and-such-a-manner. Only now are we given any access to *properties* or the like. When an assertion has given a definite character to something present-at-hand, it says something about it *as* a "what"; and this "what" is drawn *from that* which is present-at-hand as such. The as-structure of interpretation has undergone a modification. In its function of appropriating what is understood, the 'as' no longer reaches out into a totality of involvements. As regards its possibilities for Articulating reference-relations, it has been cut off from that significance which, as such, constitutes environmentality. The 'as' gets pushed back into the uniform plane of that which is merely present-at-hand. It dwindles to the structure of just letting one see what is present-at-hand, and letting one see it in a definite way. This levelling of the primordial 'as' of circumspective interpretation to the "as" with which presence-at-hand is given a definite character is the speciality of assertion. Only so does it obtain the possibility of exhibiting something in such a way that we just look at it.

Thus assertion cannot disown its ontological origin from an interpretation which understands. The primordial 'as' of an interpretation (ἑρμηνεία) which understands circumspectively we call the "existential-*hermeneutical* 'as' " in distinction from the "*apophantical* 'as' " of the assertion.

Between the kind of interpretation which is still wholly wrapped up in concernful understanding and the extreme opposite case of a theoretical assertion about something present-at-hand, there are many intermediate gradations: assertions about the happenings in the environment, accounts of the ready-to-hand, 'reports on the Situation', the recording and fixing of the 'facts of the case', the description of a state of affairs, the narration of something that has befallen. We cannot trace back these 'sentences' to theoretical statements without essentially perverting their meaning. Like the theoretical statements themselves, they have their 'source' in circumspective interpretation.

With the progress of knowledge about the structure of the λόγος, it was inevitable that this phenomenon of the apophantical 'as' should come into view in some form or other. The manner in which it was proximally seen was not accidental, and did not fail to work itself out in the subsequent history of logic.

When considered philosophically, the λόγος itself is an entity, and, according to the orientation of ancient ontology, it is something present-at-hand. Words are proximally present-at-hand; that is to say, we come across them just as we come across Things; and this holds for any sequence of words, as that in which the λόγος expresses itself. In this first search for the structure of the λόγος as thus present-at-hand, what was found was the *Being-present-at-hand-together* of several words. What establishes the unity of this "together"? As Plato knew, this unity lies in the fact that the λόγος is always λόγος τινός. In the λόγος an entity is manifest, and with a view to this entity, the words are put together in *one* verbal whole. Aristotle saw this more radically: every λόγος is both σύνθεσις and διαίρεσις, not just the one (call it 'affirmative judgment') or the other (call it 'negative judgment'). Rather, every assertion, whether it affirms or denies, whether it is true or false, is σύνθεσις *and* διαίρεσις equiprimordially. To exhibit anything is to take it together and take it apart. It is true, of course, that Aristotle did not pursue the analytical question as far as the problem of which phenomenon within the structure of the λόγος is the one that permits and indeed obliges us to characterize every statement as synthesis and diaeresis.

Along with the formal structures of 'binding' and 'separating'—or, more precisely, along with the unity of these—we should meet the phenomenon of the 'something as something', and we should meet this as a phenomenon. In accordance with this structure, something is understood with regard to something: it is taken together with it, yet in such a way that this confrontation which *understands* will at the same time take apart what has been taken together, and will do so by Articulating it *interpretatively*. If the phenomenon of the 'as' remains covered up, and, above all, if its existential source in the hermeneutical 'as' is veiled, then Aristotle's phenomenological approach to the analysis of the λόγος collapses to a superficial 'theory of judgment', in which judgment becomes the binding or separating of representations and concepts.

Binding and separating may be formalized still further to a 'relating'. The judgment gets dissolved logistically into a system in which things are 'co-ordinated' with one another; it becomes the object of a 'calculus'; but it does not become a theme for ontological Interpretation. The possibility and impossibility of getting an analytical understanding of σύνθεσις and διαίρεσις—of the 'relation' in judgment generally—is tightly linked up with whatever the current status of the ontological problematic and its principles may be.

How far this problematic has worked its way into the Interpretation of the λόγος, and how far on the other hand the concept of 'judgment' has (by a remarkable counter-thrust) worked its way into the ontological problematic, is shown by the phenomenon of the *copula*. When we consider this 'bond', it becomes clear that proximally the synthesis-structure is regarded as self-evident, and that it has also retained the function of serving as a standard for Interpretation. But if the formal characteristics of 'relating' and 'binding' can contribute nothing phenomenally towards the structural analysis of the λόγος as subject-matter, then in the long run the phenomenon to which we allude by the term "copula" has nothing to do with a bond or binding. The Interpretation of the 'is', whether it be expressed in its own right in the language or indicated in the verbal ending, leads us therefore into the context of problems belonging to the existential analytic, if assertion and the understanding of Being are existential possibilities for the Being of Dasein itself. When we come to work out the question of Being (cf. Part I, Division 3),[30] we shall thus encounter again this peculiar phenomenon of Being which we meet within the λόγος.

By demonstrating that assertion is derived from the interpretation and understanding, we have made it plain that the 'logic' of the λόγος is rooted in the existential analytic of Dasein; and provisionally this has been sufficient. At the same time, by knowing that the λόγος has been Interpreted in a way which is ontologically inadequate, we have gained a sharper insight into the fact that the methodological basis on which ancient ontology arose was not a primordial one. The λόγος gets experienced as something present-at-hand and Interpreted as such, while at the same time the entities which it points out have the meaning of presence-at-hand. This meaning of Being is left undifferentiated and uncontrasted with other possibilities of Being, so that Being in the sense of a formal Being-something becomes fused with it simultaneously, and we are unable even to obtain a clear-cut division between these two realms.

34. Being-there and Discourse. Language

The fundamental *existentialia* which constitute the Being of the "there", the disclosedness of Being-in-the-world, are states-of-mind and understanding. In understanding there lurks the possibility of interpretation—that is, of appropriating what is understood. In so far as a state-of-mind is equiprimordial with an act of understanding, it maintains itself in a certain understanding. Thus there corresponds to it a certain capacity for getting interpreted. We have seen that assertion is derived from interpretation, and is an extreme case of it. In clarifying the third signification of assertion as communication (speaking forth), we were led to the concepts of "saying" and "speaking", to which we had purposely given no attention up to that point. The fact that language *now* becomes our theme *for the first time* will indicate that this phenomenon has its roots in the existential constitution of Dasein's disclosedness. *The existential-ontological foundation of language is discourse or talk.*[31] This phenomenon is one of which we have been making constant use already in our foregoing Interpretation of state-of-mind, understanding, interpretation, and assertion; but we have, as it were, kept it suppressed in our thematic analysis.

Discourse is existentially equiprimordial with state-of-mind and understanding. The intelligibility of something has always been articulated, even before there is any appropriative interpretation of it. Discourse is the

Articulation of intelligibility. Therefore it underlies both interpretation and assertion. That which can be Articulated in interpretation, and thus even more primordially in discourse, is what we have called "meaning". That which gets articulated as such in discursive Articulation, we call the "totality-of-significations" [*Bedeutungsganze*]. This can be dissolved or broken up into significations. Significations, as what has been Articulated from that which can be Articulated, always carry meaning [. . . *sind* . . . *sinnhaft*]. If discourse, as the Articulation of the intelligibility of the "there", is a primordial *existentiale* of disclosedness, and if disclosedness is primarily constituted by Being-in-the-world, then discourse too must have essentially a kind of Being which is specifically *worldly*. The intelligibility of Being-in-the-world—an intelligibility which goes with a state-of-mind—*expresses itself as discourse*. The totality-of-significations of intelligibility is *put into words*. To significations, words accrue. But word-Things do not get supplied with significations.

The way in which discourse gets expressed is language.[32] Language is a totality of words—a totality in which discourse has a 'worldly' Being of its own; and as an entity within-the-world, this totality thus becomes something which we may come across as ready-to-hand. Language can be broken up into word-Things which are present-at-hand. Discourse is existentially language, because that entity whose disclosedness it Articulates according to significations, has, as its kind of Being, Being-in-the-world—a Being which has been thrown and submitted to the 'world'.

As an existential state in which Dasein is disclosed, discourse is constitutive for Dasein's existence. *Hearing* and *keeping silent* [*Schweigen*] are possibilities belonging to discursive speech. In these phenomena the constitutive function of discourse for the existentiality of existence becomes entirely plain for the first time. But in the first instance the issue is one of working out the structure of discourse as such.

Discoursing or talking is the way in which we articulate 'significantly' the intelligibility of Being-in-the-world. Being-with belongs to Being-in-the-world, which in every case maintains itself in some definite way of concernful Being-with-one-another. Such Being-with-one-another is discursive as assenting or refusing, as demanding or warning, as pronouncing, consulting, or interceding, as 'making assertions', and as talking in the way of 'giving a talk.'[33] Talking is talk about something. That which the discourse is *about* [*das Worüber der Rede*] does not necessarily or even for the most part serve as the theme for an assertion in which one gives something a definite character. Even a command is given about something; a wish is about something. And so is intercession. What the discourse is about is a structural item that it necessarily possesses; for discourse helps to constitute the disclosedness of Being-in-the-world, and in its own structure it is modelled upon this basic state of Dasein. What is talked about [*das Beredete*] in talk is always 'talked to' [*"angeredet"*] in a definite regard and within certain limits. In any talk or discourse, there is *something said-in-the-talk* as such [*ein Geredetes als solches*]—something said as such [*das . . . Gesagte als solches*] whenever one wishes, asks, or expresses oneself about something. In this "something said", discourse communicates.

As we have already indicated in our analysis of assertion,[34] the phenomenon of *communication* must be understood in a sense which is ontologically broad. 'Communication' in which one makes assertions—giving information, for instance—is a special case of that communication which is grasped in principle existentially. In this more general kind of communication, the Articulation of Being with one another understandingly is constituted. Through it a co-state-of-mind [*Mitbefindlichkeit*] gets 'shared', and so does the understanding of Being-with. Communication is never anything like a conveying of experiences, such as opinions or wishes, from the interior of one subject into the interior of another. Dasein-with is already essentially manifest in a co-state-of-mind and a co-understanding. In discourse Being-with becomes 'explicitly' *shared*; that is to say, it *is* already, but it is unshared as something that has not been taken hold of and appropriated.[35]

Whenever something is communicated in what is said-in-the-talk, all talk about anything has at the same time the character of *expressing itself* [*Sichaussprechens*]. In talking, Dasein *expresses* itself [*spricht sich . . . aus*] not because it has, in the first instance, been encapsulated as something 'internal' over against something outside, but because as Being-in-the-world it is already 'outside' when it understands. What is expressed is precisely this Being-outside—that is to say, the way in which one currently has a state-of-mind (mood), which we have shown to pertain to the full disclosedness of Being-in. Being-in and its state-of-mind are made known in discourse and indicated in language by intonation, modulation, the tempo of talk, 'the way of speaking'. In 'poetical' discourse, the communication of the existential possibilities of one's state-of-mind can become an aim in itself, and this amounts to a disclosing of existence.

In discourse the intelligibility of Being-in-the-world (an intelligibility which goes with a state-of-mind) is articulated according to significations; and discourse is this articulation. The items constitutive for discourse are: what the discourse is about (what is talked about); what is said-in-the-talk, as such; the communication; and the making-known. These are not properties which can just be raked up empirically from language. They are existential characteristics rooted in the state of Dasein's Being, and it is they that first make anything like language ontologically possible. In the factical linguistic form of any definite case of discourse, some of these items may be lacking, or may remain unnoticed. The fact that they often do *not* receive 'verbal' expression, is merely an index of some definite kind of discourse which, in so far as it is discourse, must in every case lie within the totality of the structures we have mentioned.

Attempts to grasp the 'essence of language' have always taken their orientation from one or another of these items; and the clues to their conceptions of language have been the ideas of 'expression', of 'symbolic form', of communication as 'assertion',[36] of the 'making-known' of experiences, of the 'patterning' of life. Even if one were to put these various fragmentary definitions together in syncretistic fashion, nothing would be achieved in the way of a fully adequate definition of "language". We would still have to do what is decisive here—to work out in advance the ontologico-existential whole of the structure of discourse on the basis of the analytic of Dasein.

We can make clear the connection of discourse with understanding and intelligibility by considering an existential possibility which belongs to talking itself—hearing. If we have not heard 'aright', it is not by accident that we say we have not 'understood'. Hearing is constitutive for discourse. And just as linguistic utterance is based on discourse, so is acoustic perception on hearing. Listening to . . . is Dasein's existential way of Being-open as Being-with for Others. Indeed, hearing constitutes the primary and authentic way in which Dasein is open for its ownmost potentiality-for-Being—as in hearing the voice of the friend whom every Dasein carries with it. Dasein hears, because it understands. As a Being-in-the-world with Others, a Being which understands, Dasein is 'in thrall' to Dasein-with and to itself; and in this thraldom it "belongs" to these.[37] Being-with develops in listening to one another [*Aufeinander-hören*], which can be done in several possible ways: following,[38] going along with, and the privative modes of not-hearing, resisting, defying, and turning away.

It is on the basis of this potentiality for hearing, which is existentially primary, that anything like *hearkening* [*Horchen*] becomes possible. Hearkening is phenomenally still more primordial than what is defined 'in the first instance' as "hearing" in psychology—the sensing of tones and the perception of sounds. Hearkening too has the kind of Being of the hearing which understands. What we 'first' hear is never noises or complexes of sounds, but the creaking wagon, the motor-cycle. We hear the column on the march, the north wind, the woodpecker tapping, the fire crackling.

It requires a very artificial and complicated frame of mind to 'hear' a 'pure noise'. The fact that motor-cycles and wagons are what we proximally hear is the phenomenal evidence that in every case Dasein, as Being-in-the-world, already dwells *alongside* what is ready-to-hand as Being-in-the-world; it certainly does not dwell proximally alongside 'sensations'; nor would it first have to give shape to the swirl of sensations to provide the springboard from which the subject leaps off and finally arrives at a 'world'. Dasein, as essentially understanding, is proximally alongside what is understood.

Likewise, when we are explicitly hearing the discourse of another, we proximally understand what is said, or—to put it more exactly—we are already with him, in advance, alongside the entity which the discourse is about. On the other hand, what we proximally hear is *not* what is expressed in the utterance. Even in cases where the speech is indistinct or in a foreign language, what we proximally hear is *unintelligible* words, and not a multiplicity of tone-data.[39]

Admittedly, when what the discourse is about is heard 'naturally', we can at the same time hear the 'diction', the way in which it is said [*die Weise des Gesagtseins*], but only if there is some co-understanding beforehand of what is said-in-the-talk; for only so is there a possibility of estimating whether the way in which it is said is appropriate to what the discourse is about thematically.

In the same way, any answering counter-discourse arises proximally and directly from understanding what the discourse is about, which is already 'shared' in Being-with.

Only where talking and hearing are existentially possible, can anyone hearken. The person who 'cannot hear' and 'must feel'[40] may perhaps be one who is able to hearken very well, and precisely because of this. Just hearing something "all around" [*Das Nur-herum-hören*] is a privation of the hearing which understands. Both talking and hearing are based upon understanding. And understanding arises neither through talking at length [*vieles Reden*] nor through busily hearing something "all around". Only he who already understands can listen [*zuhören*].

Keeping silent is another essential possibility of discourse, and it has the same existential foundation. In talking with one another, the person who keeps silent can 'make one understand' (that is, he can develop an understanding), and he can do so more authentically than the person who is never short of words. Speaking at length [*Viel-sprechen*] about something does not offer the slightest guarantee that thereby understanding is advanced. On the contrary, talking extensively about something, covers it up and brings what is understood to a sham clarity—the unintelligibility of the trivial. But to keep silent does not mean to be dumb. On the contrary, if a man is dumb, he still has a tendency to 'speak'. Such a person has not proved that he can keep silence; indeed, he entirely lacks the possibility of proving anything of the sort. And the person who is accustomed by Nature to speak little is no better able to show that he is keeping silent or that he is the sort

of person who can do so. He who never says anything cannot keep silent at
any given moment. Keeping silent authentically is possible only in genuine
discoursing. To be able to keep silent, Dasein must have something to
say—that is, it must have at its disposal an authentic and rich disclosedness
of itself. In that case one's reticence [*Verschwiegenheit*] makes something
manifest, and does away with 'idle talk' ["*Gerede*"] As a mode of discoursing, reticence Articulates the intelligibility of Dasein in so primordial
a manner that it gives rise to a potentiality-for-hearing which is genuine,
and to a Being-with-one-another which is transparent.

Because discourse is constitutive for the Being of the "there" (that
is, for states-of-mind and understanding), while "Dasein" means Being-
in-the world, Dasein as discursive Being-in, has already expressed itself.
Dasein has language. Among the Greeks, their everyday existing was
largely diverted into talking with one another, but at the same time they
'had eyes' to see. Is it an accident that in both their pre-philosophical and
their philosophical ways of interpreting Dasein, they defined the essence of
man as ζῷον λόγον ἔχον ? The later way of interpreting this definition of
man in the sense of the *animal rationale*, 'something living which has reason', is not indeed 'false', but it covers up the phenomenal basis for this
definition of "Dasein". Man shows himself as the entity which talks. This
does not signify that the possibility of vocal utterance is peculiar to him,
but rather that he is the entity which is such as to discover the world and
Dasein itself. The Greeks had no word for "language"; they understood
this phenomenon 'in the first instance' as discourse. But because the λόγος
came into their philosophical ken primarily as assertion, *this* was the kind
of *logos* which they took as their clue for working out the basic structures
of the forms of discourse and its components. Grammar sought its foundations in the 'logic' of this *logos*. But this logic was based upon the ontology
of the present-at-hand. The basic stock of 'categories of signification',
which passed over into the subsequent science of language, and which in
principle is still accepted as the standard today, is oriented towards discourse as assertion. But if on the contrary we take this phenomenon to have
in principle the primordiality and breadth of an *existentiale*, then there
emerges the necessity of re-establishing the science of language on foundations which are ontologically more primordial. The task of *liberating* grammar from logic requires *beforehand* a *positive* understanding of the basic *a
priori* structure of discourse in general as an *existentiale*. It is not a task
that can be carried through later on by improving and rounding out what
has been handed down. Bearing this in mind, we must inquire into the basic
forms in which it is possible to articulate anything understandable, and to
do so in accordance with significations; and this articulation must not be
confined to entities within-the-world which we cognize by considering
them theoretically, and which we express in sentences. A doctrine of signi-

fication will not emerge automatically even if we make a comprehensive comparison of as many languages as possible, and those which are most exotic. To accept, let us say, the philosophical horizon within which W. von Humboldt made language a problem, would be no less inadequate. The doctrine of signification is rooted in the ontology of Dasein. Whether it prospers or decays depends on the fate of this ontology.[iv]

In the last resort, philosophical research must resolve to ask what kind of Being goes with language in general. Is it a kind of equipment ready-to-hand within-the-world, or has it Dasein's kind of Being, or is it neither of these? What kind of Being does language have, if there can be such a thing as a 'dead' language? What do the "rise" and "decline" of a language mean ontologically? We possess a science of language, and the Being of the entities which it has for its theme is obscure. Even the horizon for any investigative question about it is veiled. Is it an accident that proximally and for the most part significations are 'worldly', sketched out beforehand by the significance of the world, that they are indeed often predominantly 'spatial'? Or does this 'fact' have existential-ontological necessity? and if it is necessary, why should it be so? Philosophical research will have to dispense with the 'philosophy of language' if it is to inquire into 'the things themselves' and attain the status of a problematic which has been cleared up conceptually.

Our Interpretation of language has been designed merely to point out the ontological 'locus' of this phenomenon in Dasein's state of Being, and especially to prepare the way for the following analysis, in which, taking as our clue a fundamental kind of Being belonging to discourse, in connection with other phenomena, we shall try to bring Dasein's everydayness into view in a manner which is ontologically more primordial.

Translated by John Macquarrie and Edward Robinson

Notes

* What follows are sections 31–34 from *Sein und Zeit*, 7th Edition (Tübingen: Max Niemeyer Verlag, 1953). The notes marked by Roman numerals are Heidegger's. All other notes are the translators'. The translators have used single quotation marks to represent Heidegger's double quotation marks, and all double quotation marks have been added by the translators to assist the reader. The translators use italics to represent Heidegger's italics, and they use wide spacing to place some emphasis of their own.—ED.

i. Cf. *Being and Time*, section 18 ["Involvement and Significance; the Worldhood of the World."—ED.]

ii. Cf. *Being and Time*, section 4 ["The Ontical Priority of the Question of Being."—ED.]

iii. Cf. *Being and Time*, section 13 ["A Founded Mode in which Being-in is Exemplified. Knowing the World."—ED.]

iv. On the doctrine of signification, cf. Edmund Husserl, *Logische Untersuchungen*, Vol. II, Investigations I, IV–VI. See further the more radical version of the problematic in his *Ideen* I, sections 123ff, pp. 255ff.

1. '. . . in der Bedeutung von "einer Sache vorstehen können", "ihr gewachsen sein", "etwas können".' The expression 'vorstehen' ('to manage', 'to be in charge') is here connected with 'verstehen' ('to understand').

2. '. . . von der Kontingenz eines Vorhandenen, sofern mit diesem das und jenes "passieren" kann.'

3. '. . . ergreift sie und vergreift sich.'

4. 'Als solches Verstehen "weiss" es, *woran* es mit ihm selbst, das heisst seinen Seinkönnen ist.'

5. '. . . *so zwar, dass dieses Sein an ihm selbst das Woran des mit ihm selbst Seins erschliesst.*'

6. '*Entwurf*'. The basic meaning of this noun and the cognate verb 'entwerfen' is that of 'throwing' something 'off' or 'away' from one; but in ordinary German usage, and often in Heidegger, they take on the sense of 'designing' or 'sketching' some 'project' which is to be carried through; and they may also be used in the more special sense of 'projection' in which a geometer is said to 'project' a curve 'upon' a plane. The words 'projection' and 'project' accordingly lend themselves rather well to translating these words in many contexts, especially since their root meanings are very similar to those of 'Entwurf' and 'entwerfen'; but while the root meaning of 'throwing off' is still very much alive in Heidegger's German, it has almost entirely died out in the ordinary English usage of 'projection' and 'project', which in turn have taken on some connotations not felt in the German. Thus when in the English translation Dasein is said to 'project' entities, or possibilities, or even its own Being 'upon' something, the reader should bear in mind that the root meaning of 'throwing' is more strongly felt in the German than in the translation.

7. '. . . zieht es herab zu einem gegebenen, gemeinten Bestand, während der Entwurf im Werfen die Möglichkeit als Möglichkeit sich vorwirft und als solche *sein* lässt.' The expression 'einem etwas vorwerfen' means literally to 'throw something forward to someone', but often has the connotation of 'reproaching him with something', or 'throwing something in his teeth'. Heidegger may have more than one of these significations in mind.

8. '"Selbsterkenntnis"'. This should be carefully distinguished from the 'Sichkennen' discussed in *Being and Time*, section 26: "The Dasein-with of Others

and Everyday Being-with.'' Perhaps this distinction can be expressed—though rather crudely—by pointing out that we are here concerned with a full and sophisticated knowledge of the Self in all its implications, while in the earlier passage we were concerned with the kind of 'self-knowledge' which one loses when one 'forgets oneself' or does something so out of character that one 'no longer knows oneself'.

9. 'konkreten'. The earlier editions have 'konkreteren' ('more concretely').

10. '*Auslegung*'. [The translators make the following comment to an earlier reference to interpretation: "Heidegger uses two words which might well be translated as 'interpretation': 'Auslegung' and 'Interpretation'. Though in many cases these may well be regarded as synonyms, their connotations are not quite the same. 'Auslegung' seems to be used in a broad sense to cover any activity in which we interpret something 'as' something, whereas 'Interpretation' seems to apply to interpretations which are more theoretical or systematic, as in the exegesis of a text. We shall preserve this distinction by writing 'interpretation' for 'Auslegung', but 'Interpretation' for Heidegger's 'Interpretation', following similar conventions for the verbs 'auslegen' and 'interpretieren'.''—ED.]

11. 'Auslegung'. The older editions have 'A u s l e g u n g'.

12. ' . . . gibt sich . . . zu verstehen, welche Bewandtnis es je mit dem Begegnenden haben kann.'

13. 'Auseinandergelegt'. Heidegger is contrasting the verb 'auslegen' (literally, 'lay out') with the cognate 'auseinanderlegen' ('lay asunder' or 'take apart').

14. ' . . . was allein so möglich ist, dass es als Aussprechbares vor-liegt.' Here we follow the reading of the earlier editions. The hyphen in 'vor-liegt' comes at the end of the line in the later editions, but is undoubtedly meant to suggest (like the italicization of the 'vor' in the previous sentence) that this verb is to be interpreted with unusual literalness.

This paragraph is noteworthy for an exploitation of the prefix 'aus' ('out'), which fails to show up in our translation. Literally an 'Aussage' ('assertion') is something which is 'said out'; an 'Auslegung' ('interpretation') is a 'laying-out'; that which is 'ausdrücklich' ('explicit') is something that has been 'pressed out'; that which is 'aussprechbar' (our 'expressible') is something that can be 'spoken out'.

The verbs 'ausdrücken' and 'aussprechen' are roughly synonymous; but 'aussprechen' often has the more specific connotations of 'pronunciation', 'pronouncing oneself', 'speaking one's mind', 'finishing what one has to say', etc. While it would be possible to reserve 'express' for 'ausdrücken' and translate 'aussprechen' by some such phrase as 'speak out', it is more convenient to use 'express' for both verbs, especially since 'aussprechen' and its derivatives have occurred very seldom before the present chapter, in which 'ausdrücken' rarely appears. On the other hand, we can easily distinguish between the more frequent 'ausdrücklich' and 'ausgesprochen' by translating the latter as 'expressed' or 'expressly', and reserving 'explicit' for both 'ausdrücklich' and 'explizit'.

15. ' . . . die durch die Auslegung herausgelegt wird.'

16. In this paragraph Heidegger introduces the important words 'Vorhabe', 'Vorsicht', and 'Vorgriff'. 'Vorhabe' is perhaps best translated by some such expression as 'what we have in advance' or 'what we have before us'; but we shall usually find it more convenient to adopt the shorter term 'fore-having', occasionally resorting to hendiadys, as in the present sentence, and we shall handle the other terms in the same manner. 'Vorsicht' ('what we see in advance' or 'fore-sight') is the only one of these expressions which occurs in ordinary German usage, and often has the connotation of 'caution' or 'prudence'; Heidegger, however, uses it in a more general sense somewhat more akin to the English 'foresight', without the connotation of a shrewd and accurate prediction. 'Vorgriff' ('what we grasp in advance' or 'fore-conception') is related to the verb 'vorgreifen' ('to anticipate') as well as to the noun "Begriff."

17. 'Die Auslegung gründet jeweils in einer *Vorsicht*, die das in Vorhabe Genommene auf eine bestimmte Auslegbarkeit hin "anschneidet".' The idea seems to be that just as the person who cuts off the first slice of a loaf of bread gets the loaf 'started', the fore-sight 'makes a start' on what we have in advance—the fore-having.

18. ' . . . eines Vorgegebenen.' Here, as in many other passages, we have translated 'vorgeben' by various forms of the verb 'to present'; but it would perhaps be more in line with Heidegger's discussion of the prefix 'vor-' to write ' . . . of something fore-given.'

19. '*Sinn ist das durch Vorhabe, Vorsicht und Vorgriff strukturierte Woraufhin des Entwurfs, aus dem her etwas als etwas verständlich wird.*' (Notice that our usual translation of 'verständlich', and 'Verständlichkeit' as 'intelligible' and 'intelligibility', fails to show the connection of the words with 'Verständnis', etc. This connection could have been brought out effectively by writing 'understandable,' 'understandability', etc., but only at the cost of awkwardness.)

20. 'Sinn "hat" nur das Dasein, sofern die Erschlossenheit des In-der-Welt-seins durch das in ihr entdeckbare Seiende "erfüllbar" ist.' The point of this puzzling and ambiguous sentence may become somewhat clearer if the reader recalls that here as elsewhere the verb 'erschliessen' ('disclose') is used in the sense of 'opening something up' so that its contents can be 'discovered'. What thus gets 'opened up' will then be 'filled in' as more and more of its contents gets discovered.

21. 'Der Sinn von Sein kann nie in Gegensatz gebracht werden zum Seienden oder zum Sein als tragenden "Grund" des Seienden, weil "Grund" nur als Sinn zugänglich wird, und sei er selbst der Abgrund der Sinnlosigkeit.' Notice the etymological kinship between 'Grund' ('ground') and 'Abgrund' ('abyss').

22. 'Gegliederte'. The verbs 'artikulieren' and 'gliedern' can both be translated by 'articulate' in English; even in German they are nearly synonymous, but in

the former the emphasis is presumably on the 'joints' at which something gets divided, while in the latter the emphasis is presumably on the 'parts' or 'members'. We have distinguished between them by translating 'artikulieren' by 'Articulate' (with a capital 'A'), and 'gliedern' by 'articulate' (with a lower-case initial).

23. ' . . . die Aussage (das "Urteil") . . . '

24. *'Einschränkung'*. The older editions have 'E n t s c h r ä n k u n g'.

25. ' . . . die "Subjektsetzung" blendet das Seiende ab auf "der Hammer da", um durch den Vollzug der Entblendung das Offenbare *in* seiner bestimmbaren Bestimmtheit sehen zu lassen.'

26. 'Zur Aussage als der so existenzial verstandenen Mit-teilung gehört die Ausgesprochenheit.'

27. Heidegger uses three words which might conveniently be translated as 'validity': 'Geltung' (our 'validity'), 'Gültigkeit' (our 'valid character'), and 'Gelten' (our 'being valid', etc.). The reader who has studied logic in English and who accordingly thinks of 'validity' as merely a property of arguments in which the premises imply the conclusion, must remember that in German the verb 'gelten' and its derivatives are used much more broadly, so as to apply to almost anything that is commonly (or even privately) accepted, so that one can speak of the 'validity' of legal tender, the 'validity' of a ticket for so many weeks or months, the 'validity' of that which 'holds' for me or for you, the 'validity' of anything that is the case. While Heidegger's discussion does not cover as many of these meanings as will be listed in any good German dictionary, he goes well beyond the narrower usage of the English-speaking logician. Of course, we shall often translate 'gelten' in other ways.

28. ' . . . *Verbindlichkeit*, "Allgemeingültigkeit".'

29. 'Woraufhin das vorgegebene Seiende anvisiert wird, das übernimmt im Bestimmungsvollzug die Funktion des Bestimmenden.'

30. This Division has never appeared.

31. *'Rede'*. As we have pointed out earlier [. . .] we have translated this word either as 'discourse' or 'talk', as the context seems to demand, sometimes compromising with the hendiadys 'discourse or talk'. But in some contexts 'discourse' is too formal while 'talk' is too colloquial; the reader must remember that there is no good English equivalent for 'Rede'. For a previous discussion see *Being and Time*, Section 7 B.

32. 'Die Hinausgesprochenheit der Rede ist die Sprache.'

33. 'Dieses ist redend als zu- und absagen, auffordern, warnen, als Aussprache, Rücksprache, Fürsprache, ferner als "Aussagen machen" und als reden in der Weise des "Redenhaltens".'

34. Reading ' . . . bei der Analyse der Aussage . . . ' with the older editions. The words 'der Aussage' have been omitted in the newer editions.

35. 'Das Mitsein wird in der Rede "ausdrücklich" *geteilt*, das heisst es *ist* schon, nur ungeteilt als nicht ergriffenes und zugeeignetes.'

36. ' . . . der Mitteilung als "Aussage" . . . ' The quotation marks around 'Aussage' appear only in the newer editions.

37. 'Als verstehendes In-der-Welt-sein mit den Anderen ist es dem Mitdasein und ihm selbst "hörig" and in dieser Hörigkeit zugehörig.' In this sentence Heidegger uses some cognates of 'hören' ('hearing') whose interrelations disappear in our version.

38. ' . . . des Folgens . . . ' In the earlier editions there are quotations marks around 'Folgens'.

39. Here we follow the reading of the newer editions: ' . . . nicht eine Mannigfaltigkeit von Tondaten.' The older editions have 'reine' instead of 'eine'.

40. The author is here alluding to the German proverb, 'Wer nicht hören kann, muss fuhlen.' (I.e., he who cannot heed, must suffer.)

Part II

Hermeneutics and
Critical Theory:
Dialogues on Methodology

6

The Universality of the Hermeneutical Problem*

Hans-Georg Gadamer

Why has the problem of language come to occupy the same central position in current philosophical discussions that the concept of thought, or "thought thinking itself," held in philosophy a century and a half ago? By answering this question, I shall try to give an answer indirectly to the central question of the modern age—a question posed for us by the existence of modern science. It is the question of how our natural view of the world—the experience of the world that we have as we simply live out our lives—is related to the unassailable and anonymous authority that confronts us in the pronouncements of science. Since the seventeenth century, the real task of philosophy has been to mediate this new employment of man's cognitive and constructive capacities with the totality of our experience of life. This task has found expression in a variety of ways, including our own generation's attempt to bring the topic of language to the center of philosophical concern. Language is the fundamental mode of operation of our being-in-the-world and the all-embracing form of the constitution of the world. Hence we always have in view the pronouncements of the sciences, which are fixed in nonverbal signs. And our task is to reconnect the objective world of technology, which the sciences place at our disposal and discretion, with those fundamental orders of our being that are neither arbitrary nor manipulable by us, but rather simply demand our respect.

I want to elucidate several phenomena in which the universality of this question becomes evident. I have called the point of view involved in this theme "hermeneutical," a term developed by Heidegger. Heidegger was continuing a perspective stemming originally from Protestant theology and transmitted into our own century by Wilhelm Dilthey.

What is hermeneutics? I would like to start from two experiences of alienation that we encounter in our concrete existence: the experience of alienation of the aesthetic consciousness and the experience of alienation of the historical consciousness. In both cases what I mean can be stated in a few words. The aesthetic consciousness realizes a possibility that as such we can neither deny nor diminish in its value, namely, that we relate ourselves, either negatively or affirmatively, to the quality of an artistic form. This statement means we are related in such a way that the judgment we make decides in the end regarding the expressive power and validity of what we judge. What we reject has nothing to say to us—or we reject it because it has nothing to say to us. This characterizes our relation to art in the broadest sense of the word, a sense that, as Hegel has shown, includes the entire religious world of the ancient Greeks, whose religion of beauty experienced the divine in concrete works of art that man creates in response to the gods. When it loses its original and unquestioned authority, this whole world of experience becomes alienated into an object of aesthetic judgment. At the same time, however, we must admit that the world of artistic tradition—the splendid contemporaneousness that we gain through art with so many human worlds—is more than a mere object of our free acceptance or rejection. Is it not true that when a work of art has seized us it no longer leaves us the freedom to push it away from us once again and to accept or reject it on our own terms? And is it not also true that these artistic creations, which come down through the millennia, were not created for such aesthetic acceptance or rejection? No artist of the religiously vital cultures of the past ever produced his work of art with any other intention than that his creation should be received in terms of what it says and presents and that it should have its place in the world where men live together. The consciousness of art—the aesthetic consciousness—is always secondary to the immediate truth-claim that proceeds from the work of art itself. To this extent, when we judge a work of art on the basis of its aesthetic quality, something that is really much more intimately familiar to us is alienated. This alienation into aesthetic judgment always takes place when we have withdrawn ourselves and are no longer open to the immediate claim of that which grasps us. Thus one point of departure for my reflections in *Truth and Method* was that the aesthetic sovereignty that claims its rights in the experience of art represents an alienation when compared to the authentic experience that confronts us in the form of art itself.

About thirty years ago, this problem cropped up in a particularly distorted form when National Socialist politics of art, as a means to its own ends, tried to criticize formalism by arguing that art is bound to a people. Despite its misuse by the National Socialists, we cannot deny that the idea of art being bound to a people involves a real insight. A genuine artistic creation stands within a particular community, and such a community is always distinguishable from the cultured society that is informed and terrorized by art criticism.

The second mode of the experience of alienation is the historical consciousness—the noble and slowly perfected art of holding ourselves at a critical distance in dealing with witnesses to past life. Ranke's celebrated description of this idea as the extinguishing of the individual provided a popular formula for the ideal of historical thinking: the historical consciousness has the task of understanding all the witnesses of a past time out of the spirit of that time, of extricating them from the preoccupations of our own present life, and of knowing, without moral smugness, the past as a human phenomenon. In his well-known essay, *The Use and Abuse of History*, Nietzsche formulated the contradiction between this historical distancing and the immediate will to shape things that always cleaves to the present. And at the same time he exposed many of the consequences of what he called the "Alexandrian," weakened form of the will, which is found in modern historical science. We might recall his indictment of the weakness of evaluation that has befallen the modern mind because it has become so accustomed to considering things in ever different and changing lights that it is blinded and incapable of arriving at an opinion of its own regarding the objects it studies. It is unable to determine its own position vis-à-vis what confronts it. Nietzsche traces the value-blindness of historical objectivism back to the conflict between the alienated historical world and the life-powers of the present.

To be sure, Nietzsche is an ecstatic witness. But our actual experience of the historical consciousness in the last one hundred years has taught us most emphatically that there are serious difficulties involved in its claim to historical objectivity. Even in those masterworks of historical scholarship that seem to be the very consummation of the extinguishing of the individual demanded by Ranke, it is still an unquestioned principle of our scientific experience that we can classify these works with unfailing accuracy in terms of the political tendencies of the time in which they were written. When we read Mommsen's *History of Rome*, we know who alone could have written it, that is, we can identify the political situation in which this historian organized the voices of the past in a meaningful way. We know it too in the case of Treitschke or of Sybel, to choose only a few prominent names from Prussian historiography. This clearly means, first of all, that the whole reality of historical experience does not find expression in the mastery of historical method. No one disputes the fact that controlling the prejudices of our own present to such an extent that we do not misunderstand the witnesses of the past is a valid aim, but obviously such control does not completely fulfill the task of understanding the past and its transmissions. Indeed, it could very well be that only *insignificant* things in historical scholarship permit us to approximate this ideal of totally extinguishing individuality, while the great productive achievements of scholarship always preserve something of the splendid magic of immediately mirroring the present in the past and the past in the present. Historical science, the second experience from which I begin, expresses only one part of our actual experience—our actual encounter with historical tradition—and it knows only an alienated form of this historical tradition.

We can contrast the hermeneutical consciousness with these examples of alienation as a more comprehensive possibility that we must develop. But, in the case of this hermeneutical consciousness also, our initial task must be to overcome the epistemological truncation by which the traditional 'science of hermeneutics' has been absorbed into the idea of modern science. If we consider Schleiermacher's hermeneutics, for instance, we find his view of this discipline peculiarly restricted by the modern idea of science. Schleiermacher's hermeneutics shows him to be a leading voice of historical romanticism. But at the same time, he kept the concern of the Christian theologian clearly in mind, intending his hermeneutics, as a general doctrine of the art of understanding, to be of value in the special work of interpreting Scripture. Schleiermacher defined hermeneutics as the art of avoiding misunderstanding. To exclude by controlled, methodical consideration whatever is alien and leads to misunderstanding—misunderstanding suggested to us by distance in time, change in linguistic usages, or in the meanings of words and modes of thinking—that is certainly far from an absurd description of the hermeneutical endeavor. But the question also arises as to whether the phenomenon of understanding is defined appropriately when we say that to understand is to avoid misunderstanding. Is it not, in fact, the case that every misunderstanding presupposes a 'deep common accord'?

I am trying to call attention here to a common experience. We say, for instance, that understanding and misunderstanding take place between I and thou. But the formulation "I and thou" already betrays an enormous alienation. There is nothing like an "I and thou" at all—there is neither the I nor the thou as isolated, substantial realities. I may say "thou" and I may refer to myself over against a thou, but a common understanding [Verständigung] always precedes these situations. We all know that to say "thou" to someone presupposes a deep common accord [tiefes Einverständnis]. Something enduring is already present when this word is spoken. When we try to reach agreement on a matter on which we have different opinions, this deeper factor always comes into play, even if we are seldom aware of it. Now the science of hermeneutics would have us believe that the opinion we have to understand is something alien that seeks to lure us into misunderstanding, and our task is to exclude every element through which a misunderstanding can creep in. We accomplish this task by a controlled procedure of historical training, by historical criticism, and by a controllable method in connection with powers of psychological empathy. It seems to me that this description is valid in one respect, but yet it is only a partial description of a comprehensive life-phenomenon that constitutes the 'we' that we all are. Our task, it seems to me, is to transcend the prejudices that underlie the aesthetic consciousness, the historical consciousness, and the hermeneutical consciousness that has been restricted to a technique for avoiding misunderstandings and to overcome the alienations present in them all.

What is it, then, in these three experiences that seemed to us to have been left out, and what makes us so sensitive to the distinctiveness of these experiences? What is the *aesthetic* consciousness when compared to the fullness of what has already addressed us—what we call "classical" in art? Is it not always already determined in this way what will be expressive for us and what we will find significant? Whenever we say with an instinctive, even if perhaps erroneous, certainty (but a certainty that is initially valid for our consciousness) "this is classical; it will endure," what we are speaking of has already preformed our possibility for aesthetic judgment. There are no purely formal criteria that can claim to judge and sanction the formative level simply on the basis of its artistic virtuosity. Rather, our sensitive-spiritual existence is an aesthetic resonance chamber that resonates with the voices that are constantly reaching us, preceding all explicit aesthetic judgment.

The situation is similar with the historical consciousness. Here, too, we must certainly admit that there are innumerable tasks of historical scholarship that have no relation to our own present and to the depths of its historical consciousness. But it seems to me there can be no doubt that the great horizon of the past, out of which our culture and our present live, influences us in everything we want, hope for, or fear in the future. History is only present to us in light of our futurity. Here we have all learned from Heidegger, for he exhibited precisely the primacy of futurity for our possible recollection and retention, and for the whole of our history.

Heidegger worked out this primacy in his doctrine of the productivity of the hermeneutical circle. I have given the following formulation to this insight: It is not so much our judgments as it is our prejudices that constitute our being.[1] This is a provocative formulation, for I am using it to restore to its rightful place a positive concept of prejudice that was driven out of our linguistic usage by the French and the English Enlightenment. It can be shown that the concept of prejudice did not originally have the meaning we have attached to it. Prejudices are not necessarily unjustified and erroneous, so that they inevitably distort the truth. In fact, the historicity of our existence entails that prejudices, in the literal sense of the word, constitute the initial directedness of our whole ability to experience. Prejudices are biases of our openness to the world. They are simply conditions whereby we experience something—whereby what we encounter says something to us. This formulation certainly does not mean that we are enclosed within a wall of prejudices and only let through the narrow portals those things that can produce a pass saying, "Nothing new will be said here." Instead we welcome just that guest who promises something new to our curiosity. But how do we know the guest whom we admit is one who has something *new* to say to us? Is not our expectation and our readiness to hear the new also necessarily determined by the old that has already taken possession of us? The concept of prejudice is closely connected to the concept of authority, and the above image makes it clear that it is in need of hermeneutical rehabilitation. Like every image, however, this one too is misleading. The nature of the hermeneutical experience is not that something is outside and desires admission. Rather, we are possessed by something and precisely by means of it we are opened up for the new, the different, the true. Plato makes this clear in his beautiful comparison of bodily foods with spiritual nourishment: while we can refuse the former (e.g., on the advice of a physician), we have always taken the latter into ourselves already.

But now the question arises as to how we can legitimate this hermeneutical conditionedness of our being in the face of modern science, which stands or falls with the principle of being unbiased and prejudiceless. We will certainly not accomplish this legitimation by making prescriptions for science and recommending that it toe the line—quite aside from the fact that such pronouncements always have something comical about them. Science will not do us this favor. It will continue along its own path with an inner necessity beyond its control, and it will produce more and more breathtaking knowledge and controlling power. It can be no other way. It is senseless, for instance, to hinder a genetic researcher because such research threatens to breed a superman. Hence the problem cannot appear as one in which our human consciousness ranges itself over against the world of science and presumes to develop a kind of antiscience. Nevertheless, we cannot avoid the question of whether what we are aware of in such apparently harmless examples as the aesthetic consciousness and the historical consciousness does not represent a problem that is also present in modern natural science and our technological attitude toward the world. If modern science enables us to erect a new world of technological purposes that transforms everything around us, we are not thereby suggesting that the researcher who gained the knowledge decisive for this state of affairs even considered technical applications. The genuine researcher is motivated by a desire for knowledge and by nothing else. And yet, over against the whole of our civilization that is founded on modern science, we must ask repeatedly if something has not been omitted. If the presuppositions of these possibilities for knowing and making remain half in the dark, cannot the result be that the hand applying this knowledge will be destructive?

The problem is really universal. The hermeneutical question, as I have characterized it, is not restricted to the areas from which I began in my own investigations. My only concern there was to secure a theoretical basis that would enable us to deal with the basic factor of contemporary culture, namely, science and its industrial, technological utilization. Statistics provide us with a useful example of how the hermeneutical dimension encompasses the entire procedure of science. It is an extreme example, but it shows us that science always stands under definite conditions of methodological abstraction and that the successes of modern sciences rest on the fact that other possibilities for questioning are concealed by abstraction. This fact comes out clearly in the case of statistics, for the anticipatory character of the questions statistics answer makes it particularly suitable for propaganda purposes. Indeed, effective propaganda must always try to influence initially the judgment of the person addressed and to restrict his possibilities of judgment. Thus what is established by statistics seems to be a language of facts, but which questions these facts answer and which facts would begin to speak if other questions were asked are hermeneutical questions. Only a hermeneutical inquiry would legitimate the meaning of these facts and thus the consequences that follow from them.

But I am anticipating, and have inadvertently used the phase, "which answers to which questions fit the facts." This phase is in fact the hermeneutical *Urphänomen*: No assertion is possible that cannot be understood as an answer to a question, and assertions can only be understood in this way. It does not impair the impressive methodology of modern science in the least. Whoever wants to learn a science has to learn to master its methodology. But we also know that methodology as such does not guarantee in any way the productivity of its application. Any experience of life can confirm the fact that there is such a thing as methodological sterility, that is, the application of a method to something not really worth knowing, to something that has not been made an object of investigation on the basis of a genuine question.

The methodological self-consciousness of modern science certainly stands in opposition to this argument. A historian, for example, will say in reply: It is all very nice to talk about the historical tradition in which alone the voices of the past gain their meaning and through which the prejudices that determine the present are inspired. But the situation is completely different in questions of serious historical research. How could one seriously mean, for example, that the clarification of the taxation practices of fifteenth-century cities or of the marital customs of Eskimos somehow first receive their meaning from the consciousness of the present and its anticipations? These are questions of historical knowledge that we take up as tasks quite independently of any relation to the present.

In answering this objection, one can say that the extremity of this point of view would be similar to what we find in certain large industrial research facilities, above all in America and Russia. I mean the so-called random experiment in which one simply covers the material without concern for waste or cost, taking the chance that some day one measurement among the thousands of measurements will finally yield an interesting finding; that is, it will turn out to be the answer to a question from which someone can progress. No doubt modern research in the humanities also works this way to some extent. One thinks, for instance, of the great editions and especially of the ever more perfect indexes. It must remain an open question, of course, whether by such procedures modern historical research increases the chances of actually noticing the interesting fact and thus gaining from it the corresponding enrichment of our knowledge. But even if they do, one might ask: Is this an ideal, that countless research projects (i.e., determinations of the connection of facts) are extracted from a thousand historians, so that the 1001st historian can find something interesting? Of course, I am drawing a caricature of genuine scholarship. But in every caricature there is an element of truth, and this one contains an indirect answer to the question of what it is that really makes the productive scholar. That he has learned the methods? The person who never produces anything new has also done that. It is imagination [*Phantasie*] that is the decisive function of the scholar. Imagination naturally has a hermeneutical function and serves the sense for what is questionable. It serves the ability to expose real, productive questions, something in which, generally speaking, only he who masters all the methods of his science succeeds.

As a student of Plato, I particularly love those scenes in which Socrates gets into a dispute with the Sophist virtuosi and drives them to despair by his questions. Eventually they can endure his questions no longer and claim for themselves the apparently preferable role of the questioner. And what happens? They can think of nothing at all to ask. Nothing at all occurs to them that is worth while going into and trying to answer.

I draw the following inference from this observation. The real power of hermeneutical consciousness is our ability to see what is questionable. Now if what we have before our eyes is not only the artistic tradition of a people, or historical tradition, or the principle of modern science in its hermeneutical preconditions but rather the whole of our experience, then we have succeeded, I think, in joining the experience of science to our own universal and human experience of life. For we have now reached the fundamental level that we can call (with Johannes Lohmann) the "linguistic constitution of the world.''[2] It presents itself as the consciousness that is effected by history [*wirkungsgeschichtliches Bewusstsein*] and that provides an initial schematization for all our possibilities of knowing. I leave out of account the fact that the scholar—even the natural scientist—is perhaps not completely free of custom and society and from all possible factors in his environment. What I mean is that precisely *within* his scientific experience it is not so much the "laws of ironclad inference" (Helmholz) that present fruitful ideas to him, but rather unforeseen constellations that kindle the spark of scientific inspiration (e.g., Newton's falling apple or some other incidental observation).

The consciousness that is effected by history has its fulfillment in what is linguistic. We can learn from the sensitive student of language that language, in its life and occurrence, must not be thought of as merely changing, but rather as something that has a teleology operating within it. This means that the words that are formed, the means of expression that appear in a language in order to say certain things, are not accidentally fixed, since they do not once again fall altogether into disuse. Instead, a definite articulation of the world is built up—a process that works as if guided and one that we can always observe in children who are learning to speak.

We can illustrate this by considering a passage in Aristotle's *Posterior Analytics* that ingeniously describes one definite aspect of language formation.[3] The passage treats what Aristotle calls the *epagoge*, that is, the formation of the universal. How does one arrive at a universal? In philosophy we say: how do we arrive at a general concept, but even words in this sense are obviously general. How does it happen that they are "words," that is, that they have a general meaning? In his first apperception, a sensuously equipped being finds himself in a surging sea of stimuli, and finally one day he begins, as we say, to know something. Clearly we do not mean that he was previously blind. Rather, when we say "to know" [*erkennen*] we mean "to recognize" [*wiedererkennen*], that is, to pick something out [*herauserkennen*] of the stream of images flowing past as being identical.

What is picked out in this fashion is clearly retained. But how? When does a child know its mother for the first time? When it sees her for the first time? No. Then when? How does it take place? Can we really say at all that there is a single event in which a first knowing extricates the child from the darkness of not knowing? It seems obvious to me that we cannot. Aristotle has described this wonderfully. He says it is the same as when an army is in flight, driven by panic, until at last someone stops and looks around to see whether the foe is still dangerously close behind. We cannot say that the army stops when one soldier has stopped. But then another stops. The army does not stop by virtue of the fact that two soldiers stop.

When does it actually stop, then? Suddenly it stands its ground again. Suddenly it obeys the command once again. A subtle pun is involved in Aristotle's description, for in Greek "command" means *archē*, that is, *principium*. When is the principle present as a principle? Through what capacity? This question is in fact the question of the occurrence of the universal.

If I have not misunderstood Johannes Lohmann's exposition, precisely this same teleology operates constantly in the life of language. When Lohmann speaks of linguistic tendencies as the real agents of history in which specific forms expand, he knows of course that it occurs in these forms of realization, of "coming to a stand" [*Zum-Stehen-Kommen*], as the beautiful German word says. What is manifest here, I contend, is the real mode of operation of our whole human experience of the world. Learning to speak is surely a phase of special productivity, and in the course of time we have all transformed the genius of the three-year-old into a poor and meager talent. But in the utilization of the linguistic interpretation of the world that finally comes about, something of the productivity of our beginnings remains alive. We are all acquainted with this, for instance, in the attempt to translate, in practical life or in literature or wherever; that is, we are familiar with the strange, uncomfortable, and tortuous feeling we have as long as we do not have the right word. When we have found the right expression (it need not always be one word), when we are certain that we have it, then it "stands," then something has come to a "stand." Once again we have a halt in the midst of the rush of the foreign language, whose endless variation makes us lose our orientation. What I am describing is the mode of the whole human experience of the world. I call this experience hermeneutical, for the process we are describing is repeated continually throughout our familiar experience. There is always a world already interpreted, already organized in its basic relations, into which experience steps as something new, upsetting what has led our expectations and undergoing reorganization itself in the upheaval. Misunderstanding and strangeness are not the first factors, so that avoiding misunderstanding can be regarded as the specific task of hermeneutics. Just the reverse is the case. Only the support of familiar and common understanding makes possible the venture into the alien, the lifting up of something out of the alien, and thus the broadening and enrichment of our own experience of the world.

This discussion shows how the claim to universality that is appropriate to the hermeneutical dimension is to be understood. Understanding is language-bound. But this assertion does not lead us into any kind of linguistic relativism. It is indeed true that we live within a language, but language is not a system of signals that we send off with the aid of a telegraphic key when we enter the office or transmission station. That is not speaking, for it does not have the infinity of the act that is linguistically creative and world experiencing. While we live wholly within a language, the fact that we do so does not constitute linguistic relativism because there is absolutely no captivity within a language—not even within our native language. We all experience this when we learn a foreign language, especially on journeys insofar as we master the foreign language to some extent. To master the foreign language means precisely that when we engage in speaking it in the foreign land, we do not constantly consult inwardly our own world and its vocabulary. The better we know the language, the less such a side glance at our native language is perceptible, and only because we never know foreign languages well enough do we always have something of this feeling. But it is nevertheless already speaking, even if perhaps a stammering speaking, for stammering is the obstruction of a desire to speak and is thus opened into the infinite realm of possible expression. Any language in which we live is infinite in this sense, and it is completely mistaken to infer that reason is fragmented because there are various languages. Just the opposite is the case. Precisely through our finitude, the particularity of our being, which is evident even in the variety of languages, the infinite dialogue is opened in the direction of the truth that we are.

If this is correct, then the relation of our modern industrial world, founded by science, which we described at the outset, is mirrored above all on the level of language. We live in an epoch in which an increasing leveling of all life-forms is taking place—that is the rationally necessary requirement for maintaining life on our planet. The food problem of mankind, for example, can only be overcome by the surrender of the lavish wastefulness that has covered the earth. Unavoidably, the mechanical, industrial world is expanding within the life of the individual as a sort of sphere of technical perfection. When we hear modern lovers talking to each other, we often wonder if they are communicating with words or with advertising labels and technical terms from the sign language of the modern industrial world. It is inevitable that the leveled life-forms of the industrial age also affect language, and in fact the impoverishment of the vocabulary of language is making enormous progress, thus bringing about an approximation of language to a technical sign-system. Leveling tendencies of this kind are irresistible. Yet in spite of them the simultaneous building up of our own world in language still persists whenever we want to say something to each other. The result is the actual relationship of men to each other. Each one is at first a kind of linguistic circle, and these linguistic circles come into contact with each other, merging more and more. Language occurs once again, in vocabulary and grammar as always, and never without the inner infinity of the dialogue that is in progress between every speaker and his partner. That is the fundamental dimension of hermeneutics. Genuine speaking, which has something to say and hence does not give prearranged signals, but rather seeks words through which one reaches the other person, is the universal human task—but it is a special task for the theologian, to whom is commissioned the saying-further [*Weitersagen*] of a message that stands written.

Translated by David E. Linge

Notes

* Hans-Georg Gadamer, "Die Universalität des hermeneutischen Problems" in *Kleine Schriften I: Philosophie. Hermeneutik* (Tübingen: J. C. B. Mohr [Paul Siebeck], 1976), pp. 101–112.—ED.

1. Cf. *Truth and Method*, translated by Garrett Barden and John Cumming (New York: The Seabury Press, 1977), p. 245.—TRANS.

2. Cf. Johannes Lohmann, *Philosophie und Sprachwissenschaft* (Berlin: Duncker and Humbolt, 1963).

3. Aristotle, *Posterior Analytics*, 100a 11–13.

7

Hermeneutics as the General Methodology of the *Geisteswissenschaften**

Emilio Betti

The Place of the Hermeneutical Problematic in Contemporary Consciousness

Hermeneutics, as the general problematic of interpretation which blossomed so richly during that glorious epoch of the unfolding of the European spirit we now call the romanticist period and which formed the common concern of those dedicated to all the humanist disciplines—a concern shared by linguists such as Wilhelm von Humboldt; theologians such as Ast, August Wilhelm Schlegel and Boeckh; jurists such as Savigny; political historians such as Niebuhr, after him Ranke, then Droysen—this time-honoured hermeneutics (as the theory of interpretation) is today in Germany no longer a living heritage within the *Geisteswissenschaften*: it appears to have become outmoded. It would appear that, with some notable exceptions, the rich hermeneutical heritage has in many cases been forgotten in present-day Germany and that the continuity with the great romanticist tradition has nearly been broken (it is difficult to gauge the extent to which this has already happened).

This cultural situation of our time appears in a particular light through a talk given on 28 January 1959 by Professor Coing in Düsseldorf in the context of the Study-Group Nordrhein-Westfalen, on "the juristic methods on interpretation and the theories of general hermeneutics" to a circle of colleagues, only half of whom were jurists. He expressed regret at the decreasing awareness among his fellow-countrymen of the hermeneutical problematic, especially so since it had been advanced considerably in recent times by German thinkers such as Wilhelm Dilthey and Georg Simmel—as is shown by the high praise their contributions attracted from the philosopher Collingwood, the sociologist Aron and the historian Marrou. Characteristic in all this was the reserved attitude of the speaker whose references to existing literature remained too vague, and who refrained from presenting his audience with an accurate account.

Objectivations of Mind

Nothing is of greater importance to man than living in mutual understanding with his fellow-men. Nothing appeals as much to his understanding as the lost traces of man that come to light again and address him. Wherever we come into contact with meaning-full forms [*sinnhaltige Formen*] through which an other mind addresses us, we find our interpretative powers stirring to get to know the meaning contained within these forms. From fleeting speech to fixed documents and mute remainders, from writing to *chiffres* and to artistic symbol, from articulated language to figurative or musical representation, from explanation to active behavior, from facial expression to ways of bearing and types of character—in short, whenever something from the mind of an Other approaches us there is a call on our ability to understand, issued in the hope of being unfolded. The different levels on which these various objectivations present themselves to us must not, of course, be confounded with one another. Statements, above all, have to be clearly distinguished from the sounds that embody them, and they have to be separated from the signs in which they are expressed. In general, we have to beware of confusing the perceptible bearer which belongs to the physical level—on a permanent basis or through being objectified only fleetingly—with the meaning-content it has been entrusted with; it is a vehicle that, as it were, carries that meaning with it as a content which belongs to a level fundamentally different from the physical.

Meaning-full Forms

On the other hand, it is equally important that we insist that an interpretation is possible only in view of meaning-full forms. "Form" is here to be understood in a wide sense as an homogeneous structure in which a number of perceptible elements are related to one another and which is suitable for preserving the character of the mind that created it or that is embodied in it. The representational function of a meaning-full form which transmits a piece of knowledge need not, by the way, be a conscious one: the meaning-content it carries can be known through its meaning-representational function in such a way that, owing to its mediation, another mind, which is nevertheless closely related to ours, can "speak" to us by addressing our ability to understand with an "appeal." It is possible to enter into a spiritual relationship with one's fellow-men only on the basis of such meaning-full forms which are either given in actual perception or can be evoked as an image in one's memory.

It would, however, be a grave materialist prejudice to envisage these forms, and, in particular, explanations, as a kind of shell or wrapping, the transmission of which would effect a transference of the thought contained within it. In truth, people do not establish mutual understanding by exchanging the material signs of objects or by the mutual production of the same thought with the help of an automatic transference, but rather through the reciprocal mobilization of corresponding elements in the chain of their conceptual universe and the striking of the same chord on their mental instrument to bring forth thoughts that correspond to those of the speaker. This is because the gates of the mind open only from the inside and on account of a spontaneous impulse; the outside contributes only the invitation to resonate in harmony.

Representational Function and Meaning of Expression

Interpretation, by the way, does not presuppose that the thought-content has been expressed with an intent towards conscious representation or towards communicating something about social life. It is nevertheless possible that thought without such an intent, or any activity which is not directed at expressing thought, can at any time become the object of interpretation, given that one is wishing to elicit the meaning expressed in that activity, or to gather its style of production or life-style. Every practical activity possesses internal meaning which may be of an unconscious but nevertheless symptomatic kind, and which becomes important if one wishes to use it as a basis for further consideration. Viewed as a symptom, it could be used for arriving at a person's fundamental conceptions and his characteristic way of perceiving and judging things around him. Without any knowledge about the circumstances of an action and the events preceding or following it, which locate it within a chain of events, it would be difficult to attempt such an inference on the basis of one single action alone; if such knowledge is, however, available then it become possible to refer to the whole personality.

Both jurists and historians are interested in such practical activity. Because of the absence of any conscious intent at representation, it provides the most genuine and reliable indication of the attitude of their author by allowing safe inferences as to the underlying mentality. In the case of the historian, such an interest is due to his task of having to provide an assessment of the relative worth of competing interests on the basis of maxims of behavior adopted by the person in question; this is because the truthful presentation of this assessment may either suffer from possible moralizing tendencies, which may elevate it to the sublime, or from an interest in leaving in the dark the motives underlying a course of action. One should be aware that the object of interpretation in the above-mentioned case is always an objective activity of thought which is recognizable in practical behavior. Since this activity is to be regarded as a mediate, or implicit manifestation of a certain way of seeing and thinking, that behavior, if considered from the point of view of its symptomatic value, can by all means be viewed as a meaning-full form in the wider sense of an objectivation of mind. Here we come to a distinction in the field of hermeneutics which is directed at the fundamental characteristics of the representational function inherent in meaning-full forms and which is concerned with finding out whether the mode of existence of this function is mediate or immediate, intentional and consciously developed or only implicit and undeveloped. This is why one differentiates within historical material between sources of information which have been transmitted in writing, by word of mouth, or in the form of an object and remnants, traces, or findings which, as fragments of the past, point beyond it; the latter is characterized by the absence of both a conscious representational function as well as a context that would connect the fragment with the whole of a past epoch.

Interpretation and Understanding

The process of interpretation is, in my opinion, destined to solve the epistemological problem of Understanding. Drawing on the familiar distinction between action and outcome, procedure and its result, we may tentatively characterize interpretation as the procedure that aims for, and results in, Understanding. Interpreting, in view of its task, is to bring something to the Understanding. To comprehend the unity of process of interpretation we need to refer to the elementary phenomenon of understanding as it is actualized through the mediation of language. This phenomenon has been unravelled with unsurpassable clarity by Wilhelm von Humboldt. It shows us that speech produced by our fellow-men cannot be regarded as a ready-made physical object simply to be received by us; it is instead the material source of a stimulation directed at our insight to re-translate what has been perceived and to reconstruct its meaning from within so that the line of argument, as it is apparent in the spoken word, can, with the help of our categories of thought, be brought to expression anew in a creative, form-giving process.

Interpretation as a Triadic Process

It is now clear that we can generalize von Humboldt's observation. To the extent that the process of interpretation is designed to solve the problem of understanding, it remains, in its essential elements, unified and homogeneous despite the differentiations required in its application. Each time there is a demand made on the mental spontaneity of the one called upon to understand, an appeal that cannot be successful without his active participation: a challenge and an appeal emanating from meaning-full forms in which mind has objectivated itself and which is directed at a subject, an active and thinking mind, whose interest in understanding has been stimulated by the variegated concerns of everyday life. The phenomenon of understanding is therefore a triadic process at the opposite ends of which we find the interpreter as an active, thinking mind, and the mind objectivated in meaning-full forms. They do not come into contact, into touch, immediately but only through the mediation of these meaning-full forms in which an objectivated mind confronts the interpreter as an unalterably other being. Subject and object of the process of interpretation, i.e., interpreter and meaning-full forms, are the same that can be found in every process of cognition; only here they are characterized by specific traits which derive from the fact that we are not dealing with just any object but with objectivations of mind, so that the task of the cognizing subject consists in recognizing the inspiring, creative thought within these objectivations, to rethink the conception or recapture the intuition revealed in them. It follows that understanding is here the re-cognition and re-construction of a meaning— and with it of the mind that is known through the forms of its objectivations—that addresses a thinking mind congenial with it on the basis of a shared humanity: it is a bridging through a kind of arc, a bringing together and reuniting of these forms with the inner totality that generated them and from which they separated; it is, of course, an internalization of these forms in which their content is transposed into the differing subjectivity of an Other.

Inversion of the Creative and Transposition into the Subjectivity of an Other

What occurs here, then, is an inversion of the creative process: in the hermeneutical process the interpreter retraces the steps from the opposite direction by re-thinking them in his inner self.

The difficulty involved in such an inversion rests in the mentioned transposition into another subjectivity that differs from the original one. This is also the basis of the antinomy of two contradictory requirements which an interpretation has to satisfy equally well. On the one side is the demand for objectivity: the interpreter's reconstruction of the meaning contained in meaning-full forms has to correspond to their meaning-content as closely as possible; for this reason, the requirement mentioned is one of honest subordination. On the other side, the requirement for objectivity can only be met thanks to the subjectivity of the interpreter and his awareness of the preconditions of his ability to understand in a manner adequate to the subject-matter. That is to say, the interpreter is called upon to reconstruct a thought and recreate it from within himself, making it his own, while at the same time having to objectify it. We therefore have here a conflict between, on the one hand, the subjective element that cannot be separated from the spontaneity of understanding, and, on the other, objectivity as the otherness of the meaning to be arrived at. It will soon become apparent how this antinomy gives rise to the whole dialectic of the process of interpretation and that it provides the starting-point for a general theory of interpretation just as the antimony between the being-for-itself of the subject and the otherness of the object leads the dialectic emerging in any process of cognition.

Guidelines for Interpretation: The Canon of the Hermeneutical Autonomy of the Object

We find that some of the criteria and guidelines, which I would like to call hermeneutical canons, relate to the object of interpretation while others relate more to the subject.

As far as the canons relating to the object are concerned, the first and basic canon is immediately apparent. Since meaning-full forms, as the object of interpretation, are essentially objectivations of mind and, in particular, manifestations of some thought-content, it is clear that they have to be understood with reference to that other mind that has been objectivated in them, and not in relation to any meaning the form itself may acquire if abstracted from the representational function it had for that mind or thought. Not so long ago, theoreticians in the field of hermeneutics formulated this canon of the 'mens dicentis' emphatically as "sensus non est inferendus sed efferendus"; the meaning to be determined may not be inferred into meaning-full forms in an arbitrary act, and in something of an underhand manner; rather it ought to be derived from it.

May I suggest that we call this first canon the canon of the hermeneutical autonomy of the object, or the canon of the immanence of the standards of hermeneutics. By this we mean that meaning-full forms have to be regarded as autonomous, and have to be understood in accordance with their own logic of development, their intended connections, and in their necessity, coherence and conclusiveness; they should be judged in relation to the standards immanent in the original intention: the intention, that is, which the created forms should correspond to from the point of view of the author and his formative impulse in the course of the creative process; it follows that they must not be judged in terms of their suitability for any other external purpose that may seem relevant to the interpreter.

The Canon of the Coherence of Meaning
(Principle of Totality)

A second fundamental canon relating to the object of interpretation was emphasized by the Roman jurist Celsus with exemplary accuracy in a famous text that contains a polemical attack against the hair-splitting activities engaged in by pleading rhetoricians. We may call the hermeneutic canon referred to in this text the canon of totality and of the coherence of meaning of hermeneutical investigations. This canon sheds some light upon the interrelations and coherence existing among the individual elements of speech, as is the case with any manifestation of thought—and upon their mutual relationship to the whole of which they are a part. It is that relationship of elements between themselves and to their common whole which allows for the reciprocal illumination and elucidation of meaning-full forms in the relationship between the whole and its parts, and vice versa.

One can assume that even plain common sense would accept that this interrelation between the whole and its parts, i.e., their coherence and synthesis, answers to an intellectual need shared by author and interpreter. A glance at romanticist hermeneutics would, furthermore, show us that the demand for totality was established by Schleiermacher in a particularly emphatic and insistent way. He stressed the hermeneutical interrelation existing between the unity of the whole and the individual elements of a work which allows it to be interpreted in such a way that clarification is achieved by reference either to the unity arising out of the ensemble of individual parts or to the meaning which each part acquires in respect of the whole. One proceeds thereby to the pre-supposition that the totality of speech, just as that of any manifestation of thought, issues from a unitary mind and gravitates towards a unitary mind and meaning. From this, and on the basis of the correspondence of the processes of creation and interpretation already referred to, we arrive at this guideline: the meaning of the whole has to be derived from its individual elements, and an individual element has to be understood by reference to the comprehensive, penetrating whole of which it is a part. Just as the signification, intensity, nuances of a word can only be comprehended in relation to the meaning-context in which it was uttered, so the signification and sense of a sentence, and sentences connected with it, can only be understood in relation to the reciprocal coherence of meaning-context, the organic composition and conclusiveness, of speech.

The principle of the reciprocal illumination of parts and whole can further be developed so that, in turn, every speech and every written work can equally be regarded as a link in a chain which can only be fully understood by reference to its place within a larger meaning-context. The comprehensive totality into which the part has to be integrated can be conceived of, if we follow Schleiermacher, as the whole life of a person. In a subjective, personal reference to the life of an author each of his actions can be understood in relation to their totality, according to their mutual effects and clarification, as one moment interconnected with all the others of the life of a whole person. A comprehensive totality can, in an objective reference, be conceived of as a cultural system which the work to be interpreted belongs to, inasmuch as it forms a link in the chain of existing continuities of meaning between works with a related meaning-content and expressive impulse. It follows that, on this higher level, too, understanding retains its tentative character at the outset and is corroborated and widened only in the further course of the interpretative procedure.

The hermeneutical canon of totality is nowadays applied in the legal sphere in the interpretation of explanations and modes of conduct as well as legal norms and other legal directives and maxims of judgment. Its field of application is, however, much wider than that. For example, there is the case concerning a criminal which is conducted in accordance with the postulate of the positive school of criminal law. This postulate requires that one concludes from the criminal act under consideration to its symptomatic value for the personality of the culprit as it reveals itself in that act. It is clear that this procedure follows the demand to refer to the whole of the matter. In the same way, one appeals to the canon of totality, more or less consciously, in the interpretation of legal norms and laws. This is especially so in cases where interpretations have to be excluded which would conflict with the consistency of a system that has been established with the aids provided by legal dogmatics, and that contains the norm in question; this is the case, for example, when the application of particular norms derivable from other legal systems—in accordance with the directives of international private law—has to be excluded in so far as it would conflict with the spirit of one's own legal order. Disregarding the peculiarly defensive attitude apparent in the introduction of extraneous norms, a look at the concept of legal order, as formed in modern legal dogmatics, leads one to the directive that each norm, or maxim for decision-making, which is to become an integral part of it will necessarily have to be related to the whole. This whole forms, in the words of Dilthey, a *Wirkungszusammenhang* [effective-structure] which generates an organic interrelationship, mutual dependency, coherence, and conclusiveness, even between norms, and groups of norms, from different areas of the law.

Analogy and Further Development

We now move from the object to the subject of interpretation, where we find a further guideline in the application of the law by a jurist. As the

theologian's task of application would confirm, it applies whenever either
an amendment to an incomplete ruling or a restriction is judged to be necessary in instances where there are either legalistic reasons for it, or when
it is disputed that a provision allows additional conclusions in cases where
it has been established or adopted in opposition to the consequence of the
law. In these situations, the task is not only to relate one part to an overarching whole—be it the whole of a legal order or universe of belief—but
to either supplement the purposive rationality of an established evaluation
by having recourse to the excess meaning evident in it, which allows for
further interrelated conclusions with regard to the social coexistence of the
members of a legal or religious community, or by restricting its applicability in view of the limitation of its basis. It is immediately apparent that the
required integration or restriction, nowadays known as analogy, extensive
and restrictive interpretation, introduces an element into the process of interpretation that goes beyond the simple task of the purely recognitive investigation of meaning, and which adds to it the further task of adaptation
and assimilation, that is, one of improvement and application aimed at the
systematic further development of legal norms and religious demands
within their existing life structures, and of bringing them closer to the actuality of contemporary life.

    Reflective consideration, then, uncovers further guidelines that have
to be followed in interpretation. Apart from the categories of the autonomy
of the object and of hermeneutical totality which respond to the need for
standards immanent in the internal coherence and totality of the object of
interpretation—which together correspond to the moment of objectivity of
the meaning arrived at—there exist guidelines which fulfill the demand for
an active involvement of the subject in this process; they consequently correspond to the moment of subjectivity referred to which is inseparable from
the spontaneity of understanding.

The Canon of the Actuality of Understanding

There is, accordingly, a third canon to be followed in every interpretation
which I would like to call the canon of the actuality of understanding, and
which Rudolf Bultmann[1] has drawn attention to recently. It states that an
interpreter's task is to retrace the creative process, to reconstruct it within
himself, to retranslate the extraneous thought of an Other, a part of the
past, a remembered event, into the actuality of one's own life, that is, to
adapt and integrate it into one's intellectual horizon within the framework
of one's own experiences by means of a kind of transformation on the basis
of the same kind of synthesis which enabled the recognition and reconstruction of that thought. It follows that the attempt of some historians to rid
themselves of their subjectivity is completely nonsensical. It would be naive

to assume, especially in the context of historical interpretation, that the task of the historian would be exhausted by a mere reporting of what is contained by his sources and to assume that the only true history is that contained in these sources. What one forgets here is that everything our mind gains possession of enters the whole structure of our representations and concepts which we already carry within ourselves. In this way, each new experience becomes an integral part of our mental universe through a process of adaptation and remains subject to its changes in relation to the interpretation of new experiences.

Affinity with the Subject-Matter and the 'Upon-Which' of Inquiry

It is, of course, correct that the interpreter's task is merely to find out the intended meaning of a manifestation of someone's thought and to understand the style of thinking and imagining apparent in it. The meaning and way of imagining is, however, not something that is simply offered to a passive interpreter by meaning-full forms and only needs to be fathered in a mechanical procedure. On the contrary, it is something that the interpreter has to recognize and reconstruct within himself with the help of his subtle intuition and on the strength of his own insight and of the categories of thought located in his own creative, practical knowledge.

One is, today, generally aware and agreed that the interpreter's attitude cannot be merely passively receptive but has to be actively reconstructive. But then, there are cases where this has, in my opinion, been taken too far. I do not mean the postulation of a so-called "*Vorverständnis*" [pre-understanding] on the part of the interpreter—a somewhat equivocal formula that could easily be made unequivocal, for all it states is that an interpreter should have an expertise in the area concerned, i.e., a living relationship with the subject-matter. This formula is, in itself, really quite harmless—until the possibility of objective knowledge in interpretation is itself being questioned. In order to avoid any misunderstanding, it should be admitted that objectivity means something quite different in the *Geisteswissenschaften* compared with the natural sciences where we are dealing with objects that are essentially different from ourselves. But it is necessary to reject the unwarranted conclusion that it is impossible to maintain a clear distinction between the knowing subject and his object, or that the 'in-itself' of an historical phenomenon is nothing more than "the illusion of objectifying thought which may be legitimate in natural science but never in the study of history."[2]

In this context it would be appropriate to refer to Bultmann's argument which amounts to the thesis that "objectivity in historical knowledge can never be achieved, not even in the sense that phenomena can be known as they are 'in-themselves' "[3]; this 'in-self' would be the illusion of objectifying thought. Such arguments are presented by Bultmann[4] in the following way: interpreting is possible only on the basis of a preceding involvement with a subject-matter directly or indirectly expressed in a text which itself determines the *Woraufhin* [upon which] of the inquiry (this is what Bultmann means by "*Vorverständnis*"—an equivocal word that had best be avoided because of its ambiguity). According to Bultmann, the interest in a subject-matter gives rise to the kind of question asked, i.e., the upon-which of inquiry. The upon-which may coincide with the intention of the text; in this case, the subject-matter under investigation is provided directly by the text. It may, however, also emerge from an interest in states of affairs contained in all kinds of texts; here, the subject-matter is provided by the text, only indirectly. (1) The upon-which of the inquiry may, for example, be given by an interest in the reconstruction of past history that can take the form of a psychological interest, which leads to the examination of a text in relation to the psychology of the individual, group or religion, and inquires into the psychological aspects of language, poetry, art, law, etc. (2) The upon-which may be given in an aesthetic interest which subjects the text to a structural analysis and studies the inner form of a work of art (it may do so in conjunction with a religious interest or remaining within the sphere of stylistic considerations). (3) The upon-which may finally be given in an interest in history "as the living sphere in which human existence takes place."[5] This would revolve around "the question of human existence as the mode of Being of the Self." Such an inquiry which would initially involve philosophical, religious and poetic texts would always be guided by a tentative understanding of human existence (existential understanding) "from which alone the categories necessary for any such inquiry would be able to emerge"—for answering questions concerning, for example, 'salvation', the 'meaning' of individual existence, ethical norms of action, the community of man, etc. One would only have to critically examine this "*Vorverständnis*" and to stake it in understanding: in the course of inquiring into a text one should submit to the questions of the text and listen to its claim.

The Question whether Objectivity of Historical Phenomena is Attainable

Bultmann bases his answer to the question "whether we can attain objectivity in our knowledge of phenomena, i.e., objectivity in (historical) interpretation" on the above-mentioned insight; it is certainly unattainable in the sense of the natural sciences. Bultmann's reasoning seems to indicate, in my opinion, a slight confusion; in any case, it does not stand up to critical examination. Historical phenomena have no existence, in Bultmann's view, without an historical subject called upon to comprehend them, "since past events can turn into historical phenomena only if they become meaningful for a subject that is itself part of, and participating in, history; i.e., if they acquire significance for someone who is connected with them in his historical existence"(!). According to Bultmann, then, "an historical phenomenon contains its own future, where it will reveal itself as that which it is." It would be acceptable if this referred to historically distant and consequential effects; but then something quite different would be meant than the historical conditioning of a phenomenon by the existence of an observing subject.

Bultmann, though, considers a phenomenon to be unequivocal in terms of scientific understanding and not open to the arbitrariness of speculative interpretation; but every historical phenomenon is seen as many-sided in that it is subject to different kinds of inquiry: intellectual history, psychological, sociological or any other kind, as long as it emerges from an historical affinity between interpreter and phenomenon. Bultmann accepts that any such kind of inquiry leads to clear, unequivocal understanding and objective knowledge—i.e., knowledge that is adequate to an object considered from a certain perspective—given that it is the result of a methodically correct interpretation.

To call an inquiry "subjective" because it has to be chosen by a subject would, however, be pointless. One has only to consider that every phenomenon presents a number of aspects, i.e., it is meaningful from various perspectives and every interpreter chooses the kind of inquiry that will yield the information he is interested in.

It follows that it is plainly absurd to require the interpreter to efface his subjectivity; all he, in fact, has to do is to exclude any personal preference concerning the result. In this respect it is, of course, necessary that interpretation, just as any scientific research, should proceed presuppositionless. Apart from this, understanding pre-necessitates the subject's vividness and the highest possible development of his individuality. Bultmann maintains that, just as the interpretation of poetry and art can succeed only if it is undertaken by someone who is stirred by them, so it is only an interpretation that questions texts about the possibility of our existence as a truly human one "that can be regarded as the understanding of historical phenomena in its ultimate and highest sense." He concludes, therefore, "that the most 'subjective' is here the most 'objective' interpretation, i.e., only he who is moved by the question about his own existence can hear the message of the text." This he follows with a remark from Fritz Kaufmann,[6] that the monuments of history "speak to us from the depth of the reality that created them only if we know, through our openness towards new experiences, of the problematic, of the finally insurmountable destitution and insecurity which form the basis and the abyss of our being-in-the-world.''

The Role of the Historian's Values:
Value-Oriented Interpretation

After this exposition of Bultmann's theory I would like to provide a critique of it. It is possible, in my opinion, to evidence in it a slight and inconspicuous shift of meaning; if this were the case, then his arguments would lose their logical conclusiveness. One can accept both an affinity with the object and the vividness of a subject who allows himself to be gripped by it and who inquires into a text in terms of the possibility of human and personal existence as the condition for the possibility of historical interpretation. It is, however, important to know more about that historical 'reproduction' of emotional and psychological contents wherever they become historically relevant. The recourse to 'feelings' makes nonsense of the principle of scientific verification as long as they cannot be transformed into a matter for precise and demonstrable judgments, i.e., into conceptually formed experiences. All it does is to bear witness to the psychological genesis of an hypothesis in the mind of the historian. As long as it remains in the state of personally felt values, there cannot be the slightest guarantee that these feelings correspond to the ones held by the historical person with whom the historian empathizes. A subjective and emotionally derived speculative interpretation [*Deutung*] of this kind does not constitute historical knowledge about actual complexities; nor is it something else which it, in fact, could be: a value-oriented interpretation.

I shall now refer to Max Weber's theory.[7] A value-oriented interpretation is, for Weber, directed at an object that can be considered from an aesthetic, ethical, intellectual, or any other cultural viewpoint. It is not part of a purely historical representation but is, from an historical standpoint, the 'formation' of an historical individual, i.e., the investigation of values which are realized in that object, and of the individual form in which they are apparent. This effort falls within the philosophy of history and is, indeed, 'subjectivizing' in the sense that we do not regard the validity of these values to be the same as the validity of empirically derived facts. A value-oriented interpretation does not aim at finding out what the people who created the object felt at the time, but what values can and should be found in the object. In the case of the latter, a value-oriented interpretation has the same aims as a normative, i.e., dogmatically oriented, approach such as aesthetics, ethics, or jurisprudence and is itself evaluative. In the case of the former, it is based on a dialectical value-analysis which is only concerned with 'possible' value-orientations of the object. Because of this orientation, it fulfills the important function of going beyond the indeterminateness of mere 'empathy' and of moving towards that kind of determinacy which knowledge about the content of individual consciousness is capable of. In contrast to mere 'feeling' and empathy, in which the vividness of the understanding subject becomes apparent, we restrict the term 'value' to something that is able to become an issue, the content of a conscious and articulated 'judgment': i.e., it is something that seeks 'validity' and that requires us to give a value-answer; something the validity of which is recognized by us as a value for us; or that is rejected as such, or is judged in intricately varied ways in an evaluative manner. This attribution of an ethical, aesthetic or juridical value always implies a 'value judgment'. It is of decisive importance for our critical considerations to state that it is the determinacy of its content that lifts the object of our value judgment out of the sphere of mere "empathy" and on to that of knowledge. The suggestion of shared value judgments concerning a state of affairs would be nonsensical if the central points of a content of a judgment were not understood in an identical way: in some way one always goes beyond mere intuitive feelings when relating something individual to a possible value. It is because an historical individual can only be an artificial unity constructed by value-orientations that 'evaluation' is the normal psychological stage of transition for intellectual understanding: it serves noetic understanding as a means and as a midwife, however much this stage in the genesis of knowledge ought to be striven for by the historian. This way I have—following Weber's hint[8]—indicated the limitations of value-oriented interpretations within the historian's process of cognition, where this subjectivizing element occupies a justifiable place.

Answer to the Historical Question Posed

The questionable character of the grounds on which the subjectivist doctrine of Bultmann seems to be resting becomes indeed apparent upon examination; one then finds them to be either inconclusive or the result of slight shifts of meaning. Firstly, it can be agreed that any view of history depends on the historian's perspective and that each historical phenomenon can be looked at from different points of view; but it is impossible to derive a conclusive objection to the objectivity of historical interpretation from the historicity of the standpoint of the historian. An historical judgment, conditioned as it is by various interests, is merely an answer which the historian is able to give to an intellectual situation and to the "historical question" (Droysen) arising out of it. Objective truth can now be glimpsed from any standpoint and point of view within the limits of their perspective; the picture that is arrived at would only be misleading if that particular perspective was claimed to represent the only admissible and legitimate one. The second objection against the objectivity of historical interpretation concerns the so-called "existential encounter with history." Here it is possible to evidence a slight shift of meaning which occurs when a condition for the possibility of historical knowledge, viz. the necessary noetic interest and the responsible participation of the historian in history entailed by it,[9] is confused with the object of knowledge itself, and when the question concerning the meaning of an historical phenomenon, in respect of its distant and consequential effects, is confused with a completely different question: that concerning its present *Bedeutsamkeit* [significance] and relevance in changing historical epochs, and changing historical conceptions about the same phenomenon in view of self-knowledge and self-education.

The Meaning of an Historical Phenomenon and Present Significance

The shift of meaning referred to in the first case is obvious when it is asserted[10] that "objectivity of historical knowledge in the sense of absolute and final knowledge is unattainable"—this contention can be accepted as justified owing to the impossibility of ever completing the hermeneutical task; but then it is added that "neither is it attainable in the sense of getting to know the phenomena as they are authentically in-themselves." The second assertion that follows on is directed at something quite different in that it negates the being-in-itself of historical phenomena—and this is obviously going too far. The task of interpretation, which depends at all times on the actuality of understanding, can, as a matter of fact, never be regarded as finished and completed because no interpretation, however convincing it may seem at first, can force itself upon mankind as the definitive one. The fact that the hermeneutical task can never be completed entails that the meaning contained within texts, monuments and fragments is constantly reborn through life and is forever transformed in a chain of rebirths; but this does not exclude the fact that the objectivated meaning-content still remains an objectivation of the creative force of an Other, to which the interpreter should seek access, not in an arbitrary way, but with the help of controllable guidelines. Here, the mind of an Other speaks to us not directly but across space and time through transformed matter that is charged with mental energy—which makes it possible for us to approach the meaning of this product, since it is part of the human spirit and is, to speak with Husserl, born of the same transcendental objectivity; but it nevertheless remains a steadfast, self-contained existence that can confront us owing to the fact that here the mind of an Other has objectivated itself in meaning-full forms.

Next, the second case of a shift in meaning, viz. the failure to distinguish between the meaning of historical phenomena on the one hand, and the significance of these phenomena for the present and for our responsibility for the future on the other, is no less apparent when it is asserted[11] that "historical phenomena are what they are, not in isolation but only in relation to the future"; "a future (it is said) in which the phenomenon will emerge as it really is" (an assertion that would make sense in view of the consequential effects of this phenomenon). But then it is added that the question is about the "meaning (more accurately: a significance) of historical events of our past in relation to our present: a present which is responsible for the future." As it is stated, "only the historian, who is open towards historical phenomena on account of his responsibility for the future, is in a position to understand history"[12] (in this sense the "most subjective interpretation would also be the most objective"). This, of course, is a paradox which we are familiar with from earlier discussions and which is irresolvable.

Dialogue and Monologue

In contrast to these views I would make the following remarks: historical phenomena do not acquire meaning if they are considered in isolation but (in accordance with the hermeneutical canon of the totality of interpretation already referred to) only within the meaning-context of their distant and consequential effects, as far as they can be assessed; this kind of meaning can be found by the historian in a completed form if sufficient time has passed since the phenomenon occurred. If, in contrast, it is asserted that the true essence of a phenomenon "will be visible only at the end of history,"[13] one then falls victim of a confusion between the point of view of an historical interpretation and the standpoint of an eschatological meaning-inference [*Sinngebung*]. It is, indeed, only from the standpoint of such a meaning-inference that the significance of a phenomenon for the present is situationally determined; this is because it only makes sense for a present, "which is responsible for the future," to ask after any present-day significance and to regard it as the product of a value-positing meaning-inference that is conditioned by the position of the observer. If one identifies the definitive meaning of an historical phenomenon (how it really was) that is given and only needs to be found, with its significance for the present and the future of an observer, which is conditioned by meaning-inference, then it can easily be discerned what, in fact, lies at the heart of this "existential encounter with history." The dialogue that should occur between the historian and the mind objectivated in his sources would fail completely and turn into a mere monologue because one partner would be missing altogether: the partner that should be represented by the text as the unchangeable mind of an Other, without whom any interpretative procedure cannot be envisaged at all. Dialogue therefore turns into monologue: the interpreter

who should inquire into the meaning of phenomena (meaning-full forms)
allows himself indeed to be questioned by the text. Is it still possible to
regard such a procedure as an interpretation? I shall leave this question
open for the moment.

Historical Interpretation and Eschatological
Meaning-Inference

Since we have distinguished between interpretation and meaning-inference,
and have used this distinction as a lever for the above critique, it is now
necessary to elucidate the concept of meaning-inference and consider the
difference between eschatology, where it comes into effect, and the study of
history. The comprehending potential of mind is actualized in both procedures—even though they fulfill different requirements. Meaning-inference
takes place in relation to the whole of existence—which is not the case
with interpretation—but mind engages in this activity in a higher and more
exact way in relation to objects of its own kind. In relation to the world, the
meaning is inferred randomly; but where man is concerned it is no longer
accidental. In the case of the world, man is not aware of the meaning he
infers, nor does he fulfill any moral obligation placed upon him by it. In the
case of his fellow-man, however, he is obliged to do justice to their esteem
of values, not so much in his actions nor even in his way of thinking, but
merely through looking, participating, appreciating or in any other way of
attending. Man can either respond to the demand for inner justice in the
answer he gives to values or he can fail to do so. He has not merely the
power to infer meaning, but he can do so by following his own free decision. He perceives the call, which he receives as an obligation that concerns
him personally and which requires his effort in doing justice, as a moral
claim which he can fulfill dutifully or sin against. Man cannot sin against
worldly goods as he passes them inattentively, but he can do so against his
fellow-man. To fail here is not merely the missing of an opportunity (a loss
that is obvious when one follows Nietzsche in thinking that "the whole
world is full of beautiful things but nevertheless very poor in beautiful moments and the opening-up of these things");[14] it is rather a case of man
wronging his fellow-man, who then feels ignored, pushed aside and excluded from real existence, the living community of minds.

What, then, can be said about eschatological meaning-inference?
What is meant by it? Here, meaning-inference concerns the '*Verbum Dei* as
viva vox', the living word of God. Since the eschaton is positioned beyond
historical time, it could appear that the historical passage of time is imma-
terial to eschatological meaning-inference; but this is not so.

I am not in a position to give judgment on eschatological problems;
but the point of issue here is the demarcation of competence between two

intellectual activities, one of which I am familiar with but not the other; the latter, however, lays claim on the former and thereby endangers its independence and questions the objectivity of its results. How, then, can one draw a line of demarcation between eschatology and history? Since eschatology does not wish to be a doctrine about an atemporal, other-worldly state of affairs but has as its object precisely the activity of God on human existence, and because man does exist within progressing time, eschatology has to incorporate the temporal course of human existence; time, as chronological progression, consequently enters the field of vision of eschatology. But how is Bultmann's postulated polarity of presence and transcendence to be understood in this context? Upon a closer look, historical progression seems to be of only secondary importance to Bultmann's eschatology. History can never provide the framework around which eschatological events can crystallize; these events occur, in fact, within existence, which cannot be determined by reference to history alone. The presence of Christ, the Parousia, is not limited by history according to Bultmann's Protestant viewpoint; this, however, does not make it something that is pregiven in the essence of man, but rather a continuing and specific encounter. The eschatological situation is characterized by the question whether one's existence is open towards the 'On-coming', or whether it remains tied to itself; through its factual openness (towards the future), existence is no longer 'transitory' but responsible and able to decide. Faith has to prove itself in the course of time: it is a venturing, meaning-inferring anticipation of the future, the trusting belief that what has already become real in respect of Christ still remains for faith beyond the struggle.[15]

Bultmann would consider this meaning-inferring approach of eschatology as completely identical with the quest for knowledge in the study of history; only the historian, who is moved by his participation in history—i.e., who is open to historical phenomena on the basis of his responsibility for the future—would be in a position to understand history. In Bultmann's view, knowledge of history and self-knowledge would correspond to one another in a characteristic way.[16] Bultmann established this peculiar correspondence and assimilation in the following way: self-knowledge is awareness of one's responsibility towards the future, and the act of self-knowing is by no means a contemplative and merely theoretical attitude but at the same time an act of decision-making—just as the venturing anticipation of the future lies at the heart of eschatology. If this is accepted, then the historicality of human existence would be completely understood only when human existence is seen as a life of responsibility for the future—and as a life within decision.

If that was the case, it would follow that historicality is not just a natural attribute of human individuals: it should be seized and realized as an opportunity that is offered to them. Any human being who lives without self-knowledge and awareness of responsibility would, according to this view, not only be someone who has failed in his task to infer meaning, but he would have delivered himself into the hands of the relativity of the historical conditions of his environment, and thereby represent "an historical Being to a far lower degree." As Bultmann concludes, following Collingwood, "true historicality means 'to live a life of responsibility', and history is a call towards historicality." The consequence that necessarily follows from these considerations can be found in a statement that would be considered the theme of the whole issue under discussion:[17] "In this kind of understanding the traditional opposition between the understanding subject and the object understood vanishes. Only as a participant and as, himself, an historical Being can the historian understand history. In such understanding of history, man understands himself. Human nature cannot be grasped through introspection; instead, what man is can only be seen in history which reveals the possibilities of human existence through the wealth of historical creations."

The Threat of Objectivity

This contention which raises a completely new problematic and which would lead to the negation of objectivity we, as historians, have to oppose with all firmness. Our outline has shown that the subjectivist position rests on a shift of meaning which identifies the hermeneutical process of historical interpretation with a situationally determined meaning-inference (as it is the case in eschatological meaning-inference) and which has the effect of confounding a condition for the possibility with the object of that process; as a result, the fundamental canon of the hermeneutical autonomy of the object is altogether removed from the work of the historian.

In this hermeneutical approach, the danger of confusion increases with the possibility of deriving only what is meaningful and reasonable to oneself and of missing what is different and specific in the Other or, as the case may be, bracketing it as a presumed myth. The objection to this is obvious: the texts which are approached with a meaning-inferring 'pre-understanding' [*Vorverständnis*] are not to be used to confirm already held opinions; we have to suppose, instead, that they have something to say that we could not know by ourselves and which exists independently of our meaning-inference.[18] It is here that the questionable character of the subjectivist position comes to full light; it is obviously influenced by contemporary existentialist philosophy and tends towards the confounding of the interpretation and meaning-inference and the removing of the canon of the autonomy of the object, with the consequence of putting into doubt the objectivity of the results of interpretative procedures in all the human sciences [*Geisteswissenschaften*]. It is my opinion that it is our duty as guardians and practitioners of the study of history to protect this kind of objectivity and to provide evidence of the epistemological condition of its possibility.

On Theological Hermeneutics and the 'Demythologization' of the *Kerygma*

The misunderstanding mentioned has been brought to light and partially resolved by some corrections Professor Ebeling[19] has made recently to the current views about hermeneutics. In order to distinguish between general and specific-theological hermeneutics he proceeds from Bultmann's point that the different 'upon-which' of the inquiry necessitates a specifically theological form of questioning that leads, owing to its particular structures and criteria, to an exegetic and dogmatic understanding of the text. This postulates, however, a demonstrable connection with a general theory of understanding; the question is, therefore, how such a connection is to be conceived. One could formulate the problem in a different way: how are the Word and Understanding related to one another; and further: what is it that is finally constitutive of hermeneutics? The answer Ebeling gives is the opposite of what is usually thought: the primary phenomenon of understanding is not the understanding of language but the understanding through language. The word is, therefore, not the 'object of understanding' but that which enables and mediates understanding; the word itself has, according to Ebeling, a 'hermeneutic function'[20]—not as the mere expression of an individual but as a message which requires two human beings (as in the case of love), as a communication that appeals to experience and leads to experience through its 'upon-which' and 'into-what'.

In this way, it is the word-event [*Wortgeschehen*] itself that is the object of hermeneutics because understanding becomes possible whenever communication takes place 'upon' and 'into' something. As a mediation of understanding, hermeneutics has to reflect upon the conditions of the possibility of understanding, i.e., the essence of the word. As a theory of understanding, hermeneutics has to be a theory of the word: a theory that regards the word, which enables understanding to take place, as constitutive when it comes to orienting oneself on states of affairs. Drawing on the Greek language Ebeling regards hermeneutics as the theory of Logos since "the Logos that dwells within object and knower provides the condition for the possibility of understanding."[21] He accordingly defines theological hermeneutics as the "theory of the Word of God."[22] Since this word is to be hermeneutically relevant, the essential structure of the Word of God should lead to the structure of understanding characteristic of theology. The question now arises as to what kind of understanding it is that emerges here. Ebeling asks himself the question:[23] should one apply the same strict criteria to the concept of the Word of God as in the case of an inter-human word-event (this is the view favored by Ebeling), or is the Word of God a mythical concept and therefore only of symbolic character with its speech structure being that of mythical speech? In Ebeling's opinion, the mythical as such cannot be brought into connection with an idea of hermeneutics that is rooted in the Greek concept of Logos. In relation to the mythical, hermeneutics would, in his opinion, have to turn into "demythologization." The question now arises: if such demythologization were to be unavoidable in order to understand, would not the *kerygma* be translated in such a procedure from the language of God into human language and thereby be transformed? And would we not have to accept certain curtailments and distortions as is often the case in translations? It is a procedure that one would like to reject on account of its arbitrariness and unclear presuppositions.[24]

In any case, the point I am trying to make is that hermeneutics, as the mediation of understanding, does not imply a *reductio ad rationem*, i.e., an Enlightenment-inspired 'rationalization' of the text to be interpreted, since that would no longer be an interpretation but an evaluative meaning-inference! One could here cite two parallel procedures, both concerned to a high degree with practical issues: one, where the biblical text, expounded in a sermon, renders hermeneutical services for the understanding of contemporary experiences; two, juridical hermeneutics concretizes abstract legal norms for contemporary jurisdiction. These issues I cannot, however, deal with within the limits set for these hermeneutical considerations.

We shall now turn our attention to the above-mentioned epistemological conditions for the possibility of objectivity in the process of interpretation. The above comments about the canon of the actuality of understanding have by no means exhausted the examination of those hermeneutical guidelines (*canones*) that relate to the subject of interpretation—as Bultmann seems to think. Spontaneity is, certainly, indispensable on the part of the interpreter; but it must not be imposed upon the object from outside since that would lead to the curtailment of its autonomy and, ultimately, endanger the cognizance of the object which here takes the forms, essentially, of comprehension and recognition.

The Recent Turn towards the Historicality of Understanding

Such danger is posed not only from the side of those theologians who are intending to 'demythologize' the Christian *kerygma* but also from the side of some scholars who are under the influence of Heidegger's existentialism and who regard the 'existential foundation of the hermeneutic circle' as a new development of the greatest importance. The danger apparent here is even greater since the new turn towards the 'historicality of understanding' cannot be contained through a delimitation of competence between historical interpretation and eschatological meaning-inference.

A recently published book provides us with the possibility of evidencing the position of Heideggerian existentialism vis-à-vis historical hermeneutics; I am referring to Hans-Georg Gadamer's *Outline of a Philosophical Hermeneutic. Truth and Method*. The author's negative point of departure is a sharp criticism of romanticist hermeneutics and its application to history; I cannot here discuss these criticisms, but they seem to be based on a biased view that leads to some misunderstanding about Schleiermacher's hermeneutics and to what is, in my view, an unjust assessment. At this point I am only dealing with the positive point of departure which the author derived from Heidegger's exposition of the so-called fore-structure of understanding and which he employs to elevate the historicality of understanding (i.e., the historical conditioning of the process of interpretation) to the principle of hermeneutics—which leads him to the paradox of having to regard prejudices as "conditions of understanding." In the author's view,[25] historical hermeneutics should commence with the dissolution of the abstract opposition between tradition and the study of history, between the historical process and the knowledge of it. The efficacy of continuing tradition and the efficacy of historical research constitute a unity, the analysis of which always arrives at a web of reciprocal action. What is required is to recognize the moment of tradition in historical activity and to determine its hermeneutic productivity. Understanding itself should not so much be regarded as a subjective activity but as an entering into the process of tradition in which past and present constantly mediate each other.[26] What, then, are the consequences of the hermeneutic condition of participating in tradition for understanding?[27]

Prejudice as the Condition of Understanding

The circular relationship that is in evidence here reminds Gadamer of the hermeneutical rule that one should understand the whole from its parts and the parts from the whole. In this way, the anticipation of meaning, by which is meant the whole of tradition, would be brought to explicit understanding in that the parts, which are determined by the whole, themselves determine that whole.[28] The author opines that "understanding that proceeds in full methodical awareness should seek not just to follow its anticipations but to become aware of them in order to control them, and to be then able to gain a correct understanding from the things themselves." This is what Heidegger means when he asks that the scientific theme be "secured" from the things themselves in the working out of *Vorhabe* [something we have in advance], *Vorsicht* [something we see in advance] and *Vorgriff* [something we grasp in advance]—thereby distorting Husserl's famous formula.

In accordance with this train of thought, Gadamer[29] sees the hermeneutic significance of temporal distance in that it wards off any excess resonance pertaining to actuality and filters out the true meaning, whereby this distance is envisaged to be in a process of continuous 'extension'. This distance has a positive hermeneutic effect, according to Gadamer,[30] as it "allows those prejudices to die off which are of a particularistic nature and allows those to come to the fore which enable veracious understanding" (the interpreter is always dealing with prejudices and it is the hermeneutic task to "separate the true prejudices from the false ones"). A hermeneutically trained historical consciousness would "raise to awareness those prejudices that guide and condition the process of understanding so that the content of tradition can mark itself off as 'different opinion' and claim recognition of its validity." What stimulates a prejudice that has so far remained unnoticed to come into the open? Gadamer answers:[31] "the encounter with tradition"; he believes that "anything that attracts our understanding (i.e., interpretation) will already have had to assert itself in its otherness." Understanding (Gadamer always means interpretation) commences with "something addressing us" which necessitates "in principle, the suspension of our own prejudices." Seen from a logical point, this would have "the structure of a question," a question the essence of which Gadamer[32] sees as "the lying-open, and keeping-open, of possibilities." The author charges historicism—which demands the "disregarding of ourselves" in order to bring to bear the Other in place of ourselves—with "naivete" because it "evades dialectical reflection and forgets its own historicality by relying on its methodical procedures." By contrast, better understanding would, according to Gadamer, "include reflection upon its own historicality." Only then would it "not chase after the phantom of an historical object, which is the object of continuing research, but, instead, learn to recognize the object as another part of the self and thereby come to know both."

One could now try to refute the dialectical procedure suggested by the author with the help of Hegel's dialectic. This is, however, not my intention. I merely wish to show how the loss of objectivity, which is the result of Gadamer's theory, cannot be offset by the subject becoming self-aware of his own historicality; in addition, the proposed yardstick for distinguishing between true and false prejudices—a yardstick and criterion of correctness which he would like to call "fore-conception of perfection"—rests on self-deception, i.e., it does not provide a reliable criterion for the correctness of understanding.

The Existential Foundation of
the Hermeneutical Circle

Let us now follow Gadamer's argument[33] more closely. The precurrent "expectation of meaning" of the interpreter of a text has to be adjusted, should the text require it, in such a way "that the text acquires its unity of meaning from another expectation of meaning." This would lead[34] to "the movement of understanding from the whole to the part and back to the whole"; the task here would be "to extend the unity of the understood meaning in concentric circles." "Harmony of all details with the whole" would be "the appropriate criterion of the correct understanding." But now Gadamer thinks,[35] by giving hermeneutics the task of "achieving an agreement that may be lacking or be disturbed," that it would be "the aim of all communication and understanding to come to an agreement about something," i.e., a substantive agreement. Here he notices[36] a fundamental difference between Schleiermacher's ideal of objectivity, that fails to take account of the concretion of the historical consciousness of the interpreter in his hermeneutical theory, and Heidegger's existential foundation of the hermeneutic circle, which, in Gadamer's view, "represents a decisive turning-point." Schleiermacher's theory requires the interpreter to adopt completely the perspective of the author so that he can dissolve any unfamiliar and disturbing elements within the text. "In contrast to this, Heidegger describes the circle of whole and part in such a way that the understanding of the text is permanently directed by the anticipatory movement of the pre-understanding." The anticipation of meaning that is thought to be directing our understanding of the text is, according to Gadamer,[37] "based on the commonality that unites us with tradition and that is constantly being developed." According to this view, the circle "describes an ontological moment of understanding." It follows that all attempts at understanding are guided by the presupposition that "only that is understandable which forms a perfect unity of meaning." This presupposition, that guides all understanding, Gadamer refers to as the "fore-conception of perfection."

The Question Concerning the Correctness of
Understanding

The obvious difficulty with the hermeneutical method proposed by Gadamer seems to lie, for me, in that it enables a substantive agreement between text and reader—i.e., between the apparently easily accessible meaning of a text and the subjective conception of the reader—to be formed without, however, guaranteeing the correctness of understanding; for that it would be necessary that the understanding arrived at corresponded fully to the meaning underlying the text as an objectivation of mind. Only then would the objectivity of the result be guaranteed on the basis of a reliable process of interpretation. It can easily be demonstrated that the proposed method cannot claim to achieve objectivity and that it is only concerned with the internal coherence and conclusiveness of the desired understanding—one only needs to follow the advice given by the author. When reading a text we proceed, in his opinion, from the presupposition of perfection; only when this presupposition is found to be irredeemable or inadequate, i.e., when the text is found to be incomprehensible, do we query it and "maybe question tradition and try to find out how to remedy it"[38] in order to arrive at an understanding of the content. It follows that the adopted "fore-conception of perfection" would itself always be one of content, too. Consequently, "what is presupposed is not only an immanent unity of meaning which directs the reader, but his understanding is always guided by transcendent expectations of meaning which spring from the relation to the truth of what is being said." By way of contrast, Gadamer thinks that "it is only the failure of the attempt to accept what is being said as true that leads us to try and 'understand' the text—historically, or psychologically—as the meaning of an Other." The "fore-conception of perfection would, therefore, not only include the formal demand that the text should express its content perfectly (i.e., clearly and coherently), but also that what is being said is the complete truth." This, then, is Gadamer's view.

His exposition presupposes that the interpreter, who is called upon to understand, claims a monopoly of truth—if not as an actual possession then, at least, in the form of a checking device. In my view, however, the interpreter should be content to comprehend and accept the differing opinion of the text as something different—even if it should contain inaccurate conceptions. The author himself[39] is forced to concede that indubitable exceptions to the supposed "grasping-in-advance" [*Vorgriff*] do exist; so, for example, in the case of a disarranged or codified piece of writing where the disarrangement can only be deciphered if the interpreter is in possession of some factual knowledge that can serve as a key. If one, furthermore, considers that human use of language generally contains excess meaning in that it is guided by unarticulated value suppositions and is, therefore, elliptical, then one has to abandon the presumed pre-supposition concerning the conciseness of speech and generalize the exception.

In addition, Gadamer's position,[40] where the case of historical interpretation is concerned, confounds the differing role of the historian of law with that of the lawyer whose task it is to apply the law, by failing to recognize the fundamental difference in interest that guides them; he is also led to regard juridical hermeneutics, because of its relatedness to the present, "as the model for the relationship between past and present,"[41] that should be emulated by the historical *Geisteswissenschaften*. Gadamer does admit that the historian who intends to find out the historical significance of a law is dealing with a legal creation that has to be understood in juridical terms. But he would like to regard the special case of an historian who considers a legal document that is still valid today as exemplary for the way in which we should view "our relationship with any tradition." He feels that "the historian who tries to understand law by reference to the situation of its historical origin cannot disregard its juridical development: it would provide him with the questions he might like to direct at historical tradition." Very well, but these are only distant and consequential effects that do not necessarily remain effective into the present and that, in any case, should neither directly influence the historian's practical engagement with the present nor his stance. For this reason, all of Gadamer's questions[42] which he poses immediately after this statement have to be answered in the negative. He asks: is it not the case with any text that it has to be understood in terms of what it says, and does that not mean that a transposition is required every time? And does not this transformation always take the form of a mediation with the present? We answer with a decisive "No." It is true that the inversion of the process of creation in interpretation requires the transposition of meaning from the original perspective of the author into the subjectivity of the interpreter. That, however, does not imply a "transformation" that has to be conceived of as a "mediation with the present." The present furthers and stimulates the interest in understanding, but it has no place in the transposition of the 'subjective stance'. The shift of meaning that intrudes into the conclusion referred to is, in my opinion, apparent in the following line of argument.[43] The object of historical understanding does not consist of events but of their significance (which is related to the present), i.e., their significance for today.[44] Such understanding would consequently not adequately be described if one talked about an object existing in-itself which is approached by a subject. More accurately, it would be the essence of historical understanding that on-coming tradition influences the present and has to be understood in this mediation of past and present—or even as this mediation of past and present.

Historical Understanding as Mediation
of Past and Present

If that was the case, then juridical hermeneutics would not be an exception but would be in a position to hand back to historical hermeneutics its full range of issues and thereby reconstitute its former unity in which jurist and theologian come to meet the philologist. That this is not so, however, is apparent from the basically differing approach of the jurist which is required of us when we move from the application of the law to the contemplative consideration of the history of law. The hermeneutical demand to understand the content of a text from within the concrete circumstances of its origin[45] is regarded by the historian of law only as the teleological evaluation of the content of a law which is in no way directed at the present or is intending to exercise any immediate normative influence on present-day modes of behavior. The relationship to the present does have, in fact, quite a different meaning for the historian.

Another questionable conclusion of Gadamer's[46] is that of the demand made upon the historian, in contrast to the philologist, to interpret tradition in a way different from what would be required by the sources themselves, i.e., to inquire into the reality evident behind the texts and their sense which they unintendedly and unconsciously reveal; he thereby fails to recognize that today philologists, too, are required to locate a text within a larger context, and that their encounter with a text is inspired by elements adopted from a model for their work which implies a following and putting-to-use [*Applikation*].[47] Gadamer believes that the relationship between the historian and his texts—i.e., his historical sources—corresponds to that obtaining between an investigative judge in a trial and a witness; he treats his historical evidence in the way the former treats a legal witness. In both cases, evidence "is an aid for arriving at a finding"; it is not "itself the actual object but merely provides the material for the task at hand; for the judge, to come to a finding—for the historian, to determine the historical significance of an event within the totality of his historical self-awareness"![48]

It follows that the difference between them would shrink to a question of degree! The use of historical methods would always be preceded by the really important things! Thanks to a characteristic shift in the meaning of the intention of a text, the author seems to regard, despite all appearance, the problem of 'application' to be crucial for the more complicated case of historical understanding, too.[49] In each and every reading[50] "there occurs an application, so that he who reads a text will himself be included in the meaning he derives from it." He, therefore, acknowledges an internal unity of history and philology, not in the historical critique of tradition as such, but in the fact that both accomplish the task of application which differs only relatively: in his opinion one would only have "to recognize the historically-effective consciousness [*wirkungsgeschichtliche Bewusstsein* (translation altered slightly)—ED.] in all the hermeneutical activity of philologist and historian"!

Call for an Applicative Use of Interpretation

This means that historians and all guardians and practitioners of historical hermeneutics, who are concerned about the objectivity of interpretation, are called upon to oppose such a presumptuous self-assertion of subjectivity that would demote the process of historical interpretation to a mere mediation of past and present. The supposed analogy of historical and normative-juridical hermeneutics is indeed based on self-deception. That the application of the law demands a legal interpretation that is related to the present and to contemporary society follows by necessity out of the function of the law as the ordering of co-existence in a human community. It is part of its essence, therefore, that it should achieve a concretion of the law; it should be practically relevant in that it is called upon to provide a legally adequate direction and directive for communal existence and behavior. The same consideration applies to the theologian and his interpretation of the Scriptures on account of their directive, i.e., normative, task: the practical activity of the community of believers requires this interpretation to be of applicative use for moral issues.[51]

Only Justified in Normatively Oriented Interpretation

All this is, however, quite different in the case of historical interpretation. Its task is purely contemplative. It is concerned with the investigation of the finalized meaning of a segment of the past. In accordance with the hermeneutical canon of totality one has to consider all distant and consequential effects of the historical events in question, given that sufficient time has elapsed—but a transposition of their meaning on to the present is out of the question. On the contrary, it is precisely phenomena relating to the dispute between past and present, such as transposition onto the present, appropriation, assimilation, re-interpretation and transformation of parts of traditional works which have not been understandable, that characterize an unhistorical position towards the past—however productive misunderstandings may be when they are motivated by the attempt to do justice to creations of the past by regarding them as 'tools of life'. Productive completion, transposition, development, are all efforts at applying knowledge that serve and enhance the life of a community. But their sphere of justified activity has to be restricted to the field of practical co-existence. Where, however, historical interpretation is concerned, which is the only dimension of relevance here, its accuracy and competence has to be categorically negated. Procedures of this kind are obviously not suited to lead us to historical truth; on the contrary, they open the door to subjective arbitrariness and threaten to cover up or misrepresent historical truth and to distort it, even if only unconsciously. The historian who has arrived at an awareness of the historicity of understanding will be more modest and refrain from any "applicative effort." Anyone who has undertaken historical research will realize that the critique of the sincerity, honesty, and reliability of historical documents belongs to a completely different dimension.

The partner in a discussion should, as a point of honour, not end his critical remarks without extending his chivalrous thanks to his opponents for their stimulating contributions. Every conscientious scientific criticism brings the disputants closer together and leads to self-criticism and better self-knowledge. Even when we are successful in enlightening our opponent and lead him to towards self-reflection, something else will have happened, maybe unnoticed: we have changed ourselves through his help and have been led to self-reflection. We should, accordingly, not engage in a direct fight but make sure that our influence on future events balances the one exerted by him.

It is in this unbiased attitude that I shall receive the further comments that Professor Gadamer has announced and which will soon appear in the *Philosophische Rundschau*.[52] I thank him and our mutual friend Walter Hellebrand for the written clarifications I have received from them. These friendly clarifications are very valuable as they make clear the intention and theme of the new philosophical hermeneutic.[53] In order to pose the question correctly it has to be mentioned, however, that the epistemological question—formulated in an exemplary form by Kant's pioneering *Critique of Pure Reason*—is not a *quaestio facti* but a *quaestio iuris*: it is concerned with the problem of justification which does not aim at ascertaining what actually happens in the activity of thought apparent in interpretation but which aims at finding out what one should do—i.e., what one should aim for in the task of interpretation, what methods to use and what guidelines to follow in the correct execution of this task. After our critical excursions we now return to our considerations of the canons of hermeneutics.

The Canon of the Hermeneutical Correspondence of Meaning (Meaning-Adequacy in Understanding)

If it is the case that mind alone can address mind, then it follows that only a mind of equal stature and congenial disposition can gain access to, and understand, another mind in a meaningfully adequate way. An actual interest in understanding is by itself not enough, however lively it may be, to establish the required communication; what is needed, in addition, is an intellectual open-mindedness that enables the interpreter to adopt the most suitable position for his investigation and understanding. This involves a stance that is both ethically and theoretically reflective and which can be identified as unselfishness and humble self-effacement, as it is apparent in the honest and determined overcoming of one's own prejudices and certain attitudes that stand in the way of unbiased understanding; seen more positively, this stance could be characterized as a broad viewpoint and wide horizon, an ability that creates a congenial and closely related outlook in relation to the object of interpretation.

This requirement is apparent in the fourth hermeneutical canon which is connected with the above-mentioned third one and, like it, concerns the subject of interpretation. I proposed to call it the canon of meaning-adequacy in understanding [*Sinnadäquanz des Verstehens*] or the canon of the hermeneutical correspondence of meaning (or harmonization). According to this canon, the interpreter should strive to bring his own lively actuality into the closest harmony with the stimulation that he receives from the object in such a way that the one and the other resonate in a harmonious way.

This aspect of the correspondence of meaning is especially apparent in the field of historical interpretation where it initially led to self-reflection. It is here that individuality, as it is expressed in an historical personality, should resonate with the personality of the interpreter if it is to be recognized by the latter. If this personality exhibits a unity in regard of the kind and degree to which the content of given objectivations are joined together, then it is precisely the congenial affinity with such a kind and degree of synthesis that presents the historian with one of the conditions for the inner reconstruction of a personality.

The canon of the harmonization of understanding we are here referring to is itself of general import and is relevant for every type of interpretation. If we focus on historical interpretation we find two possible orientations: one, the interpretation of sources of historical knowledge or of historical remnants; two, the interpretation of modes of behavior requiring an historical interest—which itself varies with the problems the historian sets out to solve—for the inquiry into the life of individuals or social communities. In our opinion it is here necessary to make a distinction according to whether the investigation into historical material, and the evaluation of the historical activity in question, is conducted solely in terms of psychological, practical, ethical and political categories—as it is the case in biography, political history and the history of custom and ethics—or whether the historical investigation and evaluation requires a problematic of a higher order, owing to the character as a *product* of the forms of life in question.

The Character as a Product of Historical Forms of Life Leads to a Problematic of a Higher Order

This is the case when the historical analysis of structures is concerned with such objects as: works of art in their various forms, linguistic works of art in all their kinds and types, different branches of science, legal constructs, economic systems, social and religious forms of organizations of societies and communities. Whenever these cultural values, which are generated by people within their living community, become the object of an historical analysis of their structure, then the process of interpretation of a part of historical existence which, after all, is the life of culture, requires a higher order and more complex problematic. The latter takes different forms in the history of art, language, literature, science, law, social, economic and religious structures, but it provides interpretation in these various fields with a common trait owing to the character as a product of these forms of life, which sharply distinguishes these interpretations from general historical interpretation.

The objects of this type of interpretation are meaning-full forms with their definite character as a product and they can be regarded as belonging to the history of culture and mind in all its forms. In order to identify successfully the type of interpretation under consideration here, it is necessary, in our opinion, to refer back to a distinction made for the first time in hermeneutical theory by the great Schleiermacher which subsequently seems to have been forgotten. In the sphere of psychological interpretation in the wider sense, Schleiermacher differentiates between the psychological aspect in the narrower sense and technical interpretation. He, of course, uses the term "technical" in its narrow sense in the context of hermeneutics as referring to the technique of expression characteristic of a work of art—a technique that guides the reflection (mediation) and construction (composition) of a linguistic work of art; he consequently does not use it in the wider sense of a semantic or representational technique which is part of meaning-full constructs different from the written word. At the same time, it is clear that the technical, i.e., morphological, moment plays a more important role in interpretation and should be applied in a wider sphere in comparison with this narrow conception. Once it is recognized that each act of understanding takes place in the form of an inversion of an act of speech or thought, in so far as one tries to trace retrospectively the train of thought that provided the basis for the linguistic act and to raise it to consciousness, then it becomes clear that one can derive from this process of inversion the general principle of the correspondence of meaning obtaining between the process of the creation of a mental product and the process of its interpretation. One then recognizes the deep truth of Vico's statement that "the whole world of culture has, for certain, been produced by the physical and mental activity of man, and for this reason one can, and, in fact, has to, find its principles and regularities within the modes of existence of the spirit of these self-same people." As a matter of fact, the variegated and typical forms which human culture brings forth in the course of its historical development in the various cultural spheres—art, language, literature, science, law, economic and social structure—have their own logos, their own law of formation and development which, at the same time, is the law of a structure and a meaning-context. In the light of this lawfulness, a form of interpretation becomes possible which aims to understand the meaning of these cultural formations in view of their respective structural problems as regards typical, recurring factors as well as individual ones, both of which are historically conditioned.

Technical-Morphological Interpretation in View of the Problems of Formation to be Solved

One could call such an interpretation that regards the various cultural products as solutions to morphological problems of formation—even though the artist himself may not have been aware that there was such a problem—a technical interpretation with an historical task, if one wanted to use Schleiermacher's criterion and expression. It would be more appropriate, from the point of view of the contemporary use of language, to call this kind of interpretation 'morphological' (Fritz Wagner[54] has recently suggested this term).

When one refers to "technical" [*Technik*] in the context of the history of civilization, it is usually material progress that one thinks of without, at the same time, including the higher forms of objective spirit within this concept. But here we are confronted with an arbitrary restriction. It is indeed possible in interpretation to employ a technique that aims at discovering the specific laws of formation of various products of mental forms of life and systems of culture from which human civilization derives nourishment; this technique could be used in the kind of interpretation that would want to recognize and reconstruct from the inside such products in their generation and formation, in their style, in the inner coherence of their structure and in their conclusiveness, and which attempted to give an overview of the historical development of styles. If the evaluations dominant in consecutive stylistic epochs form a mental horizon which is determined by an historically conditioned perspective, then one may assume that the activities of feeling, comprehending and visualizing are directed by hermeneutical guidelines, not only in linguistic expressions but also in all other mental spheres of life and systems of culture; even though these activities are not subjected to atemporal and unchangeable categories they are, nevertheless, directed by hermeneutical guidelines of the kind that are part of the relationship between man and his environment, and which change in line with their historically conditioned context. The problem confronting the historian therefore consists in finding out whether these manifold changes in conception, modes of representation, feeling and thinking, theories and doctrines, institutions and structures, are subject to a developmental law and to such developmental tendencies as can be investigated with phenomenological means, and especially whether there are tendencies that make apparent a succession of styles.

Indeed, on the level of objective spirit there are operative laws of development that cannot be comprehended through psychological interpretation alone. In the history of art, literature, science, jurisprudence, economic and social systems, historical facts are not limited merely to the individual experience of given personalities; they rather constitute an entity that embodies a value, i.e., it contains meaning, value and its character as a product. It is necessary, above all, to understand its inner unity of style and the close relationship of its meaning with other, connected, values and products from within itself, independently of the conditioning circumstances of its appearance in time and of the chronological relationship to earlier and later times. If one wishes to arrive at the historical context and line of development that exhibits the main sequence of style, then one is faced, from the beginning, with the task of having to understand the character of the product, its conception and structure in relation to the particular lawfulness that objectively underlies the product, and of having to reconstruct the spiritual web of meaning into which it is woven.

Technical-morphological interpretation, as it has been proposed, contributes to a correct disposition towards historical knowledge in so far as it considers the various creations of the imagination, of thought and of active life, as solutions to problems which, in a wider sense, could be referred to as morphological problems of formation. A technical-artistic interpretation of pictorial works of art, for example, serves in the preparation of a history of the various arts from the point of view of their respective problems of expression. Equally, a linguistic, i.e., technical-literary, interpretation of linguistic works of art contributes to the construction of a history of language and literature with reference to the various language-areas and types of literature. Despite the criticisms levelled against it, such a history possesses a justifiable orienting function to the extent to which it corresponds to the various types of linguistic communication as they are determined by the direction and purpose of the language used in communicating one's own thoughts to one's fellow-men. Similar considerations apply to technical-scientific interpretation in the history of law and of economics as well as to sociological interpretation. The interpretation of theories and systems can equally serve a history of the scientific problems dealt with in the various areas of knowledge. Technical-juridical interpretation, that concerns itself with concept-formation in dogmatics, is, similarly, interested in presenting the history of social and economic structures; the task here is to recognize tendentially constant relationships between historical facts, which may be chronologically separate, by trying to bring together morphological problems of social existence which emerge in given areas of investigation according to perspectives which correspond to a specific interest within historical or comparative research.

In this way, specialists in the various *Geisteswissenschaften* develop hermeneutical key-concepts and ideal-types in the course of technical-morphological interpretation which they then employ in order to understand the history of the multitudinous expressions of human civilization as the history of the problems of formation and the solutions to problems which govern the creation and development of products and structures. In this context I only have to refer to Heinrich Wölfflin's seminal *Kunstgeschichtliche Grundbegriffe* and the highly fruitful *Grundbegriffe der Poetik* by Emil Staiger.

Meaning-Structure and Style as Products of the Autonomy of Mental Powers

It is obvious that only an interpreter who is familiar with the problems of artistic expression from his own experience and who possesses a cultivated artistic sensitivity and some expert knowledge is able to unfold problems that have not been consciously solved in a work of art, and to understand its meaning-content. By the same token, it is only because of his familiarity with the conceptual tools of legal dogmatics, which a legal expert has acquired in the course of his training and practice, that an historian of law is in a position to tackle the problem of the formation of legal constructs and legal opinion when he concerns himself with separating the function which these constructs have acquired over time from their structure. Only the mind of a sociologist who has considered the morphological problems of the organization of social life enables an historian of civilization to be in a position to become fully aware of constant, typically recurring factors and developmental tendencies which are operative in the historical change of social structures and which account for the fact that a community existing in a given environment will react in the same way to the same conditions of power and position. An analogous demand was made by philologists and historians of the classical age in their call for a contemporary hermeneutics of figurative (sculptured or painted) works; the aim here was to go beyond the immediate semantical content of these meaning-full forms and their excess of representational content through the complementary interpretation of literary texts. It is equally the case that only a theologian who is able to do more than just perceive external or internal changes is in a position to understand the immanent development of religions. He who is able to retrace the rise of forms of meaning and of their bearers with the fine sense of an historian can gain an idea of the laws according to which the dialectic of becoming proceeds as it submits itself to a general regularity while at the same time following an individual law.

In all these cases we are concerned with a meaning-content of historical interest which cannot be explored and fully comprehended with normal psychological and ethical categories. In respect of such meaning-content, a technical-morphological interpretation satisfies the requirement of the adequacy of meaning of understanding, or that of the hermeneutical correspondence of meaning, which traces the surplus meaning of cultural products and which constitutes, as has already been indicated, a fundamental canon of interpretation. It is the task of the historian of art, language, literature, law, economy and religion as well as that of the sociologist to understand a work of art, a formation, a typical behavior respectively in its inner coherence and validity, in its relationship with similar meaning-full forms and types, and to characterize it in its 'style' as the product of autonomous mental forces. In this way, a technical interpretation turns into the structural analysis of meaning-full forms; this analysis helps us to comprehend their character as a product and to explain how something that is sharply separated by value-criticism into valuable and worthless can appear, in the light of technical-morphological interpretation, as something that is united by a shared essence with equally justifiable elements. It is possible to consider in this way the products of individuals and of a communal spirit. The interpreter can derive from them only as much as his training and expertise enable him to register, and whatever becomes clear to him about linguistic works, works of art, law, and religion in the course of his sincere encounter with them. Interpretations which differ from one another always indicate that a genuine, organically developed work of art has remained alive within its confines. We, in addition, may remind ourselves of the eternal truth expressed by Goethe when he stated that it is only the whole of mankind that is in a position to completely understand a human product.

The fact of the matter is, that the subjective mind of an individual human being is taken up to heights and down into depths by objectivations of mind which would remain inaccessible to his own experiencing since they are situated beyond his own resources for making experiences. The deepening and elevation, expansion and enrichment which the interpreter receives in the course of understanding are clearly different from those which a human being reaches in the course of his own immanent development. The crucial point remains that it is an objectivated meaning-content, matter charged with mind, that touches us in its purity and depth. The gain we derive for our own education and self-development from great works of art is one thing; another is the realization that within the cosmos of objectivations of mind we can find meaning-contents which we acknowledge to be superior to our subjectivity and which we approach through understanding—not so much out of our own strength, but through being raised by them. Just as primitive man carries magic powers around with him in his fetish, so civilized man is surrounded by products which are infinitely greater than he is.[55]

If we think of all meaning-full forms as together forming the unity of human civilizations, then we can take in, at a glance, the tension between familiarity and unfamiliarity existing within the dialectical relationship between subjective and objectivated mind. Any given human being may well try to reap the yield of the past, but he will have come to realize that the treasures of thought accumulated through the gigantic effort of past generations contain meaning-contents which, although they are of human origin, are also of overwhelming meaning and significance. If one can state that the knowledge of history and of oneself correspond to one another in a peculiar and characteristic way,[56] then it has to be part of the essence of acquiring self-knowledge that the human mind can complete this process only if he brings forth an objective meaning-content which can confront him and which arises out of human existence as something superior to and different from himself. The return of our mind towards self-knowledge is possible only through the impetus received during the journey through objective meaning-contents; historical knowledge is not only man's route to himself but also, and at the same time, the path to something superior which far transcends individual human beings, in accordance with Goethe's famous dictum.

A common hermeneutical problematic, which takes different forms in different areas, therefore comes into sight in the field of the *Geisteswissenschaften*. I shall remain content, here, with having given the thoughtful guardians and practitioners of these sciences an indication of its possibility.

Translated by Josef Bleicher

Notes

*Emilio Betti, *Die Hermeneutik als Allgemeine Methodik der Geisteswissenschaften* (Tübingen: J. C. B. Mohr, 1972).—ED.

1. In *Geschichte und Eschatologie* (1958).

2. *Ibid.*, p. 130.

3. *Ibid.*, p. 136.

4. In "Das Problem der Hermeneutik," in *Glauben und Verstehen*, Vol. II, p. 211, and see pp. 227–30.

5. *Ibid.*, p. 228.

6. In *Geschichtsphilosophie der Gegenwart* (1931), p. 41.

7. "Über Knies und das sogennante Irrationalitätsproblem," in *Gesammelte Aufsätze zur Wissenschaftslehre*, pp. 119–22 and 245.

8. *Ibid.*, pp. 122–25.

9. Similarly Gadamer, *Wahrheit und Methode*, 4th ed. (Tübingen: J. C. B. Mohr, 1975), p. 311 [English translation: *Truth and Method*, pp. 292–93. Hereafter, all references to the English translation will appear as *TM* followed by the page numbers.—ED.]; cf. Nietzsche, *Menschliches, Allzumenschliches* [*Human, All-too-Human*], Vol. II, section 223.

10. Bultmann, *Geschichte und Eschatologie*, p. 136.

11. *Ibid.*, p. 135.

12. *Ibid.*, p. 137.

13. *Ibid.*, p. 135.

14. In *Die fröhliche Wissenschaft* [*The Gay Science*], section 339.

15. Cf. Joh. Körner, *Eschatologie und Geschichte* (1957), p. 52ff.

16. Bultmann, *Geschichte und Eschatologie*, p. 162.

17. *Ibid.*, p. 139.

18. Cf. K. Löwith, *Heidegger, Denker in dürftiger Zeit* (1953), p. 83.

19. In "Wort Gottes und Hermeneutik," *Zeitschrift für Theologie und Kirche*, Vol. 56, pp. 224–51.

20. *Ibid.*, pp. 236–238.

21. *Ibid.*, p. 239.

22. *Ibid.*, p. 242.

23. *Ibid.*, p. 242.

24. *Ibid.*, p. 224.

25. Gadamer, *Wahrheit und Methode*, pp. 267, 279 [*TM*, pp. 251, 262].

26. *Ibid.*, p. 274 [*TM*, p. 258].

27. Asks the author, *ibid.*, p. 275 [*TM*, p. 258].

28. *Ibid.*, p. 254 [*TM*, p. 239].

29. *Ibid.*, p. 275ff [*TM*, p. 258ff]; Gadamer, *Heidegger-Festschrift*, p. 32.

30. *Heidegger-Festschrift*, p. 33.

31. *Ibid.*, p. 33.

32. *Ibid.*, p. 34. [Gadamer (*Wahrheit und Methode*, 1975, p. 283) refers to *Offenlegen* (opening-up, laying-open); in Betti (p. 41) here it is quoted as *Offenliegen* (lying-open).—TRANS.]

33. *Wahrheit und Methode*, pp. 275–79 [*TM*, pp. 258–63].

34. Gadamer thinks, *ibid.*, p. 275 [*TM*, pp. 258–59].

35. *Ibid.*, p. 276 [*TM*, p. 260].

36. *Ibid.*, p. 277 [*TM*, pp. 260–61].

37. *Ibid.*, p. 277 [*TM*, pp. 260–61].

38. *Ibid.*, p. 278 [*TM*, p. 261].

39. *Ibid.*, p. 278, note 2 [*TM*, p. 524, note 196].

40. *Ibid.*, pp. 308–10 [*TM*, pp. 290–92].

41. *Ibid.*, p. 311 [*TM*, p. 292].

42. *Ibid.*, p. 311 [*TM*, p. 293].

43. *Ibid.*, p. 311 [*TM*, p. 293].

44. Gadamer's agreement with Bultmann's train of thought is symptomatic here.

45. *Ibid.*, p. 317 [*TM*, p. 299].

46. *Ibid.*, pp. 319–21 [*TM*, pp. 301–303].

47. *Ibid.*, p. 321 [*TM*, p. 303].

48. *Ibid.*, p. 321 [*TM*, p. 303. This note was inadvertently cited as pp. 319–21 in the original translation.—ED.]

49. *Ibid.*, p. 322 [*TM*, pp. 303–04].

50. *Ibid.*, p. 323 [*TM*, p. 304].

51. This is where the concept of 'application' originates; cf. Joachim Wach, *Das Verstehen*, Vol. II, p. 19; also Ebeling, "Wort Gottes und Hermeneutik," *Zeitschrift für Theologie und Kirche*, Vol. 56, p. 249.

52. "Hermeneutik und Historismus," *Philosophische Rundschau*, Vol. 9 (1962), pp. 241–76; [English translation as Appendix in Gadamer, *Truth and Method*, pp. 460–91—TRANS.].

53. Bleicher does not translate Betti's footnote 118 (pp. 51–52), which includes the texts of letters of Gadamer (18 February 1961) and Hellebrand (6 April 1961). A translation of part of Gadamer's letter appears in "Hermeneutics and Historicism," included as a supplement to the English edition of *TM*, pp. 465–66—ED.

54. In *Archiv für Kunstgeschichte*, Vol. 38 (1956), p. 261.

55. Freyer, *Theorie des objectiven Geistes*, p. 87.

56. Bultmann has recently made this point, *Geschichte und Eschatologie*, p. 137.

8

Truth and Method*

Hans-Georg Gadamer

Introduction

These studies are concerned with the problem of hermeneutics. The phenomenon of understanding and of the correct interpretation of what has been understood is not just a problem proper to the methodology of the human sciences. For a long time, there has been a theological and a legal hermeneutics, which were not so much theoretical as related to, and an aid to, the practical activity of the judge or clergyman who had completed his theoretical training. From its historical origin, the problem of hermeneutics goes beyond the limits that the concept of method sets to modern science. The understanding and the interpretation of texts is not merely a concern of science, but is obviously part of the total human experience of the world. The hermeneutic phenomenon is basically not a problem of method at all. It is not concerned with a method of understanding, by means of which texts are subjected to scientific investigation like all other objects of experience. It is not concerned primarily with the amassing of ratified knowledge which satisfies the methodological ideal of science—yet it is concerned, here, too, with knowledge and with truth. In understanding tradition not only are texts understood, but insights are gained and truths acknowledged. But what kind of insight and what kind of truth?

In the face of the dominant position of modern science in the philosophical clarification and justification of the concept of knowledge and the concept of truth, this question does not appear legitimate. Yet it is unavoidable, even within the sciences. The phenomenon of understanding not only pervades all human relations to the world. It also has an independent validity within science and resists any attempt to change it into a method of science. The following investigation starts with the resistance within modern science against the universal claim of scientific method. It is concerned to seek that experience of truth that transcends the sphere of the control of scientific method wherever it is to be found, and to inquire into its legitimacy. Hence the human sciences are joined with modes of experience which lie outside science: with the experiences of philosophy, of art, and of history itself. These are all modes of experience in which a truth is communicated that cannot be verified by the methodological means proper to science.

Contemporary philosophy is well aware of this. But it is quite a different question how far the claim to truth of these modes of experience outside science can be philosophically legitimated. The current interest in the hermeneutic phenomenon rests, I think, on the fact that only a more profound investigation of the phenomenon of understanding can provide this legitimation. This conviction is strongly supported by the importance attached in contemporary philosophical work to the history of philosophy. In regard to the historical tradition of philosophy, we encounter understanding as a superior experience enabling us easily to see through the appearance of historical method characteristic of philosophico-historical research. It is part of the elementary experience of philosophy that when we try to understand the classics of philosophical thought, they posit, of themselves, a claim of truth that the contemporary consciousness can neither reject nor transcend. The naive self-respect of the present moment may rebel against the idea that the philosophical awareness admits the possibility that one's own philosophical insight may be inferior to that of Plato or Aristotle, Leibniz, Kant or Hegel. One might think it a weakness in contemporary philosophy that it seeks to interpret and assimilate its classical heritage with this acknowledgement of its own weakness. But it is undoubtedly a far greater weakness of philosophical thinking not to face this kind of investigation into oneself, but foolishly to play at being Faustus. It is clear that in the understanding of the texts of these great thinkers, a truth is recognised that could not be attained in any other way, even if this contradicts the yardstick of research and progress by which science measures itself.

The same thing is true of the experience of art. Here the scientific research pursued by the 'science of art' is aware from the start that it can neither replace nor surpass the experience of art. That truth is experienced through a work of art that we cannot attain in any other way constitutes the philosophic importance of art, which asserts itself against all reasoning. Hence together with the experience of philosophy, the experience of art issues the most pressing challenge to the scientific consciousness to acknowledge its own limits.

Hence the following investigation starts with a critique of aesthetic consciousness, in order to defend that experience of truth that comes to us through the work of art against the aesthetic theory that lets itself be restricted to a scientific concept of truth. But the book does not stop at the justification of the truth of art; instead it tries to develop from this starting-point a concept of knowledge and of truth which corresponds to the whole of our hermeneutic experience. Just as in the experience of art we are concerned with truths that go essentially beyond the range of methodical knowledge, so the same thing is true of the whole of the human sciences, in which our historical tradition in all its forms is certainly made the object of investigation, but at the same time in it truth comes to speech. The experience of historical tradition goes quite beyond that in it which can be investigated. It is true or untrue not only in the sense concerning which historical criticism decides—it always mediates truth, in which one must try to share.[Translation altered slightly.—ED.]

Hence these studies on hermeneutics, which start from the experience of art and of historical tradition, seek to present the hermeneutic phenomenon in its full extent. It is a question of recognising in it an experience of truth that must not only be justified philosophically, but which is itself a mode of philosophizing. The hermeneutics developed here is not, therefore, a methodology of the human sciences, but an attempt to understand what the human sciences truly are, beyond their methodological self-consciousness, and what connects them with the totality of our experience of world. If we make understanding the object of our reflection, the aim is not an art or technique of understanding, as traditional literary and theological hermeneutics sought to be. Such an art or technique would fail to recognise that, in view of the truth that speaks to us out of tradition, the formalism of artistic ability would arrogate to itself a false superiority. Even though in the following I shall demonstrate how much there is of event in all understanding, and how little the traditions in which we stand are weakened by modern historical consciousness, it is not my intention to make prescriptions for the sciences or the conduct of life, but to try to correct false thinking about what they are.

I hope in this way to reinforce an insight that is threatened with oblivion in our swiftly changing age. What changes forces itself far more on the attention than what remains the same. That is a general law of our intellectual life. Hence the perspectives which come from the experience of historical change are always in danger of distortion because they forget the hidden constants. I feel that we are living in a state of constant overstimulation of our historical consciousness. It is a consequence of this over-stimulation and, as I hope to show, a bad short-circuit if one reacts to this over-estimation of historical change by invoking the eternal orders of nature and summoning the naturalness of man to legitimate the idea of natural law. It is not only that historical tradition and the natural order of life constitute the unity of the world in which we live as men; the way that we experience one another, the way that we experience historical traditions, the way that we experience the natural givenness of our existence and of our world, constitutes a truly hermeneutic universe, in which we are not imprisoned, as if behind insurmountable barriers, but to which we are opened.

A reflection on what truth is in the human sciences must not seek to derive itself from the tradition, the validity of which it has recognised. Hence it must, for its own method of working, endeavour to acquire as much historical self-transparency as possible. In its concern to understand the universe of understanding better than seems possible under the modern scientific notion of cognition, it has to try to establish a new relation to the concepts which it uses. It must be aware of the fact that its own understanding and interpretation is not a construction out of principles, but the development of an event which goes back a long way. Hence it will not be able to use its concepts unquestioningly, but will have to take over whatever features of the original meaning of its concepts have come down to it.

The philosophical endeavour of our day differs from the classical tradition of philosophy in that it is not a direct and unbroken continuation of it. In spite of all its connections with its historical origin, philosophy today is well aware of the historical distance between it and its classical models. This is found, above all, in its changed attitude to the concept. However important and fundamental were the transformations which took place with the Latinisation of the Greek concepts and with the translation of Latin conceptual language into the modern languages, the emergence of historical consciousness over the last few centuries is a much more radical development. Since then, the continuity of the Western philosophical tradition has been effective only in a fragmentary way. We have lost that naive innocence with which traditional concepts were made to support one's own thinking. Since that time, the attitude of science towards these concepts has become strangely detached, whether its concern with them is a scholarly, not to say self-consciously archaic, recording process, or a technical handling which makes its own use of concepts as tools. Neither of these truly satisfies the hermeneutic experience. The conceptual world in which philosophizing develops has already influenced us in the same way that the language in which we live conditions us. If thought is to be conscientious, it must become aware of these anterior influences. It is a new critical consciousness that now has to accompany all responsible philosophizing and which takes the linguistic and thinking habits built up in the individual in his communication with his environment and places them before the forum of the historical tradition to which we all belong.

The following investigation tries to satisfy this demand by combining as closely as possible an inquiry into the history of concepts with a factual exposition of its theme. That conscientiousness of phenomenological description which Husserl has made a duty for us all; the breadth of the historical horizon on which Dilthey has placed all philosophizing; and, not least, the penetration of both these influences by the impulse received from Heidegger, indicate the yardstick by which the writer desires to be measured, and which, despite all imperfection in the execution, he would like to see applied without reservation.

Foreword to the Second Edition

The second edition of *Truth and Method* is virtually unaltered. Its readers include its critics, and the attention that it has received undoubtedly obliges the author to improve the whole by drawing on all the really valuable suggestions they have offered.[1] And yet a line of thought that has matured over many years has its own stability. However much one tries to see through the critic's eyes, one's own generally pervasive viewpoint prevails.

The three years that have passed since the publication of the first edition have proved too short a time for the author to put the whole again in question, and to use effectively all that he has learned from criticism and from his own more recent work.[2]

Perhaps I may briefly outline the intention and claim of the work. My revival of the expression 'hermeneutics', with its long tradition, has apparently led to some misunderstandings.[3] I did not intend to produce an art or technique of understanding, in the manner of the earlier hermeneutics. I did not wish to elaborate a system of rules to describe, let alone direct, the methodical procedure of the human sciences. Nor was it my aim to investigate the theoretical foundation of work in these fields in order to put my findings to practical ends. If there is any practical consequence of the present investigation, it certainly has nothing to do with an unscientific 'commitment'; instead, it is concerned with the 'scientific' integrity of acknowledging the commitment involved in all understanding. My real concern was and is philosophic: not what we do or what we ought to do, but what happens to us over and above our wanting and doing.

Hence the methods of the human sciences are not at issue here. My starting point is that the historic human sciences, as they emerged from German romanticism and became imbued with the spirit of modern science, maintained a humanistic heritage which distinguishes them from all other kinds of modern research and brings them close to other, quite different, extra-scientific experiences, and especially those proper to art. In Germany (which has always been pre-revolutionary) the tradition of aesthetic humanism remained vitally influential in the development of the modern conception of science. In other countries more political consciousness may have entered into 'the humanities', *lettres*: in short, everything formerly known as the *humaniora*.

This does not prevent the methods of modern natural science from having an application to the social world. Possibly the growing rationalisation of society and the scientific techniques of its administration are more characteristic of our age than the vast progress of modern science. The methodical spirit of science permeates everywhere. Therefore I did not remotely intend to deny the necessity of methodical work within the human sciences [*Geisteswissenschaften*]. Nor did I propose to revive the ancient dispute on method between the natural and the human sciences. It is hardly a question of a contrast of methods. To this extent, Windelband and Rickert's question concerning the limits of concept-formation in the natural sciences seems to me misconceived. The difference that confronts us is not in the method, but in the objectives of the knowledge. The question I have asked seeks to discover and bring into consciousness something that methodological dispute serves only to conceal and neglect, something that does not so much confine or limit modern science as precede it and make it possible. This does not make its own immanent law of advance any less decisive. It would be vain to appeal to the human desire for knowledge and the human capacity for achievement to be more considerate in their treatment of the natural and social orders of our world. Moral preaching in the guise of science seems rather absurd, as does the presumption of a philosopher who deduces from principles the way in which 'science' must change in order to become philosophically legitimate.

Therefore it seems quite erroneous in this connection to invoke the famous Kantian distinction between *quaestio juris* and *quaestio facti*. Kant certainly did not wish to lay down for modern science what it must do in order to stand honourably before the judgment-seat of reason. He asked a philosophic question: What are the conditions of our knowledge, by virtue of which modern science is possible, and how far does it extend? Thus the following investigation also asks a philosophic question. But it does not ask it only of the so-called human sciences (among which precedence would then be accorded to certain traditional disciplines.) It does not ask it only of science and its modes of experience, but of all human experience of the world and human living. It asks (to put it in Kantian terms): How is understanding possible? This is a question which precedes any action of understanding on the part of subjectivity, including the methodical activity of the 'understanding sciences' [*verstehende Geisteswissenschaften*] and their norms and rules. Heidegger's temporal analytics of human existence [*Dasein*] has, I think, shown convincingly that understanding is not just one of the various possible behaviours of the subject, but the mode of being of There-being [*Da-sein*] itself. This is the sense in which the term 'hermeneutics' has been used here. It denotes the basic being-in-motion of There-being which constitutes its finiteness and historicity, and hence includes the whole of its experience of the world. Not caprice, or even an elaboration of a single aspect, but the nature of the thing itself makes the movement of understanding comprehensive and universal.

I cannot agree with those who maintain that the limits of the hermeneutical aspect are revealed in confrontation with extra-historical modes of being, such as the mathematical or aesthetic.[4] Admittedly it is true that, say, the aesthetic quality of a work of art depends on structural laws and a level of embodied form and shape which ultimately transcend all the limitations of its historical origin or cultural context. I shall not discuss how far, in relation to a work of art, the 'sense of quality' represents an independent possibility of knowledge, or whether, like all taste, it is not only formally developed, but also shaped and fashioned.[5] At any rate, taste is necessarily formed by something that does not indicate for what the taste is formed. To that extent, it may always include particular, preferred types of content and exclude others. But in any case it is true that everyone who experiences a work of art gathers this experience wholly within himself: namely, into the totality of his self-understanding, within which it means something to him. I go so far as to assert that the achievement of understanding, which in this way embraces the experience of the work of art, surpasses all historicism in the sphere of aesthetic experience. Of course there appears to be an obvious distinction between the original world structure established by a work of art, and its continued existence in the changed circumstances of the world thereafter.[6] But where exactly does the dividing line lie between the present world and the world that comes to be? How is the original life-significance transformed into the reflected experience that is cultural significance? It seems to me that the concept of aesthetic non-differentiation, which I have coined in this connection, is wholly valid; that here there are no clear divisions, and the movement of understanding cannot be restricted to the reflective pleasure prescribed by aesthetic differentiation. It should be admitted that, say, an ancient image of the gods that was not displayed in a temple as a work of art in order to give aesthetic, reflective pleasure, and is now on show in a museum, contains, in the way it stands before us today, the world of religious experience from which it came; the important consequence is that its world is still part of ours. It is the hermeneutic universe that embraces both.[7]

There are other respects in which the universality of the hermeneutical aspect cannot be arbitrarily restricted or curtailed. No mere artifice of composition persuaded me to begin with the experience of art in order to assure the phenomenon of understanding that breadth which is proper to it. Here the aesthetics of genius has done important preparatory work in showing that the experience of the work of art always fundamentally surpasses any subjective horizon of interpretation, whether that of the artist or that of the recipient. The mens auctoris is not admissible as a yardstick for the meaning of a work of art. Even the idea of a work-in-itself, divorced from its constantly renewed reality of being experienced, always has something abstract about it. I think I have already shown why this idea only describes an intention, but does not permit a dogmatic solution. At any rate, the purpose of my investigation is not to offer a general theory of interpretation and a different account of its methods (which E. Betti has done so well) but to discover what is common to all modes of understanding and to show that understanding is never subjective behaviour toward a given 'object', but towards its effective history—the history of its influence; in other words, understanding belongs to the being of that which is understood.

Therefore I do not find convincing the objection that the reproduction of a musical work of art is interpretation in a different sense from, say, the process of understanding when reading a poem or looking at a painting. All reproduction is primarily interpretation and seeks, as such, to be correct. In this sense it, too, is 'understanding'.[8]

I believe that the universality of the hermeneutical viewpoint cannot be restricted even where it is a question of the multitude of historical concerns and interests subsumed under the science of history. Certainly there are many modes of historical writing and research. There is no question of every historical observation being based on a conscious act of reflection on effective-history. The history of the North American Eskimo tribes is certainly quite independent of whether and when these tribes influenced the 'universal history of Europe'. Yet one cannot seriously deny that reflection on effective-history will prove to be important even in relation to this historical task. Whoever reads, in fifty or a hundred years, the history of these tribes as it is written today will not only find it old-fashioned (for in the meantime he will know more or interpret the sources more correctly); he will also be able to see that in the 1960s people read the sources differently because they were moved by different questions, prejudices and interests. Ultimately historical writing and research would be reduced to nullity if withdrawn from the sphere of the study of effective-history. The very universality of the hermeneutical problem precedes every kind of interest in history, because it is concerned with what is always fundamental to the historical question.[9] And what is historical research without the historical question? In the language that I use, justified by investigation into semantic history, this means application is an element of understanding itself. If, in this connection, I put the legal historian and the practising lawyer on the same level, I do not deny that the former has exclusively a 'contemplative', and the other a practical, task. Yet application is involved in the activities of both. How could the legal meaning of a law be different for either? It is true that, for example, the judge has the practical task of passing judgment, and many considerations of legal politics may enter in, which the legal historian (with the same law before him) does not consider. But does that make their legal understanding of the law any different? The judge's decision, which has a practical effect on life, aims at being a correct and never an arbitrary application of the law; hence it must rely on a 'correct' interpretation, which necessarily includes the mediation between history and the present in the act of understanding itself.

The legal historian, of course, will also have to evaluate 'historically' a law correctly understood in this way, and this always means that he must assess its historical importance; since he will always be guided by his own historical fore-understanding and prejudices, he may do this 'wrongly'. That means that again there is mediation between the past and the present: that is, application. The course of history, to which the history of research belongs, generally teaches us this. But it obviously does not mean that the historian has done something which he should not have done, and which he should or could have been prevented from doing by some hermeneutical canon. I am not speaking of the errors of legal history, but of accurate findings. The legal historian—like the judge—has his 'methods' of avoiding mistakes, in which I agree entirely with the legal historian.[10] But the hermeneutical interest of the philosopher begins only when error has been successfully avoided. Then both historians and dogmaticians testify to a truth that extends beyond what they know, insofar as their own transient present is discernible in what they do.

From the viewpoint of philosophical hermeneutics, the contrast between historical and dogmatic method has not absolute validity. This raises the question of the extent to which the hermeneutical viewpoint itself enjoys historical or dogmatic validity.[11] If the principle of effective-history is made into a general structural element in understanding, then this thesis undoubtedly includes no historical relativity, but seeks absolute validity—and yet a hermeneutical consciousness exists only under specific historical conditions. Tradition, part of whose nature is the handing-on of traditional material, must have become questionable for an explicit consciousness of the hermeneutic task of appropriating tradition to have been formed. Hence we find in Augustine such a consciousness in regard to the Old Testament; and, during the reformation, Protestant hermeneutics developed from an insistence on understanding scripture solely on its own basis [sola scriptura] as against the principle of tradition held by the Roman church. But certainly since the birth of historical consciousness, which involves a fundamental distance between the present and all historical transmission, understanding has been a task of requiring methodical direction. My thesis is that the element of effective-history is operative in all understanding of tradition, even where the methodology of the modern historical sciences has been largely adopted, which makes what has grown historically and has been transmitted historically an object to be established like an experimental finding—as if tradition were as alien and, from the human point of view, as unintelligible, as an object of physics.

Hence there is a certain legitimate ambiguity in the concept of the consciousness of history, as I have used it. This ambiguity is that it is used to mean at once the consciousness obtained in the course of history and determined by history, and the very consciousness of this gaining and determining. Obviously the burden of my argument is that this quality of being determined by effective-history still dominates the modern, historical and scientific consciousness and that beyond any possible knowledge of this domination. The effective-historical consciousness is so radically finite that our whole being, achieved in the totality of our destiny, inevitably transcends its knowledge of itself. But that is a fundamental insight which ought not to be limited to any specific historical situation; an insight which, however, in the face of modern historical research and of the methodological ideal of the objectivity of science, meets with particular resistance in the self-understanding of science.

We are certainly entitled to ask the reflective historical question: Why, just now, at this precise moment in history, has this fundamental insight into the element of effective-history in all understanding become possible? My investigations offer an indirect answer to this question. Only after the failure of the naive historicism of the very century of historicism does it become clear that the contrast between unhistorical-dogmatic and historical, between tradition and historical science, between ancient and modern, is not absolute. The *famouse querelle des anciens et des modernes* ceases to be a real alternative.

Hence what is here asserted, the universality of the hermeneutic aspect and especially what is elicited about language as the form in which understanding is achieved, embraces the 'pre-hermeneutic' consciousness as well as all modes of hermeneutic consciousness. Even the naive appropriation of tradition is a 'retelling', although it ought not to be described as a 'fusion of horizon'.

And now to the basic question: How far does the aspect of understanding itself and its linguisticity reach? Can it support the general philosophical inference in the proposition, 'Being that can be understood is language'? Surely the universality of language requires the untenable metaphysical conclusion that 'everything' is only language and language event? True, the obvious reference to the ineffable does not necessarily affect the universality of the language. The infinity of the dialogue in which understanding is achieved makes any reference to the ineffable itself relative. But is understanding the sole and sufficient access to the reality of history? Obviously there is a danger that the actual reality of the event, especially its absurdity and contingency, will be weakened and seen falsely in terms of sense-experience.

Hence it was my purpose to show that the historicism of Droysen and Dilthey, despite all the opposition of the historical school to Hegel's spiritualism, was seduced by its hermeneutic starting-point into reading history as a book: as one, moreover, intelligible from the first letter to the last. Despite all its protest against a philosophy of history in which the necessity of the idea is the nucleus of all events, the historical hermeneutics of Dilthey could not avoid letting history culminate in intellectual history. That was my criticism. Yet surely this danger recurs in regard to the present work? However, the traditional formation of ideas, especially the hermeneutic circle of whole and part, which is the starting-point of my attempt to lay the foundations of hermeneutics, does not necessarily require this conclusion. The idea of the whole is itself to be understood only relatively. The totality of meaning that has to be understood in history or tradition is never the meaning of the totality of history. The danger of docetism seems banished when historical tradition is not conceived as an object of historical knowledge or of philosophical conception, but as an effective moment of one's own being. The finite nature of one's own understanding is the manner in which reality, resistance, the absurd, and the unintelligible assert themselves. If one takes this finiteness seriously, then one must also take the reality of history seriously.

The same problem makes the experience of the 'Thou' so decisive for all self-understanding. The section on experience has a systematic and a key position in my investigations. There the experience of the 'Thou' also throws light on the idea of the effective-historical experience. The experience of the 'Thou' also manifests the paradoxical element that something standing over against me asserts its own rights and requires absolute recognition; and in that very process is 'understood'. But I believe that I have shown correctly that this understanding does not at all understand the 'Thou', but what the 'Thou' truly says to us. One truth I refer to is the truth that becomes visible to me only through the 'Thou', and only by my letting myself be told something by it. It is the same with historical tradition. It would not deserve the interest we take in it if it did not have something to teach us that we could not know by ourselves. It is in this sense that the statement 'being that can be understood is language' is to be read. It does not intend an absolute mastery over being by the one who understands but, on the contrary, that being is not experienced where something can be constructed by us and is to that extent conceived, but that it is experienced where what is happening can merely be understood.

This involves a question of philosophical procedure, which was raised in a number of critical comments on my book. I should like to call it the 'problem of phenomenological immanence'. It is true that my book is phenomenological in its method. This may seem paradoxical inasmuch as Heidegger's criticism of the transcendental question and his thinking of 'reversal' form the basis of my treatment of the universal hermeneutic problem. I consider, however, that the principle of phenomenological demonstration can be applied to this usage of Heidegger's, which at last reveals the hermeneutic problem. I have therefore preserved the term 'hermeneutics', which the early Heidegger used, not in the sense of a methodical art, but as a theory of the real experience that thinking is. Hence I must emphasize that my analyses of play or of language are intended in a purely phenomenological sense.[12] Play is more than the consciousness of the player; and so it is more than a subjective attitude. Language is more than the consciousness of the speaker; so it, too, is more than a subjective attitude. This is what may be described as an experience of the subject and has nothing to do with 'mythology' or 'mystification'.[13]

This fundamental methodical approach has nothing to do with any metaphysical conclusions. In writings published subsequently, especially in my research reports 'Hermeneutik und Historismus'[14] [. . .] and 'Die phanomenologische Bewegung' (in the *Philosophische Rundschau*), I have recorded my acceptance of the conclusions of Kant's *Critique of Pure Reason*, and regard statements that proceed by wholly dialectical means from the finite to the infinite, from human experience to what exists in itself, from the temporal to the eternal, as doing no more than set limits, and consider that philosophy can derive no actual knowledge from them. Nevertheless, the tradition of metaphysics and especially of its last great creation, Hegel's speculative dialectic, remains close to us. The task, the 'infinite relation', remains. But the mode of demonstrating it seeks to free itself from the embrace of the synthetic power of the Hegelian dialectic, and even from the 'logic' which developed from the dialectic of Plato, and to take its stand in the movement of that discourse in which word and idea first become what they are.[15]

Hence the demand for a reflexive self-grounding, as made from the viewpoint of the speculatively conducted transcendental philosophy of Fichte, Hegel and Husserl, is unfulfilled. But is the discourse with the whole of our philosophical tradition, in which we stand, and which, as philosophers, we are, purposeless? Do we need to justify what has always supported us?

This raises a final question which concerns less the method than the contents of the hermeneutic universalism that I have outlined. Does not the universality of understanding involve a onesidedness in its contents, inasmuch as it lacks a critical principle in relation to tradition and, as it were, espouses a universal optimism? However much it is the nature of tradition to exist only through being appropriated, it still is part of the nature of man to be able to break with tradition, to criticise and dissolve it, and is not what takes place in the work of remaking the real into an instrument of human purpose something far more basic in our relationship to being? To this extent, does not the ontological universality of understanding result in a certain one-sidedness? Understanding certainly does not mean merely the assimilation of traditional opinion or the acknowledgment of what tradition has made sacred. Heidegger, who first described the idea of understanding as the universal determinateness of There-being, means the very projective character of understanding, i.e., the futural character of There-being. I shall not deny, however, that within the universal context of the elements of understanding I have emphasized the element of the assimilation of what is past and handed down. Heidegger also, like many of my critics, would probably feel the lack of an ultimate radicality in the drawing of conclusions. What does the end of metaphysics as a science mean? What does its ending in science mean? When science expands into a total technocracy and thus brings on the 'cosmic night' of the 'forgetfulness of being', the nihilism that Nietzsche prophesied, then may one look at the last fading light of the sun that is set in the evening sky, instead of turning around to look for the first shimmer of its return?

It seems to me, however, that the onesidedness of hermeneutic universalism has the truth of a corrective. It enlightens the modern attitude of making, producing and constructing about the necessary conditions to which it is subject. In particular, it limits the position of the philosopher in the modern world. However much he may be called to make radical inferences from everything, the role of prophet, of Cassandra, of preacher or even of know-all does not suit him.

What man needs is not only a persistent asking of ultimate questions, but the sense of what is feasible, what is possible, what is correct, here and now. The philosopher, of all people, must, I think, be aware of the tension between what he claims to achieve and the reality in which he finds himself.

The hermeneutic consciousness, which must be awakened and kept awake, recognises that in the age of science the claim of superiority made by philosophic thought has something vague and unreal about it. But it seeks to confront the will of man, which is more than ever intensifying its criticism of what has gone before to the point of becoming a utopian or eschatological consciousness, with something from the truth of remembrance: with what is still and ever again real.

Translated by Garrett Barden and John Cumming

Notes: Foreword to the Second Edition

* Hans-Georg Gadamer, "Einleitung" und "Vorwort zur 2. Auflage," *Wahrheit und Methode*, Second Edition (Tübingen: J. C. B. Mohr [Paul Siebeck], 1965).—ED.

1. As well as personal communications I think of the following:
K. O. Apel, *Hegelstudien*, II, Bonn, 1963, pp. 314–22.
O. Becker. 'Die Fragwürdigkeit der Transzendierung der ästhetischen Dimension der Kunst (im Hinblick auf den I Teil von *Wahrheit und Methode*)', *Phil. Rundsch.* 10, 1962, pp. 225–38.
E. Betti, *Die Hermeneutik als allegemeine Methodik der Geisteswissenschaften*, Tübingen, 1962.
W. Hellebrand, 'Der Zeitbogen', *Arch. F. Rechts- u. Sozialphil.* 49, 1963, pp. 55–76.
H. Kuhn, 'Wahrheit und geschichtliches Verstehen', *Histor. Ztschr.* 193/2, 1961, pp. 376–89.
J. Möller, *Tübinger Theol. Quartalschr.* 5, 1961, pp. 471–76.
W. Pannenberg, 'Hermeneutik und Universalgeschichte', *Ztschr. f. Theol. u. Kirche* 69, 1963, pp. 90–121.
O. Pöggeler, *Philos. Literaturanzeiger*, 16, pp. 6–16.
A. de Waelhens, 'Sur une herméneutique de l'herméneutique', *Rev. philos. de Louvain*, 60, 1962, pp. 573–91.
F. Wieacker, 'Notizen zur rechtshistorischen Hermeneutik', *Nachr. d. Ak. d. W.* Göttingen, phil.-hist. KL. 1963, pp. 1–22.

2. Postscript to Martin Heidegger, *Der Ursprung des Kunstwerkes*, Stuttgart, 1960.
'Hegel und die antike Dialektik', *Hegel-Stud.* I, 1961, pp. 173–99.
'Zur Problematik des Selbstverständnisses', *Festschrift G. Krüger: Einsichten*, Frankfurt, 1962, pp. 71–85.
'Dichten und Deuten', *Jb. d. Dtsch. Ak. f. Sprache u. Dichtung*, 1960, pp. 13–21.
'Hermeneutik und Historismus', *Phil. Rundschau* 9, 1961; [reprinted in *Truth and Method* as Supplement I, pp. 460–91.—ED.]
'Die phänomenologische Bewegung', *Phil. Rundsch.* 11, 1963, p. 1ff.
'Die Natur der Sache und die Sprache der Dinge', in *Problem der Ordnung*, Dt. Kongr. f. Phil. 6, Munich, 1960, Meisenheim, 1962.
'Über die Möglichkeit einer philosophischen Ethik', *Sein und Ethos*, Walberger Stud.* I, 1963, pp. 11–24.

PART II ✻ DIALOGUES ON METHODOLOGY

'Mensch und Sprache', *Festschrift D. Tschizewski*, Munich, 1964.
'Martin Heidegger und die Marburger Theologie', *Festschrift R. Bultmann*, Tübingen, 1964.
'Ästhetik und Hermeneutik', a lecture at the Aesthetics Congress, Amsterdam, 1964. [Many of the essays cited here are translated by David E. Linge in Hans-Georg Gadamer, *Philosophical Hermeneutics* (Berkeley: University of California Press, 1976).—ED.]

3. E. Betti, *op. cit.*; F. Wieacker, *art. cit.*

4. Becker, *art. cit.*

5. In his *Traktat vom Schönen*, Frankfurt, 1935, Kurt Riezler attempted a transcendental deduction of the 'sense of quality'.

6. See H. Kuhn's recent work: *Vom wesen des Kunstwerkes* (1967).

7. The vindication of allegory, which is pertinent here, began some years ago with Walter Benjamin's major work, *Der Ursprung des deutschen Trauerspiels* (1927).

8. On this point I can invoke Hans Sedlmayr's papers despite their admittedly different emphasis, now collected as *Kunst und Wahrheit* (Rowohlts Deutsche Enzyclopädie, 71) especially p. 87ff.

9. H. Kuhn, *loc. cit.*

10. Betti, Wieacker, Hellebrand, *op. cit.*

11. K. O. Apel, *op. cit.*

12. Wittgenstein's concept of 'language games' seemed quite natural to me when I came across it. Cf. 'The Phenomenological Movement' [pp. 175–177 in *Philosophical Hermeneutics*—ED.].

13. My postscript to the Reclam edition of Heidegger's essay on the work of art (p. 108f) and, more recently, the essay in the F.A.Z. of September 26, 1964. See also *Die Sammlung* 1965, no. 1.

14. See *Truth and Method*, Supplement I, pp. 460–91.—ED.

15. O. Pöggeler has made an interesting suggestion (*art. cit.* p. 12ff), about what Hegel would have said about this, through the mouth of Rosenkranz.

9

A Review of Gadamer's *Truth and Method**

Jürgen Habermas

I

General linguistics is not the only alternative to a historically oriented language analysis that immerses itself in the pluralism of language games without being able to justify the language of analysis itself. To break through the grammatical barriers of individual linguistic totalities we do not need to follow Chomsky in leaving the dimension of ordinary language. Not only the distance of a theoretical language from the primary languages secures the unity of analytical reason in the pluralism of language games. Apparently every ordinary language grammar itself furnishes the possibility to transcend the language it determines, that is, to translate from and into other languages. To be sure, the anguish of translation brings to consciousness in a particularly clear manner the objective connection of linguistic structure and world-conception, the unity of word and thing. To procure a hearing for a text in a foreign language requires often enough a new text rather than a translation in the ordinary sense. Since Humboldt the sciences of language have been informed with the intention of demonstrating the close correlation of linguistic form and world view. But even this demonstration of the individuality of linguistic structure, leading to resignation in the face of the "untranslatability" of traditional formulations, is based on the daily experience that we are never locked within a single grammar. Rather, the first grammar that we learn to master already puts us in a position to step out of it and to interpret what is foreign, to make comprehensible what initially is incomprehensible, to assimilate in our own words what at first escapes them. The relativism of linguistic world views and the monadology of language games are equally illusory. For we become aware of the boundaries drawn for us by the grammar of ordinary language by means of the same grammar—Hegel's dialectic of the limit formulates the experience of the translator. The concept of translation is itself dialectical;

only where we lack transformation rules permitting the establishment of a deductive relation between languages through substitution and where an exact "translation" is excluded do we need that kind of interpretation that we commonly call translation. It expresses in one language a state of affairs that cannot be literally expressed in it, but can nevertheless be rendered "in other words." H.-G. Gadamer calls this experience, which is at the basis of hermeneutics, the hermeneutic experience.

> Hermeneutic experience is the corrective through which thinking reason escapes the spell of language; and it is itself linguistically constituted . . . To be sure, the multiplicity of languages with which linguistics is concerned also poses a question for us. But this is merely the single question: how is every language, in spite of its differences from other languages, supposed to be in a position to say everything it wants? Linguistics teaches us that every language does this in its own way. For our part, we pose the question: how does the same unity of thought and speech assert itself everywhere in the multiplicity of these ways of saying, in such a way that every written tradition can be understood?[1]

Hermeneutics defines its task as a countermove to the linguistic descriptions of different grammars. However, to preserve the unity of reason in the pluralism of languages, it does not rely on a metatheory of ordinary language grammars, as does the program of general linguistics. Hermeneutics mistrusts any mediatizing of ordinary languages and refuses to step out of their dimension; instead it makes use of the tendency to self-transcendence embedded in linguistic practice. Languages themselves possess the potential of a reason that, while expressing itself in the particularity of a specific grammar, simultaneously reflects on its limits and negates them as particular. Although always bound up in language, reason always transcends particular languages; it lives in language only by destroying the particularities of languages through which alone it is incarnated. Of course, it can cleanse itself of the dross of one particularity only in passing over into another. This intermittent generality is certified in the act of translation. It is reflected formally in a characteristic that is common to all traditional languages and guarantees their transcendental unity, namely, in the fact that they are in principle intertranslatable.

Wittgenstein, the logician, interpreted "translation" as a transformation according to general rules. Since the grammar of language games cannot be reconstructed according to general rules, he conceived linguistic understanding [*Sprachverstehen*] from the point of view of socialization, as training in a cultural form of life. It makes sense to conceive of the learning of ''language in general'' according to this model. But we can study the problem of linguistic understanding by focusing initially on the less fundamental process of learning a foreign language. To learn a language is not identical with learning to speak; it already presupposes the mastery of at least one language. With this primary language we have learned the rules that make it possible not only to achieve understanding within the framework of this one grammar but also to make foreign languages understandable. In learning a specific language, we have at the same time learned how one learns languages in general. We assimilate foreign languages through translation. Of course, as soon as we have mastered them, we no longer need translation. Translations are necessary only when understanding is disturbed. On the other hand, difficulties in achieving understanding arise even in conversations within our own language. Communication takes place according to rules that are shared by the partners in discussion. But these rules not only make consensus possible; they also include the possibility of putting an end to situations of disturbed understanding. To converse means both: to understand one another in principle and to be able to make oneself understood when necessary. The role of the discussion partner includes virtually the role of the interpreter, that is, of someone who can not only converse in one language but can bring about an understanding between different languages. The role of the interpreter is not different in principle from that of the translator. Translation is only the extreme variant of an achievement upon which every normal conversation must depend.

> Thus the case of translation makes us conscious of linguisticality [*Sprachlichkeit*] as the medium in which understanding is achieved; for in translation understanding must first be artfully produced through an explicit contrivance. [It] is certainly not the normal case of conversation. Translation is also not the normal case of our behavior toward a foreign language. . . . When one really masters a language, there is no longer a need for translation; indeed translation seems impossible. To understand a language is thus not yet at all a real understanding and does not include any interpretative process; it is rather an accomplishment of life [*Lebensvollzug*]. For one understands a language in living in it—a proposition that holds true not only for living languages but, as is well known, for dead languages as well. The hermeneutic problem is thus not a problem of the correct mastery of language but one of correctly coming to an understanding about what happens in the medium of language . . . Only where it is possible to come to an understanding in language, through talking to one another, can understanding and coming to an understanding be at all a problem. Being dependent on the translation of an interpreter is an ex-

treme case that doubles the hermeneutic process, the conversation: It involves a conversation of the interpreter with one's discussion partner and one's own conversation with the interpreter.[2]

The hermeneutic border-line case of translation, which at the same time provides the model for scientific interpretation, discloses a form of reflection that we implicitly carry out in every linguistic communication. It remains, to be sure, concealed in naive conversation; for understanding in reliably institutionalized language games rests on an unproblematic foundation of mutual understanding [Verständigtseins]—it is "not an interpretive process, but an accomplishment of life."

Wittgenstein analyzed only this dimension of the language game as a form of life. For him understanding was limited to the virtual repetition of the training through which "native" speakers are socialized into their form of life. For Gadamer this understanding of language is not yet at all a "real understanding" [Verstehen] because the accompanying reflection on the application of linguistic rules emerges only when a language game becomes problematic. Only when the intersubjectivity of the validity of linguistic rules is disturbed is an interpretive process set in motion that reestablishes consensus. Wittgenstein conflated this hermeneutic understanding with the primary process of learning to speak. Correspondingly, he was convinced that learning a foreign language has the same structure as growing up in one's mother tongue. This identification was necessary for him because he lacked a dialectical concept of translation. For translation is not a transformation that permits the reduction of statements in one language system to statements in another. Rather, the act of translation highlights a productive achievement to which language always empowers those who have mastered its grammatical rules: to assimilate what is foreign and thereby to further develop one's own linguistic system. This happens daily in situations in which discussion partners must first find a "common language." This language is the result of coming to an understanding [Verständigung], the structure of which is similar to translation.

> Coming to an understanding in conversation involves a readiness on the part of the participants and an attempt by them to make room for what is foreign and contrary. When this is mutually the case, and each partner weighs the counterarguments while simultaneously holding fast to his own, then we can finally come to a common language and a common judgment in an imperceptible and spontaneous reciprocal transference of points of view. (We call this an exchange of opinions.) In just the same way, the translator must hold fast to the rights of his mother tongue into which he translates and yet allow its

own worth to what is foreign, even contrary, in the text and its mode of expression. But this description of the activity of the translator is perhaps already too abbreviated. Even in such extreme situations of translating from one language into another, the matter under discussion [*Sache*] can scarcely be separated from the language. Only that translator will translate in a truly genuine sense who gives voice to the subject matter disclosed in the text; but this means: who finds a language that is not his own but one adequate to the original.[3]

Gadamer sees in grammatical rules not only institutionalized forms of life but delimitations of horizons. Horizons are open, and they shift; we enter into them and they in turn move with us. This Husserlian concept presents itself as a way of accentuating the assimilative and generative power of language vis-à-vis its structural accomplishments. The life-worlds that determine the grammar of language games are not closed forms of life, as Wittgenstein's monadological conception suggests.

Wittgenstein showed how the rules of linguistic communication imply the conditions of possibility of their own application. They are at the same time rules for the instructional practice through which they can be internalized. But Wittgenstein failed to appreciate that the same rules also include the conditions of possibility of their interpretation. It is proper to the grammar of a language game not only that it defines a form of life but that it defines a form of life as one's own over against others that are foreign. Because every world that is articulated in a language is a totality, the horizon of a language also encompasses that which it is not—it discloses itself as particular among particulars. For this reason, the limits of the world that it defines are not irrevocable; the dialectical confrontation of what is one's own with what is foreign leads, for the most part imperceptibly, to revisions. Translation is the medium in which these revisions take place, and language is continuously developed further. The inflexible reproduction of language and form of life at the level of the immature is only a boundary case of the flexible renewal to which a transmitted language is continually exposed, in that those who have already mastered it bridge disturbances of communication, respond to new situations, assimilate what is foreign, and find a common language for divergent tongues.

Translation is necessary not only at the horizontal level, between competing linguistic communities, but between generations and epochs as well. Tradition [*Überlieferung*], as the medium in which languages propagate themselves, takes place as translation, namely, as the bridging of distances between generations.[4] The process of socialization, through which the individual grows into his language, is the smallest unity of the process of tradition. Against this background we can see the foreshortening of perspective to which Wittgenstein succumbed; the language games of the young do not simply reproduce the practice of the aged. With the first fundamental rules of language the child learns not only the conditions of possible consensus but at the same time the conditions of a possible interpretation of these rules, which permit him to overcome, *and thereby also to express*, distance. Linguistic understanding [*Sprachverstehen*] is based not only upon a primary mutual understanding [*Verständigtsein*] but also upon a hermeneutic understanding [*Verstehen*] that is only articulated when there are disturbances in communication.

Hermeneutic self-reflection goes beyond the socio-linguistic stage of language analysis marked by the later Wittgenstein. When the transcendental construction of a pure language was shattered, language gained a new dimension through the pluralism of language games. The grammar of a language game no longer regulated only the connection of symbols but at the same time their institutionalized application in interaction. But Wittgenstein still conceived this dimension of application too narrowly. He saw only invariant linkages of symbols and activities and failed to appreciate that the application of rules includes their interpretation and further development. To be sure, Wittgenstein first made us aware—in opposition to the positivist bias—that the application of grammatical rules cannot in turn be defined at the symbolic level according to general rules; it can only be inculcated as a complex of language and practice and internalized as part of a form of life. But he remained enough of a positivist to conceive of this practice as the reproduction of fixed patterns—as if socialized individuals were subsumed under a total system composed of language and activities. In his hands the language game congeals to an opaque unity.

Actually, language spheres are not monadically sealed off but are inwardly as well as outwardly porous. The grammar of a language cannot contain a rigid design for its application. Whoever has learned to apply its rules has not only learned to express himself but also to interpret expressions in this language. Both translation (outwardly) and tradition (inwardly) must be possible in principle. Along with their possible application, grammatical rules simultaneously imply the necessity of interpretation. Wittgenstein failed to see this; as a consequence he conceived the practice of language games unhistorically. With Gadamer language gains a third dimension—grammar governs an application of rules, which, for its part, further develops the system of rules historically. The unity of language, submerged in the pluralism of language games, is reestablished dialectically in the context of tradition. Language exists only as transmitted [*tradierte*]. For tradition mirrors on a large scale the life-long socialization of individuals in their language.

Despite the abandonment of an ideal language, the concept of a language game remains bound to the unacknowledged model of formalized languages. Wittgenstein tied the intersubjectivity of ordinary language communication to the intersubjective validity of grammatical rules. To follow a rule means to apply it in the same way. The ambiguity of ordinary language and the imprecision of its rules are, for Wittgenstein, only apparent; every language game is completely ordered. The language analyst can rely on this order as a standard for his critique. Even though ordinary language cannot be reconstructed in less formal language without being destroyed as such, its grammar is still no less precise and unequivocal than that of a calculus. This assumption is plausible only for someone who—contrary to Wittgenstein's own intention—has a prior commitment to the standard of formalized language. For one who ties linguistic analysis to the self-reflection of ordinary language the opposite is plainly the case. The unequivocal character of calculi is purchased with their monadological structure, that is, with a construction that excludes conversations. Strictly deductive systems permit implications, not communications. Dialogue is replaced, at best, with the transfer of information. Only dialogue-free languages have a complete order. Ordinary languages are incomplete and provide no guarantee for the absence of ambiguity. Consequently, the intersubjectivity of ordinary language communication is always "broken." It exists because consensus [*Einverständnis*] is in principle possible; and it does not exist because it is in principle necessary to achieve effective communication [*Verständigung*]. Hermeneutic understanding [*Verstehen*] is applied to the points of rupture; it compensates for the brokenness of intersubjectivity.

Whoever starts from the normal case of conversation—and not from the model of a precision language—immediately grasps the open structure of ordinary language. An "unbroken" intersubjectivity of the grammar in force would certainly make possible identity of meaning, and thereby constant relations of understanding; but it would at the same time destroy the identity of the self in communication with others. Klaus Heinrich has examined ordinary language from this perspective of the dangers of a complete integration of individuals.[5] Languages that are no longer inwardly porous and have hardened into rigid systems remove the breaks in intersubjectivity and, simultaneously, the hermeneutic distance of individuals from one another. They no longer permit the vulnerable balance between separation and union in which the identity of every ego has to develop. The problem of an ego-identity that can be established only through identifications—and this means through alienations [*Entäusserungen*] of identity—is at the same time the problem of a linguistic communication that permits the saving balance between speechless union and speechless alienation [*Entfremdung*], between the sacrifice of individuality and the isolation of the individualized. Experiences of imminent loss of identity refer to experiences of the reification of linguistic communication. In the sustained nonidentity of a successful communication the individual can develop a precarious ego identity and preserve it against the risks of reification or formlessness. Heinrich analyzes primarily one side: the conditions of protest against the self-destruction of a society sinking back into indifference, a society that obliterates through forced integration the distance of individuals from one another. This is the situation of dictated language regulation and unbroken intersubjectivity that cancels out the subjective range of application. Wittgenstein's conception of a language game would be realized in this way. For a strictly regulated language, that inwardly closes all gaps, must be monadically sealed off outwardly. The speech of protest is, thus, the other side of hermeneutic understanding; the latter bridges a sustained distance and prevents the breaking off of communication. The power of reconciliation is intrinsic to translation. It marshals the unifying power of language against its disintegration into a number of dispersed languages, which, as isolated systems, would exact the penalty of immediate unity.[6]

II

Gadamer uses the image of a horizon to capture the basic hermeneutic character of every concrete language—far from having a closed boundary, each concrete language can in principle incorporate what is linguistically foreign and at first incomprehensible. Each of the partners among whom communication must be brought about lives in a horizon. For this reason Gadamer represents effective hermeneutic communication [*Verständigung*] with the image of a fusion [*Verschmelzung*] of horizons. This holds true for the vertical plane in which we overcome historical distance through understanding as well as for the horizontal plane in which understanding mediates geographical or cultural-linguistic distance. The appropriation [*Aneignung*] of a tradition through understanding follows the pattern of translation. The horizon of the present is not, so to speak, extinguished but fused with the horizon from which the tradition comes.

> To understand a tradition requires, to be sure, a historical horizon. But there can be no question of gaining this horizon by transposing oneself [*sich versetzen*] into a historical situation. It is, rather, necessary to have a horizon already if one is to be able to transpose oneself in this way. For what does it mean to "transpose oneself"? Certainly

not simply to disregard oneself. Of course, this is necessary insofar as one must really keep the other situation before one's eyes. But one must bring *oneself* into this other situation. Only that consummates the meaning of "transposing oneself." If one transposes oneself, for instance, into the situation of another, one will understand him, i.e., become conscious of the otherness, indeed the inextinguishable individuality of the other, precisely through transposing oneself into his situation. Such self-transposition is neither the empathetic projection of one individuality into another nor the subjection of the other to one's own standards; it means, rather, rising to a higher level of generality on which not only one's own particularity but that of the other is overcome. The concept of horizon presents itself here because it expresses the superior farsightedness that the one who is understanding must possess. To acquire a horizon means that one learns to see beyond the near and the all-too-near not in order to overlook it but in order better to see it in a larger whole and with a more accurate sense of its proportions. Nietzsche's account of the many changing horizons into which one needs to transpose oneself is not a correct description of historical consciousness. Whoever overlooks himself in this way has precisely no historical horizon.[. . .] To acquire a historical horizon certainly demands effort on one's part. We are always preoccupied, hopefully and fearfully, with what is closest to us; and we always approach the testimony of the past with this bias. Thus we have continually to curb the precipitous assimilation of the past to our own expectations of meaning. Only then will one hear the tradition as it makes itself audible in its own, distinct meaning.[. . .] Actually, the horizon of the present is constantly being developed to the extent that we must continually put our prejudices to the test. Not the least of these tests is the encounter with the past and the understanding of the tradition out of which we come. Thus the horizon of the present is not formed without the past. There is no more a separate horizon of the present than there are historical horizons that have to be acquired. Rather, understanding is always the process of fusing such supposedly self-sufficient horizons.[7]

This interlacing of horizons cannot be methodologically eliminated; it belongs to the very conditions of hermeneutic work. This becomes evident in the circular relation of prior understanding [*Vorverständnis*] to the explication of what is understood. We can decipher the parts of a text only if we anticipate an understanding—however diffuse—of the whole; and conversely, we can correct this anticipation [*Vorgriff*] only to the extent to which we explicate individual parts.

Thus the circle is not a formal circle. It is neither subjective nor objective but describes understanding as the interplay between the
movement of tradition and that of the interpreter. The anticipation of
meaning that guides our understanding of a text is not an action of
subjectivity; it is determined instead by the common bond that links
us with the tradition. This common bond, however, is constantly being developed in our relationships to tradition.[8]

The interpreter is a moment of the same fabric of tradition as his
object. He appropriates a tradition from a horizon of expectations that is
already informed by this tradition. For this reason we have, in a certain
way, already understood the tradition with which we are confronted. And
only for this reason is the horizon opened up by the language of the interpreter not merely something subjective that distorts our interpretation. In
opposition to theoretically oriented language analysis, hermeneutics insists
that we learn to understand a language from the horizon of the language we
already know. In a way, we repeat virtually those learning processes
through which the native was socialized into his language. However, we are
not drawn into these learning processes immediately [unvermittelt] but
through the mediation of the rules that we internalized in our own socialization processes. Hermeneutics comprehends the mediation of what the interpreter brings with him, with what he appropriates, as a further
development of the same tradition which the interpreter seeks to appropriate. Hermeneutics avoids the embarrassment of a language analysis that
cannot justify its own language game; for it starts with the idea that learning the language games can never succeed abstractly but only from the basis
of the language games that the interpreter has already mastered. Hermeneutic understanding is the interpretation of texts in the knowledge of already understood texts. It leads to new learning processes
[Bildungsprozesse] out of the horizon of already completed learning processes. It is a new step of socialization that takes previous socialization as
its point of departure. In appropriating tradition, it continues tradition. Because hermeneutic understanding itself belongs to the objective context that
is reflected in it, the overcoming of temporal distance cannot be interpreted
as a construction of the knowing subject. The continuity of tradition already
bridges the distance of the interpreter from his object. From the perspective
of hermeneutic self-reflection, the phenomenological and linguistic foundations of interpretive [verstehenden] sociology move to the side of historicism. Like the latter, they succumb to objectivism, since they claim for the
phenomenological observer and the language analyst a purely theoretical
attitude. But both are connected with their object domain through communication experience alone and cannot, therefore, lay claim to the role of

uninvolved spectators. Impartiality is guaranteed only through reflected participation, that is, by monitoring the initial situation [*Ausgangssituation*] of the interpreter—the sounding-board from which hermeneutic understanding cannot be detached. At the level of communication, the possible objectivity of experience is endangered precisely to the degree that the interpreter is seduced by the illusion of objectivism into concealing from himself the methodologically indissoluble bond to the hermeneutic initial situation. Gadamer's first-rate critique of the objectivistic self-understanding of the cultural sciences [*Geisteswissenschaften*] hits not only historicism but also the false consciousness of the phenomenological and linguistic executors of its legacy. The pluralism of life-worlds and language games is only a distant echo of the world views and cultures projected by Dilthey onto a fictive plane of simultaneity.

In the second part of his work, Gadamer discusses the romantic empathy theory of hermeneutics and its application to history (Schleiermacher and Droysen). Using Dilthey, he demonstrates the paradoxical consequences of a historical consciousness that—while transcending the psychological approach to understanding expressions in favor of an analysis of constellations of meaning--remains dependent on the deceptive capacity for an all-understanding reproduction of any objectivated meaning-content whatever. Against Schleiermacher's and Dilthey's aestheticizing of history and against their anaesthetizing of historical reflection, Gadamer brings to bear, subtly and relentlessly, Hegel's insight that the restitution of past life is possible only to the extent that it is a reconstruction of the present out of its past. In the place of an illusory reproduction of the past, we have its reflective mediation with present life.

> Subsequent understanding is in principle superior to the original production and can, therefore, be formulated as a "better understanding." This is not so much due to a subsequent bringing-to-consciousness that places us on a par with the author (as Schleiermacher thought). On the contrary, it describes the ineradicable difference between the author and the interpreter that is given with historical distance. Each time will have to understand a transmitted text in its own way; for the text belongs in the whole of the tradition that is of substantive interest to the age and in which it tries to understand itself. The actual meaning of a text, as it speaks to the interpreter, is not dependent on the occasion represented by the author and his original public. At least it is not exhausted by it; for the meaning is also determined by the historical situation of the interpreter and thus by the whole of the objective course of history. An author like Chladenius, who has not yet submerged understanding in past history,

takes this naively and artlessly into account when he suggests that an
author need not himself recognize the true meaning of his text and,
therefore, that the interpreter often can and must understand more
than he. But this is of fundamental significance. The meaning of a
text goes beyond its author, not only occasionally, but always. Understanding is therefore not merely reproductive but also productive.[9]

Objectivism conceals the complex of historical influences [*den
wirkungsgeschichtlichen Zusammenhang*] in which historical consciousness
itself is located. The principle of the historical influence [*Wirkungsgeschichte*] of a text becomes for Gadamer a basic methodological axiom for
the interpretation of the text itself. This is not a question of an auxiliary
discipline that supplies additional information but of research fundamental
to the interpretation itself. For "historical influence" refers to the chain of
past interpretations through which the prior understanding of the interpreter
is objectively mediated with his object, even if behind his back. Transmitted [*überlieferte*] documents and historical events do not acquire their meaning—which hermeneutic understanding endeavors to grasp descriptively—
independently of the events and interpretations that follow them. Meaning
[*Sinn*] is in principle incomplete, that is, open for sedimentations from future perspectives. Historians and philologists who reflect on historical influences take into account the openness of the horizon of meaning. They
anticipate that the progress of events will bring out new aspects of their
object. This is the rational core of the philologist's experience that the content of transmitted texts is "inexhaustible."[10] Corresponding to this is the
historian's experience that he cannot in principle give a conclusive description of any event.

> Completely to describe an event is to locate it in all the right stories,
> and this we cannot do. We cannot because we are temporally provin-
> cial with regard to the future.[11]

A. C. Danto corroborates Gadamer's principle of historical influence
through an analysis of the form of historical statements. Historical accounts
make use of narrative statements. They are called narrative because they
present events as elements of stories [*Geschichten*]. Stories have a beginning and an end; they are held together by an action. Historical events are
reconstructed within the reference system of a story. They cannot be presented without relation to other, later events. Narrative statements are in
general characterized by the fact that they refer to at least two events with
different temporal indices, the earlier of these being the theme of the description. Narrative statements describe an event with the aid of categories

under which it could not have been observed. The sentence, "The Thirty Years War began in 1618," presupposes that at least those events have elapsed which are relevant for the history of the war up to the Peace of Westphalia, events that could not have been narrated by any observer at the outbreak of the war. According to the context, the expression "Thirty Years War" signifies not only a military happening that extended through three decades but the political collapse of the German Empire, the postponement of capitalist development, the end of the Counter-Reformation, the motif for a Wallenstein drama, etc., etc. The predicates with which an event is narratively presented require the appearance of later events in the light of which the event in question appears as an historical event. Consequently, the historical description of events becomes in the course of time richer than empirical observation at the moment of their happening permits.

In the reference system of theories of empirical science events are described only with categories that could be used to record an observation of these events. A scientifically predicted event can only be identified in an observation language that is neutral with respect to the time of its happening. A historical account of the same event—a solar eclipse, let us say—has to relate to the languages of interpretation of all those for whom it has acquired historical significance, i.e., relevance in the framework of a story. If the historian wanted to proceed like the astronomer or physicist in describing an event and to use a temporally neutral observation language, he would have to assume the role of an ideal chronicler. Danto introduces this fiction; he places at the disposal of the historian a machine that records all events at each moment, stores them, and retrieves them. This ideal eyewitness notes down in an observation language everything that historically happens and how it happens. Notwithstanding, this fabulous machine would be almost worthless for our historian; for the perfect eyewitness reports would be meaningless if they were not constructions of at least one single living eyewitness who could make use of narrative statements. The ideal chronicler is not in a position to describe intentional actions, for that would presuppose anticipating events beyond the time of observation. Such a machine is unable to establish causal relationships, for this would require that an event could be described retrospectively—the observation of a temporally later event is the necessary condition for identifying a previous event as its cause. The mechanical chronicler cannot tell a single story because relations between events with different temporal indices escape its observation; it cannot see the beginning, crisis, and end of an action complex because it lacks a point of view for possible interpretation.

Of course, the descriptions of the ideal eyewitness would also have to be interpretations. But a temporally neutral observation language excludes that mode of interpretation that alone makes it possible to comprehend an observed event as an historical event. Two successive historical events can be understood as the relation of a past-present to a past-future only by retrospectively applying the reference system of acting subjects who assess present conditions with a view to anticipated future conditions. When we speak of the outbreak of the Thirty Years War, we grasp the events of 1618 from the retrospective of a war ended thirty years later. For a contemporary of 1618 this expression could have had only a prospective significance. Thus we describe the event in categories that would have been relevant for a contemporary not as an observer but as an actor who could anticipate something in the future. To comprehend events historically, i.e., to present them in the form of narrative statements, means that we comprehend them in the schema of possible action.

In doing this, the historian limits himself of course to the actual intentions of the actor. As someone who has been born later, he has already transcended the horizon of history as it presented itself to the actor. But even the unintended components and consequences of intentional complexes are grasped from the point of view of possible intentionality as soon as they enter the historical horizon of one who has come later. Gadamer demonstrates the transition from the psychological to the hermeneutic foundation of the cultural sciences with this point: "The problem of history is not how relationships are in general experiencable and knowable but how relationships that no one has experienced as such should be knowable."[12] Danto discusses this relation of subjectively intended meaning to objective meaning through the example of the romantic traits subsequently discovered in the works of classicism.

> It is a discovery for which we require the concept of romanticism and criteria for identifying the romantic. But a concept of romanticism would naturally not have been available in the heyday of classicism. [. . .] Whatever in classical writings turns out to fall under the concept of romanticism was doubtless put in those works intentionally. But they were not intentional under the description "putting in romantic elements," for the authors lacked that concept. This is an important limitation on the use of *Verstehen*. It was not an intention of Aristarchus to anticipate Copernicus, nor of Petrarch to open the Renaissance. To give such descriptions requires concepts which were only available at a later time. From this it follows that even having access to the minds of the men whose action he describes will not enable the Ideal Chronicler to appreciate the significance of those actions.[13]

The historian does not observe from the perspective of the actor but describes events and actions out of the experiential horizon of a history that

goes beyond the actor's horizons of expectations. But the meaning that retrospectively accrues to events in this way emerges only in the schema of
possible action, that is, only if the events are viewed as if this meaning
had—with the knowledge of those who were born later—been intended.
Thus the language in which the historian presents events does not primarily
express observations but the interrelations of a series of interpretations. The
interpretation of contemporary observers is the last rung on a ladder of
interpretations. Its first rung is the reference system of the historian, which,
insofar as he is himself an acting subject, cannot be independent of his
horizon of expectations. The ladder itself is the relationship of tradition that
connects the historian with his object. It is constructed from the retrojec-
tions of those coming later who, knowing better, have reconstructed what
happened in the schema of possible action. The historian is no chronicler
restricted to observation; he is engaged in communicative experiences. Instead of the uninvolved recording of events, we have the task of hermeneutic understanding. At the level of historical presentation it proves to be
meaningless to want to separate something like a pure description of the
chronicler from interpretation. Danto criticizes such a conception

> that, in a way, accepts the ideal of imitation of the past but wants to
> insist that there is something beyond giving accounts, even perfect
> accounts, of the past or parts of the past, which is also the aim of
> history to do. For in addition to making true statements about the
> past, it is held, historians are interested in giving interpretations of
> the past. And even if we had a perfect account, the task of interpre-
> tation would remain to be done. The problem of just giving descrip-
> tions belongs to a humbler level of historical work; it is, indeed, the
> work of chroniclers. That is a distinction I am unable to accept. For I
> wish to maintain that history is all of a piece. It is all of a piece in the
> sense that there is nothing one might call a pure description in con-
> trast with something else to be called an interpretation. Just to do
> history at all is to employ some overarching conception that goes be-
> yond what is given. And to see that this is so is to see that history as
> an imitation or duplication of the past is an impossible ideal.[14]

A series of events acquires the unity of a story only from a point of
view that cannot be taken from those events themselves. The actors are
caught in their histories; even for them—if they tell their own stories—the
point of view from which the events can take on the coherence of a story
arises only subsequently. The story has a meaning, of course, only for
someone who is in general capable of acting. As long as new points of view
arise, the same events can enter into other stories and acquire new significations. We could give a definitive and complete description of a historical

event only if we could be certain that new points of view would no longer appear, that is, that we could anticipate all the relevant points of view that would emerge in the future. In this sense, philosophy of history anticipates the point of view that could guide the last historian at the close of history as a whole. Since we are unable to anticipate the future course of events, we are also unable to anticipate, with good grounds, the point of view of the last historian. But without philosophy of history no historical event can be completely represented.

> Any account of the past is essentially incomplete. It is essentially incomplete, that is, if its completion would require the fulfillment of a condition that simply cannot be fulfilled. And my thesis will be that a complete account of the past would presuppose a complete account of the future so that one could not achieve a complete historical account without also achieving a philosophy of history. So that if there cannot be a legitimate philosophy of history, there cannot be a legitimate and complete historical account. Paraphrasing a famous result in logic, we cannot, in brief, consistently have a complete historical account. Our knowledge of the past, in other words, is limited by our knowledge (or ignorance) of the future. And this is the deeper connection between substantive philosophy of history and ordinary history.[15]

As long as the choice of descriptive expressions is determined by a theoretical system of reference, incompleteness of descriptions is no defect. Because, however, historians do not have at their disposal theories like those in the empirical sciences, their incomplete descriptions are in principle also arbitrary.

> Completely to describe an event is to locate it in all the right stories, and this we cannot do. We cannot because we are temporally provincial with regard to the future. We cannot for the same reasons that we cannot achieve a speculative philosophy of history. The complete description then presupposes a narrative organization, and narrative organization is something that we do. Not merely that, but the imposition of a narrative organization logically involves us with an inexpungeable subjective factor. There is an element of sheer arbitrariness in it. We organize events relative to some events which we find significant in a sense not touched upon here. It is a sense of significance common, however, to all narratives and is determined by the topical interests of this human being or that.[16]

These implications are plausible, however, only if we accept the ideal of complete description as a meaningful historiographical ideal. Danto develops the *idea of all possible histories* through the hypothetical role of the last historian. But for the last historian, as for every historian before him, the series of past events can take the shape of a story only from a point of view that he does not acquire from these events themselves. Only if he himself acts in a horizon of expectations can he delineate the last of all possible reference systems for the presentation of historical events. But as soon as the historian acts at all, he produces new relationships that combine into a further story from a new retrospective. The definitive and complete description would thereby be subjected to a revision. Consequently, the historical presentation of history as a whole would require a qualification that is per se incompatible with the end of history. The ideal of complete description cannot be consistently formulated; it ascribes to history a claim to contemplation that it not only cannot redeem but that is illegitimate as a claim.

Every historian is in the role of the last historian. Hermeneutic deliberations about the inexhaustibility of the horizon of meaning and the new interpretations of future generations remain empty; they have no consequences for what the historian has to do. For he does not at all organize his knowledge according to standards of pure theory. He cannot grasp anything that he can know historically independently of the framework of his own life-practice [*Lebenspraxis*]. In this context the future exists only as a horizon of expectations. And these expectations fuse hypothetically the fragments of previous traditions into an intuitively grasped totality of universal history, in the light of which every relevant event can in principle be described as completely as is possible for the practically effective self-understanding of a social life-world. Implicitly every historian proceeds in the way that Danto wishes to forbid to the philosopher of history. From the viewpoints of practice he anticipates end-states from which the multiplicity of events coalesces smoothly into action-orienting stories. Precisely the openness of history, that is, the situation of the actor, permits the hypothetical anticipation of history as a whole, without which the retrospective significance of the parts would not emerge. Dilthey already saw this.

> We grasp the significance of a moment of the past. It is significant insofar as a linkage to the future was achieved in it, through action or through an external event. . . . The individual moment [has] significance through its connection with the whole, through the relation of past and future, of individual being and mankind. But what constitutes the peculiar nature of this relation of part to whole within life? It is a relation that is never entirely completed. One would have to await the end of one's life and could only in the hour of death survey the whole from which the relation of the parts could be determined.

One would have to await the end of history to possess all the material needed for determining its significance. On the other hand, the whole is only there for us to the extent that it becomes comprehensible from the parts. Understanding moves constantly between these two modes of consideration. Our interpretation of the meaning of life changes constantly. Every plan of life is an expression of a comprehension of the significance of life. What we set as the goal of our future conditions the determination of the past's significance.[17]

Of course these goal-settings, i.e., the hermeneutic anticipations rooted in the interests of life-practice, are not arbitrary. For they can hold good only to the degree that reality does not escape their grasp. Moreover, it is the peculiar achievement of hermeneutic understanding that—in relation to the successful appropriation of traditions—the prejudices that are attached to the initial situation of the interpreter are also rendered transparent in their emergence from tradition, and thus absorbed into reflection.

III

Historical accounts that have the form of narrative statements can appear to be in principle incomplete and arbitrary only if they are measured against a mistaken ideal of description. The statements of empirical science do not themselves meet this standard of contemplative comprehension and corresponding representation. Their accuracy depends on criteria that determine the validity of technically utilizable knowledge. Correspondingly, if we examine the validity of hermeneutic statements in the framework proper to them, the framework of knowledge that has consequences for practice, then what Danto has to regard as a defect proves to be a transcendental condition of possible knowledge. Only because we project the provisional end-state of a system of reference out of the horizon of life-practice can the interpretation of events (which can be organized into a story from the point of view of the projected end) as well as the interpretation of parts (which can be described as fragments from the point of view of the anticipated totality) have any information content at all for that life-practice. I find Gadamer's real achievement in the demonstration that hermeneutic understanding is linked with transcendental necessity to the articulation of an action-orienting self-understanding.

The immanent connection of understanding and application can be seen in the examples of theology and jurisprudence. Both the interpretation of the Bible in preaching and the interpretation of positive law in adjudication serve simultaneously as guideposts of how to apply the evidence in a given situation. The practical life-relation to the self-understanding of the clients—the church congregation or the legal community—is not simply a subsequent corollary to the interpretation. Rather, the interpretation is realized in the application itself. Gadamer does not want to restrict the scope of this constitutive connection between understanding and practical transposition into life only to certain traditions that (like the sacred texts of a canonical tradition or the valid norms of positive law) are already institutionally binding. Nor does he want to extend it merely to the interpretation of works of art or the explication of philosophical texts. He persuades us that the applicative understanding of distinguished traditions endowed with a claim to authority provides the model for hermeneutic understanding in general.

> The close relationship that originally linked philological hermeneutics with legal and theological hermeneutics was based on a recognition of application as an integrating moment of all understanding. Constitutive for both legal and theological hermeneutics is the tension between the fixed text—of the law or of revelation—on the one hand and, on the other hand, the meaning acquired through its application in the concrete instant of interpretation, whether in preaching or in the legal judgment. A law is not to be understood historically but is supposed to be concretized in its legal validity through interpretation. Similarly, a religious revelation is not to be interpreted merely as a historical document but is supposed to be understood in such a way that it exercises its redemptive influence. In both cases, this involves that the text (the law or the message of salvation), if it is to be understood properly, i.e., corresponding to the claim that the text puts forward, must be understood anew and otherwise at each moment, i.e., in each concrete situation. Understanding is here always application. We took as our point of departure the knowledge that the understanding exercised in the cultural sciences is only essentially historical, that is, that there too a text is understood only if it is understood each time in another way. The task of a historical hermeneutics was characterized precisely by the fact that it reflects on the tension between the sameness of the shared reality [*Sache*] and the changing situation in which it is supposed to be understood.[18]

Gadamer explains the applicative knowledge engendered by hermeneutic understanding through the Aristotelian determinations of practical knowledge.[19] Hermeneutic knowledge has three features in common with that political-ethical knowledge that Aristotle distinguished from both science and technical knowledge.[20] *In the first place*, practical knowledge has a *reflective* form; it is simultaneously "knowing oneself." For this reason we experience mistakes in the areas of practical knowledge in ourselves. False opinions have the habitual form of false consciousness. Deficient insight has the objective power of delusion. The *second* aspect is connected with this—practical knowledge is *internalized*. It has the power to fix drives and to shape passions. In contrast, technical knowledge remains external. We forget technical rules as soon as we fall out of practice. Practical rules, once mastered, become by contrast components of our personality structure. For this reason practical knowledge can also not be gained in the same presuppositionless way as theoretical knowledge: it must fasten on to a structure of prejudgments or prejudices [*Vorurteilsstruktur*]. Only the hearer who has already acquired a foreknowledge [*Vorwissen*] on the basis of appropriated traditions and experienced situations can be enlightened by lectures in practical philosophy. Practical knowledge fastens on to a socialization process and develops it further. The *third* aspect becomes comprehensible at this point—practical knowledge is *global*. It refers not to particular aims that can be specified independently of the means for their realization. The action-orienting goals, as well as the ways in which they can be realized, are components of the same form of life [*bios*]. This is always a social form of life that is developed through communicative action. Practical knowledge orients by way of rules of interaction. These transmitted [*tradierten*] rules are acquired by training; but the historically changing conditions of their use call for an application that, for its part, further develops the rules through interpretation.

If the hermeneutic sciences occupy the same position with respect to tradition as a practical philosophy that, enlightened by historical consciousness, has abandoned an ontologically grounded natural law, then the Aristotelian determinations can be claimed for hermeneutics as well.

> The interpreter who is occupied with a tradition seeks to apply the latter to himself. But here too this does not mean that the traditional text is for him given and understood in its general nature and only afterwards put to particular uses. Rather, the interpreter wants nothing other than to understand this general sense—the text, i.e., to understand what the tradition says, in what the meaning and significance of the text consist. In order to understand this, however, he cannot disregard himself and his concrete hermeneutic situation. He must relate the text to this situation if he wants to understand at all.[21]

Hermeneutic understanding is structurally oriented toward eliciting from tradition a possible action-orienting self-understanding of social groups. It makes possible a form of consensus on which communicative action depends. It eliminates the dangers of a communication breakdown in two directions: vertically, in one's own tradition, and horizontally, in the mediation between traditions of different cultures and groups. If these communication flows come to an end and the intersubjectivity of understanding either hardens or falls apart, an elementary condition of survival is disrupted—the possibility of agreement without constraint and recognition without force.

The dialectic of the general and the particular, which also obtains in the appropriation of traditions and the corresponding application of practical rules, shows once again the brokenness of intersubjectivity. That something like tradition exists at all involves an aspect of nonobligation—the tradition must also be revisable; otherwise what is nonidentical in the sustained group identity would be destroyed. Ego-identities can be formed and maintained in linguistic communication only if the related group-identity can constitute itself, vis-à-vis the collective other of its own past, as simultaneously identical with and different from it. For this reason the global generality of practical rules requires a concretizing interpretation through which, in the given situation, it is molded into a concrete generality that is intersubjectively valid.

A technical rule is abstractly general. It can be compared to a theoretical sentence whose conditions of application are formulated in general terms. Intersubjectivity is established at the theoretical level by a prior definition of fundamental predicates and at the operational level by invariant rules of application. The identification of states of affairs to which the sentence can be applied does not affect its semantic content. We can thus subsume cases under something abstractly general. It is otherwise with practical rules. We compare them with traditional meaning-contents, which are only understood when we have arrived at a consensus about their significance; only then do they have intersubjective validity in a social group. Understanding becomes a problem in this case because both the binding definition of fundamental predicates and the invariant rules of application are lacking. A prior understanding guides us in the search for states of affairs in which the meaning can be made precise; but this identification of the range of application qualifies in turn the semantic content. The global generality, which we must already have understood diffusely, determines the subsumed particular only to the degree to which it is itself first concretized by this particular. Only through this does it gain intersubjective recognition in a given situation; the recognition is tied to this situation. A new situation demands a renewal of intersubjectivity through repeated understanding. And intersubjectivity does not come to pass arbitrarily; it is, rather, the result of thoughtful mediation of the past with present life.

To be sure, Hegel could speak of thought in this connection with greater legitimacy than Gadamer. It is difficult to fix the moment of knowledge in hermeneutic understanding independently of the absolute movement of reflection. If the framework of tradition as a whole is no longer regarded

as a production of reason apprehending itself, then the further development
of tradition fostered by hermeneutic understanding cannot eo ipso count as
rational. It would, however, be precipitous to take the logical dependence of
interpretation on application and the interlacing of normative anticipation
with cognitive experiences as sufficient cause for banishing hermeneutic
understanding from the realm of substantial research and possible knowledge. At the level of hermeneutic understanding, the mobile relation that
makes cognitive processes at all possible is not yet shut down—the relation
between the formation of standards and description according to standards.
The methodology of the empirical sciences pulls the two apart—theoretical
constructions from the observations on which they can founder. But both
aspects are previously coordinated in a transcendental framework. Proto-
physics makes an interpretation of reality binding, a reality that has been
previously constituted under the conception of possible objects of technical
control. With this constitution, the rules according to which theoretical sentences can be applied to facts are predecided; thus they are unproblematic
within the sciences. Application is problematic and inseparable from interpretation wherever a transcendental framework that coordinates sentences
and facts is not yet established once and for all but is undergoing transformation and must be determined ad hoc.[22]

The appropriation of traditional meaning-contents proceeds on a level
at which schemata of possible world-conceptions are decided. This decision
is not made independently of whether such a schema proves itself in a given
and preinterpreted situation. It is therefore senseless to assign hermeneutic
understanding either to theory or to experience; it is both and neither. What
we have called communicative experience will normally take place within a
language whose grammar fixes a connection of such schemata. But the brokenness of intersubjectivity renders the continuous coordination of views in
a common schema a permanent task. Only in extreme cases does this in-
conspicuously ever-present transformation and development of transcendental schemata of world-interpretation become a problem that has to be
explicitly mastered through hermeneutic understanding. Such cases appear
when traditions are disrupted or foreign cultures are encountered—or when
we analyze familiar traditions and cultures as if they were foreign. A controlled distanciation [Verfremdung] can raise understanding from a prescien-
tific experience to the rank of a reflected procedure. In this way
hermeneutic procedures enter into the social sciences. They are unavoidable
as soon as data is [sic] gathered at the level of communicative experience.
They are equally important for the selection of a categorial framework if
we do not want to behave naively in the face of the unavoidably historical
content of even the most general categories.

Gadamer unwittingly obliges the positivistic devaluation of hermeneutics. He joins his opponents in the view that hermeneutic experience

"transcends the range of control of scientific method."[23] In the preface to the second edition of his work he sums up his investigations in the thesis

> that the moment of historical influence is and remains effective in all understanding of tradition, even where the method of the modern historical sciences has gained ground and makes what has become historically into an "object" that has to be "ascertained" like an experimental finding—as if tradition were foreign and, humanly regarded, incomprehensible in the same sense as the object of physics.[24]

This correct critique of a false objectivistic self-understanding cannot, however, lead to a suspension of the methodological distanciation of the object, which distinguishes a self-reflective understanding from everyday communicative experience. The confrontation of "truth" and "method" should not have misled Gadamer to oppose hermeneutic experience abstractly to methodic knowledge as a whole. As it is, hermeneutic experience is the ground of the hermeneutic sciences. And even if it were feasible to remove the humanities entirely from the sphere of science, the sciences of action could not avoid linking empirical-analytic with hermeneutic procedures. The claim which hermeneutics legitimately makes good against the practically influential absolutism of a general methodology of the empirical sciences, brings no dispensation from the business of methodology in general. This claim will, I fear, be effective *in* the sciences or not at all. The ontological—in Heidegger's sense—self-understanding of hermeneutics that Gadamer expresses in the preface mentioned above does not, it seems to me, suit his intentions.

> I did not want to develop a system of rules of skill that would be able to describe or even to guide the methodological procedure of the cultural sciences. It was also not my intention to investigate the theoretical foundations of work in the humanities in order to turn the knowledge gained to practical ends. If there is a practical implication of the investigations presented here, it is not an implication for unscientific "engagement" but for the "scientific" honesty to admit to oneself the engagement operative in every understanding. But my real claim was and is a philosophical one. Not what we are doing, not what we ought to be doing but what happens with us beyond our wanting and doing, is in question.[25]

This thesis is grounded with the statement:

> Understanding itself should be thought of not so much as an action of subjectivity but as entering into the happening of tradition

[*Überlieferungsgeschehen*] in which past and present are constantly mediated. It is this that must be acknowledged in hermeneutic theory, which is much too strongly dominated by the idea of a procedure, a method.[26]

In Gadamer's view, on-going tradition and hermeneutic inquiry merge to a single point. Opposed to this is the insight that the reflected appropriation of tradition breaks up the nature-like [*naturwüchsige*] substance of tradition and alters the position of the subject in it.[27] Gadamer knows that the hermeneutic sciences first developed in reaction to a decline in the binding character of traditions. When he emphasizes, nevertheless, that traditions are not rendered powerless by historical consciousness, then he overlays the justified critique of the false self-understanding of historicism with the unjustified expectation that historicism is without consequences. Certainly, Scheler's grounding of the thesis that historical traditions lose their nature-like efficacy through scientific objectivation is methodologically false. And compared with this, the hermeneutic insight is certainly correct, viz., the insight that understanding—no matter how controlled it may be—cannot simply leap over the interpreter's relationships to tradition. But from the fact that understanding is structurally a part of the traditions that it further develops through appropriation, it does not follow that the medium of tradition is not profoundly altered by scientific reflection. Even in traditions whose efficacy is unbroken, what is at work is not simply an authority detached from insight and blindly asserting itself. Every tradition must be woven with a sufficiently wide mesh to allow for application, i.e., for prudent transposition with regard to changed situations. But the methodic cultivation of prudence in the hermeneutic sciences shifts the balance between authority and reason. Gadamer fails to appreciate the power of reflection that is developed in understanding. This type of reflection is no longer blinded by the illusion of an absolute, self-grounded autonomy and does not detach itself from the soil of contingency on which it finds itself. But in grasping the genesis of the tradition from which it proceeds and on which it turns back, reflection shakes the dogmatism of life-practices.

Gadamer turns the insight into the structure of prejudgments [*Vorurteilsstruktur*] involved in understanding into a rehabilitation of prejudice as such. But does it follow from the unavoidability of hermeneutic anticipation eo ipso that there are legitimate prejudices? Gadamer is motivated by the conservatism of that first generation, by the impulse of a Burke that has not yet been turned against the rationalism of the eighteenth century; he is convinced that true authority need not be authoritarian. It distinguishes itself from false authority through recognition [*Anerkennung*]: "indeed, authority has immediately nothing to do with obedience but with cognition [*Erkenntnis*].''[28] This strikingly harsh statement expresses a basic philosophical conviction that is not covered by hermeneutics itself but at most by its absolutization.

Gadamer has in mind the type of educational process through which tradition is transferred into individual learning processes and appropriated as tradition. Here the person of the educator legitimates prejudices that are inculcated in the learner with authority—and this means, however we turn it around, under the potential threat of sanctions and with the prospect of gratifications. Identification with the model creates the authority that alone makes possible the internalization of norms, the sedimentation of prejudices. The prejudices are in turn the conditions of possible knowledge. This knowledge is raised to reflection when it makes the normative framework itself transparent while moving around in it. In this way hermeneutics also makes us conscious of that which is already historically prestructured by inculcated tradition in the very act of understanding. At one point Gadamer characterizes the task of hermeneutics as follows: it has to return along the path of Hegel's phenomenology of spirit in such a way that it demonstrates the substantiality that underlies and shapes all subjectivity.[29] However, the substantiality of what is historically pregiven does not remain unaffected when it is taken up in reflection. A structure of preunderstanding or prejudgment that has been rendered transparent can no longer function as a prejudice. But this is precisely what Gadamer seems to imply. That authority converges with knowledge means that the tradition that is effectively behind the educator legitimates the prejudices inculcated in the rising generation; they could then only be confirmed in this generation's reflection. In assuring himself of the structure of prejudgment, the mature individual would transfer the formerly unfree recognition of the personal authority of the guardian to the objective authority of a traditional framework. But then it would remain a matter of authority, for reflection could only move within the limits of the facticity of tradition. The act of recognition that is mediated through reflection would not at all have altered the fact that tradition as such remains the only ground of the validity of prejudices.

Gadamer's prejudice for the rights of prejudices certified by tradition denies the power of reflection. The latter proves itself, however, in being able to reject the claim of tradition. Reflection dissolves substantiality because it not only confirms, but also breaks up, dogmatic forces. Authority and knowledge do not converge. To be sure, knowledge is rooted in actual tradition; it remains bound to contingent conditions. But reflection does not wrestle with the facticity of transmitted norms without leaving a trace. It is condemned to be after the fact; but in glancing back it develops retroactive power. We can turn back upon internalized norms only after we have first learned, under externally imposed force, to follow them blindly. Reflection recalls that path of authority along which the grammars of language games were dogmatically inculcated as rules for interpreting the world and for action. In this process the element of authority that was simply domination can be stripped away and dissolved into the less coercive constraint of insight and rational decision.

This experience of reflection is the unforgettable legacy bequeathed to us by German Idealism from the spirit of the eighteenth century. One is tempted to lead Gadamer into battle against himself, to demonstrate to him hermeneutically that he ignores that legacy because he has taken over an undialectical concept of enlightenment from the limited perspective of the German nineteenth century and that with it he has adopted an attitude which vindicated for us (Germans) a dangerous pretension to superiority separating us from Western tradition. But the matter is not this simple; Gadamer has a systematic argument at hand. The right of reflection demands that the hermeneutic approach restrict itself. It calls for a reference system that goes beyond the framework of tradition as such; only then can tradition also be criticized. But how could a reference system be legitimated except, in turn, out of the appropriation of tradition?

IV

Wittgenstein subjected linguistic analysis first to a transcendental and then to a socio-linguistic self-reflection. Gadamer's hermeneutics marks a third stage of reflection, the historical. At this stage the interpreter and his object are conceived as elements of the same complex. This objective complex presents itself as tradition or historical influence. Through it, as a medium of linguistic symbols, communications are historically propagated. We call this process "historical" because the continuity of tradition is preserved only through translation, through a large-scale philology proceeding in a nature-like manner. The intersubjectivity of ordinary language communication is broken and must be restored again and again. This productive achievement of hermeneutic understanding, whether implicitly or explicitly carried through, is for its part motivated by the tradition that it further develops in this way. Tradition is not a process that we learn to master but a transmitted language in which we live.

> The mode of being of tradition is not, of course, one of sensuous immediacy. It is language; and the hearing that understands it in interpreting texts draws its truth into its own linguistic behavior-in-the-world [*Weltverhalten*]. Linguistic communication between the present

and tradition is, as we have shown, the happening that extends its trajectory in all understanding. Hermeneutic experience must, as genuine experience, take on everything that is present to it. It does not have the freedom to select and disallow before the fact. But it also cannot claim an absolute freedom in that tolerant neutrality that appears to be specific to understanding. It cannot undo the happening that it is.[30]

The hermeneutic self-reflection of language analysis overcomes the transcendental conception that Wittgenstein clung to even in the face of the plurality of grammars of language games. As tradition, language encompasses all specific language games and promotes unity in the empirical multiplicity of transcendental rules. At the level of objective spirit, language becomes a contingent absolute. It can no longer comprehend itself as absolute spirit; it only impresses itself on subjective spirit as absolute power. This power becomes objective in the historical transformation of horizons of possible experience. Hegel's experience of reflection shrinks to the awareness that we are delivered up to a happening in which the conditions of rationality change irrationally according to time and place, epoch and culture. Hermeneutic self-reflection embroils itself in this irrationalism, however, only when it absolutizes hermeneutic experience and fails to recognize the transcending power of reflection that is also operative in it. Reflection can, to be sure, no longer reach beyond itself to an absolute consciousness, which it then pretends to be. The way to absolute idealism is barred to a transcendental consciousness that is hermeneutically broken and plunged back into the contingent complex of traditions. But must it for that reason remain stuck on the path of a relative idealism?

The objectivity of a ''happening of tradition'' that is made up of symbolic meaning is not objective enough. Hermeneutics comes up against the walls of the traditional framework from the inside, as it were. As soon as these boundaries have been experienced and recognized, cultural traditions can no longer be posed as absolute. It makes good sense to conceive of language as a kind of metainstitution on which all social institutions are dependent; for social action is constituted only in ordinary language communication.[31] But this metainstitution of language as tradition is evidently dependent in turn on social processes that are not reducible to normative relationships. Language is *also* a medium of domination and social power; it serves to legitimate relations of organized force. Insofar as the legitimations do not articulate the power relations whose institutionalization they make possible, insofar as these relations merely manifest themselves in the legitimations, language is *also* ideological. Here it is a question not of deceptions within a language but of deception with lan-

guage as such. Hermeneutic experience that encounters this dependency of
the symbolic framework on actual conditions changes into critique of ideology.

The nonnormative forces that infiltrate language as a metainstitution
originate not only from systems of domination but also from social labor. In
this instrumental sphere of action monitored by success, experiences are
organized that evidently motivate linguistic interpretations and can change
traditional interpretations through operational constraints. A change in the
mode of production entails a restructuring of the linguistic world view. This
can be studied, for instance, in the expansion of the realm of the profane in
primitive societies. Of course, revolutions in the reproductive conditions of
material life are for their part linguistically mediated. But a new practice is
not only set in motion by a new interpretation; old patterns of interpretation
are also weakened and overturned "from below" by a new practice.[32] Today the institutionalized research practice of the empirical sciences secures
a flow of information that was formerly accumulated prescientifically in
systems of social labor. This information digests natural or contrived experiences that are constituted in the behavioral system of instrumental action.
I suspect that the institutional changes brought about by scientific-technical
progress indirectly exert an influence on the linguistic schemata of world-comprehension not unlike that formerly exerted by changes in the mode of
production. For science has become first among the productive forces. The
empirical sciences simply do not represent an arbitrary language game.
Their language interprets reality from the anthropologically deep-seated
vantage point of technical mastery. Through them the factual constraints of
the natural conditions of life impinge on society. To be sure, even the statements of the theories of empirical science refer to ordinary language as
final metalanguage; but the system of activities that they make possible, the
techniques of mastering nature, also react back on the institutional framework of society as a whole and alter the language.

An interpretive [*verstehende*] sociology that hypostasizes language to
the subject of forms of life and of tradition ties itself to the idealist presupposition that linguistically articulated consciousness determines the material practice of life. But the objective framework of social action is not
exhausted by the dimension of intersubjectively intended and symbolically
transmitted meaning. The linguistic infrastructure of a society is part of a
complex that, however symbolically mediated, is also constituted by the
constraint of reality—by the constraint of outer nature that enters into procedures for technical mastery and by the constraint of inner nature reflected
in the repressive character of social power relations. These two categories
of constraint are not only the object of interpretations; behind the back of
language, they also affect the very grammatical rules according to which

we interpret the world. *Social actions can only be comprehended in an objective framework that is constituted conjointly by language, labor, and domination.* The happening of tradition appears as an absolute power only to a self-sufficient hermeneutics; in fact it is relative to systems of labor and domination. Sociology cannot, therefore, be reduced to interpretive sociology. It requires a reference system that, on the one hand, does not suppress the symbolic mediation of social action in favor of a naturalistic view of behavior that is merely controlled by signals and excited by stimuli but that, on the other hand, also does not succumb to an idealism of linguisticality [*Sprachlichkeit*] and sublimate social processes entirely to cultural tradition. Such a reference system can no longer leave tradition undetermined as the all-encompassing; instead, it comprehends tradition as such and in its relation to other aspects of the complex of social life, thereby enabling us to designate the conditions outside of tradition under which transcendental rules of world-comprehension and of action empirically change.

A descendant of Marburg neo-Kantianism, Gadamer is prevented by the residues of Kantianism still present in Heidegger's existential ontology from drawing the consequences that his own analyses suggest. He avoids the transition from the transcendental conditions of historicity to the universal history in which these conditions are constituted. He does not see that in the dimension of the "happening of tradition" he must also conceive as mediated what, according to the ontological difference, cannot be mediated—linguistic structures and the empirical conditions under which they change historically. Only on that account can Gadamer conceal from himself that the practical [*lebenspraktische*] connection of understanding with the hermeneutic vantage point of the interpreter makes necessary the hypothetical anticipation of a philosophy of history with a practical intent.[33]

Translated by Fred R. Dallmayr and Thomas McCarthy

Notes

*Jürgen Habermas, "Zu Gadamers *Wahrheit und Methode*," in *Zur Logik der Sozialwissenschaften*, pp. 251–90. Copyright 1970 by Suhrkamp Verlag, Frankfurt am Main.—ED.

1. H.-G. Gadamer, *Wahrheit und Methode*, 2nd. ed. (Tübingen, 1965), p. 380. [Cf. *Truth and Method*, translation by Garrett Barden and John Cumming (New York: The Seabury Press, 1975), pp. 363–64. All references to the English translation will follow in brackets Habermas's references to the German text.—ED.]

2. *Ibid.*, p. 362ff. [p. 346f.].

3. *Ibid.*, p. 364 [p. 348–49].

4. *Überlieferung* is the nominal form of *überliefern*: deliver up, hand down, pass on, transmit. Because the German term retains the aspect of activity or process, of something that is done or happens, while the English "tradition" has largely lost the connotation of delivery or transmission present in its Latin roots, there are some difficulties in translation. In this sentence, for example, to speak of tradition as taking place or being carried out is odd; whereas a (literal) passing-on, handing-down or transmission might, perhaps, be spoken of in this way. When similar problems arise below, the German term will be noted in the text. As will become evident, Habermas uses *Überlieferung* and *Tradition* interchangeably.— TRANS.

5. K. Heinrich, *Versuch über die Schwierigkeit nein zu sagen* (Frankfurt, 1964).

6. Cf. my review of Heinrich reprinted in *Zur Logik der Socialwissenschaften* (Frankfurt, 1970), p. 322ff. This examination shows that hermeneutic self-reflection passes over freely into a dialectical theory of language. Bruno Liebrucks's planned six-volume work, *Sprache und Bewusstsein*, promises to provide such a theory. To date there have appeared volume 1, *Einleitung und Spannweite des Problems* (Frankfurt, 1964), and volume 2, *Sprache* (Frankfurt, 1965). Liebrucks's critique of Gehlen's anthropology is important for the methodology of the sciences of action. Because Liebrucks accepts a restricted concept of practice—which he foreshortens to instrumental action—he ends up with an abstract opposition between language and action. The peculiar connection of language and practice, which Wittgenstein and Mead worked out in the symbolically mediated interaction of language games and of communicative action, has not yet been given its due in those volumes which have appeared.

7. Gadamer, *Wahrheit und Methode*, p. 288ff. [pp. 271–73]. [The German word translated here as "prejudices" is *Vorurteile*. This is somewhat misleading, since the English term now has an almost exclusively pejorative connotation, whereas Gadamer—while allowing for the similar connotation of the German term—attempts to elaborate a positive sense of the concept. A *Vor* + *urteil* is literally a prejudgment; as Gadamer uses the term, its meaning corresponds more closely to the etymological meaning of prejudice (Latin: *prae* + *judicium*) than to current usage. The accent here, as in the case of the other key hermeneutical concepts compounded from *vor*, is on this prefix (e.g., *Vorverständnis*—"prior understanding"; *Vorgriff*—"anticipation"; *Vorbegriffe*—"preconceptions"). This is meant to bring out the fact that the interpreter's own language, practice, form of life, etc. are *pre*conditions for understanding. They belong to the initial situation (*Ausgangssituation*) from which interpretation proceeds. Cf. *Wahrheit und Methode*, p. 255 [p. 240] for Gadamer's elucidation of the concept of a *Vorurteil*.—TRANS.]

8. Gadamer, *Wahrheit und Methode*, p. 277 [p. 261].

9. *Ibid.*, p. 280 [pp. 263–64].

10. Cf. *Ibid.*, p. 355 [p. 336].

11. A. C. Danto, *Analytical Philosophy of History* (Cambridge, 1965), p. 142.

12. Gadamer, *Wahrheit und Methode*, p. 211 [p. 198].

13. Danto, *Analytical Philosophy of History*, p. 169.

14. *Ibid.*, p. 115.

15. *Ibid.*, p. 17ff.

16. *Ibid.*, p. 142.

17. W. Dilthey, *Der Aufbau der geschichtlichen Welt in den Geisteswissenschaften*, in *Gesammelte Schriften*, Vol. 3, p. 233.

18. Gadamer, *Wahrheit und Methode*, p. 292 [pp. 275–76].

19. Cf. especially the *Nicomachean Ethics*, VI, 3–10.

20. The comparison of *phronēsis* and *technē* is particularly timely, since science—which was once reserved for contemplation—has become methodologically obligated to the attitude of the technician.

21. Gadamer, *Wahrheit und Methode*, p. 307 [p. 289].

22. Habermas's conception of the different "transcendental frameworks" guiding different types of inquiry is developed in his theory of cognitive interests. Cf. especially *Knowledge and Human Interests* (Boston, 1971). He argues there that "empirical-analytic" inquiry is ultimately grounded in the structure of human labor whereas "historico-hermeneutic" inquiry is rooted in the structure of human interaction. Both "anthropologically deep-seated structures of human action" give rise to "cognitive strategies" that determine the different logics of inquiry. In the one case there is an "orientation toward technical control," and in the other, an "orientation toward mutual understanding in the conduct of life."—TRANS.

23. Gadamer, *Wahrheit und Methode*, Introduction [see p. 198 above].

24. *Ibid.*, p. xix [p. 207 above].

25. *Ibid.*, p. xiv [p. 202 above].

26. *Ibid.*, p. 274ff. [p. 258].

27. There is no precise English equivalent for the term *naturwüchsig*. The suffix *-wüchsig* (from *wachsen*: to grow) means literally "growing." The term is used by neo-Marxists to refer to processes that develop without reflection or plan. It is employed by way of contrast to consciously directed processes or structures that are the result of human will and consciousness.—TRANS.

28. Gadamer, *Wahrheit und Methode*, p. 264 [p. 248].

29. *Ibid.*, p. 286 [p. 269].

30. *Ibid.*, p. 439 [p. 420].

31. This is the point of view adopted by K. O. Apel in his critique of Gehlen's institutionalism. Cf. Apel, "Arnold Gehlen's Philosophie der Institution," in *Philosophische Rundschau*, Vol. 10 (1962), p. 1ff.

32. Cf. J. O. Hertzler, *A Sociology of Language* (New York, 1965), especially chapter 7: "Sociocultural Change and Changing Language."

33. W. Pannenberg has seen this: "It is an odd spectacle to witness how a clear-sighted and profound author has his hands full keeping his thoughts from taking the direction in which they themselves point. This spectacle is presented by Gadamer's book in its efforts to avoid Hegel's total mediation of present truth through history. These efforts are indeed grounded by the reference to the finitude of human experience, which can never be transcended in absolute knowledge. But strangely enough, the phenomena described by Gadamer push again and again in the direction of a universal conception of history which he—with Hegel's system before his eyes—would precisely like to avoid." (W. Pannenberg, "Hermeneutik und Universalgeschichte," in *Zeitschrift für Theologie und Kirche*, Vol. 60 [1963], p. 90ff.) In recent Protestant theology the reception of Ernst Bloch's work has, as far as I can see, given an impetus to overcoming the ontology of historicity (Bultmann, Heidegger) through a reflection on the dependence of the transcendental conditions of understanding on the objective complex of universal history. In addition to the works of Pannenberg, cf. also J. Moltmann, *Theologie der Hoffnung* (1964).

10

The Hermeneutic Claim to Universality*

Jürgen Habermas

I

Hermeneutics refers to an "ability" we acquire to the extent to which we learn to "master" a natural language: the art of understanding linguistically communicable meaning and to render it comprehensible in cases of distorted communication. The understanding of meaning is directed at the semantic content of speech as well as the meaning-content of written forms or even of non-linguistic symbolic systems, in so far as their meaning-content can, in principle, be expressed in words. It is no accident that we speak of the art of understanding and of making-oneself-understood, since the ability to interpret meaning, which every language-user possesses, can be stylized and developed into an artistic skill. This art is symmetric with the art of convincing and persuading in situations where decisions have to be reached on practical questions. Rhetoric, too, is based on an ability which is part of the communicative competence of every language user and which can be stylized into a special skill. Rhetoric and hermeneutics have both emerged as teachable arts which methodically discipline and cultivate a natural ability.

This is not so in the case of a philosophical hermeneutic:[1] it is not a practical skill guided by rules but a critique, for its reflexive engagement brings to consciousness experiences of our language which we gain in the course of exercising our communicative competence, that is, by moving within language. It is because rhetoric and hermeneutics serve the instruction and disciplined development of communicative competence that hermeneutic reflection can draw on this sphere of experience. But the reflection upon skilled understanding and making-oneself-understood on the one hand (1), and upon convincing and persuading on the other (2), does not serve the establishing of a teachable art, but the philosophical consideration of the structures of everyday communication.

245

(1) The art of understanding and making-oneself-understood provides a philosophical hermeneutic with its characteristic insight that the means of natural language are, in principle, sufficient for elucidating the sense of any symbolic complex, however unfamiliar and inaccessible it may initially appear. We are able to translate from any language into any language. We are able to make sense of objectivations of the most remote epoch and the most distant civilization by relating them to the familiar, i.e., pre-understood, context of our own world. At the same time, the actual distance to other traditions is part of the horizon of every natural language. In addition, the already understood context of one's own world can at any time be exposed as being questionable; it is, potentially, incomprehensible. Hermeneutic experience is circumscribed by the conjunction of these two moments: the intersubjectivity of everyday communication is principally as unlimited as it is restricted; it is unlimited because it can be extended *ad libitum*; it is restricted because it can never be completely achieved. This applies to contemporary communication both within a socio-culturally homogeneous language community and across the distance between different classes, civilizations and epochs.

Hermeneutic experience brings to consciousness the position of a speaking subject *vis-à-vis* his language. He can draw upon the self-referentiality of natural languages for paraphrasing any changes metacommunicatively.

It is, of course, possible to construct hierarchies of formal languages on the basis of everyday language as the "last metalanguage" which would relate to one another as object—to meta, to metametalanguage, etc. The formal construction of such language systems excludes the possibility that for individual sentences the rules of application be determined ad hoc, commented on or changed; and the type-rule prohibits metacommunication about sentences of a language on the level of this object language. Both these things are, however, possible in everyday language. The system of natural language is not closed, but it allows the rules of application for any utterance to be determined ad hoc, commented on or changed; and metacommunication has to employ the language which itself is made the object: every natural language is its own metalanguage. This is the basis for that reflexivity which, in the face of the type-rule, makes it possible for the semantic content of linguistic utterances to contain, in addition to the manifest message, an indirect message as to its application. Such is, for example, the case in a metaphoric use of language. Thanks to the reflexive structure of natural languages, the native speaker is provided with a unique metacommunicative maneuvering space.

The reverse side of this freedom of movement is a close bond with linguistic tradition. Natural languages are informal; for this reason, speaking subjects cannot confront their language as a closed system. Linguistic competence remains, as it were, behind their backs: they can make sure of a meaning-complex explicitly only to the extent to which they also remain tied to a dogmatically traditioned and implicitly pregiven context. Hermeneutical understanding cannot approach a subject-matter free of any prejudice; it is, rather, unavoidably pre-possessed by the context within which the understanding subject has initially acquired his interpretative schemes. This pre-understanding can be thematized and it has to prove itself in relation to the subject-matter in the course of every analysis undertaken with hermeneutic awareness. But even the modification of these unavoidable preconceptions does not break through the objectivity of language *vis-à-vis* the speaking subject: in the course of improving his knowledge he merely develops a new pre-understanding which then guides him as he takes the next hermeneutical step. This is what Gadamer means when he states that the "awareness of effective-history is unavoidably more being than consciousness."[2]

(2) The art of convincing and persuading, in turn, provides a philosophical hermeneutic with the characteristic insight that it is possible not only to exchange information through the medium of everyday language, but also that, through it, action-orienting attitudes are formed and changed. Rhetoric is traditionally regarded as the art of bringing about a consensus on questions which cannot be settled through compelling reasoning. This is why the classical age reserved the realm of the merely "probable" for rhetoric, in contrast to the realm in which the truth of statements is discussed theoretically. We are consequently here dealing with practical questions which can be traced to decisions about the acceptance or rejection of standards, of criteria for evaluation and norms of action. These decisions, if arrived at in a rational process, are made neither in a theoretically compelling nor in a merely arbitrary way: they have, in effect, been motivated by convincing speech. The peculiar ambivalence between conviction and persuasion, which attaches to any consensus arrived at through rhetorical means, not only evidences the element of force which to this day has not been removed from the determination of socio-political objectives—however much it is based on discussion. More importantly, this equivocality is also an indication of the fact that practical questions can only be resolved dialogically and for this reason remain within the context of everyday language. Rationally motivated decisions can be arrived at only on the basis of a consensus that is brought about by convincing speech; and that means depending on the both cognitively and expressively appropriate means of everyday language.

We can also learn from our experience of rhetoric about the relationship between a speaking subject and his language. A speaker can make use of the creativity of natural language to respond spontaneously to changing situations and to define new situations in principally unpredictable statements. A formal prerequisite for this is a language-structure which makes possible the generation and understanding of an infinite number of sentences by following general rules and by drawing on a finite number of elements. This productivity extends, however, not only to the immediate generation of sentences in general, but also to the long-term process of the formation of interpretative schemes which are formulated in everyday language and which both enable and pre-judge the making of experiences. A good speech which leads to a consensus about decisions on practical questions merely indicates the point where we consciously intervene in this natural-innate process and attempt to alter accepted interpretative schemes with the aim of learning (and teaching) to see what we pre-understood through tradition in a different way and to evaluate it anew. This type of insight is innovatory through the choice of the appropriate word. Thanks to the creativity of natural language the native speaker gains a unique power over the practical consciousness of the members of a community. The career of sophistry reminds us that it can be used for mind-fogging agitation as well as for enlightening people.

There is, however, another side to this power: the specific lack of power of the speaking subject *vis-à-vis* habitualized language-games; they cannot be modified unless one participates in them. This in turn can be successful only to the extent that the rules which determine a language-game have been internalized. To enter into a linguistic tradition necessitates, at least latently, the efforts of a process of socialization: the "grammar" of language-games has to become part of the personality structure. The sway of a good speech over practical consciousness rests with the fact that a natural language cannot be adequately comprehended as a system of rules for the generation of systematically ordered and semantically meaningful symbolic contexts; an immanent necessity ties it, in addition, to the context of action and bodily expressions. Rhetoric experience teaches us, in this way, the interconnection of language and praxis. Everyday communication would not only be incomplete but impossible outside the, grammatically ruled, connection with normatively guided interaction and accompanying, intermittent expressions of experiences. The insight that language and action mutually interpret each other is, of course, developed in Wittgenstein's concept of a language-game which is, at the same time, a life-form. The grammar of language-games, in the sense of a complete life-praxis, regulates not only the combining of symbols but, at the same time, the interpretation of linguistic symbols by actions and expressions.[3]

These remarks should serve as a reminder that a philosophical hermeneutic develops those insights into the structure of natural languages which can be gained from the reflexive use of communicative competence: *reflexivity and objectivity are fundamental traits of language, as are creativity and the integration of language into life-praxis*. Such reflexive knowledge, which is comprised by the "hermeneutic consciousness," is obviously different from a skill in understanding and speech. A philosophical hermeneutic differs equally from linguistics.

Linguistics is not concerned with communicative competence, that is, the ability of native speakers to participate in everyday communication through understanding and speaking; it restricts itself to linguistic competence in the narrower sense. This expression was introduced by Chomsky[4] to characterize the ability of an ideal speaker who has a command of the abstract system of rules of natural language. The concept of a language system in the sense of *langue* leaves out of account the pragmatic dimension in which *langue* is transformed into *parole*. It is precisely experiences a speaker makes in this dimension that a philosophical hermeneutic is concerned with. Furthermore, linguistics aims at a reconstruction of the system of rules that allows the generation of all the grammatically correct and semantically meaningful elements of a natural language, whereas a philosophical hermeneutic reflects upon the basic experiences of communicatively competent speakers whose linguistic competence is tacitly presupposed. This distinction between rational reconstruction and self-reflection I would like to introduce by just giving one intuitive example.

Through *self-reflection* a subject becomes aware of the unconscious pre-suppositions of completed acts. Hermeneutic consciousness is thus the outcome of a process of self-reflection in which a speaking subject recognized his specific freedom from, and dependence on, language. This leads to the dissolution of a semblance, both of a subjectivist and an objectivist kind, which captivates naive consciousness. Self-reflection throws light on experiences a subject makes while exercising his communicative competence, but it cannot explain this competence. The rational *reconstruction* of a system of linguistic rules, in contrast, is undertaken with the aim of explaining linguistic competence. It makes explicit those rules which a native speaker has an implicit command of; but it does not as such make the subject conscious of suppositions he is not aware of. The speaker's subjectivity, constituting the horizon within which reflexive experience can be gained, remains excluded in principle. One could say that a successful linguistic reconstruction makes us conscious of the apparatus of language that is functioning without us being aware of it. This would, however, be an inauthentic use of language, since the consciousness of the speaker is not changed by this linguistic knowledge. What, then, is the relevance of hermeneutic consciousness if a philosophical hermeneutic is as little concerned with the art of understanding and of speech as it is with linguistics, i.e., if its usefulness is equally limited in relation to the pre-scientific exercise of communicative competence as it is for the scientific study of language?

It is nevertheless possible to cite four aspects in which a philosophical hermeneutic is relevant to the sciences and the interpretation of their results. (1) Hermeneutic consciousness destroys the objectivist self-understanding of the traditional *Geisteswissenschaften*. It follows from the hermeneutic situatedness of the interpreting scientist that objectivity in understanding cannot be secured by an abstraction from preconceived ideas, but only by reflecting upon the context of effective-history which connects perceiving subjects and their object.[5] (2) Hermeneutic consciousness furthermore reminds the social sciences of problems which arise from the symbolic pre-structuring of their object. If the access to data is no longer mediated through controlled observation but through communication in everyday language, then theoretical concepts can no longer be operationalized within the framework of the pre-scientifically developed language-game of physical measuring. The problems that arise on the level of measuring recur on the level of theory-construction: the choice of a categorical framework and of basic theoretical predicates has to correspond to a tentative preconception of the object.[6] (3) Hermeneutic consciousness also affects the scientistic self-understanding of the natural sciences but not, of course, their methodology. The insight that natural language represents the "last" metalanguage for all theories expressed in formal language elucidates the epistemological locus of everyday language within scientific activity. The legitimation of decisions which direct the choice of research strategies, the construction of theories and the methods for testing them, and which thereby determine the "progress of science," is dependent on discussions within the community of scientists. These discussions, which are conducted on the level of meta-theory, are nevertheless tied in principle to the context of natural language and to the explicative forms of everyday communication. A philosophical hermeneutic can show the reason why it is possible to arrive at a rationally motivated but not at a peremptory consensus on this theoretic level. (4) Hermeneutic consciousness is, finally, called upon in one area of interpretation more than in any other and one which is of great social interest: the translation of important scientific information into the language of the social life-world. "What would we know of modern physics which so visibly alters our existence from physics alone? Its portrayal, which aims beyond the circle of experts, is dependent on a rhetorical element for its impact. . . . All science that hopes to be of practical use is dependent on rhetoric."[7]

The objective need to rationally relate technically utilizable knowledge to the practical knowledge of the life-world is explained by the function which scientific-technological progress has acquired for the maintenance of the system of developed industrial societies. It is my opinion that a philosophical hermeneutic tries to satisfy this need with its claim to universality. Hermeneutic consciousness can open the path towards "integrating again the experience of science into our own general and human life-experience"[8] only when it is possible to consider "the universality of human linguisticality as an element that is itself unlimited and that supports everything, not just linguistically transmitted cultural objects."[9] Gadamer refers to Plato's saying that he who considers objects in the mirror of speech arrives at their whole and uncurtailed truth—"in the mirror of language everything that exists is reflected."[10]

This specific historical theme, which itself led to the efforts of a philosophical hermeneutic, does not, however, correspond to Plato's statement. It is obviously the case that modern science can legitimately claim to arrive at true statements about "things" by proceeding monologically instead of considering the mirror of human speech: that is, by formulating theories which are monologically constructed and which are supported by controlled observation. It is because hypothetic-deductive systems of propositions of science do not form an element of everyday speech that the information derived from them is removed from the life-world which is articulated in natural language. Of course, the transference of technically utilizable knowledge into the context of the life-world requires that monologically generated knowledge be made intelligible within the dimension of speech, i.e., within the dialogue of everyday language; and this transference does, of course, represent a hermeneutic problem—but it is a problem that is new to hermeneutics itself. Hermeneutic consciousness does, after all, emerge from a reflection upon our own movement *within* natural language, whereas the interpretation of science on behalf of the life-world has to achieve a mediation *between* natural language *and* monological language systems. This process of translation transcends the limitations of a rhetorical-hermeneutical art which has only been dealing with cultural products that were handed down and which are constituted by everyday language. Going beyond hermeneutic consciousness, that has established itself in the course of the reflective exercise of this art, it would be the task of a philosophical hermeneutic to clarify the conditions for the possibility to, as it were, step outside the dialogical structure of everyday language and to use language in a monological way for the formal construction of theories and for the organization of purposive rational action.

At this stage I would like to include, parenthetically, some considerations. Jean Piaget's[11] genetic epistemology uncovers the non-linguistic roots of operative thought. It is certainly the case that the latter can only reach maturity through the integration of cognitive schemes, which emerge pre-linguistically within the sphere of instrumental action, with the linguistic systems of rules. But there is sufficient indication that language merely "sits upon" categories such as space, time, causality and substance, and rules for the formal-logical combination of symbols which possess a *pre-*linguistic basis. With the help of this hypothesis it is possible to understand the monological use of language for the organization of purposive-rational action and for the construction of scientific theories; in these cases, natural language is, in a manner of speaking, removed from the structure of inter-subjectivity; without its dialogue-constitutive elements and separated from communication it would be solely under the conditions of operative intelligence. The clarification of this issue is still to be completed; it will, in any case, be of relevance for deciding upon our question. If it is the case that operative intelligence goes back to pre-linguistic, cognitive schemes, and is therefore able to use language in an instrumental way, then the hermeneutic claim to universality would find its limit in the linguistic systems of science and the theories of rational choice. On the basis of this pre-supposition it could be made plausible why monologically constructed systems of language, even though they cannot be interpreted without recourse to natural language, can nevertheless be "understood" while by-passing the hermeneutic problem; the conditions for understanding would not, at the same time, be the conditions for everyday communication. That would only be the case once the content of rigorously constructed theories were to be translated into the context of the life-world of speech.

I cannot deal with this problem now, but I would like to put the question concerning the validity of the hermeneutic claim to universality in a different way. Can there be an understanding of meaning in relation to symbolic structures formulated in everyday language that is not tied to the hermeneutic pre-supposition of context-dependent processes of understanding, an understanding that in this sense by-passes natural language as the last metalanguage? Since hermeneutical understanding always has to proceed in an ad hoc way and cannot be developed into a scientific method—it can at best be developed in an art—this question is equivalent to the problem of whether there can be a theory appropriate to the structure of natural languages on which a methical understanding of meaning can be based.

I can envisage two ways which promise success in looking for a solution.

On the one hand we hit upon a non-trivial limit to the sphere of hermeneutical understanding in cases which are dealt with by psychoanalysis—or the critique of ideology where collective phenomena are concerned. Both deal with objectivations in everyday language in which the subject does not recognize the intentions which guided his expressive activity. These manifestations can be regarded as parts of systematically distorted communication. They are comprehensible only to the extent to which the general conditions of the pathology of everyday communication are known. A theory of everyday communication would first of all have to beat a path through to the pathologically blocked meaning-context. If the claim to represent such a theory were justified, then an explanatory understanding would be possible which transcended the limit of the hermeneutical understanding of meaning.

On the other hand, representatives of generative linguistics have for more than a decade been working on a renewed programme of a general theory of natural languages. This theory is meant to provide a rational reconstruction of a regulative system that adequately defines general linguistic competence. If this claim could be fulfilled in such a way that each element of a natural language can definitely be attached to structural descriptions formulated in theoretical language, then the latter could take the place of the hermeneutical understanding of meaning.

I cannot deal with this problem either in the present context. In the following, I shall only consider the question whether a critical science such as psychoanalysis can by-pass the way skillful interpretation is tied to the natural competence of everyday communication with the help of a theoretically based semantic analysis—and thereby refute the hermeneutic claim to universality. These investigations will help us to establish more precisely in what sense it is nevertheless possible to defend the basic hermeneutic tenet that we cannot transcend "the dialogue which we are," to use Gadamer's romanticist formulation.

II

Hermeneutic consciousness remains incomplete as long as it does not include a reflection upon the limits of hermeneutic understanding. The experience of a hermeneutical limitation refers to specifically incomprehensible expressions. This specific incomprehensibility cannot be overcome by the exercise, however skillful, of one's naturally acquired communicative competence; its stubbornness can be regarded as an indication that it cannot be explained by sole reference to the structure of everyday communication that hermeneutic philosophy has brought to light.

In this case it is not the objectivity of linguistic tradition, the finite horizon of a linguistically articulated understanding of life, the potential incomprehensibility of what is implicitly regarded as self-evident, that stands in the way of the interpretative effort.

In cases where understanding proves difficult owing to great cultural, temporal or social distance it is still possible for us to state in principle what additional information we require in order to fully understand: we know that we have to decipher an alphabet, get to know a vocabulary or rules of application which are specific to their context. Within the limits of tolerance of normal everyday communication it is possible for us to determine what we do not—yet—know when we try to make sense of an incomprehensible complex of meaning. This hermeneutic consciousness proves inadequate in the case of systematically distorted communication: incomprehensibility is here the result of a defective organization of speech itself. Openly pathological speech defects which are apparent, for example, among psychotics, can be disregarded by hermeneutics without impairment of its self-conception. The area of applicability of hermeneutics is congruent with the limits of normal everyday speech, as long as pathological cases are excluded. The self-conception of hermeneutics can only be shaken when it appears that patterns of systematically distorted communication are also in evidence in "normal," let us call it pathologically unobtrusive, speech. This is the case in the pseudo-communication in which the participants cannot recognize a breakdown in their communication; only an external observer notices that they misunderstand one another. Pseudo-communication generates a system of misunderstandings that cannot be recognized as such under the appearance of a false consensus.

Hermeneutics has taught us that we are always a participant as long as we move within the natural language and that we cannot step outside the role of a reflective partner. There is, therefore, no general criterion available to us which would allow us to determine when we are subject to the false consciousness of a pseudo-normal understanding and consider something as a difficulty that can be resolved by hermeneutical means when, in fact, it requires systematic explanation. The experience of the limit of hermeneutics consists of the recognition of systematically generated misunderstanding as such—without, at first, being able to "grasp" it.

Freud has drawn on this experience of systematically distorted communication in order to demarcate a sphere of specifically incomprehensible expressions. He always regarded dreams as the "standard model" for those phenomena which themselves extend innocuous pseudo-communication and parapraxes in everyday life to the pathological manifestations of neuroses, mental illness and psychosomatic complaints. In his writings on the theory of civilization Freud extended the sphere of systematically distorted communication and he used the insights gained in dealing with clinical phenomena as a key for pseudo-normality, i.e., the hidden pathology of societal systems. We shall first of all focus on the sphere of neurotic manifestations that has received the fullest explanation.

There are available three criteria for demarcating neurotically distorted, which here means specifically incomprehensible, forms of expression. On the level of linguistic symbols, distorted communication is apparent in the application of rules which deviate from the publicly accepted rule-system. It is possible for an isolated semantic content or complete fields of meaning, in extreme cases even the syntax, to be affected. Freud examined the content of dreams mainly in relation to condensation, displacement, a-grammaticality and the role of contraries. On the level of the behaviour, a deformed language game is noticeable because of its rigidity and compulsion to repeat. Stereotyped patterns of behaviour recur in situations with the same stimuli which give rise to affective impulses. This inflexibility is an indication that the semantic content of a symbol has lost its specifically linguistic situational independence. When we consider the system of distorted communication as a whole it becomes apparent that there exists a characteristic discrepancy between the levels of communication: the usual congruence between linguistic symbols, actions and accompanying expressions has disintegrated. Neurotic symptoms are merely the most stubborn and manifest evidence of this dissonance. No matter on what level of communication these symptoms appear—in linguistic expression, body-language or compulsive behaviour—it is always the case that a content, which has been excommunicated from its public usage, assumes independence. This content expresses an intention which remains incomprehensible according to the rules of public communication, and is, in this sense, privatized; but it also remains inaccessible to its author. There exists within the self a barrier to communication between the "I" who is linguistically competent and who participates in intersubjectively established language-games, and that "inner exile" (Freud) that is represented by the symbolic system of a private or protogenic language.

Alfred Lorenzer has examined the analytical dialogue between doctor and patient from the point of view of psychoanalysis as a linguistic analysis.[12] He conceives of the depth-hermeneutical decoding of the meaning of specifically incomprehensible objectivations as an understanding of analogous scenes. The aim of analytical interpretation, seen hermeneutically, consists of the clarification of the incomprehensible meaning of symptomatic expressions. As far as neuroses are concerned, these expressions represent part of a deformed language-game within which the patient "acts": he enacts an incomprehensible scene by contravening, in a conspicuous and stereotyped way, existing expectations of behaviour. The analyst tries to render understandable the meaning of a symptomatic scene by relating the latter to analogous scenes in a situation which contains the key to the coded relationship between the symptomatic scene which the adult patient enacts outside his treatment on the one hand, and to the original scene of his early childhood on the other, in the transfer situation. This is because the analyst is pushed into the role of the conflict-charged primary object. In his role as reflective partner the analyst can interpret the transference as a repetition of scenes of early childhood and can thereby draw up a lexicon of the meanings of these symptomatic expressions which are formulated in a private language. Scenic understanding proceeds, therefore, from the insight that the patient behaves in his symptomatic scenes as he does in certain transference scenes; it aims at a reconstruction of the original scene which the patient validates in an act of self-reflection.

As Lorenzer has demonstrated by reference to the phobia of Little Hans whom Freud examined, the reconstructed original scene is typically a situation in which a child suffers an intolerable conflict which he then represses. This defense is connected with a process of desymbolization and of symptom-formation. The child excludes the experience of conflictive object-relations from public communication (and thereby renders it inaccessible even to his own Ego); it splits off the part of the representation of the object that is charged with conflict and, in a way, desymbolizes the meaning of the relevant object. The gap that appears in the semantic field is closed by a symptom, in that an unsuspicious symbol takes the place of the symbolic content that has been split off. This symbol is, however, as conspicuous as a symptom since it has gained a private meaning and can no longer be used in accordance with the rules of public language. Scenic understanding establishes an equivalence of meaning between the elements of three patterns: everyday scene, transference scene and original scene; it thereby breaks through the specific incomprehensibility of the symptom and assists in the resymbolization, i.e., the re-introduction into public communication of a symbolic content that has been split off. The latent meaning underlying the present situation is rendered comprehensible by reference to the unmutilated meaning of the original scene in infancy. Scenic understanding makes possible the "translation" into public communication of the sense of a pathologically petrified pattern of communication which has so far remained inaccessible, but which determined behaviour.

Scenic understanding is distinguishable from the elementary hermeneutical understanding of meaning by its explanatory potential; it makes accessible the meaning of specifically incomprehensible forms of expression only to the extent to which it is possible to clarify the conditions for the emergence of nonsense in conjunction with the reconstruction of the original scene. The "what," the meaning-content of systematically distorted expressions, can only be "understood" when it is possible to answer, at the same time, the "why" question, i.e., to "explain" the emergence of the symptomatic scene by reference to the initial conditions of the systematic distortion itself.

This understanding can acquire an explanatory function in the narrow sense only if the analysis of meaning does not rely solely on the skilled application of communicative competence but is guided by theoretical as sumptions. I name two points of evidence to show that scenic understanding relies on theoretical pre-suppositions which in no way follow automatically from the natural competence of a native speaker.

Scenic understanding is, first of all, tied to a specific hermeneutical form of experimentation. The analytical rule introduced by Freud guarantees a form of communication between doctor and patient which, as it were, fulfills experimental conditions; virtualization of an actual situation and free association on the part of the patient, and goal-inhibited reaction and reflective participation by the analyst, make it possible that a transference occurs which can be used as a foil for the task of "translation." Secondly, the analyst's pre-understanding is directed at a small segment of possible meanings: viz. early, conflictive object-relations. The linguistic material that emerges in talks with the patient is classified within a closely circumscribed context of possible double meaning. This context consists of a general interpretation of infant patterns of interaction which is correlated with a theory of personality that exhibits specific phases of development. Both these aspects show that scenic understanding cannot be regarded in the same way as hermeneutical understanding, i.e., as a non-theoretical application of communicative competence which makes theorizing possible in the first place.

The theoretical assumptions tacitly underlying depth-hermeneutical language analysis can be developed in relation to three aspects. The psychoanalyst has a pre-conception of the structure of undistorted everyday communication (1); he traces the systematic distortion of communication back to the confusion of pre-linguistic and linguistic organization of symbols which are separated as two stages in the developmental process (2); he explains the emergence of deformations with the aid of a theory of deviant processes of socialization which extends onto the connection of patterns of infant interaction with the formation of personality (3). I need not here develop these theoretical assumptions in a systematic way; but I would like to illustrate briefly the aspects just mentioned.

(1) The first set of theoretical assumptions refers to the structural conditions that have to be met when talking about "normal" everyday communication.

(a) In non-deformed language-games there exists a congruence of expression on all three levels of communication; those utterances symbolized linguistically, those that are presented in actions, and those embodied in physical expressions do not contradict but complement one another metacommunicatively. Intended contradictions, which themselves contain a message, are, in this sense, regarded as normal. It is a further aspect of the normal form of everyday communication that a part of extra-verbal meanings, which varies with its socio-cultural context but which remains constant within a language-community, is intentional, i.e., in principle verbalizable.

(b) Normal everyday language follows intersubjectively valid rules: it is public. Communicated meanings are, in principle, identical for all members of a language-community. Verbal utterances are formed in agreement with the valid system of grammatical rules and are applied in a specific context; there also exists a lexicon for all extra-verbal utterances not following grammatical rules which varies within limits between socio-cultural contexts.

(c) In normal speech, the speakers are aware of the categorical difference between subject and object. They differentiate between outer and inner speech and separate private and public existence. The differentiation between reality and appearance is, in addition, dependent on the difference between the linguistic symbol, its meaning-content (signification) and the object referred to by the symbol (referent, denotation). Only on this basis is it possible to use linguistic symbols independently of a given situation (decontextualization). The speaking subject becomes capable of distinguishing between reality and appearance to the extent to which language acquires for him an existence separate from the denoted objects and the represented state of affairs as well as from private experiences.

(d) It is in normal everyday communication that the intersubjectivity of relations which secures the identity of individuals who mutually recognize one another is formed and maintained. Whereas the analytical use of language allows the identification of states of affairs (i.e., the categorization of objects by means of the identification of the specific, the subsumption of elements under classes, and the inclusion of aggregates, the reflexive use of language secures the relationship of speaking subject to a language-community, which is something that cannot be adequately represented with the mentioned analytical operations. The intersubjectivity of a world, which the subjects can inhabit on the strength of their communication in everyday language alone, is not a generality under which individuals are subsumed in the same way as elements under a class. It is, rather, the case that the relations between I, You (other I) and We (I and the other Is) are established through an analytically paradoxical achievement. The speakers identify themselves with two mutually incompatible dialogic roles and thereby secure the identity of the I as well as that of the group. The one (I) affirms his absolute non-identity *vis-à-vis* the other (You); but at the same time both recognize their own identity by accepting one another as irreplaceable individuals. In this process they are connected by something they share (We), i.e., a group which itself affirms its individuality *vis-à-vis* other groups, so that the same relations are established on the level of intersubjectively united collectives as exist between individuals.[13]

The specific point about linguistic intersubjectivity is that individuated persons can communicate on the basis of it. In the reflexive use of language we formulate what is inalienable and individual in general categories; we do this in such a way that we, as it were, metacommunicatively retract (and confirm with reservation) our direct message in order to express indirectly that part of the I that is non-identical and that cannot be represented by general determinations—even though they are the only means for expressing it.[14] The analytical use of language is embedded within the reflexive use, since the intersubjectivity of everyday communication cannot be maintained without the reciprocal self-representation of speaking subjects. A speaker can distinguish between reality and appearance to the extent to which he has a mastery of those indirect means of communication on the level of metacommunication. It is possible for us to communicate directly about states of affairs, but the subjectivity we encounter in the course of talking to one another appears only as a surface-phenomenon in direct forms of communication. The categorial meaning of indirect forms of communication which give expression to that which is individualized and unsayable is merely ontologized in the concept of an entity that exists in its appearances.

(e) Finally, it is characteristic of normal speech that the sense of substance and causality, space and time differs depending on whether these categories are applied to objects in the world or to the linguistically constituted world of speaking subjects itself. The interpretative scheme "substance" has a different sense in the identity of objects which can be categorized in an analytically unequivocal way from the one it has for speaking and acting subjects whose Ego-identity cannot be captured in analytically unequivocal operations. The causal interpretative scheme leads to the concept of physical "cause" if applied to the empirical consequences of events, and also to the concept of "motive" in the context of intentional action. Space and time are, analogously, schematized differently in respect of the physically measurable properties of objects and events than in respect of the intersubjective experience of contexts of symbolically mediated interaction. In the first case categories are employed as a system of co-ordinates for observations which are checked by the success of instrumental action; in the second case they serve as a frame of reference for subjective experiences of social space and historical time. The parameter of possible experiences in the field of intersubjectivity changes complementary to the parameter of possible experiences about objectivated objects and events.

(2) The second set of assumptions refers to the relationship between two genetically consecutive stages of the human organization of
symbols.

(a) The earlier organization of symbols which does not allow the
transposition of its contents into grammatically regulated communication
can only be investigated through data about the pathology of speech and on
the basis of an analysis of the content of dreams. We are here concerned
with symbols which direct behaviour and not just with signs since symbols
possess an authentic meaning-function; they represent experiences gained in
interaction. This layer of paleo-symbols is, however, devoid of all the properties of normal speech.[15] Paleo-symbols are not integrated into a system of
grammatical rules. They are unordered elements and do not arise within a
system that could be transformed grammatically. It is for this reason that
the functioning of pre-linguistic symbols has been compared with that of
analogy computers in contrast to digital computers. Freud had already no-
ticed the lack of logical connections in his analyses of dreams. In particular,
he points to contraries which have preserved, on the linguistic level, the
genetically earlier characteristic of an ensemble of logically irreconcilable,
that is contrary, meanings.[16] Pre-linguistic symbols are highly charged affectively and are tied to specific scenes; there is also no separation between
linguistic symbol and bodily expression. They are tied to a specific context,
so closely that symbols cannot vary freely in relation to actions.[17] Even
though paleo-symbols represent the pre-linguistic basis for the intersubjectivity of co-existence and collective action they do not lend themselves to
public communication in the strict sense. This is because the constancy of
meaning is low while the proportion of private meanings is, at the same
time, high: they cannot yet guarantee an intersubjectively binding identity
of meaning. The privatism of the pre-linguistic organization of symbols,
which is apparent in all forms of pathological speech, can be traced back to
the fact that the distance which is maintained in everyday speech between
addressor and addressee has not yet been developed, and neither has the
distinction between symbolic sign, semantic content and referent. Nor is it
as yet possible, by means of paleo-symbols, to differentiate clearly between
the level of reality and that of appearance, and between public and private
world (adualism).

Pre-linguistic organization of symbols does not, finally, allow any satisfactory categorization of the experienced world of objects. Among the
disorders of communication and thought processes apparent in psychotics[18]
one can find two extreme forms of malfunctioning; in both cases, the analytical operation of classification is disturbed. There exists, firstly, a struc-

ture of fragmentation that does not allow the comprehension of disintegrated individual elements into classes by following general criteria. Secondly, one can find an amorphous structure that does not allow any analysis of aggregates of objects which resemble each other superficially and which are vaguely grouped together. The use of symbols has not become impossible in its entirety. But the inability to form hierarchies of classes and to identify elements of classes indicates in both cases the collapse of the analytical use of language. It is, of course, possible to conclude on the basis of the second variation that an archaic formation of classes is possible by means of pre-linguistic symbols. In any case, we can find so-called primary classes, which are not formed on the abstract basis of the identity of properties, in the early stages of ontogenetic and phylogenetic development and in cases of speech-pathology. The aggregates in question, in fact, comprehend concrete objects in view of an overarching, subjectively convincing context of motivation irrespective of their identifiable properties. Animistic cosmologies are organized in accordance with such primary classes. Since comprehensive intentional structures cannot be developed without any experience of interaction one can assume that early forms of intersubjectivity are already developed in the pre-linguistic stage of symbol-organization. Paleo-symbols are, apparently, formed in contexts of interaction before they are incorporated into a system of grammatical rules and connected to operative intelligence.

(b) The organization of symbols described above, which is genetically prior to language, is a theoretical construction. It can nowhere be observed. The psychoanalytic decoding of systematically distorted communication pre-supposes such a construction, however, since depth-hermeneutics comprehends confusions of normal speech either as forced regression to earlier stages of communication or as the intrusion of an earlier form of communication into language. Basing himself on an analyst's experience of neurotic patients, Alfred Lorenzer sees the essence of psychoanalysis, as has been already shown, as the attempt to re-integrate split-off symbolic contents, which led to a privatistic narrowing of public communication, into the general usage of language. Analysis helps to achieve a "resymbolization" by retracing, and thereby undoing, the process of repression; the latter can, therefore, be regarded as a process of "desymbolization." The patient reacts against the analyst's cogent interpretation by the defense mechanism of repression, which is analogous to a taking to flight; this is an operation that takes place through and against language—otherwise it would be impossible to undo the defensive process by hermeneutical means, i.e., through the analysis of language. The fleeing Ego that in situations of conflict is forced to submit to the claims of external reality hides before itself by removing the representatives of the claims of unwelcome drives from the text of its everyday self-understanding. By means of this censorship, the representation of the tabooed object of love is excommunicated from the public use of language and, as it were, pushed back into the genetically earlier stage of paleo-symbols.

The assumption that neurotic behaviour is guided by paleo-symbols and is only subsequently rationalized by linguistic interpretation also provides an explanation for the characteristics of this form of behaviour: for its status as pseudo-communication, stereotyped and compulsive behaviour, emotional attachment, expressive content and inflexible situational tie.

If repression can be regarded as desymbolization then it is possible to provide a language-analytical interpretation for a complementary defensive mechanism that is not directed at the self but at external reality, viz. projection and disavowal. Whereas in the first case the public use of language is mutilated by symptoms that have been formed in place of excommunicated linguistic elements, distortion in the second case is directly attributable to the uncontrolled intrusion of paleo-symbolic derivatives into language. Language analysis does not aim here at the re-transformation of desymbolized contents into linguistically articulate meaning, but at a consciously undertaken excommunication of pre-linguistic elements. In both instances, systematic distortion of everyday communication can be explained by reference to semantic contents which are tied to paleo-symbols and which encyst within language like alien bodies. It is the task of language analysis to dissolve these syndromes, i.e., to isolate both levels of language.

In processes of linguistic creation, however, there occurs a genuine integration; the meaning-potential tied to paleo-symbols is publicly retrieved in the creative use of language, and is utilized for the grammatically guided use of symbols.[19] The transference of semantic contents from the pre-linguistic to the linguistic state of aggregation widens the sphere of communicative action at the expense of the unconsciously motivated one. The moment of successful, creative use of language is one of emancipation.

This is not so in the case of jokes. The laughter with which we almost compulsively respond to a joke is witness to the liberative experience of the transition from the stage of paleo-symbols to that of linguistic thought; the funny element consists in the demasking of the ambiguity of the joke which resides in the teller enticing us to regress to the stage of pre-linguistic symbolism, i.e., to confuse identity and resemblance, and at the same time to convict us of the mistake of this regression. The ensuing laughter is one of relief. In our response to a joke, which leads us to retrace, virtually and experimentally, the dangerous passage across the archaic boundary between pre-linguistic and linguistic communication, we become reassured of the control we have achieved over the dangers of a superseded stage of consciousness.

(3) Depth-hermeneutics, which clarifies the specific incomprehensibility of distorted communication, can, strictly speaking, no longer be considered in relation to the model of translation, as is the case with ordinary hermeneutical understanding. This is because the controlled "translation" or pre-linguistic symbolism into language removes obscurities which do not arise within language but through language itself; it is the structure of everyday communication, which provides the basis of translation, which is itself affected. Depth-hermeneutical understanding requires, therefore, a systematic pre-understanding that extends onto language in general, whereas hermeneutical understanding always proceeds from a pre-understanding that is shaped by tradition and which forms and changes itself within linguistic communication. The theoretical assumptions which relate, on the one hand, to two stages in the organization of symbols and, on the other hand, to processes of de- and re-symbolization, to the intrusion of paleo-symbolic elements into language and the conscious excommunication of these interspersals, as well as to the integration of pre-linguistic symbolic contents—these theoretical assumptions can be integrated into a structural model which Freud derived from his experiences gained in the analysis of the mechanism of defense. The constructions of the "Ego" and the "Id" interpret the analyst's experience of resistance on the part of the patient.

"Ego" is the portion of the personality that fulfills the task of examining reality and of censuring drives. "Id" is the name for those parts of the self which have been separated from the Ego and the existence of which becomes accessible in connection with the mechanism of defense. The "Id" is indirectly represented by symptoms which fill the gaps in normal discourse that appeared in the course of de-symbolization; it is directly represented by those delusory paleo-symbolic elements which enter language through projection and disavowal. The same clinical experience of "resistance" which led to the construction of the structures Ego and Id now also shows that defensive processes occur mainly unconsciously. This is why Freud introduced the category of "Super-ego": an agency of defense unknown to the Ego which is formed through the open-ended identification with the expectations of the primary object. All three categories, Ego, Id and Super-ego, are consequently tied to the specific sense of a systematically distorted communication which analyst and patient enter into with the aim of initiating a dialogical process of enlightenment, and to encourage and guide the patient towards self-reflection. Metapsychology can only be established as meta-hermeneutics.[20]

The structural model implicitly relies upon a model of the deformation of everyday intersubjectivity; the dimensions of Id and Super-ego within the structure of personality clearly correspond to the deformation of that structure of intersubjectivity which is apparent in communication free from domination. The structure model which Freud introduced as the categorial frame of metapsychology can, consequently, be traced back to a theory of the distortion of communicative competence.

Metapsychology consists, in the main, of assumptions about the formation of personality structures which, too, can be explained by reference to the meta-hermeneutical role of psychoanalysis. The understanding of the analyst derives, as we have seen, its explanatory force from the fact that the clarification of systematically inaccessible sense can succeed only to the extent that the origin of this non-sense can itself be explained. The reconstruction of the original scene can do both at the same time; it makes it possible to understand the meaning of deformed language-games and, together with it, to explain the origin of this deformation. This is why scenic understanding pre-supposes a metapsychology in the sense of a theory of the formation of the structures of Ego, Id and Super-ego.

On the sociological level, this finds its correspondence in the theory of the acquisition of the basic qualifications for role-guided behaviour. But both theories are part of a meta-hermeneutic which traces back the psychological development of personality structures and the acquisition of the basic qualifications for role-guided behaviour to the development of communicative competence; this is the socializing introduction into, and practicing of, forms of the intersubjectivity of everyday communication. It is now possible to answer our original question: explanatory understanding, in the sense of the depth-hermeneutical decoding of specifically inadequate expressions, does not only necessitate the skilled application of naturally acquired communicative competence, as it is the case with elementary hermeneutical understanding, but also pre-supposes a theory of communicative competence. The latter covers the forms of the intersubjectivity of language and causes of its deformation. I cannot say that a theory of communicative competence has up until now been attempted in a satisfactory way, never mind been explicitly developed. Freud's metapsychology would have to be freed of its scientist self-miscomprehension before it could be utilized as a part of a meta-hermeneutic. I would say, however, that each depth-hermeneutical interpretation of systematically distorted communication, irrespective of whether it appears in an analytic encounter or informally, implicitly relies on those demanding theoretical assumptions which can only be developed and justified within the framework of a *theory of communicative competence*.

III

What follows from this hermeneutic claim to universality? Is it not the case that the theoretical language of a meta-hermeneutic is subject to the same reservation as all other theories: that a given non-reconstructed everyday language remains the last metalanguage? And would not the application of general interpretations, which are deducible from such theories, to material given in everyday language still require basic hermeneutical understanding which is not replaceable by any generalized measuring procedure? Neither of these questions would any longer have to be answered in accordance with the hermeneutic claim to universality if the knowing subject, who necessarily has to draw on his previously acquired linguistic competence, could assure himself explicitly of this competence in the course of a theoretical reconstruction. We have so far bracketed this problem of a general theory of natural language. But we can already refer to this competence, which the analyst (and the critic of ideologies) has to employ factually in the disclosure of specifically incomprehensible expressions, in advance of all theory construction. Already the *implicit knowledge of the conditions of systematically distorted communication*, which is presupposed in an actual form in the depth-hermeneutical use of communicative competence, *is sufficient for the questioning of the ontological self-understanding of the philosophical hermeneutic* which Gadamer propounds by following Heidegger.

Gadamer turns the context-dependency of the understanding of meaning, which hermeneutic philosophy has brought to consciousness and which requires us always to proceed from a pre-understanding that is supported by tradition as well as to continuously form a new pre-understanding in the course of being corrected, to the ontologically inevitable primacy of linguistic tradition.[21] Gadamer poses the question: "Is the phenomenon of understanding adequately defined when I state that to understand is to avoid misunderstanding?" Is it not, rather, the case that something like a "supporting consensus" precedes all misunderstanding?[22] We can agree on the answer, which is to be given in the affirmative, but not on how to define this preceding consensus.

If I understand correctly, then Gadamer is of the opinion that the hermeneutical clarification of incomprehensible or misunderstood expressions always has to lead back to a consensus that has already been reliably established through converging tradition. This tradition is objective in relation to us in the sense that we cannot confront it with a principled claim to truth. The pre-judgmental structure of understanding not only prohibits us from questioning that factually established consensus which underlies our misunderstanding and incomprehension, but makes such an undertaking appear senseless. It is a hermeneutical requirement that we refer to a concrete pre-understanding which itself, in the last analysis, goes back to the process of socialization, i.e., the introduction into a shared tradition. None of this is, in principle, beyond criticism; but neither can it be questioned abstractly. This would only be possible if we could examine a consensus that has been achieved through mutual understanding by, as it were, looking into it from the side and subjecting it, behind the backs of the participants, to renewed demands for legitimation. But we can only make demands of this kind in the face of the participants by entering into a dialogue with them. In this case we submit, yet again, to the hermeneutic demand to accept, for the time being, the clarifying consensus which the resumed dialogue might arrive at, as a supporting agreement. It would be senseless to abstractly suspect this agreement, which, admittedly, is contingent, of being false consciousness since we cannot transcend the dialogue which we are. This leads Gadamer to conclude to the ontological priority of linguistic tradition over all possible critique; we can consequently criticize specific traditions only on the basis that we are part of the comprehensive context of the tradition of a language.

On first sight, these considerations seem plausible. They can, however, be shaken by the depth-hermeneutical insight that a consensus achieved by seemingly "reasonable" means may well be the result of pseudo-communication. Albrecht Wellmer has pointed out that the Enlightenment tradition generalized this insight which is hostile to tradition. However much the Enlightenment was interested in communication, it still demanded that Reason be recognized as the principle of communication, free from force in the face of the real experience of communication distorted by force: "The Enlightenment knew what a philosophical hermeneutic forgets—that the 'dialogue' which we, according to Gadamer, 'are,' is also a context of domination and as such precisely no dialogue. . . . The universal claim of the hermeneutic approach [can only] be maintained if it is realized at the outset that the context of tradition as a locus of possible truth and factual agreement is, at the same time, the locus of factual untruth and continued force."[23]

It would only be legitimate for us to equate the supporting consensus which, according to Gadamer, always precedes any failure at mutual understanding with a given factual agreement, if we could be certain that each consensus arrived at in the medium of linguistic tradition has been achieved without compulsion and distortion. But we learn from depth-hermeneutic experience that the dogmatism of the context of tradition is subject not only to the objectivity of language in general but also to the repressivity of forces which deform the intersubjectivity of agreement as such and which systematically distort everyday communication. It is for this reason that every consensus, as the outcome of an understanding of meaning, is, in principle, suspect of having been enforced through pseudo-communication: in earlier days, people talked about delusion when misunderstanding and self-misunderstanding continued unaffected under the appearance of factual agreement. Insight into the pre-judgmental structure of the understanding of meaning does not cover the identification of actually achieved consensus with a true one. It, rather, leads to the ontologization of language and to the hypostatization of the context of tradition. A critically enlightened hermeneutic that differentiates between insight and delusion incorporates the meta-hermeneutic awareness of the conditions for the possibility of systematically distorted communication. It connects the process of understanding to the principle of rational discourse, according to which truth would only be guaranteed by *that* kind of consensus which was achieved under the idealized conditions of unlimited communication free from domination and could be maintained over time.

K.-O. Apel rightly emphasized that hermeneutical understanding can, at the same time, lead to the critical ascertainment of truth only to the extent to which it follows the regulative principle: to try to establish universal agreement within the framework of an unlimited community of interpreters.[24] Only this principle can make sure that the hermeneutic effort does not cease until we are aware of deceptions within a forcible consensus and of the systematic distortion behind seemingly accidental misunderstanding. If the understanding of meaning is not to remain *a fortiori* indifferent towards the idea of truth then we have to anticipate, together with the concept of a kind of truth which measures itself on an idealized consensus achieved in unlimited communication free from domination, also the structures of solidary co-existence in communication free from force. Truth is that characteristic compulsion towards unforced universal recognition; the latter is itself tied to an ideal speech situation, i.e., a form of life, which makes possible unforced universal agreement. The critical understanding of meaning thus has to take upon itself the formal anticipation of a true life. This has already been expressed by G. H. Mead:[25]

> Universal discourse is the formal ideal of communication. If communication can be carried through and made perfect, then there would exist the kind of democracy . . . in which each individual would carry just the response in himself that he knows he calls out in the community. That is what makes communication in the significant sense the organising process in the community.

The idea of truth, which measures itself on a true consensus, implies the idea of the true life. We could also say: it includes the idea of being-of-age [*Mündigkeit* (original, *Münd* = mouth) here refers to one's ability as a competent, self-determining speaker—TRANS.]. It is only the formal anticipation of an idealized dialogue, as the form of life to be realized in the future, which guarantees the ultimate supporting and contra-factual agreement that already unites us; in relation to it we can criticize every factual agreement, should it be a false one, as false consciousness. It is, however, only when we can show that the anticipation of possible truth and a true life is constitutive for every linguistic communication which is not monological that we are in a position not merely to demand but to justify that regulative principle of understanding. Basic meta-hermeneutic experience makes us aware of the fact that critique, as a penetrating form of understanding which does not rebound off delusions, orients itself on the concept of ideal consensus and thereby follows the regulative principle of rational discourse. But to justify the view that we not only do, but indeed have to, engage in that formal anticipation in the course of every penetrating understanding, it is not enough to merely refer to experience alone. To attempt a systematic justification we have to develop the implicit knowledge, that always and already guides the depth-hermeneutical analysis of language, into a theory which would enable us to deduce the principle of rational discourse from the logic of everyday language and regard it as the necessary regulative for any actual discourse, however distorted it may be.

Even without anticipating a general theory of natural language, the above considerations would suffice to criticize two conceptions which follow not so much from hermeneutics itself but from what seems to me to be a false ontological self-understanding of it.

(1) Gadamer deduced the rehabilitation of prejudice from his hermeneutic insight into the pre-judgmental structure of understanding. He does not see any opposition between authority and reason. The authority of tradition does not assert itself blindly but only through its reflective recognition by those who, while being part of tradition themselves, understand and develop it through application. In response to my criticism,[26] Gadamer clarifies his position once again:[27]

> I grant that authority exercises force in an infinite number of forms of domination. . . . But this view of obedience to authority cannot tell us why these forms all represent ordered states of affairs and not the disorder of the brachial use of force. It seems to me to follow necessarily when I consider recognition as being determined in actual situations of authority. . . . One only needs to study such events as the loss or decay of authority . . . to see what authority is and what sus-

tains it; it is not dogmatic force but dogmatic recognition. But what is dogmatic recognition, however, if it is not that one concedes to authority a superiority of knowledge.

The dogmatic recognition of tradition, and this means the acceptance of the truth-claims of this tradition, can be equated with knowledge itself only when freedom from force and unrestricted agreement about tradition have already been secured within this tradition. Gadamer's argument presupposes that legitimizing recognition and the consensus on which authority is founded can arise and develop free from force. The experience of distorted communication contradicts this pre-supposition. Force can, in any case, acquire permanence only through the objective semblance of an unforced pseudo-communicative agreement. Force that is legitimated in such a way we call, with Max Weber, authority. It is for this reason that there has to be that principal proviso of a universal agreement free from domination in order to make the fundamental distinction between dogmatic recognition and true consensus. Reason, in the sense of the principle of rational discourse, represents the rock which factual authorities have so far been more likely to crash against than build upon.

(2) If, then, such opposition between authority and reason does in fact exist, as the Enlightenment has always claimed, and if it cannot be superseded by hermeneutic means, it follows that the attempt to impose fundamental restrictions upon the interpreter's commitment to enlightenment becomes problematic, too. Gadamer has, in addition, derived the reabsorption of the moment of enlightenment into the horizon of currently existing convictions, from his insight into the pre-judgmental structure of understanding. The interpreter's ability to understand the author better than he had understood himself is limited by the accepted and traditionally established certitudes of the socio-cultural life-world of which he is part:[28]

How does the psychoanalyst's knowledge relate to his position within the social reality to which he belongs? The emancipatory reflection which he initiates in his patients necessitates that he inquires into the more conscious surface interpretations, breaks through masked self-understanding, sees through the repressive function of social taboos. But when he conducts this reflection in situations which are outside the legitimate sphere of an analyst and where he is himself a partner in social interaction, then he is acting out of part. Anyone who sees through his social partners to something hidden to them, i.e., who does not take their role-acting seriously, is a "spoilsport" who will be avoided. The emancipatory potential of reflection which the psychoanalyst draws on therefore has to find its limit in the social consciousness within which both the analyst and his patient are in agreement with everyone else. As hermeneutic reflection has shown us, social communality, despite existing tensions and defects, always refers us back to a consensus on the basis of which it exists.

There is, however, reason to assume that the background consensus of established traditions and of language-games may be a forced consensus which resulted from pseudo-communication; this may be so not only in the individual, pathological case of disturbed family systems, but also in societal systems. The range of a hermeneutical understanding that has been extended into critique must, consequently, not be tied to the radius of convictions existing within a tradition. A depth-hermeneutic which adheres to the regulative principle of rational discourse has to seek out remaining natural-historical traces of distorted communication which are still contained even within fundamental agreements and recognized legitimations; and since it can find them there, too, it follows that any privatization of its commitment to enlightenment, and the restriction of the critique of ideology to the role of a treatment as it is institutionalized in the analyst-patient relationship, would be incompatible with its methodic point of departure. The enlightenment, which results from radical understanding, is always political. It is, of course, true that criticism is always tied to the context of tradition, which it reflects. Gadamer's hermeneutic reservations are justified against monological self-certainty which merely arrogates to itself the title of critique. There is no validation of depth-hermeneutical interpretation outside of the self-reflection of all participants that is successfully achieved in a dialogue. The hypothetical status of general interpretations leads, indeed, to *a priori* limitations in the selection of ways in which the given immanent commitment of critical understanding to enlightenment can at any time be realized.[29]

In present conditions it may be more urgent to indicate the limits of the false claim to universality made by criticism rather than that of the hermeneutic claim to universality. Where the dispute about the grounds for justification is concerned, however, it is necessary to critically examine the latter claim, too.

Translated by Josef Bleicher

Notes

* Jürgen Habermas, "Der Universalitätsanspruch der Hermeneutik" in Karl-Otto Apel et al., eds., *Hermeneutik und Ideologiekritik* (Frankfurt: Suhrkamp, 1971), pp. 120–158.—ED.

1. H. G. Gadamer, "Rhetorik, Hermeneutik und Ideologiekritik," in *Kleine Schriften* I (Tübingen: J. C. B. Mohr, 1967), pp. 113–30.

2. *Ibid.*, p. 127.

3. Cf. J. Habermas, *Erkenntnis und Interesse* (Frankfurt: Suhrkamp, 1968), p. 206. [Cf. *Knowledge and Human Interests*, translated by Jeremy J. Shapiro (Boston: Beacon Press, 1971), p. 162.—ED.]

4. N. Chomsky, *Aspects of the Theory of Syntax* (Cambridge: MIT Press, 1965).

5. Gadamer shows this in the second part of *Truth and Method*.

6. Cf. J. Habermas, "Zur Logik der Sozialwissenschaften," in *Philosophische Rundschau*, Supplement 5 (1967), Ch. III.

7. H. G. Gadamer, "Rhetorik, Hermeneutik und Ideologiekritik," p. 117f.

8. H. G. Gadamer, "Die Universalität des hermeneutischen Problems," in *Kleine Schriften* I, p. 109 [translated in this book as "The Universality of the Hermeneutical Problem," see p. 154 above—ED.].

9. H. G. Gadamer, "Rhetorik, Hermeneutik und Ideologiekritik," p. 118.

10. *Ibid.*, p. 123.

11. Cf. H. G. Furth's excellent examination, *Piaget and Knowledge* (Englewood Cliffs, N. J.: Prentice-Hall, 1969.)

12. A. Lorenzer, *Sprachzerstörung und Rekonstruktion. Vorarbeiten zu einer Metatheorie der Psychoanalyse* (Frankfurt: Suhrkamp, 1970.)

13. This is also apparent in our relationship with foreign languages. We can, in principle, learn every foreign language since all natural languages can be traced back to a general system of generative rules. But, yet, we acquire a foreign language only to the extent to which we, at least potentially, undergo at a late stage the process of socialization of native speakers—and, thereby, again at least potentially, grow into an individual language community; natural language can be general only as something concrete.

14. For the concept of non-identity, see T. W. Adorno, *Negative Dialektik* (Frankfurt: Suhrkamp, 1966) [translated as *Negative Dialectics* (London: Routledge and Kegan Paul, 1973)—TRANS.].

15. Cf. S. Arieti, *The Intrapsychic Self* (New York: Basic Books, 1967), especially Ch. 7 and Ch. 16; also H. Werner and B. Kaplan, *Symbol Formation* (New York: Wiley, 1967); P. Watzlawick, J. H. Beavin, D. D. Jackson, *Pragmatics of Human Communication* (New York: Norton, 1967), especially Ch. 6 and Ch. 7.

16. Cf. A. Gehlen, *Urmensch und Spätkultur* (Bonn, 1956); A. S. Diamond, *The History and Origin of Language* (London, 1959).

17. Lorenzer (*Kritik des psychoanalytischen Symbolsbegriff* [Frankfurt: Suhrkamp, 1970], p. 87ff.) finds the same characteristics in the unconscious representatives which direct neurotic modes of behaviour: the confusion of living expression and symbol, the close co-ordination with a particular mode of behaviour, the scenic content, context-dependency.

18. Cf. S. Arieti, op. cit., p. 286; Werner and Kaplan, op. cit., p. 253ff; and L. C. Wynne, "Denkstörung und Familienbeziehung bei Schizophrenen," in *Psyche* (May, 1965), p. 82ff.

19. S. Arieti, op. cit., p. 327ff.

20. Cf. J. Habermas, *Erkenntnis und Interesse*, p. 290ff. [Cf. *Knowledge and Human Interests*, p. 237ff.—ED.].

21. Cf. C. v. Bormann, "Die Zweideutigkeit der hermeneutischen Erfahrung," in *Philosophische Rundschau*, Vol. 16 (1969), p. 92ff (also in Apel et al., *Hermeneutik und Ideologiekritik* [Frankfurt: Suhrkamp, 1971], pp. 83–119) for Gadamer's meta-critique to my objections to the third part of *Truth and Method*, where he gives an ontological interpretation of the hermeneutic consciousness.

22. H. G. Gadamer, "Die Universälitat des hermeneutischen Problems," p. 104 [see p. 150 above—ED.].

23. A. Wellmer, *Kritische Gesellschaftstheorie und Positivismus* (Frankfurt, 1969), p. 48f [translated as *Critical Theory of Society* (New York: Seabury Press, 1974).—TRANS.].

24. K.-O. Apel, "Szientismus oder transzendentale Hermeneutik?" in Rüdiger Bubner et al., *Hermeneutik und Dialektik* (Tübingen: Mohr, 1970), Vol. II, p. 105; also in Apel, *Transformation der Philosophie* (Frankfurt: Suhrkamp, 1973), Vol. II.

25. G. H. Mead, *Mind, Self and Society* (Chicago: University of Chicago Press, 1934), p. 327.

26. J. Habermas, "Zur Logik der Sozialwissenschaften," p. 174ff.

27. H. G. Gadamer, "Rhetorik, Hermeneutik und Ideologiekritik," p. 124.

28. *Ibid.*, p. 129f.

29. Cf. Habermas, *Protestbewegung und Hochschulreform* (Frankfurt: Suhrkamp, 1969), Introduction, p. 43, note 6.

11

Reply to My Critics*

Hans-Georg Gadamer

Hermeneutics is the art of agreement. That notwithstanding, it seems to be especially difficult to reach agreement about the problem of hermeneutics, at least as long as unclarified concepts of science, criticism, and reflection dominate the discussion. We live in an age in which science achieves, in ever greater degrees, the domination of nature and regulates the way in which human coexistence is governed. Science, the pride of our civilization, tirelessly remedies the shortcomings in its successes and constantly produces new tasks for scientific research, ventures which are the basis for progress, planning, and which keep us from harm. Because of this, the power of science develops the power of a genuine delusion. By obstinately sticking to the path of structuring the world in terms of progress, a system perpetuates itself in which an individual's practical consciousness surrenders with resignation and without insight, defends itself.

Clearing up this delusion has nothing to do with the romantic criticism of culture which turns against science itself and its technical emanations. Whether one is considering ''the eclipse of reason,'' the increasing ''forgetfulness of being,'' or the tension of ''truth and method,'' only scientific consciousness worked up to the point of delusion can fail to recognize that the controversy about the goals of human society, or the question of being within the ascendancy of the manufactured, or existence within our historical heritage and future, point to a knowledge that is not science. It is a knowledge which guides all human living *praxis*, especially where this living *praxis*, *ex professo*, allies itself with the results and ways of science.

To be sure, since the seventeenth century modern science has ushered in a new world. Modern science decisively turned its back on the knowledge of substances and limited itself to the mathematical plan of nature and the methodological employment of measurement and experiment; thus it opened up the constructive path to the mastery of nature. Through this was introduced the world-wide dissemination of technical civilization. But, it has only been in our century that the rising successes have increasingly intensified the tension between our scientific progress consciousness and our socio-political consciousness. Be that as it may, the conflict between the former and the latter types of knowledge is a very old problem. It cost Socrates his life, demonstrating the ignorance of the artisans' specialized knowledge about that which is really worth knowing, i.e., the good. This repeats itself in the Platonic portrait of Socrates. Plato contrasted the dialectic, the art of leading a discussion, not only with the limited, specialized knowledge of the professional, but also with mathematics, although he saw mastery of mathematics as the unconditional precondition for turning towards the last 'dialectical' questions concerning true being and the highest good.

And yet even in the *Ethics* of Aristotle, where the fundamental clarification of the difference between productive wisdom [*technē*] and practical wisdom [*phronēsis*] is worked out, it remains in many points unclear how the political wisdom of the statesman, political activity, and the technical knowledge of the professional man are to be related to each other. To be sure, there seems to be a clear hierarchy, in which, e.g., the general, in whose service all the "arts" are employed, is himself only active in the service of peace, while the statesman acts for the happiness of all in peace as in war. But here is yet another question: who is the statesman? Is it the expert who has achieved the highest rung of the ladder of political office, or the citizen who, as a part of the true sovereignty, reaches his decision through the vote (and through this has his "citizens' " profession)? In the *Charmides* Plato leads the ideal expert in political knowledge, which is supposed to be the science of all sciences, into absurdities.[1] Obviously the type of wisdom which concerns itself with practical-political decisions cannot be approached by following the model of productive wisdom. Following this path will not allow a glimpse of the highest technical knowledge [*technisches Wissen*], namely, the knowledge of the production of human happiness. Something such as this cannot be directly taught, as Plato loved to demonstrate to the sons of the great men of Athens. Aristotle, although not a citizen of Athens, also taught this within the city, even though he spurned and described as sophists (not *Politologen*) the itinerant experts on the ideal founding of the state and constitutions. In fact these experts were anything but statesmen, i.e., anything but leading citizens in their own *polis*. But even if all this was crystal clear for Aristotle and he had masterfully worked out the structure of practical wisdom in contrast to that of technical wisdom, a question still remains: What type of wisdom or science is it within which Aristotle encounters, and then teaches, these distinctions? In what sense is practical and political science, from its own point of view, a science?

Such knowledge is not simply an application at a higher level of that practical wisdom which Aristotle has described and analyzed as *phronēsis*. Nonetheless, Aristotle explicitly differentiates 'practical philosophy' from theoretical science, and does so quite obviously by arguing that the 'object' [*Gegenstand*] of this science is not the eternally existing and highest enduring principles and axioms. Rather, its 'object' is the constant change which underlies all human *praxis*. But in a certain sense this is nonetheless theoretical, insofar as it does not teach an actual doctrine of action which clarifies and resolves a concrete situation of *praxis*. Rather, it brings about 'general' knowledge of human behavior and the forms of its 'political' existence [*Dasein*]. In this way, '*scientia practica*', practical philosophy, is found throughout the tradition of Western history of science as its own form of science. It is neither theoretical science, nor can it be adequately characterized as being '*praxis* based'. It most certainly is not, as a doctrine, a 'doctrine of action'.[2] But is it nothing but technique or 'technical doctrine' [*Kunstlehre*]? It cannot be compared with grammar or rhetoric which have at their disposal the technical consciousness of rules required for technical abilities such as reading or writing. On the one hand this consciousness of rules makes possible the control of *praxis*, and on the other, makes possible its doctrine. Despite the superiority of all these technical doctrines over mere experience, they all seem to acknowledge the final authority of speaking or writing. So is it with every other technique, with the knowledge of every other trade, that it is subordinated to the use to which one puts the manufactured product. Practical philosophy is not knowing of rules for human-social *praxis* in the sense that grammatical or rhetorical technical doctrines are a knowing of rules. It is much rather a reflection upon human-social *praxis*, and as such, in the final analysis, is 'general' and 'theoretical'. On the other side are doctrines and discussions influenced by their specific conditions, to the degree that all knowledge of moral philosophy and all the attendant general political science are based on the investigator's particular conditions of experience. Aristotle fully endorsed the position that such a 'discussion in general', which is, in its most intimate details, concrete *praxis*, is only justified when one is dealing with students who are mature enough to participate with autonomous responsibility on the basis of the concrete circumstances of their own life experience. Practical science is thus really a 'general' knowledge, but obviously a knowledge which one would refer to less as a productive wisdom than as criticism.

The present circumstances of philosophical hermeneutics seem to be the same. So far as hermeneutics is defined as the art of understanding, and the exercise of this art is understood, like the art of reading or writing, as a skilled procedure, then such knowledge can be brought under the discipline of consciously employed rules and thus be deemed a technical doctrine. In this way even Schleiermacher and his followers understood hermeneutics as a 'technical doctrine'. But this is not 'philosophical' hermeneutics. Philosophical hermeneutics would not elevate an ability to the consciousness of rules. Moreover, such an 'elevation' remains a peculiarly ambivalent process, to the extent that the consciousness of rules always turns itself about, 'elevating' itself once again to an 'automatic' ability. In contrast to this, a philosophical hermeneutics reflects about this ability and the knowledge upon which it rests. Thus it no longer serves the purpose of overcoming particular problems of understanding encountered in texts or in conversation with other humans. Rather, philosophical hermeneutics attempts, as Habermas calls it, a "critical reflective knowledge." But what does this mean?

Let us provide ourselves with a concrete view of what is meant. Reflection which employs a philosophical hermeneutic would generally be critical in that it uncovers the naive objectivism within which historical sciences, taking their bearings from the self-understanding of the natural sciences, are trapped. In the socio-critical interpretation of prejudice's constraint of all understanding, the critique of ideology makes use of hermeneutic reflection. Or, hermeneutic reflection discovers false hypostatizations of words, in the way Wittgenstein criticized psychology's concepts by returning to the original hermeneutic situation of *praxis*-related speaking. Such a critique of language's bewitching powers justifies a self-understanding which renders our experience easier to come to terms with. Hermeneutics makes critical reflection possible, e.g., where intelligible discourse is defended from misguided demands of logic. Such a case occurs when specific standards of the calculus of utterances are brought to bear on philosophical texts. Carnap or Tugendhat attempt to demonstrate that Heidegger's or Hegel's talk of nothing is meaningless because it fails to fulfill logical conditions. In this case philosophical hermeneutics can critically show that such objections do not correspond to hermeneutic experience, and thus fail to recognize what should be understood. The 'nothing which nothings' [*das 'nichtende Nichts'*], e.g., does not express, as Carnap contends, a feeling, but rather the way in which a movement of thought is to be valued. In this way hermeneutic reflection seems to me productive—productive, to take an example, in the way in which someone closely examines the logical cogency of Socratic argumentation in Platonic dialogue. Hermeneutic reflection reveals in this that the communicative movement [*Vorgang*] of such Socratically led conversations is a movement of understanding and agreement, something which is completely missed in the epistemological goal of the logical analyst.[3] In all these cases reflective critique plainly refers to an instance represented through hermeneutic experience and its linguistic execution. It elevates to critical consciousness the '*scopus*' of the expression under consideration and the hermeneutic efforts which its claim to truth demands.

What is at issue is the correction of self-understanding. Such hermeneutic reflection is 'philosophical', not because it lays claim to a specific, proprietary philosophical legitimation, but to the contrary, because it disputes a specific 'philosophical' claim. What it criticizes is not a scientific procedure as such, e.g., the research of nature or research conducted by logical analysis, but rather the deficiency of the methodological justification found in the uses described above. To base philosophical legitimation upon such a critical enterprise is, after all, nothing novel. There is really no justification for philosophizing except by reference to the fact that mankind always has pursued philosophy, and even when this has frequently been under the negative sign of opposition to the claim of metaphysics, e.g., in the case of skepticism, the critique of language, or of scientific theory.

But the claim of a philosophical hermeneutic extends even further. It makes the claim to universality. This claim rests on the view that understanding and agreement are not primarily and originally a way of behaving towards a text acquired through methodical training. Rather, they are the culminating form of human social life, which in its final formalization is a speech community. Nothing is left out of this speech community; absolutely no experience of the world is excluded. Neither the specialization and increasingly esoteric operations of the modern sciences nor material labor and its form of organization, nor the political institutions of domination and governance which bind the society together find themselves outside this universal medium of practical reason (or unreason). Now the only thing which remains in contention is the universality of the hermeneutic experience. Is it not limited by its linguistic culmination to a circle of communicative understanding, which, it would seem, could be circumvented in a variety of ways? One has only to consider the fact of the sciences themselves and their theory building. Habermas immediately sees in this an objection: "Obviously modern science can raise the legitimate charge that in order to achieve true statements about 'things' it needs to proceed monologically rather than heeding the mirror of human discourse."[4] He nonetheless recognizes that such 'monologically' constructed theories of science must be rendered understandable in everyday dialogue. But, he sees in this a new problem for hermeneutics, one which it acquires in its intercourse with such theoretical languages. Hermeneutics is alleged to be concerned, both originally and exclusively, with colloquially constituted and transmitted culture. It is supposed to be a new undertaking to explain how language emerges from the dialogue structure and how it makes possible the construction of rigorous theory.

I do not understand these statements. The difference between technical and colloquial speech has certainly existed for thousands of years. Is
mathematics something new? Has it not always been that the professional,
the shaman, the doctor have been defined through their use of ways of understanding which are not generally understandable? What can be seen as a
modern problem is, at most, that the professional no longer sees it as his
task to translate his knowledge into general colloquial speech. Thus this
task of hermeneutic integration becomes its own special task. However, the
hermeneutic task as such is not altered by this.—Or perhaps Habermas only
means that theoretical constructions like those which appear in the fields of
mathematics and the mathematically oriented contemporary natural sciences can be 'understood' without recourse to colloquial speech. This is
certainly indisputable. It would be absurd to assert that all our experience
of the world is nothing other than a linguistic process or that something like
the development of our sense of color would consist entirely of the differentiation of color words we use.[5] In addition, genetic discoveries such as
those of Piaget, to which Habermas refers, and which make it likely that
there exists an operational use of categories which is pre-linguistic, render
ridiculous every thesis which seeks to deny other extra-linguistic forms of
understanding by appealing to a linguistic universality. Lending additional
support to the genetic discoveries such as Piaget's are all non-linguistic
forms of communication such as those examined by Helmuth Plessner,[6]
Michael Polanyi,[7] and Hans Kunz.[8] Speaking is, in contrast to this linguistic universality, communicated existence. And it is indeed in the communi-
cability of understanding that the theme of hermeneutics lies, as Habermas
himself correctly recognizes. If the desire is to avoid an argument about
words, one is better advised to renounce the use of quotation marks and,
e.g., not imply that artificial systems of symbols are 'understood' in the
same way as our linguistic interpretation of the world is understood. Of
course it can then no longer be said that the natural sciences can make
assertions about 'the things' without "heeding the mirror of human discourse." What kind of 'things' are known by the natural sciences? Hermeneutics' claim is, and remains, the same. It claims to integrate into the
unity of linguistic world interpretation that which is not understood, or that
which is uncommon: 'understandable' only to the initiates. Modern science
has developed its own specialized and discipline-specific languages, its own
artificial symbolic systems. Within these languages and systems it does operate 'monologically', i.e., it does attain 'understanding' and 'agreement'
independently of all colloquial communication. However, this cannot be
taken seriously as a legitimate objection against the claim of hermeneutics.
Habermas, who raises this objection, knows himself that such 'understanding' and expertise (which constitute the pathos of modern social engineers

and experts) lack precisely the kind of reflection which could give it social accountability.

He is so well aware of this that in order to assist reflection to secure its proper rights he provides a broadly painted example of a critical reflective science, one which is intended to serve as an example for social reflection: psychoanalysis. Psychoanalysis exercises critical, emancipatory reflection in its attempts to free through reflection defective communication from its obstructions and in its attempts to re-establish communication. Such emancipatory reflection is also to be encountered in the social sphere. It is not only the neurotic patient who, in the defense of his neurosis, suffers from systematically distorted communication. Indeed, every social consciousness that finds itself in agreement with the ruling social system, thereby supporting its coercive character, also suffers fundamentally from such systematically distorted communication. This is the presupposition, itself never discussed, of Habermas' argumentation.

It is the task of the psychoanalyst to engage the patient, a person compelled to seek out the analyst by the desire to become well, in a project of reflection. This project is one of the highest responsibility, and at the same time a liberating activity. This also holds true in the social realm, where every form of the coerciveness of power must be made conscious and must be dissolved. Habermas and Giegel in particular make this concrete in a variety of ways under the basic theme of being able to get behind language. By this they mean primarily a certain sense of understanding coming under the influence of technology, through which the ambiguity of spoken communication would be overcome. But that is not all. Habermas does indeed touch on such metalinguistic possibilities, but to him the significance of psychoanalysis is something else again, namely its methodological peculiarity of being at the same time an explanatory science (and therewith possibly a technology) and an emancipatory reflection. In his view psychoanalysis must be able to get behind language. This is required in the case of neurosis, as here we find such a fundamental and systematic disruption of communication that the therapeutic dialogue would surely fail if it did not proceed under wholly special and complicated conditions. In such a dialogue there is a supporting agreement[9] which binds together the participants. This cannot be dismissed, even if in the end the analysis receives its justification in the patient's affirmation, even if the patient returns to normal communicative ability after the symptoms are eliminated. On this point Habermas makes extensive use of Lorenzer's illuminating descriptions of 'speech disruption' ['*Sprachzerstörung*'].

However, where it concerns his own work, he adds that just as the patient learns to see through the concealed constraint, to dissolve inhibitions and consciously overcome them, in the social realm concealed constraint and societal power relationships can be seen through and overcome through a critique of ideology. Philosophical hermeneutics' trusting optimism concerning dialogue cannot accomplish this. It only perpetuates a pseudo-understanding based on the prevailing societal prejudices. It does not possess critical reflection. What is required is a depth-hermeneutic interpretation of "systematically distorted communication." This is required, as we "have reason to be convinced that the background consensus of long-established traditions and language games can be a coercively integrated consciousness and a result of pseudo-communication not only in isolated instances of pathologically disturbed family systems, but also in entire social systems."[10] Habermas resists the supposition that communication is limited to the "traditional realm of accepted convictions," and in this sees the impossible claim of depth-hermeneutics to offer explanation and understanding on the basis of its own resources alone. It is in this sense that he has obviously understood my suggestions concerning the social role of the doctor and the limiting conditions of psychotherapy.

In fact, this objection is close to that which I made concerning the relationship between patient and doctor. Insofar as the work of emancipatory reflection is to proceed within the context of professional responsibility, the patient and the doctor are operating within, and confined to, a specific set of social roles. It cannot fall within the socially legitimate function of the doctor, or the lay analyst, to move outside of the professionally therapeutic situation and 'treat' others as 'ill' by engaging in emancipatory reflection concerning their social consciousness. [. . .] Such 'treatment' is not to be described as a technique, but rather as a common work of reflection. I also recognize that the analyst cannot simply set aside his analytic experience and knowledge when he, no longer a doctor, plays his social role as a partner in society. But this alters nothing regarding the disruptive character of the infiltration of psychoanalytic competence into social intercourse. I do not claim that this is avoidable. We write letters to handwriting experts, exposing ourselves to them, without intending to appeal to their professional competence. Further, when outside of such specific areas of competence, while engaged in dialogue, listening to explanations, and while being affectively influenced by others, we do not refrain from bringing into play our knowledge of humanity, information from various quarters and independent observations. This does not mean that the openness required for 'pure' rational conversation has been curtailed. One has only to think about something like Sartre's famous discussion of the look of the other.

Nonetheless, the hermeneutic situation found in the relationship of social partnership is very different from that evident in the analytical relationship. When I tell someone of a dream, and I am not led to do so by some analytic intention or even by being in the role of a patient, then what

I say obviously is not meant to invite an analytic dream interpretation. If this is done the listener has failed to maintain himself within the proper hermeneutic scope. The intention is much rather to share one's own unconscious play of dream fantasies, just as one takes part in the fantasies of fairy tales or literary imagination. This hermeneutic claim is legitimate, and has nothing to do with the phenomenon of resistance which is so well known in analysis. It is thoroughly justified to put this aside if one is not prepared to enter into the hermeneutic situation. It is justified, e.g., rather than attempting to understand Jean-Paul's works of fantasy as the pregnant play of the power of imagination, to interpret them as the gravely serious unconscious symbolization of a disturbed biography. Such a hermeneutic critique of the legitimacy of depth-psychology is in no way limited to the aesthetic joys of erudition. For example, when one seeks to convince another with passionate emotion in a political question, indeed with arguments so sharp that they reach the point of anger, the former has a hermeneutic claim to counter-arguments and not the rejoinder that "He who becomes angry is in the wrong." We will later return to this relationship between psychoanalytic and hermeneutic reflection and the dangers of confusing these two 'language games'.

Now the exemplary significance which psychoanalysis, in its role of emancipatory reflection, is supposed to have for the critique of hermeneutics and the critique of societal communication is its therapeutic function. Reflection liberates one from that which remains incomprehensible, from that which dominates one, by making it comprehensible. This is obviously a different sense of critical reflection than is meant in hermeneutic reflection, which, as I have described, destroys self-understanding and reveals a lack of methodological justification. And, even though the leading psychoanalytically oriented criticism does not contradict such hermeneutic criticism, I would nonetheless like to show that hermeneutic criticism must reject the former's claim to provide an exemplary model. However, psychoanalytic critique is not adequate for hermeneutics. The hermeneutic sciences defend themselves with hermeneutic reflection against the thesis that their procedures are unscientific, that it denies the 'objectivity' of science. On this point the critique of ideology and philosophical hermeneutics are in agreement. But the former turns its critique against hermeneutics insofar as the latter is alleged to perpetuate unremitting adherence to all things traditional and to prejudices transmitted from the past. However, since the irruption of the industrial revolution and of science into social life the element of tradition is supposed to have played only a secondary role.

K. O. Apel most certainly expresses such a critique, and in doing so obviously misunderstands what hermeneutics means when it speaks of application [*Applikation*].[11] Application concerns itself with an implicit moment of all understanding. One should really take seriously my analysis of hermeneutic experience. Hermeneutic experience has as its object the successful *praxis* of the hermeneutic sciences; in this there is certainly no 'conscious application' at work from which one could fear an ideological corruption of knowledge. Betti has already upset himself over this misunderstanding. Obviously an unclarity in the concept of conscious application is at work here. It is completely true, as Apel ascertains, that bringing conscious application into a relationship with the objectivistic self-understanding of the sciences of understanding [*der verstehenden Wissenschaften*] is a hermeneutic demand. And, in just the same way, hermeneutics demands that conscious application be brought to bear upon the living *praxis* of understanding. A philosophical hermeneutic, as I have attempted to develop it, is 'normative' to the degree that it aims to replace a bad philosophy with a better one. But, it does not propagate a new *praxis*, and it is certainly out of the question to think that at times hermeneutic *praxis*, in the concrete, is guided by a consciousness of application or an intention directed at application, let alone application directed at the conscious legitimation of an accepted tradition.

Certainly a false self-understanding has repercussions on practical activity, and just as surely an appropriate self-understanding has the opposite effect. From a theoretical point of view the latter destroys practical distortions which have arisen from the theory. However, it is by no means the task of an effective-historical reflection to strive for actualization and attempt to bring about 'application'. To the contrary, its task is to impede and undermine all attempts to understand the tradition in terms of the most tempting, seductive opportunities which are being actualized. Its tools are not only the formal discipline of the scientific method, but also concrete, substantive reflection. Apel and I are in complete agreement when he says: "An interpretive method conscious of the role of application has a sphere of responsibility. Entirely within that sphere is the necessity, under some circumstances, to hinder the present understanding of the latest application. This is done in the service of an unlimited understanding." I would go even further and say instead that under all circumstances this must be the case. I say under all circumstances not because I see this as a fundamental rule of conscious application, but because it is necessary for fulfillment of the true duty to the scientific. This duty seems to me to be obviously violated in those instances in which ideological prejudices remain in the background and yet remain effective as a *vis à tergo*, remaining so because a pseudo-exact methodological deliberation refuses to acknowledge it. In these points I, along with Apel, see a danger of corruption. Whether this, as Apel claims, applies to the hermeneutic human sciences he calls 'existential' I cannot say, as I do not know what he means. However, this certainly does not apply to those human sciences from which a philosophical hermeneutic takes its bearings, or even to itself. Here, in contrast, hermeneutic reflection may even become 'practical': it renders every ideology suspect in that it makes prejudices conscious.

The best way to test such things is with concrete examples. In order to remain within my area of competence let us examine the history of presocratic thought in this century. Here every interpretation brings particular prejudices into play: in Joel the scientific-religious prejudice, in Karl Reinhardt the prejudice of the logical enlightenment, Werner Jaeger's unexamined religious monotheism, as W. Bröcker in his *Aristoteles* has shown, and my own prejudices when I myself attempt to understand 'the divinities' in light of classical philosophy and philosophical thought, inspired certainly by Heidegger's exposition of the question of being. Certainly in all these cases a guiding prejudice is to be observed, one that becomes productive precisely because it corrects previously held prejudices. In these cases previously determined meanings are not applied to texts; rather, one seeks to understand what is there, indeed to understand better by seeing through the prejudice of another. But this perspicacity can only be achieved by seeing with new eyes what is there. Hermeneutic reflection cannot be detached from hermeneutic *praxis*.

Accordingly, one must be careful to avoid the inclination to understand this type of hermeneutic movement of research according to the model of immediate progress. Apel has greatly enriched the discussion of the hermeneutical problematic in his accounts of Peirce and Royce. He has done so by working out the relations of *praxis* in all understanding of meaning, and he is completely correct in his attendant claim for the idea of an unlimited community of interpretation. Certainly only such a community is suited to legitimize the claims to truth made by those attempting to achieve agreement. Nonetheless, I doubt whether it is justified to link this legitimation with the idea of progress. The multiplicity of interpretive possibilities to be tested in no way excludes the possibility that they may mutually overshadow each other. In addition, the fact that dialectical antitheses in the process of interpretive *praxis* emerge is no guarantee of an approach to a true synthesis. In these areas of the human sciences one must view the 'results' of the interpretive process not so much in terms of progress, as it always offers only a partial perspective, but rather as the sinking away and decay of projects which stand in the way of knowledge; it is the revival of language and the reacquisition of meaning that has been given by tradition. It is only according to the measuring stick of an absolute knowledge, something foreign to us, that this is a threatening relativism.

Thus the attempt to equate the naive application of tradition, which before the rise of historical consciousness ruled the movement of tradition, with the moment of application in all understanding also seems to me a misunderstanding. Without a doubt the *praxis* of understanding has been modified by the rupture of tradition and the rise of historical consciousness. Nonetheless it seems to me, as before, not entirely convincing that historical consciousness and its outgrowth in the historical human sciences should be considered the reason that the power of tradition was eroded. Rather, it seems much more likely that the rupture of tradition is determinative for the beginning of the modern period and reaches its first radical peak in the French Revolution. It seems far more likely to me that the historical human sciences found their direction as a reaction to this rupture of tradition. Certainly it is correct that the human sciences, despite their romantic heritage, are themselves a broken phenomenon of tradition, and in a certain sense continue the critical enlightenment. I called this time of theirs a re-reflection of the enlightenment. But on the other hand within them are obviously active impulses of the romantic restoration. Whether one applauds this or deplores it does not alter in the slightest the fact that these specific epistemological elements are able to emerge at this time. One might refer to something in the vein of Raumer's *History of the Staufer Epoch* [*Geschichte der Stauferzeit*]. That is anything but conscious application. It is much rather an inner penetration of critical enlightenment which belongs to the essence of the historical sciences. It criticizes the naive extension of delivered opinion, of traditions which continue to be effective, co-determining the historical horizons, and it does not do this just in the homeland of the romantic human sciences. For example, the history of Athens in the Peloponnesian Wars, the way one judges Pericles or 'Cleon the Tanner', appears astonishingly different in the tradition of imperial Germany than in that of American democracy, despite how young both of these traditions are. This is no different for the tradition of Marxism. [. . .] Hermeneutic reflection is limited to opening up opportunities for knowledge which would otherwise remain unperceived. Hermeneutic reflection is not itself a criterion of truth.

In other areas the discussion of conscious application is also sufficiently filled with misunderstanding. It remains quite astonishing to me that in cases of a director or a musician Apel even mentions actualization in the sense of conscious application. This suggests that the entire interpretation must be guided by the idea that the interpretation itself will be unaffected by the fact that the work is once again coming to life. However, we actually praise a theatrical production or a musical performance as a successful interpretation because the work itself, in its true substance, is newly expressed. And when, to the contrary, it is demanded of us that we produce or perform a work in accord with current tendencies and consciously incorporate allusions to the present we find this, justifiably, to be inappropriate.

On the other hand it seems to me that the image we have of the simultaneous translator, which is indeed given as the model for the hermeneutic task, is vastly under-interpreted when it is misunderstood to be just a task of translation. Rather, the translator has the task of bringing the selection to be interpreted into a language which the other can comprehend. This seems to me to indicate that at times an objectivistic concept of meaning and transparency of meaning dominates here, something which is not really appropriate to the situation.

Hermeneutic experience has a tension within itself originating not with the science of the modern period, but a tension which has been there since the inception of hermeneutic questioning; and, indeed, this is a tension which will never be dissipated. Hermeneutic experience does not go so far as to allow itself to be classified within the idealistic schema of obtaining self knowledge through the being of others that meaning can be completely grasped and passed on. [. . .] Has not the impetus of hermeneutics always been to 'understand', through interpretation, the foreign, the unfathomable will of the gods, the message of salvation, or the works of the classic authors? And does this not mean that one who understands will always be in a subordinate position in respect to one who speaks and who will be understood?

Certainly this original meaning of hermeneutics has been cast into sharp relief by the modern period's break with tradition and the emergence of a completely different type of exact ideal of knowledge. But the fundamental presupposition of the hermeneutic project, a presupposition which no one wants to acknowledge and which I am attempting to restore, has always been the appropriation of a dominant meaning. It is not something especially original when in my investigation I support the hermeneutic productivity of temporal distance and fundamentally emphasize the finitude and openendedness of all understanding and effective-historical reflection. That is nothing more than exposing the true hermeneutic thematic, which finds its real legitimation completely in the experience of history. This has nothing to do with the transparency of meaning, and 'history' must always guard itself against humanistic attenuation. The experience of history is not the experience of meaning and plans and reason; only under the eternalizing gaze of the philosopher of absolute knowledge could the claim be raised to grasp reason in history. And thus the experience of history truly places the hermeneutic project right back in its proper place. It is its task to ever again decipher history's fragments of meaning, fragments which border on the dark contingency of facticity and which relentlessly advance upon the twilight into which the future of every present consciousness fades. Even the 'fore-conception of completion', which belongs to the structure of understanding, stresses in its 'fore-conception' that the dominance of that which is to be understood cannot be entirely retrieved by an interpretation. Thus one is surprised when according to Apel, Habermas, and with a significant modification according to Giegel, hermeneutic reflection elevates in glistening light an explanatory science of full idealistic transparency of meaning. This is the result of the exemplary role which these authors grant to psychoanalysis.

With this we return to the legitimacy of emancipatory reflection's transference and application of psychoanalysis to the social sphere. Much depends upon how far the legitimacy of psychoanalysis' knowledge extends. Upon it depends whether history is impenetrable contingency, denied by those who are clever enough to foresee it and prophesy, or whether this fact represents only a not-yet, no longer affecting a humanity grown reasonable. Certainly it is no accident that this science has found great regard within the discussion of hermeneutics, and Apel's, Habermas' and Giegel's presentations are richly informative. But the question remains whether their anthropological results have been correctly formulated. Apel says, in effect, that the natural organism is entirely sublated in the conscious control of the instincts. The ideal represented in this depends upon the legitimacy of the transference of psychoanalysis to this sphere. Mankind is, after all, a social being.

In order to support this, Habermas lays the broad foundation of a meta-hermeneutical theory of communicative competence. After he has sketched a theory of the origination of the ego-id-super-ego structure on the basis of the experience of depth-psychology, the transition to the social realm appears to him entirely unquestionable. On the basis of such a general theory of communicative competence a "theory of the acquisition of the fundamental qualifications of role-guided behavior" becomes the counter-piece. I do not know if I understand Habermas correctly. The expression 'communicative competence' is obviously modeled after that of Chomsky's linguistic competence and means a facile mastery of the activities of understanding and agreement, equally facile as the master of speech that Chomsky intends with his expression. Within Chomsky's thought the linguistic ideal consists of developing a theory of linguistic competence, and in the end constructively explaining all exceptional occurrences and modifications of speech. Following this lead, all colloquial agreement would necessarily accomplish something similar. Even though research has not yet advanced sufficiently far, it would not alter the fundamental situation that with the help of the knowledge of the conditions of systematically disrupted communication, agreement of an ideal dimension would be reached, one which would necessarily bring about consensus. By itself such a consensus could be a rational criterion of truth. Without such a theory to combat it, one would fall prey to a 'supporting agreement' of forced consensus without being able to see through it.

In the final analysis the theory of communicative competence serves the legitimation of the claim to see through distorted social communication, and corresponds to psychoanalysis' accomplishments in therapeutic discussion. Nonetheless, there is one thing which is not quite correct. Here we are dealing with groups, groups formed of individuals living in agreement. Between groups agreement is destroyed and sought again. But, this does not occur between individuals and the speech community, a community from which they are split apart by their neuroses. Who is it here who has been split apart? What desymbolization must occur, for instance with the word 'democracy'? On the basis of what competence will this be done? It goes without saying that behind these notions there must be a concept of freedom for all. Habermas says accordingly: rational speech free from coercion always presupposes a certain anticipation of the right life. Only then can such speech be successful. "The idea of truth, which measures itself on true consensus, includes the idea of coming of age."[12]

This criterion of truth appears to me to be clearly recognizable as metaphysical in origin; it derives the idea of the true from the idea of the good, and Being from the concept of 'pure' intelligence. The concept of pure intelligence has its origin in the Middle Ages' doctrine of intelligence, and is incorporated in the angel, who has the decisive advantage of being able to see God in his essence. It is difficult for me not to charge Habermas with false ontological self-understanding, something which also seems to me to occur in Apel's sublation of natural being into rationality. Of course Habermas accuses me of false ontologizing, e.g., because I am not able to see authority and enlightenment as mutually exclusive. According to Habermas, this is false as it presupposes that legitimizing recognition can come into play both without force and without the agreement that is the foundation of authority.[13] According to Habermas, one is not allowed to make this presupposition. Is one really never allowed to do this? Does not Habermas make the same presupposition when he recognizes that such a non-forceful agreement would come about under the guiding idea of social life free from coercion and dominance? I myself did not have such 'ideal' conditions in mind, but rather all the circumstances of concrete experience in terms of which one speaks of natural authority and the following which it finds. It seems to me a dogmatic prejudice concerning what one means by human 'reason' to always speak in such cases of coercive communication; e.g., where love, the choice of ideals, submissiveness, voluntary superiority or subordination have reached a level of stability. Thus, I am not able to see how communicative competence and its theoretical mastery in the social sphere are supposed to eliminate the barriers between groups, groups which in reciprocal critique charge each other with harboring a coercive character in their present ways of understanding. In this instance "the gentle power of productivity"[14] seems indispensable, and along with it the acceptance of the claim of a completely different type of competence, specifically that of political activity. The goal of this activity is to bring about possibilities of communication where they had previously been absent. [. . .]

Now it is obvious that the phrase which I occasionally use, that much depends on establishing a connection with tradition, promotes misunderstanding. Contained within this is in no sense a preference for that which is customary, to which one must be blindly subservient. On the contrary, the phrase 'connection to tradition' means only that the tradition is not exhausted by the heritage one knows and is conscious of. In this way tradition cannot be relegated to an adequate consciousness of history. Alteration of the existing conditions is no less a form of connection to tradition than is a defense of existing conditions. Tradition exists only in constantly becoming other than it is. To 'establish a connection' with tradition suggests itself forcefully as a formulation of an experience in which our plans and wishes constantly outstrip reality, that is, they are without connection to reality. Such a connection depends, therefore, upon the mediation between the anticipations of the desirable and the possibilities of what can be done, between empty wishes and real wants, i.e., upon imagining our anticipations into the stuff of reality.

This does not truly happen without critical discrimination [*Unterscheiden*]. Indeed, I would say that only what is 'determined' ['*entscheidet*'] in such a relation of *praxis* remains real critique. A critique which in general opposes the prejudices of another individual or the dominant social prejudices because of their coercive character and, on the other hand, claims to dissolve such a delusory relation by communication finds itself [. . .] in very bad circumstances. It must ignore fundamental differences. In the case of psychoanalysis the patient's suffering and desire to be cured is given as a supporting foundation for the therapeutic activity of her doctor. The doctor interposes his authority and, not without necessity, insistently presses for the unshrouding of repressed motivations. In this situation the voluntary subordination of one to the other is the supporting basis. In social life, on the contrary, the resistance of the opponent, and the resistance directed against the opponent, is a general presupposition held by all.

This seems to me so self-evident that I am amazed that my critics, certainly Giegel and fundamentally even Habermas, say of me that on the basis of my hermeneutics I am inclined to dispute the legitimacy of revolutionary consciousness and the will to bring about change. Against Habermas I would argue that the doctor-patient relationship is not an adequate model for social dialogue. In opposition to his analogy I pose the following question: "With respect to which self-interpretation of social conscious-ness—and all convention is such—is covert questioning and deception, as might be found in the revolutionary desire for change, not out of place, and in respect to which is it out of place?" The response to this question, in the case of the psychoanalyst, is given in terms of the authority of the knowl-edgeable doctor. However, in the sphere of the social and political the spe-cial basis of communicative analysis is lacking by which the ill voluntarily give themselves over to treatment because of an insight into their illness. And thus such questions seem to me to be hermeneutically unanswerable. They rest upon political-social convictions. This does not in any sense mean that the revolutionary will to change, as distinguished from the endorse-ment of tradition, cannot be legitimated. Neither the former conviction nor the latter is capable of, nor requires, a theoretical legitimation through hermeneutics. The theory of hermeneutics cannot decide from within itself whether or not the presupposition is correct that society is ruled by class conflict and that no basis for dialogue exists between the classes. Obviously my critics have misconstrued the claim of legitimacy implicit in reflection on the hermeneutic experience. Otherwise they could take offense at the thesis that wherever agreement is possible solidarity is presupposed. They make the same presupposition. There is no support for the insinuation that with 'supporting agreement' I recognize one side more than the other, that I acknowledge conservative solidarity but fail to equally acknowledge revolutionary solidarity. It is the idea of reason itself that cannot give up the idea of general agreement. That is the solidarity which unites us all. [. . .]

Let us return to something which can be discussed, viz., the theoret-ical foundations of what is hermeneutic *praxis*. In one point I agree with my critics, and have them to thank for forcing me to raise this point: As the critique of ideology moves the 'artificial doctrine' of understanding over into self-reflection, it also seems to me that hermeneutic reflection is an integral moment of understanding itself, and indeed to such a great degree that the division of reflection from *praxis* contains a dogmatic error, an error which applies equally to the concept of 'emancipatory reflection'. This is also the reason why I find the concept of 'emancipation' a poor description of the step by step movement through various forms that devel-oping spirit takes in Hegel's *Phenomenology*. Certainly in Hegel one finds operative the experience of the dialectic as change through the becoming of consciousness. However, it seems to me that Bubner is quite justified in raising a point concerning the phenomenological dialectic of Hegel, namely that one form of spirit which is derived from another is not truly derived from the other, but rather unfolds another immediacy.[15] The step by step movement of the forms of spirit is postulated, as it were, from the point of view of their completion, and cannot be deduced from their beginning. This is what brought me to argue that it is crucial to read the *Phenomenology of Spirit* backwards, the way in which it was truly thought. That is to say, to read it moving from the subject to the substance extended within it and the consciousness appropriate to it. This tendency of reversal contains a fundamental critique of the idea of absolute knowledge. The absolute transparency of knowledge amounts to the same thing as an idealistic concealment of a bad infinity in which the finite being man makes his experiences.

I express myself in the language of Hegel. This has become an object of critical attention, [. . .] because I remove the conceptual-linguistic materials from its systematic context.[16] This critique is not without justification, and is especially cogent in the case of Hegel, as my critical engagement with Hegel in *Truth and Method* is certainly quite unsatisfactory.[17] All the same, in this case I would also like to defend the descriptive benefit of thought being engaged with the classical figures. Insofar as I apply Hegel's description of the concept of dialectical experience of consciousness to the widest sense of experience, my critical point vis-à-vis Hegel emerges, in my view, decisively. Completed experience is not the completion of knowledge, but rather the completed openness for new experience. That is the truth which hermeneutic experience presses home against the concept of absolute knowledge. In this truth is not ambiguous.

Concerning the talk of emancipation, the situation is the same. The concept of reflection which is used in this context seems to me not undogmatic. It does not express the becoming of consciousness, which belongs alone to *praxis*, but rests, as Habermas once expressed it, upon a 'counterfactual agreement'. Contained within is the claim to foreknowledge—before the practical confrontation—foreknowledge of that about which one does not agree. However, it is not the meaning of hermeneutic *praxis* to take such a counter-factual agreement as its beginning, but rather to make such agreement possible and then bring it about, which, in fact, means nothing other than to convince by means of concrete critique. The dogmatic character of the concept of reflection which Habermas takes as a foundation comes forth in the following example. In a critique, which I take to be justified, of society's superstitious belief in experts he demands that society: "free itself from the reflective stage of a technologically limited rationality."[18] In this is implied a concept of stages which seems false to me. This is also the case concerning the "new function of science" in which society is considered to be that which lies in the rational consensus of the citizens; and in this the rationality of being able to make, to bring about, what Aristotle called '*technē*', is another, not a lower, type of reflection. Hermeneutic reflection is directed specifically at the illumination of these matters. This cannot be truly attained without a constant, reciprocal playing out of critical arguments, but in a way that reflects the concrete convictions of the partners in conversation.

The ideal of the removal, the sublation, of a natural certainty in rational, conscious motivation represents, in my view, a dogmatic exaggeration which is incompatible with the *condition humaine*. This is the case even in the areas of individual and depth-psychology. Already supposed in the contrast between sickness and health, between the prescription of medical help and restoration through healing, is that analysis is limited in its extent—just as the analyst himself, as the doctrine of 'counter-transference' recognizes, is never completely analyzed. I do not feel competent to draw the anthropological-psychological consequences from this fundamental situation of depth-psychology, and would refer only to the concept of equilibrium and the form of being of play around the situation of equilibrium, which in other circumstances I have used as an ontological characteristic of health.[19]

On the other hand, when Habermas speaks of "depth-hermeneutics" I must heed my own thesis to the extent that I find the reduction of hermeneutics to "cultural transmission" and the ideal of the transparency of meaning, characterizations allegedly legitimate in this context, to be idealistically diluted. To limit the understanding of meaning neither to *mens auctoris* nor to *mens actoris* is a point dear to me. To be sure this does not mean that understanding peaks in the explication of unconscious motive, but rather, that understanding draws out the thread of meaning in all directions, beyond the limited horizon of the individual so that the transmission of history will speak. As Apel has correctly emphasized, the hermeneutic dimension of meaning is bound to the unending conversation of an ideal interpretive community. In *Truth and Method*,[20] I have attempted to demonstrate why Collingwood's re-enactment theory cannot be carried out. Accordingly, I must examine a confusion of language games, frequently the opening of a real comic sewer, comprised of depth-psychological interpretations of literary works or the historical activities of their authors. Hermeneutic *praxis* and its discipline differentiates itself from the way in which a simple technique is learned, whether this is called a social technique or a critical method, insofar as hermeneutic *praxis* always contains within it an effective historical factor which co-determines the consciousness of understanding. However, in this situation a reversal is also found. That which is understood always develops a certain persuasive power which takes a part in the development of new convictions. In no sense do I deny that the abstraction of understanding from one's own specialized meaning represents a justified effort. He who will understand does not need to endorse what he understands. And nonetheless I maintain that hermeneutic experience teaches us that the power of abstraction is always a limited power. That which one understands always also speaks for itself. It is upon just this that the richness of the hermeneutic universe rests. As it, within the full dimensions of its field of play, brings itself into action, it forces he who understands to place his prejudices at stake. All these are the results of reflection which have grown out of *praxis*, and out of *praxis* alone. One should be lenient with me, the old philologist, in my characterization of all this as 'being towards the text'. The hermeneutic experience truly is woven completely and utterly into the general being of human *praxis*. Although the understanding of that which is written is significant, it is included only in a secondary fashion. This extends just as far as the willingness of rational beings to engage in rational discussion extends.

With this I note the lack of recognition of the fact that hermeneutics and rhetoric share this area, the area of convincing arguments (although not the logically convincing arguments). In the modern scientific culture the defense of rhetoric is difficult. [. . .] Even though the art of speaking is concerned with affects, as has been clear since antiquity, it nonetheless does not in any way fall from the rational sphere, and Vico rightly presses home a unique value found here: the *copia*, the abundance of viewpoints. On the other side, an assertion such as Habermas' to the effect that rhetoric contains a coercive character and must be circumvented in the interest of coercion-free rational dialogue seems to me to be shockingly unrealistic. If it is the case that rhetoric contains a coercive moment then it is nonetheless certain that social *praxis*—and in truth also revolutionary *praxis*—would not even be conceivable without this coercive moment. I find it noteworthy that the scientific culture of our epoch has not diminished the importance of rhetoric, but rather has, in a supplementary fashion, increased it, as a glance at the mass-media, or even Habermas' cogent analysis of 'public opinion', shows.

The concept of manipulation is in this context genuinely ambiguous. Every emotional influence occurring through speech is in a certain sense such a manipulation. And this is not just an empty social technique, just as rhetoric was an integral moment of social life at one time. Aristotle had already characterized rhetoric as not a *technē*, but rather a *dynamis*, so strongly did it belong to the *zoon logon echon*. Even the technical forms of shaping opinion which our industrial society has developed always contain at some point a moment of consent, be it on the side of the consumer who can withhold his agreement, or be it, and this is decisive, in the way our mass media are not simply extensions of a unitary political will, but rather are the showplace of political controversies, which for their part both reflect and determine political occurrences in society. A theory of depth-hermeneutics is supposed to justify a socio-critical emancipatory reflection, or from it is even expected a universal theory of natural language. In contrast to these expectations, such a theory is alleged to endorse "the principle of rational discourse as necessarily regulative of each real discourse, and even, if it is so distorted, to derive such a principle."[21] This implies, and against its will—especially in regards to the organization of the modern social state and the ways in which public opinion is formed within the state—the role of the social engineer who creates without liberating. This would place a depth-hermeneutic in the position of being the keeper of the means of public information and would give its supposed truth the power of monopoly on public opinion. This is indeed no fictitious assumption. Rhetoric cannot be argued away as if it were not needed or as if nothing depended upon it.

Now it is certain that rhetoric as well as hermeneutics are not, as culminating forms of life, independent of what Habermas calls the anticipation of the right life. Such a thing lies at the foundation of all social partnership and its attempts to reach agreement. But also the same holds true for this, that the same ideal of reason that must guide every attempt to convince, regardless of the side from which it starts, forbids one from claiming for oneself the correct insight on the basis of the delusion of the other. The ideal of living together in coercion-free communication is thus just as binding as it is indeterminate. The life goals included within these formal frames differ greatly. It is also true that the anticipation of the correct life, which in fact is essential for all practical reason, must make itself concrete. That is to say, it must consciously appropriate the sharp contrast between the empty desires of wish and the true goals of active volition.

What is important here, it seems to me, can be recognized as an old problem that Aristotle already had in mind in his critique of Plato's universal Idea of the Good. The human good is something to be encountered in human *praxis*, and it is indeterminable without the concrete situation in which one thing is preferred to another. This alone, and not a counterfactual agreement, is the critical experience of the Good. It must be worked through in the concrete circumstances of the situation. Such an idea of the correct life as a universal idea is 'empty'.[22] Herein lies the portentous fact that the knowledge of practical wisdom is not a knowledge that is conscious of its ascendancy over the ignorant. Moreover, one finds that everyone claims to know the right for all. For the living together of humans in society this means that others must be convinced. This is certainly not in the sense that politics and the shaping of social life would be nothing other than a mere discussion group, acting as if discussion free from coercion and the oppressiveness of power is the true remedy. Politics demands from reason that it guide our interests in the service of the development of the will. Further, all social and political manifestations of the will are dependent upon rhetoric's construction of public convictions. This includes, and I mean by this that it belongs to the concept of reason, that one must always reckon with the possibility that the opposite conviction, whether of the individual or in the social realm, could be correct. The way of hermeneutic experience has led me to put forth a claim for a concept that obviously is of the widest application. I readily admit that specific elements of the Western cultural tradition have worked themselves into this concept. I refer here to the concept of play. We know this concept from other contexts beyond that of the modern economic theory of play. This concept reflects, in my view, much more than this; it reflects the plurality which is tied to the exercise of human reason, as well as the plurality which brings together opposing powers into a unity of the whole. The play of powers supplements itself through the play of convictions, argumentation, and experiences. In its right application the fruitfulness of the schema of dialogue is maintained. In the exchange of powers as in the self evaluation of one's views a community forms itself, a community which surpasses the individual and the group to which he belongs.

Translated by George H. Leiner

Notes

*This essay, originally titled "Replik," was the final contribution to a discussion volume addressing *Hermeneutik und Ideologiekritik* (Frankfurt: Suhrkamp Verlag, 1971), pp. 283–317. Other contributors to the volume included Karl-Otto Apel, Claus v. Bormann, Rüdiger Bubner, Hans Joachim Giegel, and Jürgen Habermas.—ED.

1. Cf. my discussion of the topic "The Boundaries of Expertise," from a talk held in Darmstadt: "Man and his Future," 1967, pp. 160–168.

2. This is just what Ernst Schmidt has correctly demonstrated in his criticism of the book *Moral Knowledge and its Methodology in Aristotle* by J. Donald Monan (*Philosophische Rundschau*, 17 Jg., 1971), p. 249ff.

3. Plato, Seventh Letter, 343 A 7: "Because it is not the 'soul' of the speaker which is refuted."

4. Gadamer refers to a remark of Habermas from "The Hermeneutic Claim to Universality" in *Hermeneutik und Ideologiekritik*, p. 129 (English translation above, p. 251).—ED.

5. Von Bormann, p. 98 [Gadamer is here referring to Claus von Bormann's "Die Zweideutigkeit der hermeneutischen Erfahrung" in *Hermeneutik und Ideologiekritik*, pp. 83–119.—ED.], goes so far to say of me "that the words which are understood are really nothing more than words,"—"without concrete meaning . . . " and traces this to a formalization of hermeneutical questioning which has gone too far. But here he falls victim to the ambiguity of which he accuses me. He underestimates the essential relationship of the philosophy of hermeneutics to hermeneutical praxis. Everyone wants to know (and not just 'believe') what has happened to themselves. The 'ambiguity' of which he accuses me in his most constructive critique is certainly due in part to my conceptual weakness, but it also in part rests on the undecided essence of hermeneutical experience, and its constant attempt to find with the most exact insight possible that which one understands to be the assertion of the other.

6. This now appears in *Philosophische Anthropologie*, "Conditio humana" (Frankfurt, 1970).

7. In *The Tacit Dimension* (New York, 1966).

8. E.g., in the critical discussion with me in *Studia philosophica*.

9. The phrase which has been translated as "supporting agreement" appears in the original as *tragendes Einverständnis*. This phrase has been translated in Habermas' writings as "supporting consensus" (See Josef Bleicher's translation of "The Hermeneutic Claim to Universality" above and Martha Matesich's translation of "Summation and Response" in *Continuum*, Vol. 8 [1970], pp. 123–133). "Supporting agreement" seems preferable for two reasons. First, it allows the English reader to distinguish between the occasions in which Gadamer and Habermas use *Einverständnis* and *Konsensus*. In the previously mentioned translations of Habermas' essays the translators do not consistently distinguish between the two. On some occasions the terms are rendered as "agreement," on others "consensus." In all instances I have translated *Einverständnis* as "agreement," and have translated *Konsensus* as "consensus." Second, "agreement" is preferable as it conveys a greater sense of the exercise of the intellect than does the terms "consensus." *Einverständnis* has as its root *verstehen*, "to understand," which even in the broad sense that Gadamer uses this term connotes an activity which involves the exercise of discursive reason. On the other hand, the etymology of "consensus" suggests a greater dependence on the emotive elements of consciousness. Its Latin roots *con-* and *sentio* suggest a coming to agreement with others based on a common 'feeling' or 'intuition' rather than on the basis of a decision. Certainly Gadamer does not wish to eliminate emotive elements from the range of human capacities which play a role in our reaching agreement with others. Nonetheless, he insists on a leading role for the more discursive capacities of human intellection. This is evident in his use of *Einverständnis* and its relation to *verstehen*. While it is true that Gadamer's notion of understanding is not limited to a narrow view of logical consistency, understanding is not based primarily on "feeling." "Agreement" thus seems a more appropriate term to use when translating *Einverständnis*—it suggests a rational de-

cision making process, while still keeping the door open for emotional elements.—TRANS.

10. See Habermas, "The Hermeneutic Claim to Universality," in *Hermeneutik und Ideologiekritik*, p. 158 (English translation above, p. 270).—ED.

11. Gadamer is commenting on Karl-Otto Apel's "Scientists, Hermeneutics, Critique of Ideology. Outline of a theory of science from a cognitive-anthropological standpoint" in *Hermeneutik und Ideologiekritik*, pp. 7–44 (English translation in Karl-Otto Apel, *Towards a Transformation of Philosophy*, translated by Glyn Adey and David Frisby [London: Routledge and Kegan Paul, 1980], pp. 46–76).—ED.

12. Habermas, "The Hermeneutic Claim to Universality," in *Hermeneutik und Dialektik* I, edited by R. Bubner, K. Cramer, and R. Wiehl (Tübingen: J. C. B. Mohr [Paul Siebeck], 1970), p. 100. [This essay was reprinted in *Hermeneutik und Ideologiekritik*, and the citation is found on page 155, although not in the precise form Gadamer quotes. Here it reads: "The idea of truth, which measures itself on true consensus, implies the idea of the true life. We could also say: it includes the idea of coming of age." See complete English translation above, p. 268.—TRANS.]

13. Von Bormann is entirely correct when he refers to the 17th and 18th Centuries, and especially to Lessing (*Hermeneutik und Ideologiekritik*, p. 89). I have myself primarily referred to Spinoza, but also to Descartes, and in other circumstances to Chladenius. I am fully convinced that I do not belong on the side of obscurantism, which the enlightenment 'rejects *in toto*' (*Hermeneutik und Ideologiekritik*, p. 115).

14. Hans Joachim Giegel, "Reflexion und Emanzipation," in *Hermeneutik und Ideologiekritik*, p. 249. Gadamer continues in the next few pages of "Replik" to respond to the specific comments made by Giegel in this essay. The absence of this essay in the present volume renders Gadamer's responses somewhat disjointed, and for that reason Gadamer's rejoinders to Giegel have been omitted in what follows.—ED.

15. See Rüdiger Bubner, " 'Philosophie ist ihre Zeit, in Gedanken erfasst,' " in *Hermeneutik und Ideologiekritik*, p. 231ff.

16. See von Bormann, "Die Zweideutigkeit der hermeneutischen Erfahrung," pp. 99, 102ff, 107ff.

17. In the meanwhile I would like to suggest the subsequently appearing work, "The Idea of Hegelian Logic," in *Kleine Schriften III*.

18. Jürgen Habermas, *Theorie und Praxis* (Neuwied, 1967), p. 232 [English translation: *Theory and Practice* by John Viertel (Boston: Beacon Press, 1973), p. 255.—ED].

19. Especially in "Apologie der Heilkunst," *Kleine Schriften I*, p. 214ff.

20. See Hans-Georg Gadamer, *Truth and Method*, translated and edited by Garrett Barden and John Cumming (New York: Seabury Press, 1977), p. 333ff.—ED.

21. See Habermas, "The Hermeneutic Claim to Universality" in *Hermeneutik und Ideologiekritik*, p. 155 [English translation above, p. 268.—ED.].

22. *Nicomachean Ethics*, A 4, *mataion to ēidos.*

12

Hermeneutics and the Critique of Ideology*

Paul Ricoeur

The debate which is evoked by this title goes well beyond the limits of a discussion about the foundations of the social sciences. It raises the question of what I shall call the fundamental gesture of philosophy. Is this gesture an avowal of the historical conditions to which all human understanding is subsumed under the reign of finitude? Or rather is it, in the last analysis, an act of defiance, a critical gesture, relentlessly repeated and indefinitely turned against "false consciousness," against the distortions of human communication which conceal the permanent exercise of domination and violence? Such is the philosophical stake of a debate which at first seems tied to the epistemological plane of the human sciences. What is at stake can be expressed in terms of an alternative: either a hermeneutical consciousness or a critical consciousness. But is it really so? Is it not the alternative itself which must be challenged? Is it possible to formulate a hermeneutics which would render justice to the critique of ideology, which would show the necessity of the latter at the very heart of its own concerns? Clearly the stake is considerable. We are not going to risk everything by beginning with terms which are too general and an attitude which is too ambitious. We shall, instead, focus on a contemporary discussion which presents the problem in the form of an alternative. Even if ultimately this alternative must be surpassed, we shall not be in ignorance of the difficulties to be overcome.

The principal protagonists in the debate are, on the side of hermeneutics, Hans-Georg Gadamer; and on the side of critique, Jürgen Habermas. The dossier of their polemic is now public, partially reproduced in the little volume entitled *Hermeneutik und Ideologiekritik*.[1] It is from this dossier that I shall extract the lines of force which characterise the conflict between hermeneutics and the critical theory of ideology. I shall take the assessment of *tradition* by each of these philosophies as the touchstone of the debate. In contrast to the positive assessment by hermeneutics, the theory of ideology adopts a suspicious approach, seeing tradition as merely the systematically distorted expression of communication under unacknowledged conditions of violence. The choice of this touchstone has the advantage of bringing to the fore a confrontation which bears upon the "claim to universality" of hermeneutics. For the critique of ideology is of interest insofar as it is a non-hermeneutical discipline, situated outside the sphere of competence of a science of philosophy of interpretation, and marking the fundamental limit of the latter.

In the first part of this essay, I shall restrict myself to presenting the contents of the dossier. I shall do so in terms of a simple alternative: either hermeneutics or the critique of ideology. I shall reserve for the second part a more personal reflection, centered on the following two questions: (1) Can hermeneutic philosophy account for the legitimate demand of the critique of ideology, and if so at what price? Must it sacrifice its claim to universality and undertake a profound reformulation of its programme and its project? (2) On what condition is the critique of ideology possible? Can it, in the last analysis, be detached from hermeneutic presuppositions?

I hasten to say that no plan of annexation, no syncretism, will preside over this debate. I readily admit, along with Gadamer, that each of the two theories speaks from a different place; but I hope to show that each can recognise the other's claim to universality in a way which marks the place of one in the structure of the other.

I. The Alternative

1. Gadamer: The hermeneutics of tradition

We may go directly to the critical point—the *Brennpunkt*—which Habermas attacks in his *Logik der Socialwissenschaften*, namely the conception of historical consciousness and the provocative rehabilitation of the three connected concepts of prejudice, authority and tradition. This text is by no means secondary or marginal. It goes directly to the central experience or, as I have just said, to the place from which this hermeneutics speaks and upon which it raises its claim to universality. This experience is the scandal constituted, on the level of modern consciousness, by the sort of *alienating distanciation—Verfremdung*—which is not merely a feeling or a mood, but rather the ontological presupposition which sustains the objective conduct of the human sciences. The methodology of these sciences ineluctably implies an assumption of distance; and this, in turn, presupposes the destruction of the primordial relation of belonging— *Zugehörigkeit*—without which there would be no relation to the historical as such. The debate between alienating distanciation and the experience of belonging is pursued by Gadamer through the three spheres into which the hermeneutical experience is divided: the aesthetic sphere, the historical sphere and the sphere of language.[. . .] So although we shall focus on the second part, it must be remembered that in a sense the debate is already played out in the aesthetic sphere, just as it only culminates in the lingual experience whereby aesthetic consciousness and historical consciousness are brought to discourse. The theory of historical consciousness is therefore an epitome of the work as a whole and a microcosm of the great debate.

At the same time that hermeneutic philosophy declares the amplitude of its aim, so too it announces the locality of its point of departure. Gadamer speaks from a place which is determined by the history of attempts to resolve the problem of the foundation of the human sciences, attempts first undertaken in German Romanticism, then in Dilthey's work, and finally in terms of Heidegger's ontology. This is readily acknowledged by Gadamer himself, even when he proclaims the universality of the hermeneutical dimension. For the universality is not abstract; it is, for each investigator, centered on a dominant problematic, a privileged experience. "My own attempt," he writes at the outset of "Rhetorik, Hermeneutik und Ideologiekritik," "is linked to the revival of the heritage of German Romanticism by Dilthey, insofar as he takes the theory of the human sciences as his theme, placing it on a new and broader foundation; the experience of art, together with the experience of contemporaneousness which is peculiar to it, provides the riposte to the historical distanciation of the human sciences."[2] Thus hermeneutics has an aim which precedes and surpasses any science, an aim testified to by "the universal linguality of behaviour relative to the world";[3] but the universality of the aim is the counterpart to the narrowness of the initial experience in which it is rooted. The fact that the localised nature of the initial experience is emphasised, as well as the claim to universality, is therefore not irrelevant to the debate with the proponents of the critique of ideology. It would have been equally possible to begin, not with historical consciousness as such, but rather with the interpretation of texts in the experience of reading, as the hermeneutics of Schleiermacher shows. In choosing this somewhat different point of departure, as I myself shall do in the second part of the essay, the problem of distanciation can be given a more positive significance than Gadamer suggests. Gadamer has specifically dismissed as less important a reflection on "being for the text" [Sein zum Texte], which he seems to reduce to a deliberation on the problem of translation, itself set up as a model of the linguality of human behaviour towards the world. However, it is to this reflection that I shall return in the second part, in the hope of deriving therefrom an orientation of thought which is less subordinated to the problematic of tradition and more receptive to the critique of ideology.

By taking historical consciousness and the question of the conditions of possibility of the human sciences as the axis of reflection, Gadamer inevitably turned hermeneutic philosophy towards the rehabilitation of prejudice and the defense of tradition and authority, placing this philosophy in a conflictual relation to any critique of ideology. At the same time the conflict itself, in spite of the modern terminology, was returned to its original formulation, as expressed in the struggle between the spirit of Romanticism and that of the *Aufklärung* [Enlightenment]. The conflict had to take the form of a repetition of the same struggle along the course of an obligatory route, beginning with Romanticism, passing through the epistemological stage of the human sciences with Dilthey, and undergoing the ontological transposition of Heidegger. In adopting the privileged experience of historical consciousness, Gadamer adopted also a certain philosophical route which, ineluctably, he had to reiterate.

The struggle between Romanticism and the Enlightenment is the source of our own problem and the milieu in which the opposition between two fundamental philosophical attitudes took shape: on one side, the *Aufklärung* and its struggle against prejudices; on the other, Romanticism and its nostalgia for the past. The problem is whether the modern conflict between the critique of ideology according to the Frankfurt School and the hermeneutics of Gadamer marks any progress in this debate.

So far as Gadamer is concerned, his declared intention is perfectly clear: the pitfalls of Romanticism must be avoided. The second part of *Truth and Method*, which culminates in the famous theory of "consciousness exposed to the effects of history" [*wirkungsgeschichtliches Bewusstsein*], contains a sharp attack on Romantic philosophy for having merely reversed the terms of the argument, without displacing the problematic itself and without changing the terrain of the debate. For "prejudice," in the double sense of precipitation (to judge too quickly) and predisposition (to follow custom or authority), is the category *par excellence* of the *Aufklärung*. Prejudice is what must be put aside in order to think, in order to dare to think—according to the famous adage *sapere aude*—so that one may reach the age of adulthood or *Mündigkeit*. To recover a less univocally negative sense of the word "prejudice" (which has become virtually synonymous with unfounded or false judgment), and to restore the ambivalence that the Latin word *praejudicium* had in the juridical tradition prior to the Enlightenment, it would be necessary to question the presuppositions of a philosophy which opposes reason to prejudice. These are, in fact, the very presuppositions of a critical philosophy; it is for a philosophy of judgment—and a critical philosophy is a philosophy of judgment—that prejudice is a predominantly negative category. What must be questioned, therefore, is the primacy of judgment in man's behavior towards the world; and the only philosophy which sets up judgment as a tribunal is one that makes objectivity, as modelled on the sciences, the measure of knowledge. Judgment and prejudice are dominant categories only in the type of philosophy, stemming from Descartes, which makes methodical consciousness the key of our relation to being and to beings. Hence it is necessary to delve beneath the philosophy of judgment, beneath the problematic of subject and object, in order to effect a rehabilitation of prejudice which is not a simple negation of the spirit of the Enlightenment.

It is here that Romantic philosophy proves to be both a first foundation and a fundamental failure. A first foundation, because it dares to challenge "the discrediting of prejudice by the *Aufklärung*" (the title of pp. 241–5 in *Truth and Method*); a fundamental failure, because it only inverts the answer without inverting the question. Romanticism wages its war on a terrain defined by the adversary, a terrain on which the role of tradition and authority in the process of interpretation are in dispute. It is on the same terrain, the same ground of inquiry, that the *mythos* is celebrated over the *logos*, that the old is defended against the new, historical Christendom against the modern state, the fraternal community against an administrative socialism, the productive unconscious against a sterile consciousness, the mythical past against a future of rational utopias, the poetic imagination against cold ratiocination. Romantic hermeneutics thus ties its destiny to everything which is associated with the Restoration.

Such is the pitfall which the hermeneutics of historical consciousness seeks to avoid. The question, once again, is whether Gadamer's hermeneutics has really surpassed the Romantic point of departure of hermeneutics, and whether his affirmation that "the finitude of man's being consists in the fact that firstly he finds himself at the heart of tradition" (*WM* 260; *TM* 244 [Here and elsewhere, page references to the German texts are supplied by Paul Ricoeur; page references to the English translations are provided by the translator.—ED.]) escapes from the play of inversions in which he sees philosophical Romanticism, confronting the claims of critical philosophy, ensnared.

In Gadamer's view, it is only with the philosophy of Heidegger that the problematic of prejudice can be reconstituted as, precisely, a problematic. The Diltheyan stage of the problem is, in this respect, not at all decisive. On the contrary, we owe to Dilthey the illusion that the natural sciences and the human sciences are characterised by two scientificities, two methodologies, two epistemologies. Hence, in spite of his debt to Dilthey, Gadamer does not hesitate to write: "Dilthey was unable to free himself from the traditional theory of Knowledge" (*WM* 261; *TM* 245). Dilthey still begins from self-consciousness; for him, subjectivity remains the ultimate point of reference. The reign of *Erlebnis* [lived experience] is the reign of a primordiality which I am. In this sense, the fundamental is the *Innesein*, the interior, the awareness of self. It is thus against Dilthey, as well as the constantly resurging *Aufklärung*, that Gadamer proclaims: "the prejudices of the individual, far more than his judgments, constitute the historical reality of his being" (*WM* 261; *TM* 245). The rehabilitation of prejudice, authority and tradition will thus be directed against the reign of subjectivity and interiority, that is, against the criteria of reflection. This anti-reflective polemic will help to give Gadamer's plea the appearance of a return to a pre-critical position. Yet however provoking—not to say provocative—this plea may be, it attests to the resurgence of the historical dimension over the moment of reflection. History precedes me and my reflection; I belong to history before I belong to myself. Dilthey could not understand that, because his revolution remained epistemological and his reflective criterion prevailed over his historical consciousness.

It may be asked nonetheless whether the sharpness of the remarks against Dilthey has the same significance as the attack on Romanticism: is not the fidelity to Dilthey more profound than the critique addressed to him? This would explain why the question of history and historicity, rather than that of the text and exegesis, continues to provide what I shall call, in a manner similar to Gadamer himself, the *primary* experience of hermeneutics. It is perhaps at this level that Gadamer's hermeneutics must be interrogated, that is, at a level where his fidelity to Dilthey is more important than his critique. We shall reserve this question for the second part, restricting ourselves here to following the movement from the critique of Romanticism and Dilthey's epistemology to the properly Heideggerian phase of the problem.

To restore the historical dimension of man requires much more than a simple methodological reform, much more than a mere epistemological legitimation of the idea of a "human science" in face of demands from the sciences of nature. Only a fundamental upheaval which subordinates the theory of knowledge to ontology can bring out the real sense of the *Vorstruktur des Verstehens*—the forestructure (or structure of anticipation) of understanding—which is the condition for any rehabilitation of prejudice.

We are all familiar with the section of *Being and Time* on understanding (section 31 [pp.115–20—ED.])[4], where Heidegger, accumulating expressions that exhibit the prefix *vor* (*Vor-habe*, *Vor-sicht*, *Vor-griffe*), proceeds to found the hermeneutical circle of the human sciences in a structure of anticipation which is part of the very position of our being within being.

Gadamer expresses it well: "the point of Heidegger's hermeneutical think-ing is not so much to prove that there is a circle as to show that this circle possesses an ontologically positive significance" (WM 251; TM 236). It is worth noting, however, that Gadamer refers not only to paragraph 31, which is still part of "the fundamental Analytic of Dasein" (the title of the first division), but also to paragraph 63, which clearly shifts the problem-atic of interpretation towards the question of temporality as such; it is no longer just a question of the Da [there] of Dasein [being-there], but of its "potentiality-for-being-a-whole" [Ganzseinskönnen], which is manifested in the three temporal ecstases of care. Gadamer is right to "inquire into the consequences which follow for the hermeneutics of the human sciences from the fact that Heidegger derives the circular structure of understanding from the temporality of Dasein" (WM 251; TM 235). But Heidegger him-self did not consider these questions, which would perhaps lead us back in an unexpected way to the critical theme that was allegedly expurgated along with purely epistemological or methodological concerns. If one fol-lows the movement of radicalisation which leads, not only from Dilthey to Heidegger, but from paragraph 31 to paragraph 63 in the very interior of Being and Time, then it seems that the privileged experience (if one can still speak in this way) is no longer the history of the historians, but rather the history of the question of the meaning of being in Western metaphysics. So it seems that the hermeneutical situation within which the interpretation unfolds is characterised by the fact that the structure of anticipation, in terms of which we interrogate being, is provided by the history of meta-physics; it is that which takes the place of prejudice. (Later we shall ask ourselves whether the critical relation that Heidegger establishes with re-spect to this tradition does not also involve a certain rehabilitation of the critique of prejudices.) Heidegger thus effects a fundamental displacement of the problem of prejudice: prejudice—Vormeinung—is part of the struc-ture of anticipation (see SZ 150; BT 190). Here the example of textual exe-gesis is more than a particular case; it is a development, in the photographic sense of the term. Heidegger may well call philological inter-pretation a "derivative mode" (SZ 152; BT 194), but it remains the touch-stone. It is there that we can perceive the necessity of drawing back from the vicious circle in which philological interpretation turns, insofar as it understands itself in terms of a model of scientificity borrowed from the exact sciences, to the non-vicious circle formed by the anticipatory struc-ture of the very being which we are.

However, Heidegger is not interested in the movement of return from the structure of anticipation which constitutes us to the hermeneutic circle in its properly methodological aspects. This is unfortunate, since it is on the return route that hermeneutics is likely to encounter critique, in particular the critique of ideology. Hence our own interrogation of Heidegger and Gadamer will begin from the difficulties raised by the movement of return, upon which the idea that philological interpretation is a "derivative mode of understanding" can alone be legitimated. Insofar as this derivation has not been attempted, it has still not been shown that the fore-structure itself is fundamental. For nothing is fundamental, so long as something else has not been derived from it.

It is on this threefold basis—Romantic, Diltheyan, Heideggerian—that *Gadamer's distinctive contribution to the problematic* must be placed. In this respect, Gadamer's text is like a palimpsest, in which it is always possible to distinguish, as in the thickness of overlaid transparencies, a Romantic layer, a Diltheyan layer and a Heideggerian layer, and which may thus be read at each of these levels. Each level, in turn, is reflected in the views which Gadamer currently espouses as his own. As his adversaries have clearly seen, Gadamer's distinctive contribution concerns, first, the link which he establishes, purely phenomenologically as it were, between prejudice, tradition and authority; second, the ontological interpretation of this sequence in terms of the concept of *wirkungsgeschichtliches Bewusstsein*, which I shall translate as "consciousness exposed to the effects of history" or "consciousness of historical efficacy," and third, the epistemological or "meta-critical" consequence, as Gadamer calls it in his *Kleine Schriften*, that an exhaustive critique of prejudice—and hence of ideology—is impossible, since there is no zero point from which it could proceed.

Let us consider each of these three points in turn: the phenomenology of prejudice, tradition and authority; the ontology of consciousness exposed to the effects of history; and the critique of critique.

Gadamer's attempt to rehabilitate prejudice, tradition and authority is not without a provocative aim. The analysis is "phenomenological" in the sense that it seeks to extract from these three phenomena an essence which the *Aufklärung*, with its pejorative appraisal, has obscured. For Gadamer, prejudice is not the opposite pole of a reason without presupposition; it is a component of understanding, linked to the finite historical character of the human being. It is false to maintain that there are only unfounded prejudices, since there are, in the juridical sense, pre-judgments which may or may not be subsequently grounded, and even "legitimate prejudices." So even if prejudices by precipitation are more difficult to rehabilitate, prejudices by predisposition have a profound significance which is missed by analyses conducted from a purely critical standpoint. Yet the prejudice against prejudice is rooted at a deeper level, namely in a prejudice against authority, which is identified too quickly with domination and violence. The concept of authority brings us to the heart of the debate with the critique of ideology. Let us recall that this concept is also at the centre of Max Weber's political sociology: the state is the institution *par excellence* which rests on a belief in the legitimacy of its authority and its right to use violence in the last instance. Now for Gadamer, the analysis of this concept has suffered, since the time of the *Aufklärung*, from a confusion between domination, authority and violence. It is here that the analysis of essence is crucial. The *Aufklärung* posits a necessary connection between authority and blind obedience:

> But this is not the essence of authority. It is true that it is primarily persons that have authority; but the authority of persons is based ultimately, not on the subjection and abdication of reason, but on acceptance and recognition—recognition, namely, that the other is superior to oneself in judgment and insight and that for this reason his judgment takes precedence, i.e., it has priority over one's own. This is connected with the fact that authority cannot actually be bestowed, but is acquired and must be acquired, if someone is to lay claim to it. It rests on consideration and hence on an act of reason itself which, aware of its own limitations, accepts that others have better understanding. Authority in this sense, properly understood, has nothing to do with blind obedience to a command. Indeed, authority has nothing to do with obedience; it rests on recognition. (*WM* 264; *TM* 248)

Thus the key concept is recognition [*Anerkennung*], which is substituted for the notion of obedience. We may note in passing that this concept implies a certain critical moment: "The recognition of authority," says Gadamer further on, "is always connected with the idea that what authority states is not irrational and arbitrary, but can be accepted in principle. This is the essence of the authority claimed by the teacher, the superior, the expert" (*WM* 264; *TM* 249). This critical moment offers the possibility of articulating the phenomenology of authority onto the critique of ideology.

However, this is not the aspect that Gadamer ultimately underlines. In spite of his earlier critique, it is to a theme of German Romanticism that Gadamer returns, linking *authority* to *tradition*. That which has authority is tradition. When he comes to this equation, Gadamer speaks in Romantic terms:

> There is one form of authority that romanticism has defended with particular ardour: tradition. That which has been sanctioned by tradition and custom has an authority that is nameless, and our finite historical being is determined by the fact that always the authority of what has been transmitted—and not only what is clearly grounded—

has power [*Gewalt*] over our attitudes and behaviour. All education depends on this . . . [Customs and traditions] are freely taken over, but by no means created by a free insight or justified by themselves. This is precisely what we call tradition: the ground of their validity. And in fact we owe to romanticism this correction of the enlightenment, that tradition has a justification that is outside the arguments of reason and in large measure determines our attitudes and behaviour. It is even a mark of the superiority of classical ethics over the moral philosophy of the modern period that it justifies the transition of ethics into "politics," the art of right government, by the indispensability of tradition. In comparison with it, the modern enlightenment is abstract and revolutionary. (*WM* 265; *TM* 249)

(Notice how the word *Gewalt* [power] is slipped into the text behind *Autorität* [authority], as well as *Herrschaft* [domination] in the expression *Herrschaft von Tradition* [*WM* 265; *TM* 250]).

Gadamer does not want, of course, to fall back into the rut of the irresolvable debate between Romanticism and the Enlightenment. We must be grateful to him for attempting to reconcile, rather than oppose, authority and reason. The real meaning of authority stems from the contribution which it makes to the maturity of free judgment: "to accept authority" is thus also to pass through the screen of doubt and critique. More fundamentally still, authority is linked to reason insofar as "tradition is constantly an element of freedom and of history itself" (*WM* 265; *TM* 250). This point is missed if the "preservation" [*Bewahrung*] of a cultural heritage is confused with the simple conservation of a natural reality. A tradition must be seized, taken up and maintained; hence it demands an act of reason: "Preservation is as much a freely-chosen action as revolution and renewal" (*WM* 266; *TM* 250).

It may be noted, however, that Gadamer uses the word *Vernunft* [reason] and not *Verstand* [understanding]. A dialogue is possible on this basis with Habermas and Karl-Otto Apel, who are also concerned to defend a concept of reason distinct from technocratic understanding which they see as subservient to a purely technological project. It may well be the case that the Frankfurt School's distinction between communicative action, the work of reason, and instrumental action, the work of technological understanding, can be sustained only by recourse to tradition — or at least to a living cultural tradition, as opposed to a tradition which is politicised and institutionalised. Eric Weil's distinction between the rationale of technology and the reasonableness of politics would be equally relevant here; for Eric Weil as well, what is reasonable emerges only in the course of a dialogue between the spirit of innovation and the spirit of tradition.

The properly "ontological" interpretation of the sequence—prejudice, authority, tradition—is crystallised, as it were, in the category of *Wirkungsgeschichte* or *wirkungsgeschichtliches Bewusstsein*, which marks the summit of Gadamer's reflection on the foundations of the human sciences.

This category does not pertain to methodology, to historical *Forschung* [inquiry], but rather to the reflective consciousness of this methodology. It is a category of the awareness of history. Later we shall see that certain of Habermas's concepts, such as the regulative idea of unrestricted communication, are situated at the same level of the self-understanding of the social sciences. It is therefore important to analyze the category of the consciousness of historical efficacy with the greatest care. In general terms, it can be characterised as the consciousness of being exposed to history and to its effects, in such a way that this action over us cannot be objectified, for the efficacy belongs to the very meaning of the action as an historical phenomenon. Thus in *Kleine Schriften* we read:

> By that I mean, first, that we cannot extricate ourselves from the historical process, so distance ourselves from it that the past becomes an object for us . . . We are always situated in history . . . I mean that our consciousness is determined by a real historical process, in such a way that we are not free to juxtapose ourselves to the past. I mean moreover that we must always become conscious afresh of the action which is thereby exercised over us, in such a way that everything past which we come to experience compels us to take hold of it completely, to assume in some way its truth.[5]

Let us analyze further the massive and global fact whereby consciousness, even before its awakening as such, belongs to and depends on that which affects it. This properly prevenient action, incorporated into awareness, can be articulated at the level of philosophical thought in terms of four themes, which seem to me to converge in the category of the consciousness of historical efficacy.

To begin with, the concept must be placed together and in tension with the notion of *historical distance*. This notion, which Gadamer elaborated in the paragraph preceding the one we quoted, is made into a methodological condition of *Forschung*. Distance is a fact; placing at a distance is a methodological attitude. The history of effects is precisely what occurs under the condition of historical distance. It is the nearness of the remote. Whence the illusion, against which Gadamer struggles, that "distance" puts an end to our collusion with the past and creates a situation comparable to the objectivity of the natural sciences, on the grounds that a loss of familiarity is a break with the contingent. Against this illusion, it is important to restore the paradox of the "otherness" of the past. Effective history is efficacy at a distance.

The second theme incorporated in the idea of historical efficacy is this: there is no *overview* which would enable us to grasp in a single glance the totality of effects. Between finitude and absolute knowledge, it is necessary to choose; the concept of effective history belongs to an ontology of finitude. It plays the same role as the "thrown project" and the "situation" play in Heidegger's ontology. Historical being is that which never passes into self-knowledge. If there is a corresponding Hegelian concept, it would not be *Wissen* (knowledge), but rather *Substanz*, which Hegel uses whenever it is necessary to speak of the unfathomable depths which come to discourse through the dialectic. To do justice to Hegel, one must retrace the course of *The Phenomenology of Mind*, rather than descend along the path towards absolute knowledge.

The third theme corrects somewhat the preceding point: if there is no overview, neither is there a situation which restricts us absolutely. Wherever there is a situation, there is an *horizon* which may contract or expand. As the visual circle of our existence attests, the landscape is organised into the near, the far and the open. It is the same in historical understanding. At one time it was thought that the concept of horizon could be accounted for by assimilating it to the methodological rule of placing oneself in the other's point of view: the horizon is the horizon of the other. It was thus thought that history had been aligned with the objectivity of the sciences: to adopt the other's point of view while forgetting one's own, is that not objectivity? Yet nothing is more disastrous than this fallacious assimilation. For the text, thus treated as an absolute object, is divested of its claim to tell us something about something. This claim can be sustained only by the idea of a prior understanding concerning the thing itself. Nothing destroys more the very sense of the historical enterprise than this objective distancing, which suspends both the tension of points of view and the claim of tradition to transmit a true speech about what is.

By restoring the dialectic of points of view and the tension between the other and the self, we arrive at the culminating concept of the *fusion of horizons*—our fourth theme. This is a dialectical concept which results from the rejection of two alternatives: objectivism, whereby the objectification of the other is premissed on the forgetting of oneself, and absolute knowledge, according to which universal history can be articulated within a single horizon. We exist neither in closed horizons, nor within an horizon that is unique. No horizon is closed, since it is possible to place oneself in another point of view and in another culture. It would be reminiscent of Robinson Crusoe to claim that the other is inaccessible. But no horizon is unique, since the tension between the other and oneself is unsurpassable. Gadamer seems to accept, at one stage, the idea of a single horizon encompassing all points of view, as in the monadology of Leibniz (*WM* 288; *TM* 271). This is, it seems, in order to combat Nietzsche's radical pluralism, which would lead to incommunicability and which would shatter the idea, essential to the philosophy of *logos*, of a "common understanding concerning the thing." In this respect, Gadamer's account is similar to Hegel's insofar as historical comprehension requires a "common understanding concerning the thing" and hence a unique *logos* of communication; but Gadamer's position is only tangential to that of Hegel, because his Heideggerian ontology of finitude prevents him from transforming this unique horizon into a knowledge. The very word "horizon" indicates an ultimate repudiation of the idea of a knowledge wherein the fusion of horizons would itself be grasped. The contrast in virtue of which one point of view stands out against the backcloth of others [*Abhebung*] marks the gulf between hermeneutics and any form of Hegelianism.

The unsurpassable concept of the fusion of horizons endows the theory of prejudice with its most peculiar characteristic: prejudice is the horizon of the present, the finitude of what is near in its openness towards the remote. This relation between the self and the other gives the concept of prejudice its final dialectical touch: only insofar as I place myself in the other's point of view do I confront myself with my present horizon, with my prejudices. It is only in the tension between the other and the self, between the text of the past and the point of view of the reader, that prejudice becomes operative and constitutive of historicity.

The epistemological implications of the ontological concept of historical efficacy are easy to discern. They concern the very status of research in the social sciences: that is what Gadamer wanted to show. *Forschung*—inquiry—scientific research does not escape the historical consciousness of those who live and make history. Historical knowledge cannot free itself from the historical condition. It follows that the project of a science free from prejudices is impossible. History poses meaningful questions to the past, pursues meaningful research and attains meaningful results only by beginning from a tradition which interpellates it. The emphasis on the word *Bedeutung* [meaning] leaves no doubt: history as science receives its meanings, at the outset as well as the end of research, from the link which it preserves with a received and recognised tradition. The action of tradition and historical investigation are fused by a bond which no critical consciousness could dissolve without rendering the research itself nonsensical. The history of the historians [*Historie*] can only bring to a higher level of consciousness the very flow of life within history [*Geschichte*]: "Modern historical research itself is not only research, but the transmission of tradition"

(*WM* 268; *TM* 253). Man's link to the past precedes and envelops the purely objective treatment of historical facts. It remains to be seen whether the ideal of unlimited and unconstrained communication, which Habermas opposes to the concept of tradition, escapes from Gadamer's argument against the possibility of a complete knowledge of history and, along with it, of history as an object in itself.

Whatever the outcome of this argument against the critique of ideology, hermeneutics ultimately claims to set itself up as a critique of critique, or meta-critique.

Why meta-critique? What is at stake in this term is what Gadamer calls, in the *Kleine Schriften*, "the universality of the hermeneutical problem." I see three ways of construing this notion of universality. It may be construed, first, as the claim that hermeneutics has the same scope as science. For universality is first of all a scientific demand, one which concerns our knowledge and our power. Hermeneutics claims to cover the same domain as scientific investigation, founding the latter in an experience of the world which precedes and envelops the knowledge and the power of science. This claim to universality is thus raised on the same ground as the critique which addresses itself to the conditions of possibility of the knowledge of science and its power. So the first universality arises from the very task of hermeneutics: "to reconnect the objective world of technology, which the sciences place at our disposal and discretion, with those fundamental orders of our being that are neither arbitrary nor manipulable by us, but rather simply demand our respect."[6] To remove from our discretion what science places at our disposal: such is the first meta-critical task.

It could be said, however, that this universality is still derived. In Gadamer's view, hermeneutics has a peculiar universality which can be attained, paradoxically, only by starting from certain privileged experiences of universal significance. For fear of becoming a *Methodik* [methodology], hermeneutics can raise its claim to universality only from very concrete domains, that is, from regional hermeneutics which must always be "deregionalised." In the process of deregionalisation, hermeneutics may encounter a resistance that stems from the very nature of the experiences with which it begins. For these are, *par excellence*, the experiences of *Verfremdung*—alienation—whether it be in the aesthetic, historical or lingual consciousness. The struggle against methodological distanciation transforms hermeneutics into a critique of critique; it must always push the rock of Sisyphus up again, restore the ontological ground that methodology has eroded away. But at the same time, the critique of critique assumes a thesis which will appear very suspect to "critical" eyes: namely that a *consensus* already exists, which founds the possibility of aesthetic, historical and lingual relations. To Schleiermacher, who defined hermeneutics as the art of overcoming misunderstanding [*Missverständnis*], Gadamer ripostes: "is it not, in fact, the case that every misunderstanding presupposes a 'deep common accord'?"[7]

This idea of a *tragendes Einverständnis* is absolutely fundamental; the assertion that misunderstanding is supported by a prior understanding is the pre-eminent meta-critical theme. It leads, moreover, to the third concept of universality which may be found in Gadamer's work. The universal element which permits the deregionalisation of hermeneutics is language itself. The accord which supports us is the understanding reached in dialogue—not so much the relaxed face-to-face situation, but the question-answer relation in its most radical form. Here we come across the primitive hermeneutical phenomenon: "No assertion is possible that cannot be understood as an answer to a question, and assertions can only be understood in this way."[8] Every hermeneutics thus culminates in the concept of *Sprachlichkeit* or the "lingual dimension," although "language" must be construed here, not as the system of languages [*langues*], but as the collection of things said, the summary of the most significant messages, transmitted not only by ordinary language but by all of the eminent languages [*langages*] which have made us what we are.

We shall approach Habermas's critique by asking whether "the dialogue which we are" is indeed the universal element that allows hermeneutics to be deregionalised, or if instead it constitutes a rather peculiar experience, enveloping both a blindness with respect to the real conditions of human communication, as well as a hope for a communication without restriction and constraint.

2. The critique of ideology: Habermas

I should like now to present the second protagonist of the debate, reduced for the sake of clarity to a simple duel. I shall discuss his *critique of ideology*, considered as an alternative to the *hermeneutics of tradition*, under four successive headings.

(1) Whereas Gadamer borrows the concept of *prejudice* from philosophical Romanticism, reinterpreting it by means of the Heideggerian notion of pre-understanding, Habermas develops a concept of *interest*, which stems from the tradition of Marxism as reinterpreted by Lukacs and the Frankfurt School (Horkheimer, Adorno, Marcuse, Apel, etc.).

(2) Whereas Gadamer appeals to the *human sciences*, which are concerned with the contemporary reinterpretation of cultural tradition, Haber-

mas makes recourse to the *critical social sciences*, directly aimed against institutional reifications.

(3) Whereas Gadamer introduces *mis-understanding* as the inner obstacle to understanding, Habermas develops a theory of *ideology*, construed as the systematic distortion of communication by the hidden exercise of force.

(4) Lastly, whereas Gadamer bases the hermeneutic task on an ontology of the "dialogue which we are," Habermas invokes the *regulative ideal* of an unrestricted and unconstrained communication which does not precede us but guides us from a future point.

I present this very schematic outline of the alternative with the aim of clarification. The debate would be without interest if the two apparently antithetical positions did not share a zone of intersection which, in my view, ought to become the point of departure for a new phase of hermeneutics, a phase which I shall sketch in the second part. But first, let us take up each of the lines of disagreement.

(1) The concept of interest invites us to say a few words about Habermas's relation to Marxism, which is roughly comparable with Gadamer's relation to philosophical Romanticism. The Marxism of Habermas is of a quite specific sort, having little in common with Althusser's and leading to a very different theory of ideology. In *Knowledge and Human Interests*, published in 1968, Marxism is placed inside an archaeology of knowledge which, unlike Foucault's, does not aim to isolate discontinuous structures that could be neither constituted nor manipulated by any subject; on the contrary, it aims to retrace the continuous history of a single problematic, that of reflection, swamped by the rise of objectivism and positivism. The book seeks to reconstruct the "pre-history of modern positivism," and thereby the history of the dissolution of the critical function, with a goal that could be called apologetic: namely, "to recover the forgotten experience of reflection."[9] Placed within the history of the achievements and the failures of reflection, Marxism can only appear as a very ambiguous phenomenon. On the one hand, it is part of the history of critical reflection; it is at one extremity of a line which begins with Kant and passes through Fichte and Hegel. I do not have the time to describe how Habermas sees this series of radicalisations of the reflective task, across the successive stages of the Kantian subject, the Hegelian consciousness and the Fichtean ego, and culminating with the synthesis of man and nature in the activity of production. This way of formulating the filiation of Marxism from the question of critique is very revealing in itself. To conceive of Marxism as a novel solution to the problem of the conditions of possibility of objectivity and the object, to say that "in materialism labour has the function of syn-

thesis," is to submit Marxism to a properly "critical" reading, in the Kantian and post-Kantian sense of the word. Hence Habermas says that the critique of political economy has the same role in Marx's work as the logic has in idealism.

Thus placed within the history of critical reflection, Marxism cannot avoid appearing both as the most advanced position of the meta-critique, insofar as man the producer takes the place of the transcendental subject and the Hegelian spirit, and as a stage in the history of the forgetting of reflection and the advance of positivism and objectivism. The defense of man the producer leads to the hypostatisation of one category of action at the expense of all others, namely instrumental action.

In order to understand this critique which claims to be internal to Marxism, it is necessary to introduce the concept of interest. Here I shall follow the 1965 essay, included as an appendix to *Knowledge and Human Interests*, before returning to the latter work.

The concept of interest is opposed to all pretensions of the theoretical subject to situate itself outside the sphere of desire, pretensions that Habermas sees in the work of Plato, Kant, Hegel and Husserl; the task of a critical philosophy is precisely to unmask the interests which underlie the enterprise of knowledge. It is evident that, however different the concept of interest may be from Gadamer's notions of prejudice and tradition, there is a certain family resemblance which will have to be clarified at a later stage. For the moment it will enable us to introduce the concept of ideology, understood as an allegedly disinterested knowledge which serves to conceal an interest under the guise of a rationalisation, in a sense similar to Freud's.

To appreciate Habermas's critique of Marx, it is important to realise that there are several interests, or more precisely a *pluralism* of spheres of interest. Habermas distinguishes three basic interests, each of which governs a sphere of *Forschung*—of inquiry—and hence a group of sciences.

There is, first, the *technical* or *instrumental interest*, which governs the "empirical-analytic sciences." It governs these sciences in the sense that the signification of possible empirical statements consists in their technical exploitability: the relevant facts of the empirical sciences are constituted by an *a priori* organization of our experience within the behavioural system of instrumental action. This thesis, close to the pragmatism of Dewey and Peirce, will be decisive for understanding the functions of what Habermas, following Marcuse, regards as the modern ideology, namely science and technology themselves. The imminent possibility of ideology arises from this correlation between empirical knowledge and the technical interest, which Habermas defines more exactly as "the cognitive interest in technical control over objectified processes."[10]

There is, however, a second sphere of interest, which is no longer technical but *practical*, in the Kantian sense of the word. In other writings, Habermas opposes communicative action to instrumental action; it is the same distinction: the practical sphere is the sphere of inter-subjective com munication. He correlates this sphere with the domain of the "historical-hermeneutic sciences." The signification of propositions produced in this domain does not proceed from possible prediction and technical exploitability, but from understanding meaning. This understanding is accomplished through the interpretation of messages exchanged in ordinary language, by means of the interpretation of texts transmitted by tradition, and in virtue of the internalisation of norms which institutionalise social roles. It is evident that here we are closer to Gadamer than to Marx. Closer to Gadamer, for, at the level of communicative action, understanding is subsumed by the interpreter to the conditions of pre-understanding, which in turn is constituted on the basis of the traditional meanings incorporated into the seizure of any new phenomenon. Even the practical emphasis which Habermas gives to the hermeneutical sciences is not fundamentally foreign to Gadamer, insofar as the latter linked the interpretation of what is distant and past to the "application" [*Anwendung*] here and now. Closer to Gadamer, we are also further from Marx. For the distinction between the two levels of interest, technical interest and practical interest, between the two levels of action, instrumental action and communicative action, between the two levels of science, empirical-analytic science and historical-hermeneutic science, provides the starting point for the internal critique of Marxism (here I return to the main text of *Knowledge and Human Interests*).

The critique claims to be internal in the sense that Habermas discerns in the work of Marx himself the outlines of his own distinction between the two types of interest, action and science. He sees this in the famous distinction between "forces of production" and "relations of production," the latter designating the institutional forms in which productive activity is carried out. Marxism in fact rests on the disjunction between force and form. The activity of production should engender one unique self-productive humanity, one unique "generic essence" of man; but the relations of production split the producing subject into antagonistic classes. Therein Habermas sees the beginnings of his own distinction, in the sense that the phenomena of domination and violence, as well as the ideological dissimulation of these phenomena and the political enterprise of liberation, take place in the sphere of the *relations* of production and not that of the *forces* of production. An awareness of the distinction between instrumental and communicative action is therefore necessary in order to account for the very phenomena which Marx analysed: antagonism, domination, dissimulation, liberation. But such an awareness is precisely what Marxism, in the understanding which it has of its own thought, lacks. In subsuming forces and relations to the same concept of *production*, it precludes the real separation of interests, and hence also of levels of action and spheres of science. In that respect, Marxism belongs explicitly to the history of positivism, to the history of the forgetting of reflection, even though implicitly it is part of the history of the awareness of reifications which affect communication.

(2) We have still not spoken of the third type of interest, which Habermas calls the *interest in emancipation*. He connects this interest with a third type of science, the *critical social sciences*.

Here we touch upon the most important source of disagreement with Gadamer; whereas the latter takes the "human sciences" as an initial point of reference, Habermas invokes the "critical social sciences." This initial choice is heavy with consequences. For the "human sciences" are close to what Gadamer calls *humaniora*, the humanities; they are essentially sciences of culture, concerned with the renewal of cultural heritage in the historical present. They are thus by nature sciences of tradition—of tradition reinterpreted and reinvented in terms of its implications here and now, but of continuous tradition nonetheless. From the outset, the destiny of Gadamer's hermeneutics is tied to these sciences. They can incorporate a critical moment, but they are inclined by nature to struggle against the alienating distanciation of the aesthetic, historical and lingual consciousness. Consequently, they forbid the elevation of the critical instance above the recognition of authority and above the very tradition reinterpreted. The critical instance can be developed only as a moment subordinated to the consciousness of finitude and of dependence upon the figures of pre-understanding which always precede and envelop it.

The situation is quite different in the critical social sciences. They are critical by constitution; it is this which distinguishes them from the empirical-analytic sciences described above. The task of the critical social sciences is to discern, beneath the regularities observed by the empirical social sciences, those "ideologically frozen" relations of dependence which can be transformed only through critique. Thus the critical approach is governed by the interest in emancipation, which Habermas also calls *self-reflection*. This interest provides the frame of reference for critical propositions: self-reflection, he says in the sketch of 1965, frees the subject from dependence on hypostatised powers. It can be seen that this is the very interest which animated the philosophies of the past; it is common to philosophy and the critical social sciences. It is the interest in *Selbständigkeit*, in autonomy, in independence. But ontology concealed this interest, buried it in the ready-made reality of a being which supports us. The interest is active only in the critical instance which unmasks the interests at work in the activities of knowledge, which shows the dependence of the theoretical subject on empirical conditions stemming from institutional constraints and which orients the recognition of these forms of constraint towards emancipation.

The critical instance is thus placed above the hermeneutical consciousness, for it is presented as the enterprise of "dissolving" the constraints arising not from nature, but from institutions. A gulf therefore divides the hermeneutical project, which puts assumed tradition above judgment, and the critical project, which puts reflection above institutionalised constraint.

(3) We are thus led, step by step, towards the third point of disagreement, which is the focus of our debate. I shall state the point as follows: the concept of ideology plays the same role in a critical social science as the concept of misunderstanding plays in a hermeneutics of tradition. It was Schleiermacher who, before Gadamer, tied hermeneutics to the concept of misunderstanding. There is hermeneutics where there is misunderstanding. But there is hermeneutics because there is the conviction and the confidence that the understanding which precedes and envelops misunderstanding has the means to reintegrate misunderstanding into understanding by the very movement of question and answer on the dialogical model. Misunderstanding is, if I may say so, homogenous with understanding and of the same genre; hence understanding does not appeal to explanatory procedures, which are relegated to the excessive claims of "methodologism."

It is otherwise with the concept of ideology. What makes the difference? Here Habermas constantly resorts to the parallel between psychoanalysis and the theory of ideology. The parallel rests on the following criteria.

First trait: in the Frankfurt School and in a tradition that could still be called Marxist in a very general sense, distortion is always related to the repressive action of an authority and therefore to violence. The key concept here is "censorship," an originally political concept which has returned to the critical social sciences after passing through psychoanalysis. The link between ideology and violence is crucial, for it introduces into the field of reflection dimensions which, without being absent from hermeneutics, are not accentuated by it, namely the dimensions of labor and power. We may say, in a broad Marxist sense, that the phenomena of class domination appear with the emergence of human labor, and that ideology expresses these phenomena in a way that will be explained shortly. In Habermas's terms, the phenomenon of domination takes place in the sphere of communicative action; it is there that language is distorted as regards its conditions of application at the level of communicative competence. Hence a hermeneutics which adheres to the ideality of *Sprachlichkeit* finds its limit in a phenomenon that affects language as such only because the relation between the three dimensions—labor, power and language—is altered.

Second trait: since the distortions of language do not come from the usage of language as such but from its relation to labor and power, these distortions are unrecognisable by the members of the community. This misrecognition is peculiar to the phenomenon of ideology. It can be analysed phenomenologically only by appealing to concepts of a psychoanalytic type: to *illusion* as distinct from error, to *projection* as the constitution of a false transcendence, to *rationalization* as the subsequent rearrangement of motivations according to the appearance of a rational justification. To say the same thing in the sphere of critical social science, Habermas speaks of "pseudo-communication" or "systematically distorted communication," as opposed to mere misunderstanding.

Third trait: if misrecognition is insurmountable by the directly dialogical route, then the dissolution of ideologies must pass through the detour of procedures concerned with explaining and not simply with understanding. These procedures invoke a theoretical apparatus which cannot be derived from any hermeneutics that remains on the level of the spontaneous interpretation of everyday speech. Here again psychoanalysis provides a good model: it is developed at length in the third part of *Knowledge and Human Interests* and in the article entitled "Der Universalitätsanspruch der Hermeneutik."[11]

Habermas adopts Alfred Lorenzer's interpretation of psychoanalysis as *Sprachanalyse*, according to which the "understanding" of meaning is accomplished by the "reconstruction" of a "primitive scene," placed in relation with two other "scenes": the "symptomatic scene" and the artificial "scene of transference." Certainly, psychoanalysis remains in the sphere of understanding, and of an understanding which culminates in the awareness of the subject; hence Habermas calls it a *Tiefenhermeneutik*, a "depth hermeneutics." But the understanding of meaning requires the detour of a "reconstruction" of the processes of "desymbolisation," which psychoanalysis retraces in the inverse direction along the routes of "resymbolisation." So psychoanalysis is not completely external to hermeneutics, since it can still be expressed in terms of desymbolisation and resymbolisation; rather it constitutes a *limit-experience*, in virtue of the explanatory force linked to the "reconstruction" of the "primitive scene." In other words, to "understand" the *what* of the symptom, it is necessary to "explain" its *why*. This explanatory phase invokes a theoretical apparatus, which establishes the conditions of possibility of explanation and reconstruction: topographical concepts (the three agencies and the three roles), economic concepts (the defense mechanism, primary and secondary repression, splitting-off), genetic concepts (the famous stages and the successive phases of symbol organisation). As regards the three agencies *ego-id-superego* in particular, Habermas says that they are connected to the sphere of communication by the dialogical process of analysis, through which the patient is led to reflect upon himself. The metapsychology, concludes Habermas, "can be founded only as meta-hermeneutics."[12]

Unfortunately, Habermas tells us nothing about the way in which the explanatory and meta-hermeneutical scheme of psychoanalysis could be transposed onto the plane of ideology. It would have to be said, I think, that the distortions of communication which are linked to the social phenomena of domination and violence also constitute phenomena of desymbolisation. Habermas sometimes speaks, very appropriately, of "excommunication," recalling the Wittgensteinian distinction between public and private language. It would also have to be shown in what sense the understanding of these phenomena requires a reconstruction which would recover certain features of "scenic" understanding, or indeed of the three "scenes" as such. In any case, it would be necessary to show that understanding requires an explanatory stage, such that the sense is understood only if the origin of the non-sense is explained. Finally, it would have to be shown how this explanation invokes a theoretical apparatus comparable to the Freudian topography or economics, and that the central concepts of this apparatus could be derived neither from the dialogical experience within the framework of ordinary language, nor from a textual exegesis grafted onto the direct understanding of discourse.

Such are the major characteristics of the concept of ideology: the impact of violence in discourse, a dissimulation whose key eludes consciousness, and the necessity of a detour through the explanation of causes. These three characteristics constitute the ideological phenomenon as a *limit-experience* for hermeneutics. Since hermeneutics can only develop a natural competence, we need a meta-hermeneutics to formulate the theory of the deformations of communicative competence. Critique is this theory of communicative competence, which comprises the art of understanding, the techniques for overcoming misunderstanding and the explanatory science of distortions.

(4) I do not want to end this very schematic presentation of Habermas's thought without saying something about what is perhaps the most profound divergence that separates him from Gadamer.

For Habermas, the principal flaw of Gadamer's account is to have *ontologised* hermeneutics; by that he means its insistence on understanding or accord, as if the *consensus* which precedes us were something constitutive, something given in being. Doesn't Gadamer say that understanding is *Sein* [being] rather than *Bewusstsein* [consciousness]? Does he not speak, with the poet, of the "dialogue which we are" [*das Gespräch, das Wir sind*]? Doesn't he regard *Sprachlichkeit* as an ontological constitution, as a milieu within which we move? More fundamentally still, does he not anchor the hermeneutics of understanding in an ontology of finitude? Habermas can have nothing but mistrust for what seems to him to be the ontological hypostatisation of a rare experience, namely the experience of being preceded in our most felicitous dialogues by an understanding which supports them. This experience cannot be canonized and made into the paradigm of communicative action. What prevents us from doing so is precisely the ideological phenomenon. If ideology were only an internal obstacle to understanding, a mere misunderstanding which the exercise of question and answer could resolve, then it could be said that "Where there is misunderstanding, there is a prior understanding."

A critique of ideology must think in terms of anticipation where the hermeneutics of tradition thinks in terms of assumed tradition. In other words, the critique of ideology must posit as a regulative idea, in front of us, what the hermeneutics of tradition conceives as existing at the origin of understanding. It is at this point that the third interest which guides knowledge, the interest in emancipation, comes into play. This interest, as we have seen, animates the critical social sciences, providing a frame of reference for all the meanings constituted in psychoanalysis and the critique of ideology. Self-reflection is the correlative concept of the interest in emancipation. Hence self-reflection cannot be founded on a prior *consensus*, for what is prior is precisely a broken communication. One cannot speak with Gadamer of the common accord which carries understanding without assuming a convergence of traditions that does not exist, without hypostatising a past which is also the place of false consciousness, without ontologising a language which has always only been a distorted "communicative competence."

The critique of ideology must be placed, therefore, under the sign of a regulative idea, that of unlimited and unconstrained communication. The Kantian emphasis is evident here; the regulative idea is more what ought to be than what is, more anticipation than recollection. It is this idea which gives meaning to every psychoanalytic or sociological critique. For there is desymbolisation only within the project of resymbolisation, and there is such a project only within the revolutionary perspective of the end of violence. Where the hermeneutics of tradition sought to extract the essence of authority and to connect it to the recognition of superiority, the interest in emancipation leads back towards the eleventh of the *Theses on Feuerbach*: "the philosophers have only interpreted the world; the point, however, is to change it." An eschatology of non-violence thus forms the ultimate philosophical horizon of a critique of ideology. This eschatology, close to that of

Ernst Bloch, takes the place of the ontology of lingual understanding in a hermeneutics of tradition.

II. Towards a Critical Hermeneutics

1. Critical reflection on hermeneutics

I should like now to offer my own reflections on the presuppositions of each position and tackle the problems posed in the introduction. These problems, we said, concern the significance of the most fundamental gesture of philosophy. The gesture of hermeneutics is a humble one of acknowledging the historical conditions to which all human understanding is subsumed in the reign of finitude; that of the critique of ideology is a proud gesture of defiance directed against the distortions of human communication. By the first, I place myself in the historical process to which I know that I belong; by the second, I oppose the present state of falsified human communication with the idea of an essentially political freedom of speech, guided by the limiting idea of unrestricted and unconstrained communication.

My aim is not to fuse the hermeneutics of tradition and the critique of ideology in a super-system which would encompass both. As I said at the outset, each speaks from a different place. Nonetheless, each may be asked to recognize the other, not as a position which is foreign and purely hostile, but as one which raises in its own way a legitimate claim.

It is in this spirit that I return to the two questions posed in the introduction: (1) Can hermeneutic philosophy account for the demands of a critique of ideology? and if so, at what price? (2) On what condition is the critique of ideology possible? Can it, in the last analysis, be detached from hermeneutical presuppositions?

The first question challenges the capacity of hermeneutics to account for a critical instance in general. How can there be critique within hermeneutics?

I shall note to begin with that the recognition of a critical instance is a vague desire constantly reiterated, but constantly aborted, within hermeneutics. From Heidegger onwards, hermeneutics is wholly engaged in *going back to the foundations*, a movement which leads from the epistemological question concerning the conditions of possibility of the human sciences to the ontological structure of understanding. It may be asked, however, whether the return route from ontology to epistemology is possible. For it is only along this route that one could confirm the assertion that questions of exegetico-historical critique are "derivative," and that the hermeneutical circle, in the sense of the exegetes, is "founded" on the fundamental anticipatory structure of understanding.

Ontological hermeneutics seems incapable, for structural reasons, of unfolding this problematic of return. In the work of Heidegger himself, the question is abandoned as soon as it is asked. Thus in *Being and Time* we read this:

> In the circle of understanding . . . is hidden a positive possibility of the most primordial kind of knowing. We genuinely take hold of this possibility only when, in our explication [*Auslegung*], we have understood that our first, last, and constant task is never to allow our fore-having, fore-sight, and fore-conception to be presented to us by fancies [*Einfälle*] and popular conceptions [*Volksbegriffe*], but rather to make this scientific theme secure by working out these anticipations in terms of the things themselves. (*SZ* 153; *BT* 195)

Here we find, posed in principle, the distinction between an anticipation according to the things themselves and an anticipation springing from fancies [*Einfälle*] and popular conceptions [*Volksbegriffe*]; these two terms have a visible link with prejudices by "precipitation" and by "predisposition." But how can this distinction be pursued when one declares, immediately afterwards, that "the ontological presuppositions of historiological knowledge transcend in principle the idea of rigour held in the most exact sciences" (*SZ* 153; *BT* 195), and thereby eludes the question of the rigour proper to the historical sciences themselves? The concern to anchor the circle more deeply than any epistemology prevents the epistemological question from being raised on ontological ground.

Is that to say that there is not, in the work of Heidegger himself, any development which corresponds to the critical moment of epistemology? Indeed there is, but the development is applied elsewhere. In passing from the Analytic of *Dasein*, which still includes the theory of understanding and interpretation, to the theory of temporality and totality, which includes the second meditation on understanding (para. 63), it seems that all critical effort is spent in the work of *deconstructing metaphysics*. The reason is clear: since hermeneutics has become the hermeneutics of being—of the meaning of being — the anticipatory structure appropriate to the question of the meaning of being is given by the history of metaphysics, which thus takes the place of prejudice. Henceforth, the hermeneutics of being deploys all its critical resources in the debate with classical and medieval substance, with the Cartesian and Kantian *cogito*. The confrontation with the metaphysical tradition of the West takes the place of a critique of prejudices. In other words, from a Heideggerian perspective, the only internal critique that can be conceived as an integral part of the enterprise of disclosure is the deconstruction of metaphysics; and a properly epistemological critique can be resumed only indirectly, insofar as metaphysical residues can be found at work in the sciences which claim to be empirical. But this critique of prejudices which originate in metaphysics cannot take the place of a real confrontation with the human sciences, with their methodology and with their epistemological presuppositions. The obsessive concern with radicality thus blocks the return route from general hermeneutics towards regional hermeneutics: towards philology, history, depth-psychology, etc.

As regards Gadamer, there is no doubt that he has perfectly grasped the urgency of this "descending dialectic" from the fundamental towards the derived. Thus he proposes, as we noted above, to "inquire into the consequences which follow for the hermeneutics of the human sciences from the fact that Heidegger derives [*Ableitung*] the circular structure of understanding from the temporality of *Dasein*" (*WM* 251; *TM* 235). It is precisely these "consequences" which interest us. For it is in the movement of derivation that the link between pre-understanding and prejudice becomes problematic and the question of critique is raised afresh, in the very heart of understanding. Thus Gadamer, speaking of the texts of our culture, repeatedly insists that these texts signify by themselves, that there is a "matter of the text" which addresses us. But how can the "matter of the text" be left to speak without confronting the critical question of the way in which pre-understanding and prejudice are mixed?

It seems to me that Gadamer's hermeneutics is prevented from embarking upon this route, not simply because, as with Heidegger, all effort of thought is invested in the radicalisation of the problem of foundation, but because the hermeneutical experience itself discourages the recognition of any critical instance.

The *primary* experience of this hermeneutics, determining the very place from which it raises its claim to universality, involves the refutation of the "alienating distanciation"—*Verfremdung*—which commands the objectifying attitude of the human sciences. Henceforth the entire work assumes a dichotomous character which is indicated even in the title, *Truth and Method*, wherein the disjunction overrides the conjunction. It is this initial dichotomous situation which, it seems to me, prevents Gadamer from really recognising the critical instance and hence rendering justice to the critique of ideology, which is the modern post-Marxist expression of the critical instance.

My own interrogation proceeds from this observation. Would it not be appropriate to shift the initial locus of the hermeneutical question, to reformulate the question in such a way that a certain dialectic between the experience of belonging and alienating distanciation becomes the main-spring, the key to the inner life, of hermeneutics?

The idea of such a shift in the initial locus of the hermeneutical question is suggested by the history of hermeneutics itself. Throughout this history, the emphasis has always come back to exegesis or philology, that is, to the sort of relation with tradition which is based on the *mediation* of texts, or documents and monuments which have a status comparable to texts. Schleiermacher was exegete of the New Testament and translator of Plato. Dilthey located the specificity of interpretation [*Auslegung*], as contrasted with the direct understanding of the other [*Verstehen*], in the phenomenon of fixation by writing and, more generally, of inscription.

In thus reverting to the problematic of the text, to exegesis and philology, we appear at first sight to restrict the aim and the scope of hermeneutics. However, since any claim to universality is raised from somewhere, we may expect that the restoration of the link between hermeneutics and exegesis will reveal its own universal features which, without really contradicting Gadamer's hermeneutics, will rectify it in a manner decisive for the debate with the critique of ideology.

I should like to sketch four themes which constitute a sort of critical supplementation to the hermeneutics of tradition.

(a) The distanciation in which this hermeneutics tends to see a sort of ontological fall from grace appears as a positive component of being for the text; it characteristically belongs to interpretation, not as its contrary but as its condition. The moment of distanciation is implied by fixation in writing and by all comparable phenomena in the sphere of the transmission of discourse. Writing is not simply a matter of the material fixation of discourse; for fixation is the condition of a much more fundamental phenomenon, that of the autonomy of the text. A threefold autonomy: with respect to the intention of the author; with respect to the cultural situation and all the sociological conditions of the production of the text; and finally, with respect to the original addressee. What the text signifies no longer coincides with what the author meant; verbal meaning and mental meaning have different destinies. This first form of autonomy already implies the possibility that the ''matter of the text'' may escape from the author's restricted intentional horizon, and that the world of the text may explode the world of its author. What is true of psychological conditions is also true of sociological conditions, even though he who is prepared to liquidate the author is less prepared to perform the same operation in the sociological sphere. The peculiarity of the literary work, and indeed of the work as such, is nevertheless to transcend its own psycho-sociological conditions of production and thereby to open itself to an unlimited series of readings, themselves situated in socio-cultural contexts which are always different. In short, the work *decontextualizes* itself, from the sociological as well as the psychological point of view, and is able to *recontextualize* itself differently in the act of reading. It follows that the mediation of the text cannot be treated as an extension of the dialogical situation. For in dialogue, the *vis-à-vis* of discourse is given in advance by the setting itself; with writing, the original addressee is transcended. The work itself creates an audience, which potentially includes anyone who can read.

The emancipation of the text constitutes the most fundamental condition for the recognition of a critical instance at the heart of interpretation; for distanciation now belongs to the mediation itself.

In a sense, these remarks only extend what Gadamer himself says, on the one hand, about "temporal distance" which, as we have seen above, is one aspect of "consciousness exposed to the efficacy of history"; and on the other hand, about *Schriftlichkeit* which, according to Gadamer himself, adds new features to *Sprachlichkeit*. But at the same time as this analysis extends Gadamer's, it shifts the emphasis somewhat. For the distanciation revealed by writing is already present in discourse itself, which contains the seeds of the distanciation of the *said* from the *saying*, to follow Hegel's famous analysis at the beginning of *The Phenomenology of Mind*: the *saying* vanishes, but the *said* persists. In this respect, writing does not represent a radical revolution in the constitution of discourse, but only accomplishes the latter's profoundest aim.

(b) If hermeneutics is to account for a critical instance in terms of its own premises, then it must satisfy a second condition: it must overcome the ruinous dichotomy, inherited from Dilthey, between "explanation" and "understanding." As is well known, this dichotomy arises from the conviction that any explanatory attitude is borrowed from the methodology of the *natural sciences* and illegitimately extended to the *human sciences*. However, the appearance of semiological models in the field of the text convinces us that all explanation is not naturalistic or causal. The semiological models, applied in particular to the theory of the narrative, are borrowed from the domain of language itself, by extension from units smaller than the sentence to units larger than the sentence (poems, narratives, etc.). Here discourse must be placed under the category, no longer of writing, but rather of the work, that is, under a category which pertains to *praxis*, to labor. Discourse is characterised by the fact that it can be produced as a work displaying structure and form. Even more than writing, the production of discourse as a work involves an objectification that enables it to be read in existential conditions which are always new. But in contrast to the simple discourse of conversation, which enters into the spontaneous movement of question and answer, discourse as a work "takes hold" in structures calling for a description and an explanation that mediate "understanding." We are here in a situation similar to that described by Habermas: *reconstruction* is the path of understanding. However, this situation is not peculiar to psychoanalysis and to all that Habermas designates by the term "depth hermeneutics"; it is the condition of the work in general. So if there is a hermeneutics—and here I oppose those forms of structuralism which would remain at the explanatory level—it must be constituted across the mediation rather than against the current of structural explanation. For it is the task of understanding to bring to discourse what is initially given as structure. It is necessary to have gone as far as possible along the route of objectification, to the point where structural analysis discloses the *depth semantics* of a text, before one can claim to "understand" the text in terms of the "matter" which speaks therefrom. The *matter* of the text is not what a naive reading of the text reveals, but what the formal arrangement of the text mediates. If that is so, then truth and method do not constitute a disjunction but rather a dialectical process.

(c) The hermeneutics of texts turns towards the critique of ideology in a third way. It seems to me that the properly hermeneutical moment arises when the interrogation, transgressing the closure of the text, is carried towards what Gadamer himself calls "the matter of the text," namely the sort of *world* opened up by it. This can be called the *referential* moment, in allusion to the Fregean distinction between sense and reference. The sense of the work is its internal organisation, whereas the reference is the mode of being unfolded in front of the text.

It may be noted in passing that the most decisive break with Romantic hermeneutics is here; what is sought is no longer an intention hidden behind the text, but a world unfolded in front of it. The power of the text to open a dimension of reality implies in principle a recourse against any given reality and thereby the possibility of a critique of the real. It is in poetic discourse that this subversive power is most alive. The strategy of this discourse involves holding two moments in equilibrium: suspending the reference of ordinary language and releasing a second order reference, which is another name for what we have designated above as the world opened up by the work. In the case of poetry, fiction is the path of redescription; or to speak as Aristotle does in the *Poetics*, the creation of a *mythos*, of a "fable," is the path of *mimēsis*, of creative imitation.

Here again we are developing a theme sketched by Gadamer himself, particularly in his magnificent pages on *play*. But in pressing to the end this mediation on the relation between *fiction* and *redescription*, we introduce a critical theme which the hermeneutics of tradition tends to cast beyond its frontiers. The critical theme was nevertheless present in the Heideggerian analysis of understanding. Recall how Heidegger conjoins understanding to the notion of "the projection of my ownmost possibilities"; this signifies that the mode of being of the world opened up by the text is the mode of the possible, or better of the power-to-be: therein resides the subversive force of the imaginary. The paradox of poetic reference consists precisely in the fact that reality is redescribed only insofar as discourse is raised to fiction.

A hermeneutics of the power-to-be thus turns itself towards a critique of ideology, of which it constitutes the most fundamental possibility. Distanciation, at the same time, emerges at the heart of reference: poetic discourse distances itself from everyday reality, aiming towards being as power-to-be.

(d) In a final way, the hermeneutics of texts indicates the place for a critique of ideology. This final point pertains to the status of subjectivity in interpretation. For if the primary concern of hermeneutics is not to discover an intention hidden behind the text but to unfold a world in front of it, then authentic self-understanding is something which, as Heidegger and Gadamer wish to say, can be instructed by the "matter of the text." The relation to the world of the text takes the place of the relation to the subjectivity of the author, and at the same time the problem of the subjectivity of the reader is displaced. To understand is not to project oneself into the text but to expose oneself to it; it is to receive a self enlarged by the appropriation of the proposed worlds which interpretation unfolds. In sum, it is the matter of the text which gives the reader his dimension of subjectivity; understanding is thus no longer a constitution of which the subject possesses the key. Pressing this suggestion to the end, we must say that the subjectivity of the reader is no less held in suspense, no less potentialised, than the very world which the text unfolds. In other words, if fiction is a fundamental dimension of the reference of the text, it is equally a fundamental dimension of the subjectivity of the reader: in reading, I "unrealise myself." Reading introduces me to imaginative variations of the *ego*. The metamorphosis of the world in play is also the playful metamorphosis of the *ego*.

In the idea of the "imaginative variation of the *ego*," I see the most fundamental possibility for a critique of the illusions of the subject. This link could remain hidden or undeveloped in a hermeneutics of tradition which introduced prematurely a concept of appropriation [*Aneignung*] directed against alienating distanciation. However, if distanciation from oneself is not a fault to be combated, but rather the condition of possibility of understanding oneself in front of the text, then appropriation is the dialectical counterpart of distanciation. Thus the critique of ideology can be assumed by a concept of self-understanding which organically implies a critique of the illusions of the subject. Distanciation from oneself demands that the appropriation of the proposed worlds offered by the text passes through the disappropriation of the self. The critique of *false consciousness* can thus become an integral part of hermeneutics, conferring upon the critique of ideology that meta-hermeneutical dimension which Habermas assigns to it.

2. *Hermeneutical reflection on critique*

I should like now to offer a similar reflection on the critique of ideology, with the aim of assessing the latter's claim to universality. I do not expect this reflection to return the critique of ideology to the fold of hermeneutics, but rather to confirm Gadamer's view that the two "universalities," that of hermeneutics and that of the critique of ideology, are interpenetrating. The question could also be presented in Habermas's terms: on what conditions can critique be formulated as meta-hermeneutics? I propose to follow the order of the theses in terms of which I sketched Habermas's thought.

(1) I shall begin with the theory of interests which underlies the critique of the ideologies of transcendental phenomenology and positivism. It may be asked what authorises the following theses: that all *Forschung* is governed by an interest which establishes a prejudicial frame of reference for its field of meaning; that there are three such interests (and not one or two or four): namely, the technical interest, the practical interest and the interest in emancipation; that these interests are anchored in the natural history of the human species, but that they mark the emergence of man out of nature, taking form in the spheres of labor, power and language; that in self-reflection, knowledge and interest are one; that the unity of knowledge and interest are one; that the unity of knowledge and interest is attested to in a dialectic which discerns the historical traces of the repression of dialogue and which constructs what has been suppressed.

Are these "theses" empirically justifiable? No, for then they would fall under the yoke of the empirical-analytic sciences which pertain to *one* interest, the technical interest. Are these theses a "theory," in the sense given to this word by psychoanalysis for example, that is, in the sense of a network of explanatory hypotheses permitting the reconstruction of a primitive scene? No, for then they would become regional theses as in any theory and would again be justified by *one* interest, the interest in emancipation perhaps; and the justification would become circular.

Is it not necessary to recognise henceforth that the disclosure of interests at the roots of knowledge, the hierarchical ordering of interests and their connection to the trilogy of labor—power—language, are dependent upon a philosophical anthropology similar to Heidegger's Analytic of *Dasein*, and more particularly to his hermeneutics of "care"? If that is so, then these interests are neither observables, nor theoretical entities like the *ego*, the *super-ego* and the *id* in Freud's work, but rather "existentiales."

Their analysis depends upon hermeneutics, insofar as they are at once "the closest" and "the most concealed," so that they must be disclosed in order to be recognised.

The analysis of interests could be called "meta-hermeneutical," if it is supposed that hermeneutics is primarily a hermeneutics of discourse, indeed an idealism of lingual life. But we have seen that it has nothing to do with this, that the hermeneutics of pre-understanding is fundamentally a hermeneutics of finitude. Hence I am quite willing to say that the critique of ideology raises its claim from a different place than hermeneutics, namely from the place where labor, power and language are intertwined. But the two claims cross on a common ground: the hermeneutics of finitude, which secures *a priori* the correlation between the concept of prejudice and that of ideology.

(2) I should like now to consider afresh the pact which Habermas establishes between critical social science and the interest in emancipation. We have sharply contrasted the positions of the critical social sciences and the historical-hermeneutic sciences, the latter inclining towards recognition of the authority of traditions rather than towards revolutionary action against oppression.

Here the question which hermeneutics addresses to the critique of ideology is this: can you assign the interest in emancipation a status as distinct as you suppose with respect to the interest which animates the historical-hermeneutic sciences? The distinction is asserted so dogmatically that it seems to create a gulf between the interest in emancipation and the ethical interest. But the concrete analyses of Habermas himself belie this dogmatic aim. It is striking that the distortions which psychoanalysis describes and explains are interpreted, at the meta-hermeneutical level where Habermas places them, as distortions of communicative competence. Everything suggests that the distortions relevant to the critique of ideology also operate at this level. Recall how Habermas reinterprets Marxism on the basis of a dialectic between instrumental and communicative action. It is at the heart of communicative action that the institutionalisation of human relations undergoes the reification which renders it unrecognisable to the participants of communication. It follows that all distortions, those which psychoanalysis discovers as well as those which the critique of ideology denounces, are distortions of the communicative capacity of men.

So can the interest in emancipation be treated as a distinct interest? It seems not, especially if one considers that taken positively as a proper motif and no longer negatively in terms of the reifications which it combats, this interest has no other content than the ideal of unrestricted and unconstrained communication. The interest in emancipation would be quite empty and abstract if it were not situated on the same plane as the historical-hermeneutic sciences, that is, on the plane of communicative action. But if that is so, can a critique of distortions be separated from the communicative experience itself, from the place where it begins, where it is real and where it is exemplary? The task of the hermeneutics of tradition is to remind the critique of ideology that man can project his emancipation and anticipate an unlimited and unconstrained communication only on the basis of the creative reinterpretation of cultural heritage. If we had no experience of communication, however restricted and mutilated it was, how could we wish it to prevail for all men and at all institutional levels of the social nexus? It seems to me that critique can be neither the first instance nor the last. Distortions can be criticised only in the name of a *consensus* which we cannot anticipate merely emptily, in the manner of a regulative idea, unless that idea is exemplified; and one of the very places of exemplification of the ideal of communication is precisely our capacity to overcome cultural distance in the interpretation of works received from the past. He who is unable to reinterpret his past may also be incapable of projecting concretely his interest in emancipation.

(3) I arrive at the third point of disagreement between the hermeneutics of tradition and the critique of ideology. It concerns the abyss which seems to separate simple misunderstanding from pathological or ideological distortion. I shall not reconsider the arguments, already mentioned above, which tend to attenuate the difference between misunderstanding and distortion; a depth-hermeneutics is still a hermeneutics, even if it is called meta-hermeneutical. I should like instead to emphasise an aspect of the theory of ideology which owes nothing to the parallel with psychoanalysis. A large part of Habermas's work is addressed, not to the theory of ideology taken abstractly, but to contemporary ideologies. Now when the theory of ideology is thus developed concretely in terms of a critique of the present, it reveals aspects which call for a concrete—and not simply a theoretical—*rapprochement* between the interest in emancipation and the interest in communication.

For what is, according to Habermas, the dominant ideology of the present day? His answer is close to that of Herbert Marcuse and Jacques Ellul: it is the ideology of science and technology. Here I shall not discuss Habermas's interpretation of advanced capitalism and of developed industrial societies; I shall go straight to the principal characteristic which, in my view, imperiously returns the theory of ideology to the hermeneutical field. In modern industrial society, according to Habermas, the traditional legitimations and basic beliefs once used for the justification of power have been replaced by an ideology of science and technology. The modern state is a state dedicated no longer to representing the interests of an oppressing class, but rather to eliminating the dysfunctions of the industrial system. To justify surplus-value by concealing its mechanism is thus no longer the primary legitimating function of ideology, as it was in the epoch of liberal capitalism described by Marx, quite simply because surplus-value is no longer the principal source of productivity and its appropriation the dominant feature of the system. The dominant feature of the system is the productivity of rationality itself, incorporated into self-regulating systems; what is to be legitimated, therefore, is the maintenance and growth of the system itself. It is precisely for this purpose that the scientific-technological apparatus has become an ideology, that is, a legitimation of the relations of domination and inequality which are necessary for the functioning of the industrial system, but which are concealed beneath all sorts of gratifications provided by the system. The modern ideology thus differs appreciably from that described by Marx, which prevailed only during the short period of liberal capitalism and possessed no universality in time. Nothing now remains of pre-bourgeois ideology, and bourgeois ideology was expressly linked to the camouflaging of domination in the legal institution of the free labor contract.

Granted this description of the modern ideology, what does it signify in terms of interest? It signifies that the sub-system of instrumental action has ceased to be a sub-system, and that its categories have overrun the sphere of communicative action. Therein consists the famous "rationalisation" of which Max Weber spoke: not only does rationality conquer new domains of instrumental action, but it subjugates the domain of communicative action. Max Weber described this phenomenon in terms of "disenchantment" and "secularisation"; Habermas describes it as the obliteration of the difference between the plane of instrumental action, which is also that of labor, and the plane of communicative action, which is also that of agreed norms, symbolic exchanges, personality structures and rational decision-making procedures. In the modern capitalist system, which here seems identical with the industrial system as such, the ancient Greek question of the "good life" is abolished in favor of the functioning of a manipulated system. The problems of *praxis* linked to communication—in particular the desire to submit important political questions to public discussion and democratic decision—have not disappeared; they persist, but in a repressed form. Precisely because their elimination is not automatic and the need for legitimation remains unfulfilled, there is still the need for an ideology to legitimate the authority that secures the functioning of the system; science and technology today assume this ideological role.

But the question which hermeneutics then addresses to the critique of contemporary ideology is this: granted that ideology today consists in disguising the difference between the normative order of communicative action and bureaucratic conditioning, hence in dissolving the sphere of interaction mediated by language into the structures of instrumental action, how can the interest in emancipation remain anything other than a pious vow, save by embodying it in the reawakening of communicative action itself? And upon what will you concretely support the reawakening of communicative action, if not upon the creative renewal of cultural heritage?

(4) The ineluctable link between the reawakening of political responsibility and the reanimation of traditional sources of communicative action leads me to say a few words, in conclusion, about what appeared to be the most formidable difference between the hermeneutical consciousness and the critical consciousness. The first, we said, is turned towards a *consensus* which precedes us and, in this sense, which exists; the second anticipates a future freedom in the form of a regulative idea which is not a reality but an ideal, the ideal of unrestricted and unconstrained communication.

With this apparent antithesis, we reach the liveliest but perhaps the most futile point in the debate. For in the end, hermeneutics will say, from where do you speak when you appeal to *Selbstreflexion*, if it is not from the place that you yourself have denounced as a non-place, the non-place of the transcendental subject? It is indeed from the basis of a tradition that you speak. This tradition is not perhaps the same as Gadamer's; it is perhaps that of the *Aufklärung*, whereas Gadamer's would be Romanticism. But it is a tradition nonetheless, the tradition of emancipation rather than that of recollection. Critique is also a tradition. I would even say that it plunges into the most impressive tradition, that of liberating acts, of the Exodus and the Resurrection. Perhaps there would be no more interest in emancipation, no more anticipation of freedom, if the Exodus and the Resurrection were effaced from the memory of mankind . . .

If that is so, then nothing is more deceptive than the alleged antinomy between an ontology of prior understanding and an eschatology of freedom. We have encountered these false antinomies elsewhere: as if it were necessary to choose between reminiscence and hope! In theological terms, eschatology is nothing without the recitation of acts of deliverance from the past.

In sketching this dialectic of the recollection of tradition and the anticipation of freedom, I do not want in any way to abolish the difference between hermeneutics and the critique of ideology. Each has a privileged place and, if I may say so, different regional preferences: on the one hand, an attention to cultural heritages, focused most decidedly perhaps on the theory of the text; on the other hand, a theory of institutions and of phenomena of domination, focused on the analysis of reifications and alienations. Insofar as each must always be regionalised in order to endow their claims to universality with a concrete character, their differences must be preserved against any conflationist tendency. But it is the task of philosophical reflection to eliminate deceptive antinomies which would oppose the interest in the reinterpretation of cultural heritages received from the past and the interest in the futuristic projections of a liberated humanity.

The moment these two interests become radically separate, then hermeneutics and critique will themselves be no more than . . . ideologies!

Translated by John B. Thompson

Notes

*Paul Ricoeur, "Herméneutique et critique des idéologies," in *Démythisation et idéologie*, edited by Enrico Castelli (Paris: Aubier Montaigne, 1973), pp. 25–64.—ED.

1. Here roughly is the history of the debate. In 1965 the second edition of Hans-Georg Gadamer's *Wahrheit und Methode* (Tübingen: J. C. B. Mohr; hereafter cited in the text as *WM*) appeared, published for the first time in 1960. [English translation: *Truth and Method* (London: Sheed and Ward, 1975; hereafter cited in the text as *TM*)—TRANS.]. This edition contains a preface which replies to a first group of critics. Habermas launched an initial attack in 1967 in *Zur Logik der Sozialwissenschaften* (Frankfurt: Suhrkamp), an attack directed against the section of *Wahrheit und Methode* on which we shall concentrate, namely the rehabilitation of prejudice, authority and tradition, and the famous theory of the "historical-effective consciousness." The same year Gadamer published, in *Kleine Schriften I* (Tübingen: J. C .B. Mohr), a lecture from 1965 entitled "Der Universalität des hermeneutischen Problems" ["The Universality of the Hermeneutical Problem," see pp. 147–58 above—ED.] as well as another essay, "Rhetorik, Hermeneutik and Ideologiekritik." Habermas replied in a long essay, "Der Universalitätsanspruch der Hermeneutik," published in the *Festschrift* in honour of Gadamer entitled *Hermeneutik und Dialektik I* (Tübingen: J. C. B. Mohr, 1970) ["The Hermeneutic Claim to Universality," see pp. 245–72 above—ED.]. (The latter two essays are reprinted in a collection edited by Habermas and others entitled *Hermeneutik und Ideologiekritik* (Frankfurt: Suhrkamp, 1971).) But the principal work of Habermas which we shall consider is called *Erkenntnis und Interesse* (Frankfurt: Suhrkamp, 1968) [English translation: *Knowledge and Human Interests*, translated by Jeremy J. Shapiro (London: Heinemann, 1972)—TRANS.]; it contains in the appendix an important exposition of principles and methods published in 1965 as "A general perspective." His conception of the contemporary form of ideology is found in "Technik und Wissenschaft als 'Ideologie,' " offered to Herbert Marcuse on his seventieth birthday in 1968 [English translation: "Technology and science as 'ideology,' " translated by Jeremy J. Shapiro, in *Toward a Rational Society* (London: Heinemann, 1971)—TRANS.].

2. Hans-Georg Gadamer, *Hermeneutik und Ideologiekritik*, p. 57.

3. *Ibid.*

4. Martin Heidegger, *Sein und Zeit* (Tübingen: Max Niemeyer, 1927; hereafter cited in the text as *SZ*) [English translation: *Being and Time*, translated by John Macquarrie and Edward Robinson (Oxford: Basil Blackwell, 1978; hereafter cited in the text as *BT*)—TRANS.].

5. Hans-Georg Gadamer, *Kleine Schriften* I, p. 158.

6. *Ibid.*, p. 101 [p. 147 above.—ED.].

7. *Ibid.*, p. 104 [p. 150 above.—ED.].

8. *Ibid.*, p. 107 [p. 153 above.—ED.].

9. Jürgen Habermas, *Knowledge and Human Interests*, p. 9.

10. *Ibid.*, p. 309.

11. Cf. *Hermeneutik und Ideologiekritik*, pp. 120ff. [see pp. 245–72 above.—ED.].

12. *Ibid.*, p. 149.

Selected Bibliography

A. Works Authored by Contributors

Ast, Friedrich. *Grundlinien der Grammatik, Hermeneutik und Kritik*. Landshut: Thomann, 1808.

――――. *Grundriss der Philologie*. Landshut: Krull, 1808.

Betti, Emilio. *Allgemeine Auslegungslehre als Methodik der Geisteswissenschaften*. Tübingen: J. C. B. Mohr (Paul Siebeck), 1967.

――――. *Die Hermeneutik als allgemeine Methodik der Geisteswissenschaften*. Tübingen: J. C. B. Mohr (Paul Siebeck), 1962.

――――. *Teoria generale della interpretazione*. 2 vol. Milan: A. Guiffrè, 1955.

――――. "The Epistemological Problem of Understanding As An Aspect of the General Problem of Knowing." Translated by Susan Noakes. In *Hermeneutics: Questions and Prospects*, edited by Gary Shapiro and Alan Sica. Amherst: University of Massachusetts Press, 1984, pp. 25–53.

――――. "Problematik einer allgemeinen Auslegungslehre als Methode der Geisteswissenschaften." In *Hermeneutik als Weg heutiger Wissenschaft*, edited by Viktor Warnach. Salzburg-Munich: Anton Pustet, 1971, pp. 15–30.

Dilthey, Wilhelm. *Descriptive Psychology and Historical Understanding*. Translated by Richard M. Zaner and Kenneth L. Heiges. The Hague: Martinus Nijhoff, 1977.

――――. *Gesammelte Schriften*. 18 vols. Stuttgart: B. G. Teubner; Göttingen: Vandenhoeck und Ruprecht, 1914–77.

――――. *Pattern and Meaning in History: Thoughts on History and Society*. Edited and introduced by H. P. Rickman. New York: Harper and Row, 1962.

――――. *Selected Writings*. Edited, translated, and introduced by H. P. Rickman. Cambridge: Cambridge University Press, 1976.

――――. *Selected Writings: Poetry and Experience*. Edited by Rudolf A. Makkreel and Frithjof Rodi. Princeton, N.J.: Princeton University Press, 1985.

Gadamer, Hans-Georg. *Die Aktualität des Schönen: Kunst als Spiel, Symbol und Fest*. Stuttgart: Reclam, 1977.

――――. *Dialogue and Dialectic*. Translated by P. Christopher Smith. New Haven, Conn.: Yale University Press, 1980.

――――. *Hegel's Dialectic: Five Hermeneutical Studies*. Translated by P. Christopher Smith. New Haven, Conn.: Yale University Press, 1976.

――――. *The Idea of the Good in Platonic-Aristotelian Philosophy*. Translated by P. Christopher Smith. New Haven, Conn.: Yale University Press, 1986.

—— . *Kleine Schriften*. Tübingen: J. C. B. Mohr, 1967–.

—— . *Philosophical Apprenticeships*. Translated by Robert R. Sullivan. Cambridge, Mass.: MIT Press, 1985.

—— . *Philosophical Hermeneutics*. Edited and translated by David E. Linge. Berkeley: University of California Press, 1976.

—— . *Philosophische Lehrjahre*. Frankfurt: Klostermann, 1977.

—— . *Plato und die Dichter*. Frankfurt: Klostermann, 1934.

—— . *Plato. Texte zur Ideenlehre*. Frankfurt: Klostermann, 1978.

—— . *Poetica*. Frankfurt: Klostermann, 1977.

—— . *Reason in the Age of Science*. Translated by Frederick G. Lawrence. Cambridge, Mass.: MIT Press, 1981.

—— . *The Relevance of the Beautiful and Other Essays*. Translated by Nicholas Walker. Edited by Robert Bernasconi. Cambridge: Cambridge University Press, 1986.

—— . *Truth and Method*. Translated by Garrett Barden and John Cumming. New York: Seabury, 1975.

—— . "The Continuity of History and the Existential Moment." *Philosophy Today* 16 (Fall 1971): 230–40.

—— . "Heidegger and the History of Philosophy." *The Monist* 64 (1981): 423–438.

—— . "Heidegger's Paths." *Philosophie Exchange* 2 (1979): 80–91.

—— . "The Hermeneutics of Suspicion." *Man and World* 17 (1984): 313–24.

—— . "Historical Transformations of Reason." In *Rationality Today*, edited by Theodore F. Geraets. Ottawa: University of Ottawa Press, 1979.

—— . "On the Problematic Character of Aesthetic Consciousness." *Graduate Faculty Philosophy Journal* 9 (1982): 31–40.

—— . "The Problem of Historical Consciousness." In *Interpretive Social Science: A Second Look*, edited by Paul Rabinow and William Sullivan. Berkeley: University of California Press, 1987 pp. 103–162.

—— . "The Power of Reason." *Man And World* 3 (February 1970): 5–15.

—— . "Summation." *Cultural Hermeneutics* 2 (1975): 329–30.

Jürgen Habermas. *Communication and the Evolution of Society*. Translated by Thomas McCarthy. Boston: Beacon Press, 1979.

—— . *Knowledge and Human Interests*. Translated by Jeremy J. Shapiro. Boston: Beacon Press, 1971.

—— . *Legitimation Crisis*. Translated by Thomas McCarthy. Boston: Beacon Press, 1975.

—— . *On the Logic of the Social Sciences*. Translated by Shierry Weber Nicholsen and Jerry A. Stark. Cambridge, Mass: MIT Press, 1988.

—— . *The Philosophical Discourse of Modernity*. Translated by Frederick G. Lawrence. Cambridge, Mass.: MIT Press, 1987.

—— . *Philosophical-Political Profiles*. Translated by Frederick Lawrence. Cambridge, Mass.: MIT Press, 1981.

—— . *Protestbewegung und Hochschulreform*. Frankfurt: Suhrkamp, 1969.

—— . *Technik und Wissenschaft als 'Ideologie'*. Frankfurt: Suhrkamp, 1969.

―――. *Theory and Practice.* Translated by John Viertel. Boston: Beacon Press, 1973.

―――. *The Theory of Communicative Practice*, vol. 1: *Reason and The Rationalization of Society.* Translated by Thomas McCarthy. Boston: Beacon Press, 1984.

―――. *The Theory of Communicative Practice*, vol. 2: *Lifeworld and System, a Critique of Function and System.* Translated by Thomas McCarthy. Boston: Beacon Press, 1987.

―――. *Toward a Rational Society: Student Protest, Science, and Politics.* Translated by Jeremy J. Shapiro. Boston: Beacon Press, 1970.

―――. "A Reply to My Critics." In *Habermas: Critical Debates,* edited by John B. Thompson and David Held. Cambridge, Mass.: MIT Press, 1987, pp. 219–83.

Heidegger, Martin. *The Basic Problems of Phenomenology.* Translated by Albert Hofstader. Bloomington: Indiana University Press, 1982.

―――. *Basic Writings.* Edited by David Farrell Krell. New York: Harper and Row, 1977.

―――. *Being and Time.* Translated by John Macquarrie and Edward Robinson. New York: Harper and Row, 1962.

―――. *Discourse on Thinking.* Translated by John M. Anderson and E. Hans Freund. New York: Harper and Row, 1966.

―――. *Early Greek Thinking.* Translated by David Farrell Krell and Frank A. Capuzzi. New York: Harper and Row, 1975.

―――. *The End of Philosophy.* Translated by Joan Stambaugh. New York: Harper and Row, 1973.

―――. *The Essence of Reasons.* Translated by Terrence Malick. Evanston, Ill.: Northwestern University Press, 1969.

―――. *Existence and Being.* Edited and introduced by Werner Brock. Chicago: Henry Regnery Company, 1949.

―――. *Hegel's Concept of Experience.* Translated by J. Glenn Gray and Fred D. Wieck. New York: Harper and Row, 1970.

―――. *Identity and Difference.* Translated by Joan Stambaugh. New York: Harper and Row, 1969.

―――. *An Introduction to Metaphysics.* Translated by Ralph Manheim. New York: Doubleday-Anchor Books, 1961.

―――. *Kant and the Problem of Metaphysics.* Translated by James S. Churchill. Bloomington: Indiana University Press, 1962.

―――. *The Metaphysical Foundations of Logic.* Translated by Michael Heim. Bloomington: Indiana University Press, 1984.

―――. *Nietzsche, vol. 1: The Will to Power as Art.* Edited and translated by David Farrell Krell. New York: Harper and Row, 1979.

―――. *Nietzsche, vol. 2: The Eternal Recurrence of the Same.* Edited and translated by David Farrell Krell. New York: Harper and Row, 1984.

―――. *Nietzsche, vol. 3: The Will to Power as Knowledge and Metaphysics.* Edited by David Farrell Krell. Translated by Joan Stambaugh, David Farrell Krell, and Frank Capuzzi. New York: Harper and Row, 1987.

—————. *Nietzsche, vol. 4: Nihilism*. Edited by David Farrell Krell. Translated by Frank Capuzzi. New York: Harper and Row, 1982.

—————. *On the Way to Language*. Translated by Peter D. Hertz and Joan Stambaugh. New York: Harper and Row, 1971.

—————. *On Time and Being*. Translated by Joan Stambaugh. New York: Harper and Row, 1972.

—————. *Poetry, Language, Thought*. Translated by Albert Hofstader. New York: Harper and Row, 1971.

—————. *The Question Concerning Technology and Other Essays*. Translated by William Lovitt. New York: Harper and Row, 1979.

—————. *The Question of Being*. Translated by William Kluback and Jean T. Wilde. New Haven, Conn.: College and University Press, 1958.

—————. *Schelling's Treatise on the Essence of Human Freedom*. Translated by Joan Stambaugh. Athens, Ohio: Ohio University Press, 1985.

—————. *What is a Thing?* Translated by W. B. Barton, Jr., and Vera Deutsch. Chicago: Henry Regnery Company, 1967.

—————. *What is Called Thinking?* Translated by Fred D. Wieck and J. Glenn Gray. New York: Harper and Row, 1968.

—————. *What is Philosophy?* Translated by William Kluback and Jean T. Wilde. New Haven, Conn.: College and University Press, 1958.

Ricoeur, Paul. *The Conflict of Interpretations: Essays in Hermeneutics*. Edited by Don Ihde. Evanston, Ill.: Northwestern University Press, 1974.

—————. *Freud and Philosophy: An Essay on Interpretation*. Translated by Denis Savage. New Haven, Conn.: Yale University Press, 1970.

—————. *History and Truth*. Translated by Charles A. Kelbley. Evanston, Ill.: Northwestern University Press, 1965.

—————. *Husserl: An Analysis of His Phenomenology*. Translated by Edward G. Ballard and Lester E. Embree. Evanston, Ill.: Northwestern University Press, 1967.

—————. *Interpretation Theory: Discourse and the Surplus of Meaning*. Fort Worth: Texas Christian University Press, 1976.

—————. *Hermeneutics and the Human Sciences*. Edited and translated by John B. Thompson. Cambridge: Cambridge University Press, 1981.

—————. *The Philosophy of Paul Ricoeur*. Edited by Charles Reagan and David Stewart. Boston: Beacon Press, 1978.

—————. *The Rule of Metaphor: Multi-disciplinary Studies of the Creation of Meaning in Language*. Translated by Robert Czerny. Toronto: University of Toronto Press, 1977.

—————. *The Symbolism of Evil*. Translated by Emerson Buchanan. New York: Harper and Row, 1967.

—————. *Du Texte à l'action: Essais d'herméneutique, II*. Paris: Éditions du Seuil, 1986.

—————. *Time and Narrative I*. Translated by Kathleen McLaughlin and David Pellauer. Chicago: University of Chicago Press, 1984.

—————. *Time and Narrative II*. Translated by Kathleen McLaughlin and David Pellauer. Chicago: University of Chicago Press, 1986.

———. *Time and Narrative III*. Translated by Kathleen McLaughlin and David Pellauer. Chicago: University of Chicago Press, 1988.

———. "Ethics and Culture: Habermas and Gadamer in Dialogue." *Philosophy Today* 17 (1973): 153–65.

———. "Narrative and Hermeneutics." In *Essays on Aesthetics: Perspectives on the Work of Monroe Beardsley*, edited by John Fischer. Philadelphia: Temple University Press, 1983.

———. "Phenomenology & Hermeneutics." *Nous* 9 (1975): 85–102.

———. "Schleiermacher's Hermeneutics." *Monist* 60 (1977): 181–97.

Ricoeur, Paul, and Gadamer, Hans-Georg. "The Conflict of Interpretations," In *Phenomenology: Dialogues & Bridges*, edited by Ronald Bruzina and Bruce Wilshire. Albany: State University of New York Press, 1982.

Schleiermacher, Friedrich D. E. *Dialektik*. Edited by Andras Arndt. Hamburg: Meiner, 1986.

———. *Hermeneutics: The Handwritten Manuscripts*. Edited by Heinz Kimmerle. Translated by James Duke and Jack Forstman. Missoula, Mont.: Scholars Press, 1977.

———. *Hermeneutik*. Edited and introduced by Heinz Kimmerle. Heidelberg: Carl Winter Universitätsverlag, 1959.

———. *Hermeneutik und Kritik mit besonderer Beziehung auf das Neue Testament*. Edited by F. Lücke. *Sämmtliche Werke*. Vol. 7. Berlin: Reimer, 1838.

———. *Hermeneutik und Kritik: Mit einem Anhang sprachphilosophischer Texte Schleiermachers*. Edited and introduced by Manfred Frank. Frankfurt: Suhrkamp, 1977.

———. *Kritische Gesamtausgabe*. Edited by Hans-Joachim Birkner, et al. Berlin: Walter de Gruyter, 1980.

B. General Works

Abel, Elizabeth, editor. *Writing and Sexual Difference*. Chicago: University of Chicago Press, 1982.

Abel, Theodore. "The Operation Called *Verstehen*." *American Journal of Sociology* 54 (1948): 211–18.

Abrams, M. H. "How to Do Things with Texts." *Partisan Review* 64 (1979): 566–88.

Adorno, Th. W., Popper, K., et al. *The Positivist Dispute in German Sociology*. Edited by Glyn Adey and David Frisby. London: Heinemann, 1976.

Albert, Hans. *Pladoyer für Kritischen Rationalismus*. Munich: Piper, 1971.

———. *Transzendentale Träumereien: Karl-Otto Apels Sprachspiele und sein hermeneutischer Gott*. Hamburg: Hoffmann und Campe, 1975.

Albrecht, Erhard. *Beiträge zur Erkenntnistheorie und das Verhältnis von Sprache und Denken*. Halle: Niemeyer, 1959.

Allison, David B. "Destruction/Deconstruction in the Text of Nietzsche." *boundary 2* 8 (Fall 1979): 197–222.

———, editor. *The New Nietzsche: Contemporary Styles of Interpretation*. 2nd ed. Cambridge, Mass.: MIT Press, 1985.

Altenhofer, Norbert. "Geselliges Betragen-Kunst-Auslegung. Anmerkungen zu Peter Szondis Schleiermacher Interpretation und zur Frage einer Materialen Hermeneutik." In *Studien zur Entwicklung einer materialen Hermeneutik*, edited by Ulrich Nassen. Munich: Fink Verlag, 1974, pp. 165–211.

Althusser, Louis, and Balibar, Étienne. *Reading Capital*. Translated by Ben Brewster. London: New Left Books, 1972.

Altieri, Charles. *Act and Quality: A Theory of Literary and Humanistic Understanding*. Amherst: University of Massachusetts Press, 1981.

———. "The Hermeneutics of Literary Indeterminacy: A Dissenting From the Orthodoxy." *New Literary History* 10 (1978-79): 71–99.

Apel, Karl-Otto. *Analytic Philosophy of Language and the Geisteswissenschaften*. Dordrecht: D. Reidel, 1967.

———. *Die Idee der Sprache in der Tradition des Humanismus von Dante bis Vico*. 2nd ed. Bonn: Bouvier, 1975.

———. *Towards a Transformation of Philosophy*. Translated by Glyn Adey and David Frisby. London and Boston: Routledge and Kegan Paul, 1980.

———. *Understanding and Explanation: A Transcendental Pragmatic Perspective*. Translated by Georgia Warnke. Cambridge, Mass.: MIT Press, 1985.

———. "The Common Presuppositions of Hermeneutics and Ethics," *Research in Phenomenology* 9 (1979): 35–53.

———. "Types of Social Science in the Light of Human Interests of Knowledge." *Social Research* 44, no. 3 (1977): 425–70.

———. "Das Verstehen." *Archiv für Begriffsgeschichte* 1 (1955): 142–99.

Arac, Jonathan, editor. *Postmodernism and Politics*. Minneapolis: University of Minnesota Press, 1986.

Argyros, Alex. "The Warp of the World: Deconstruction and Hermeneutics." *Diacritics* 16, no. 3 (Fall 1986): 46–55.

Aristotle. *The Basic Works*. Edited by Richard McKeon. New York: Random House, 1941.

———. *Categories* and *De Interpretatione*. Translation with notes by J. L. Ackrill. London: Clarendon Press, 1966.

Arthur, Christopher E. "Gadamer and Hirsch: The Canonical Work and the Interpreter's Intention." *Cultural Hermeneutics* 4 (1977): 183–97.

Attridge, Derek, Bennington, Geoff, and Young, Robert, editors. *Post-Structuralism and the Question of History*. Cambridge: Cambridge University Press, 1987.

Auerbach, Erich. *Mimesis: The Representation of Reality in Western Literature*. Princeton, N.J.: Princeton University Press, 1953.

Ball, Terrence, editor. *Political Theory and Praxis: New Perspectives*. Minneapolis: University of Minnesota Press, 1977.

Ballard, Edward G. *Principles of Interpretation*. Athens: Ohio University Press, 1983.

Bar-Hillel, Y. "On Habermas' Hermeneutic Philosophy of Language." *Synthese 26* (1973): 1–12.

Barnes, Annette. *On Interpretation: A Critical Analysis*. Oxford: B. Blackwell, 1986.

Barthes, Roland. *Critical Essays*. Translated by Richard Howard. Evanston, Ill.: Northwestern University Press, 1972.

———. *Mythologies*. Translated by Richard Howard. Evanston, Ill.: Northwestern University Press, 1972.

———. *The Pleasure of the Text*. Translated by Richard Miller. New York: Hill and Wang, 1975.

———. *On Racine*. Translated by Richard Howard. New York: Hill and Wang, 1977.

———. *Roland Barthes*. Translated by Richard Howard. New York: Hill and Wang, 1977.

———. *Sade/Fourier/Loyola*. Translated by Stephen Heath. New York: Hill and Wang, 1977.

———. *S/Z*. Translated by Richard Miller. New York: Hill and Wang, 1975.

———. *Writing Degree Zero/Elements of Semiology*. Translated by Annette Lavers and Colin Smith. Boston: Beacon Press, 1970.

Bauman, Zygmunt. *Hermeneutics and Social Science*. New York: Columbia University Press, 1978.

Bernstein, Richard J. *Beyond Objectivism and Relativism: Science, Hermeneutics, and Praxis*. Philadelphia: University of Pennsylvania Press, 1983.

———. *Praxis and Action*. Philadelphia: University of Pennsylvania Press, 1971.

———. *The Restructuring of Social and Political Theory*. New York: Harcourt Brace Jovanovich, 1976.

———. "From Hermeneutics to Praxis." *Review of Metaphysics* 35 (1982): 823–45.

———. "Philosophy in the Conversation of Mankind." *Review of Metaphysics* 33 (1980): 745–76.

———. "Why Hegel Now?" *Review of Metaphysics* 31 (1977): 29–60.

Binswanger, Ludwig. *Grundformen und Erkenntnis menschlichen Daseins*. Munich and Basel: Ernst Reinhardt Verlag, 1962.

Blanchette, Oliva. "Language, the Primordial Labor of History: A Critique of Critical Social Theory in Habermas." *Cultural Hermeneutics* 1 (February 1974): 325–82.

Bleicher, Josef. *Contemporary Hermeneutics: Hermeneutics as method, philosophy, and critique*. London: Routledge and Kegan Paul, 1980

———. *The Hermeneutic Imagination: Outline of a Positive Critique of Scientism and Sociology*. London: Methuen, 1982.

Blondel, Eric. *Nietzsche: le "cinquième 'évangile' "?* Paris: Bergers et Mages, 1980.

———. *Nietzsche, le corps et la culture*. Paris: Presses Universitaires de France, 1986.

———. "Nietzsche: Life as Metaphor." In *The New Nietzsche: Contemporary Styles of Interpretation*, edited by David Allison. Cambridge, Mass.: MIT Press, 1985, pp. 150–175.

———. "Nietzsche's Style of Affirmation: The Metaphors of Genealogy." In *Nietzsche as Affirmative Thinker*, edited by Yirmiyahu Yovel. Dordrecht: Nijhoff, 1986, pp. 132–146.

Bloom, Harold. *A Map of Misreading*. New York: Oxford University Press, 1975.
Bloom, Harold, de Man, Paul, Derrida, Jacques, Hartman, Geoffrey, and Miller, J. Hillis, editors. *Deconstruction and Criticism*. New York: Seabury Press, 1979.
Blumenberg, Hans. *The Legitimacy of the Modern Age*. Translated by Robert Wallace. Cambridge, Mass.: MIT Press, 1983.
Boeckh, Philip August. *On Interpretation and Criticism*. Translated and edited by John Paul Pritchard. Norman: University of Oklahoma Press, 1968.
Boehler, Dietrich. "Das Dialogische Prinzip als Hermeneutische Maxime." *Man and World* 11 (1978): 131–64.
————. "Zum Problem des 'Emancipatorischen Interesses' und seiner gesellschaftlichen Wahrnehmung." *Man and World* 3 (1970): 26–53.
Bollnow, Otto Friedrich. *Dilthey: Eine Einführung in seine Philosophie*. 3rd rev. ed. Stuttgart: Kohlhammer, 1968.
————. *Die Lebensphilosophie*. Berlin: Springer, 1958.
————. *Die Methode der Geisteswissenschaften*. Mainz: Gutenberg, 1950.
————. *Das Verstehen: Drei Aufsätze zur Theorie der Geisteswissenschaften*. Mainz: Kirchheim, 1949.
————. "Über das Kritische Verstehen." *Deutsche Vierteljahresschrift für Literaturwissenschaft* 22: 1–29.
————. "What Does it Mean to Understand a Writer Better than He Understood Himself?" *Philosophy Today* 23 (1979): 16–28.
Bontekoe, Ron. "A Fusion of Horizons: Gadamer and Schleiermacher." *International Philosophical Quarterly*, 27 (March 1987):3–16.
Bornkamm, Günther. "Die Theologie Rudolf Bultmanns in neueren Diskussion. Zum Problem der Entmythologisierung und Hermeneutik." *Theologische Rundschau*, n.s. (1963): 33–141.
Borsche, Tilman. *Sprachansichten. Der Begriff der menschlichen Rede in der Sprachphilosophie Wilhelm von Humboldts*. Stuttgart: Klett-Cotta, 1981.
Bourdieu, Pierre. *Outline of a Theory of Practice*. Translated by Richard Nice. Cambridge: Cambridge University Press, 1977.
Bové, Paul. *Destructive Poetics: Heidegger and Modern American Poetry*. New York: Columbia University Press, 1980.
Brandt, Reinhard. *Die aristotelische Urteilslehre: Untersuchungen zur "Hermeneutik."* Marburg: Görich und Weiershäuser, 1965.
Brenkman, John. *Culture and Domination*. Ithaca: Cornell University Press, 1987.
Brinckmann, Hennig. *Mittelalterliche Hermeneutik*. Tübingen: Niemeyer, 1980.
Brunner, August. *Geschichtlichkeit*. Bern and Munich: Francke, 1961.
Bubner, Rüdiger. *Essays in Hermeneutics and Critical Theory*. Translated by Eric Matthews. New York: Columbia University Press, 1987.
————. *Modern German Philosophy*. Translated by Eric Matthews. Cambridge: Cambridge University Press, 1981.
————. *Theorie und Praxis, eine nachhegelsche Abstraktion*. Frankfurt: Klostermann, 1971.
————. "Action and Reason." *Ethics*, 83 (1973): 224–236.

———. "Transzendentale Hermeneutik?" In *Wissenschaftstheorie in den Geistes-wissenschaften. Konzeptionen, Vorschläge, Entwürfe*, edited by R. Simon Schaefer and W. Ch. Zimmerli. Hamburg: Hoffmann und Campe, 1975.

———. "Was ist Kritische Theorie?" *Philosophische Rundschau* (December 1969): 213–248.

Bubner, Rüdiger., Cramer, K., and Weihl, R., editors. *Hermeneutik und Dialektik.* Vols. 1 and 2. Tübingen: J. C. B. Mohr, 1970.

Buck, Günther."Hermeneutics of Texts and Hermeneutics of Action." *New Literary History* 4, no. 1 (1980): 87–96.

———. "The Structure of Hermeneutic Experience and the Problems of Tradition." *New Literary History* 10, no. 1 (1978): 31–47.

Bultmann, Rudolf. *Essays, Philosophical and Theological*. Translated by J. C. G. Greig. London: SCM Press; New York: Macmillan, 1955.

———. *Existence and Faith: Shorter Writings of Rudolf Bultmann*. Selected, translated, and introduced by Schubert M. Ogden. New York: Meridian Books, 1960.

———. *Faith and Understanding*. Edited and introduced by Robert W. Funk. Translated by Louise Pettibone Smith. New York: Harper and Row, 1969.

———. *Jesus and the Word*. Translated by Louise Pettibone Smith and E. Huntress. New York: Charles Scribner's Sons, 1958.

———. *Theology of the New Testament*. 2 vols. Translated by K. Grobel. New York: Charles Scribner's Sons, 1951–1955.

Byrum, Charles Stephen. "Philosophy as Play." *Man and World* 8 (1975): 315–26.

Capurro, Rafael. *Hermeneutik der Fachinformation*. Freiburg: Alber, 1986.

Caputo, John D. *Radical Hermeneutics: Repetition, Deconstruction, and the Hermeneutic Project*. Bloomington: Indiana University Press, 1987.

———. "Hermeneutics as the Recovery of Man." *Man and World* (1982): 343–67.

———. "Husserl, Heidegger, and the Question of a 'Hermeneutic' Phenomenology." *Husserl Studies* 1 (1984): 157–78.

Carr, David. *Phenomenology and the Problem of History*. Evanston, Ill.: Northwestern University Press, 1974.

———. "Interpretation and Self-Evidence." *Analecta Husserliana* 11 (1980): 133–148.

Cassirer, Ernst. *The Philosophy of Symbolic Forms*. 3 vols. Translated by Ralph Manheim. New Haven, Conn.: Yale University Press, 1953–57.

Castelli, Enrico, editor. *Herméneutique et tradition*. Paris: Vrin, 1963.

Caws, Peter. *The Philosophy of Science, a Systematic Account*. Princeton, N.J.: Van Nostrand, 1965.

———. *Sartre*. London and New York: Routledge and Kegan Paul, 1979.

———. *Science and The Theory of Value*. New York: Random House, 1967.

———, editor. *Two Centuries of Philosophy: American Philosophy Since the Revolution*. Totowa, N.J.: Rowman and Littlefield, 1980.

———. "Flaubert's Laughter." *Philosophy and Literature* 8 (October 1984): 167–180.

———— . "Oracular Lives: Sartre and the 20th Century." *Revue Internationale de Philosophie* 39 (1985): 172–183.

Chladenius, Johann Martin. *Einleitung zur richtigen Auslegung vernünftiger Reden und Schriften*. Facsimile reprint of the Leipzig edition of 1742. With an introduction by Lutz Geldsetzer. Vol. 5 of the Series Hermeneutica, Instrumenta Philosophica. Düsseldorf: Stern Verlag, 1969.

Chomsky, Noam. *Aspects of the Theory of Syntax*. Cambridge, Mass.: MIT Press, 1963.

———— . *Cartesian Linguistics. A Chapter in the History of Rationalist Thought*. New York: Harper and Row, 1966.

Cicourel, Aaron. *Cognitive Sociology: Language and Meaning in Social Interaction*. New York: The Free Press, 1974.

Coreth, Emrich. *Grundfragen der Hermeneutik*. Freiburg: Herder, 1969.

Corngold, Stanley. *The Fate of the Self*. New York: Columbia University Press, 1986.

———— . "Error in Paul de Man." *Critical Inquiry* 8 (Spring 1982): 489–513.

Corrington, Robert S. "Horizontal Hermeneutics and the Actual Infinite." *Graduate Faculty Philosophy Journal* 8 (Spring 1982): 36–97.

Cosgrove, Stephen. "Styles of Thought: Science, Romanticism, and Modernization." *British Journal of Sociology* 29 (1978): 358–71.

Crother, Paul. "Experience of Art: Some Problems and Possibilities of Hermeneutical Analysis." *Philosophy and Phenomenological Research* 43 (1983): 347–62.

Crowley, Charles B. *Universal Mathematics in Aristotelian-Thomistic Philosophy: The Hermeneutics of Aristotelian Texts Relative to Universal Mathematics*. Washington, D.C.: University Press of America, 1980.

Culler, Jonathan. *On Deconstruction*. Ithaca, N.Y.: Cornell University Press, 1982.

Dallmayr, Fred R. *Critical Encounters: Between Philosophy and Politics*. Notre Dame, Ind.: University of Notre Dame Press, 1987.

———— . *Polis and Praxis: Essays in Contemporary Political Theory*. Cambridge, Mass.: MIT Press, 1985.

———— , editor. *Materialien zu Habermas' 'Erkenntnis und Interesse'*. Frankfurt: Suhrkamp, 1974.

———— . "Hermeneutics and Historicism: Reflections on Winch, Apel, and Vico." *The Review of Politics* 39 (1977): 60–81.

———— . "Reason and Emancipation: Notes on Habermas." *Man and World* (Fall 1972): 79–109.

Dallmayr, Fred R., and McCarthy, Thomas A., editors. *Understanding and Social Inquiry*. Notre Dame, Ind.: University of Notre Dame Press, 1977.

Dannhauer, Johann Conrad. *Idea boni interpretis (1670)*. Strasbourg: n.p., 1670.

Danto, Arthur C. "Deep Interpretation." *Journal of Philosophy* 78 (1981): 691–706.

———— . "Philosophy as/and/of Literature." In *Post-Analytic Philosophy*, edited by John Rajchman and Cornel West. New York: Columbia University Press, 1985, pp. 63–83.

Davidson, Donald. *Inquiries into Truth and Interpretation*. Oxford: Oxford University Press, 1984.

De George, Richard T., and Fernande, M., editors. *The Structuralists: From Marx to Lévi-Strauss*. Garden City, N.Y.: Anchor Books, 1972.

Deleuze, Gilles, and Guattari, Félix. *Kafka: Toward a Minor Literature*. Translated by Dana Parker. Minneapolis: University of Minnesota Press, 1986.

De Man, Paul. *Allegories of Reading*. New Haven, Conn.: Yale University Press, 1979.

———. *Blindness and Insight*. 2nd ed. Minneapolis: University of Minnesota Press, 1983.

Derrida, Jacques. *Dissemination*. Translated by Barbara Johnson. Chicago: University of Chicago Press, 1981.

———. *The Ear of the Other: Otobiography, Transference, Translation*. English edition edited by Christie V. McDonald. Translated by Avital Ronell and Peggy Kamuf. New York: Schocken, 1985.

———. *Glas*. Translated by John P. Leavey, Jr. Lincoln: University of Nebraska Press, 1987.

———. *Margins of Philosophy*. Translated by Barbara Johnson. Chicago: University of Chicago Press, 1981.

———. *Memoires for Paul De Man*. Translated by Cecile Lindsay, Jonathan Culler, and Eduardo Cadava. New York: Columbia University Press, 1986.

———. *Of Grammatology*. Translated Gayatri Chakravorty Spivak. Baltimore, Md.: The Johns Hopkins University Press, 1974.

———. *Otobiographies: L'enseignement de Nietzsche et la politique du nom propre*. Paris: Éditions Galilée, 1984.

———. *Positions*. Translated by Alan Bass. Chicago: University of Chicago Press, 1981.

———. *The Post Card: From Socrates to Freud and Beyond*. Translated by Alan Bass. Chicago: University of Chicago Press, 1987.

———. *Speech and Phenomena*. Translated by David B. Allison. Evanston, Ill.: Northwestern University Press, 1973.

———. *Spurs: Nietzsche's Styles/Éperons: Les Styles de Nietzsche*. Translated by Barbara Harlow. Chicago: University of Chicago Press, 1979.

———. *Truth in Painting*. Translated by Geoff Bennington and Ian McLeod. Chicago: University of Chicago Press, 1987.

———. *Writing and Difference*. Translated by Alan Bass. Chicago: University of Chicago Press, 1978.

———. "Fors." *Georgia Review* 31 (Spring 1977): 64–116.

———. "Limited Inc a b c . . . " *Glyph 2* (1977): 162–254.

———. "The *Retrait* of Metaphor." *Enclitic*, 2, no. 2. (Fall 1978): 5–33.

Descombes, Vincent. *Modern French Philosophy*. Cambridge: Cambridge University Press, 1981.

Diderot, Denis, and d'Alembert, Jean Le Rond. "Interpretation." *Encyclopédie*. Vol. 8. 1765.

Diwald, Hellmut. *Wilhelm Dilthey: Erkenntnistheorie und Philosophie der Geschichte*. Göttingen: Musterschmidt, 1963.

Dockhorn, Klaus. "Hans-Georg Gadamer's *Truth and Method*." *Philosophy and Rhetoric* 13 (1980): 160–80.

Doppelt, Gerald. "Kuhn's Epistemological Relativism: An Interpretation and Defense." *Inquiry* 21 (1978): 33–86.

Dostel, Robert J. "The World Never Lost: The Hermeneutics of Trust." *Philosophy and Phenomenological Research* 47 (March 1987):413–34.

Dray, William H. *Laws and Explanations in History*. Oxford: Oxford University Press, 1957.

——. "Explaining What Is History." In *Theories of History*. edited by Patrick Gardiner. Glencoe, Ill.: The Free Press, 1959.

Dreyfus, Hubert L. "Holism and Hermeneutics." *Review of Metaphysics* 34 (1980): 3–55.

Dreyfus, Hubert, and Rabinow, Paul. *Michel Foucault: Beyond Structuralism and Hermeneutics*. Chicago: University of Chicago Press, 1982.

Droysen, Johann Gustav. *Historik: Rekonstruktion der ersten vollständigen Fassung der Vorlesungen (1857), Grundriss der Historik* (1857/1858). Historical and critical edition by Peter Leyh. Stuttgart-Bad Cannstatt: Frommann-Holzboog, 1977.

——. *Outline of the Principles of History*. Translated and introduced by E. Benjamin Andrews. Boston: Ginn and Co., 1897.

Dufrenne, Mikel. *The Notion of the A Priori*. Translated by Edward S. Casey. Evanston, Ill.: Northwestern University Press, 1966.

——. *The Phenomenology of Aesthetic Experience*. Translated by Edward S. Casey, et al. Evanston, Ill.: Northwestern University Press, 1973.

——. *La Poétique*. Paris: Presses Universitaires de France, 1963.

Ebeling, G. "Hermeneutik." *Religion in Geschichte und Gegenwart* 3 (1959): 242–62.

Ebner, Ferdinand. *Schriften*. 3 vols. Munich: Kösel, 1963, 1965.

Eco, Umberto. *The Role of the Reader: Explorations in the Semiotics of Texts*. Bloomington: Indiana University Press, 1979.

——. *A Theory of Semiotics*. Bloomington: Indiana University Press, 1976.

Ermarth, Michael. *Wilhelm Dilthey: The Critique of Historical Reason*. Chicago: University of Chicago Press, 1978.

——. "The Transformation of Hermeneutics." *Monist* 64, no. 2 (April 1981): 175–194.

Ernesti, Johann August. *Institutio interpretis Novi Testamenti*. 4th ed. With observations by Christopher Fr. Ammon. Leipzig: Weidmann, 1792. English translation by Moses Stuart, *Elements of Interpretation*, 3rd ed.; Andover, England: M. Newman, 1827. 4th ed., New York: Dayton and Saxton, 1842. Another English translation by Charles H. Terrot, *Principles of Biblical Interpretation*, 2 vols.; Edinburgh: T. Clark, 1832–33.

Farrar, Fredric W. *History of Interpretation*. Grand Rapids, Mich.: Baker Book House, 1961.

Felman, Shoshana, editor. *Literature and Psychoanalysis: The Question of Reading: Otherwise*. Baltimore, Md.: Johns Hopkins, 1982.

Feyerabend, Paul. *Against Method: Outline of an Anarchistic Theory of Knowledge*. London: NLB, 1975.

Figl, Johann. *Interpretation als philosophisches Prinzip: Friedrich Nietzsches universale Theorie der Auslegung im späten Nachlass.* Berlin: Walter de Gruyter, 1982.

——. "Nietzsche und die philosophische Hermeneutik des 20. Jahrhunderts." *Nietzsche-Studien* 10–11. Berlin: Walter de Gruyer, 1981–82, pp. 408–30.

Fink, Eugen. *Sein, Wahrheit, Welt. Vor-Fragen zum Problem des Phänomen-Begriffs.* The Hague: Nijhoff, 1958.

——. *Spiel als Weltsymbol.* Stuttgart: Kohlhammer, 1960.

Fischer-Lichte, Erika. *Bedeutung. Probleme einer semiotischen Hermeneutik und Aesthetik.* Munich: C. H. Beck, 1979.

Fish, Stanley. *Is There A Text In This Class?* Cambridge, Mass.: Harvard University Press, 1980.

——. "Literature in the Reader: Affective Stylistics." *New Literary History* 1 (1970): 123–62.

Flanagan, Kieran. "Hermeneutics: A Sociology of Misunderstanding." *Philosophical Studies* (Ireland) 30 (1984): 270–81.

Flashar, Hellmut, Gründer, Karlfried, and Horstmann, Axel, editors. *Philologie und Hermeneutik im 19. Jahrhundert. Zur Geschichte und Methodologie des Geisteswissenschaften.* Göttingen: Vandenhoeck und Ruprecht, 1979.

Forget, Phillipe, editor. *Text und Interpretation.* Munich: Fink Verlag, 1984.

Foster, Hal, editor. *The Anti-Aesthetic: Essays on Postmodern Culture.* Port Townsend, Wash.: Bay Press, 1983.

Foucault, Michel. *The Archaeology of Knowledge* and *The Discourse on Language.* Translated by A. M. Sheridan Smith. New York: Pantheon, 1972.

——. *Discipline and Punish: The Birth of the Prison.* Translated by Alan Sheridan. New York: Vintage Books, 1977.

——. *The History of Sexuality*, vol. 1: *An Introduction.* Translated by Robert Hurley. New York: Vintage Books, 1980.

——. *The History of Sexuality*, vol. 2: *The Uses of Pleasure.* Translated by Robert Hurley. New York: Pantheon, 1985.

——. *The History of Sexuality*, vol. 3: *The Care of the Self.* Translated by Robert Hurley. New York: Pantheon, 1987.

——. *Language, Counter-Memory, Practice.* Edited by Donald F. Bouchard. Translated by Donald F. Bouchard and Sherry Simon. Ithaca, N.Y.: Cornell University Press, 1977.

——. *Madness and Civilization: A History of Madness in the Age of Reason.* Translated by Richard Howard. New York: Vintage, 1973.

——. *The Order of Things: An Archaeology of the Human Sciences.* New York: Pantheon, 1970.

——. *Power/Knowledge.* Edited by Colin Smith. New York: Pantheon, 1977.

——. *This Is Not A Pipe.* Translated and edited by James Harkness. Berkeley: University of California Press, 1983.

Frank, Manfred. *Das individuelle Allgemeine. Textstrukturierung und –interpretation nach Schleiermacher.* Frankfurt: Suhrkamp, 1977.

——. *Das Problem 'Zeit' in der deutschen Romantik. Zeitbewusstsein und Bewusstsein von Zeitlichkeit in der frühromantischen Philosophie und in Tiecks Dichtung.* Munich: Winkler, 1972.

———— . *Das Sagbare und das Unsagbare. Studien zur neuesten französischen Hermeneutik und Texttheorie.* Frankfurt: Suhrkamp, 1980.

———— . *Die unendliche Fahrt. Ein Motiv und sein Text.* Frankfurt: Suhrkamp, 1979.

———— . *Der unendliche Mangel an Sein. Schellings Hegelkritik und die Anfänge der Marxschen Dialektik.* Frankfurt: Suhrkamp, 1975.

———— . *Die Unhintergehbarkeit von Individualität. Reflexionen über Subjekt, Person und Individuum aus Anlass ihrer 'postmodernen' Toterklärung.* Frankfurt: Suhrkamp, 1986.

———— . *What is Neostructuralism?* Translated by Sabine Wilke and Richard T. Gray. Minneapolis: University of Minnesota Press, 1989.

———— . "The Infinite Text." Translated by Michael Schwerin. *Glyph 7* (1980): 70–101.

———— . "The Text and Its Style: Schleiermacher's Hermeneutic Theory of Language," *boundary 2* 11, no. 3 (Spring 1983): 11–28.

Franklin, James. "Natural Sciences of Textual Interpretation: The Hermeneutics of the Natural Sign." *Philosophy and Phenomenological Research* 44 (1984): 509–20.

Frei, Hans W. *The Eclipse of Biblical Narrative: A Study of Eighteenth and Nineteenth Century Hermeneutics.* New Haven, Conn.: Yale University Press, 1974.

Friedrich, Christoph. *Sprache und Geschichte. Untersuchungen zur Hermeneutik von Johann Martin Chladenius.* Meisenheim am Glan: Hain, 1978.

Freundlieb, Dieter. *Zur Wissenschaftstheorie der Literaturwissenschaft: eine Kritik der transzendentalen Hermeneutik.* Munich: Fink Verlag, 1978.

Fruchon, Pierre. *Herméneutique, langage et ontologie: Un disiernment du Platonisme chez H.-G. Gadamer.* Paris: Éditions du Seuil, 1975.

Fuchs, Ernst. *Hermeneutik.* Bad Cannstatt: R. Müllerschön, 1963.

Funk, Robert W., editor. *History and Hermeneutic* (Journal for Theology and the Church, vol. 4). Tübingen: J. C. B. Mohr, 1967; New York: Harper and Row, 1967.

———— . *Schleiermacher as Contemporary* (Journal for Theology and the Church, vol. 7). New York: Herder and Herder, 1970.

Funke, Gerhard. "Problem und Theorie der Hermeneutik: Auslegen, Verstehen in E. Bettis 'Teoria generale della interpretazione.' " In *Studi in Onore di Emilio Betti.* Milan: A. Giuffrè, 1962.

Fynsk, Christopher. *Heidegger: Thought and Historicity.* Ithaca, N.Y.: Cornell University Press, 1986.

Gallop, Jane. *The Daughter's Seduction: Feminism and Psychoanalysis.* Ithaca, N.Y.: Cornell University Press, 1982.

———— . *Reading Lacan.* Ithaca, N.Y.: Cornell University Press, 1985.

Gasché, Rodolphe. *The Tain of the Mirror.* Cambridge, Mass.: Harvard University Press, 1987.

Geertz, Clifford. *The Interpretation of Culture.* New York: Basic Books, 1973.

———— . *Local Knowledge: Further Essays in Interpretive Anthropology.* New York: Basic Books, 1985.

————. "From the Native's Point of View: On the Nature of Anthropological Understanding." In *Interpretive Social Science: A Second Look*, edited by Paul Rabinow and William Sullivan. Berkeley: University of California Press, 1987.

Gethmann, C. F. *Verstehen und Auslegung: Das Methodenproblem in der Philosophie Martin Heideggers*. Bonn: Bouvier, 1974.

Giddens, Anthony. *New Rules of Sociological Method*. London: Hutchinson, 1976.

————. *Profiles and Critiques in Social Theory*. Berkeley: University of California Press, 1982.

Glowinski, Michael. "Reading, Interpretation, Reception." *New Literary History* (Anniversary Issue II) 9 (1980): 76–81.

Gooch, G. P. *History and Historians in the Nineteenth Century*. Boston: Beacon Press, 1959.

Goodman, Nelson. *Ways of Worldmaking*. Indianapolis, Ind.: Hackett Press, 1978.

Greisch, Jean. *Herméneutique et grammatologie*. Paris: Éditions du CNRS, 1977.

Griswald, Charles. "Gadamer and the Interpretation of Plato." *Ancient Philosophy* 2 (1981): 121–28.

Grondin, Jean. *Hermeneutische Wahrheit?* Königstein: Athenäum, 1982; Bern: Francke, 1947.

Grunbaum, Adolf. *The Foundations of Psychoanalysis*. Berkeley: University of California Press, 1984.

Gründer, K. R. "Hermeneutik und Wissenschaftstheorie." *Philosophisches Jahrbuch der Gorres-Gesellschaft* 75: 152–65.

Guattari, Félix. "Postmodern Impasse and Postmodern Transition." *Filozof Istraz* 16 (1986): 97–102.

Gusdorf, Georges. *Speaking (La Parole)*. Translated and introduced by Paul T. Brockelman. Evanston, Ill.: Northwestern University Press, 1965.

Gutting, Gary. "Paradigms and Hermeneutics: A Dialogue on Kuhn, Rorty and the Social Sciences." *American Philosophical Quarterly* 21 (1984): 1–16.

Güttinger, Fritz. *Zielsprache: Theorie und Technik des Übersetzens*. Zürich: Manesse, 1963.

Haering, Theodor. *Philosophie des Verstehens. Versuch einer systematisch-erkenntnistheoretischen Grundlegung alles Erkennens*. Tübingen: Niemeyer, 1963.

Hamacher, Werner. "'Disgregation of the Will': Nietzsche on the Individual and Individuality." Translated by Jeffrey Librett. In *Reconstructing Individualism: Autonomy, Individuality, and the Self in Western Thought*, edited by Thomas C. Heller, Morton Susna, and David E. Wellberg. Palo Alto, Calif.: Stanford University Press, 1986, pp. 106-139.

————. "Journal Politics: Notes on Paul de Man's Wartime Journalism." Translated by Susan Bernstein, et al. In *Responses: On Paul de Man's Wartime Journalism*, edited by Werner Hamacher, Neil Hertz, and Thomas Keenan. Lincoln, Neb.: University of Nebraska Press, 1989, pp. 438–467.

————. "*Pleroma*—zu Genesis und Struktur einer dialektischen Hermeneutik." In G. W. F. Hegel, *Der Geist des Christentums. Schriften 1796–1800*, edited by Werner Hamacher. Berlin: Ullstein, 1978.

——— . "The World *Wolke*—If It Has One." *Studies in Twentieth Century Literature* 11, No., 1 (Fall, 1986): 133–62.

Handleman, Susan. "Jacques Derrida and the Heretic Hermeneutic." *Displacement: Derrida and After*, edited by Mark Krupnick. Bloomington: Indiana University Press, 1983, pp. 98–129.

Harari, Josué. *Textual Strategies: Perspectives in Post-Structuralist Criticism*. Ithaca, N.Y.: Cornell University Press, 1979.

Harney, Maurita. "Psychoanalysis and Hermeneutics." *Journal of the British Society for Phenomenology* 9 (1978): 71–81.

Hartmann, Eduard von. *Über die dialektische Methode. Historisch-kritische Untersuchungen*. Darmstadt: Wissenschaftliche Buchgesellschaft, 1963.

Hass Jaeger, H.-E. "Studien zur Frühgeschichte der Hermeneutik." *Archiv für Begriffsgeschichte* 18 (1974):35–84.

Haw, Alan R. "Dialogue as Productive Limitation in Social Theory: The Habermas-Gadamer Debate." *Journal of the British Society for Phenomenology* 11 (1980):131–43.

Heelan, Patrick A. "Continental Philosophy of Science." In *Current Research in Philosophy of Science*, edited by P. Asquith. Ann Arbor, Mich.: Edwards, 1979.

——— . "Horizon, Objectivity and Reality in the Physical Sciences." *International Philosophical Quarterly* 7 (Summer 1967): 375–412.

——— . "Perception as a Hermeneutical Art." *Review of Metaphysics* 37 (1983): 61–76.

——— . "Towards a Hermeneutics of Science." *Main Currents* 28 (January–February 1971): 85–93.

Heeschen, Volker. *Die Sprachphilosophie Wilhelm von Humboldts*. Ph.D. diss., Bochum, 1972.

Heinrich, D., Schultz, W., Volkmann-Schluck, K-H., editors. *Die Gegenwart der Griechen im neueren Denken: Festschrift für Hans-Georg Gadamer zum 60, Geburtstag*. Tübingen: J.C.B. Mohr, 1960.

Hekman, Susan J. *Hermeneutics and the Sociology of Knowledge*. Notre Dame, Ind.: University of Notre Dame Press, 1986.

Henn, Claudia. " 'Sinnreiche Gedanken.' Zur Hermeneutik des Chladenius." *Archiv für Geschichte der Philosophie* 58 (1976): 240–63.

Henrichs, Norbert. *Bibliographie der Hermeneutik und ihrer Anwendungsbereiche seit Schleiermacher. Kleine Bibliographien aus dem Philosophischen Institut der Universität Dusseldorf*. Dusseldorf: Philosophia-Verlag, 1968.

Herrmann, Friedrich Wilhelm Von. *Die Selbstinterpretation Martin Heideggers*. Meisenheim: Anton Hain, 1964.

——— . *Subjekt und Dasein. Interpretationen zu 'Sein und Zeit'*. Frankfurt: Klostermann, 1974.

Hinman, Lawrence M. "Quid facti or quid juris?: The Fundamental Ambiguity of Gadamer's Understanding of Hermeneutics." *Philosophy and Phenomenological Research* 40 (1980): 512–35.

Hirsch, E. D., Jr. *The Aims of Interpretation*. Chicago: University of Chicago Press, 1976.

————. *Validity in Interpretation.* New Haven, Conn.: Yale University Press, 1967.

Hodges, H. A. *The Philosophy of Wilhelm Dilthey.* London: Routledge and Kegan Paul, 1952.

Hogan, John. "Gadamer and the Hermeneutical Experience." *Philosophy Today* 20 (1976): 3–12.

Hollinger, Robert, editor. *Hermeneutics and Praxis.* Notre Dame, Ind: University of Notre Dame Press, 1985.

————. "Practical Reason and Hermeneutics." *Philosophy and Rhetoric* 18, no. 2 (1985): 113–22.

Hookway, Christopher, and Pettit, Philip, editors. *Action and Interpretation.* Cambridge: Cambridge University Press, 1978.

Howard, Roy J. *Three Faces of Hermeneutics: An Introduction to Current Theories of Understanding.* Berkeley: University of California Press, 1982.

Hoy, David Couzens. *The Critical Circle. Literature, History, and Philosophical Hermeneutics.* Berkeley: University of California Press, 1978.

————. "Forgetting the Text: Derrida's Critique of Hermeneutics." *boundary 2* 8 (Fall 1979): 223–35.

————. "Hermeneutic Circularity, Indeterminacy and Incommensurability." *New Literary History* 10, no.1 (1978):161–73.

————. "Must We Say What We Mean?" *Review of the University of Ottawa* 50 (1980): 411–26.

————. "Taking History Seriously: Foucault, Gadamer, Habermas." *Union Seminary Quarterly Review* 34 (Winter 1979): 85–95.

Hufnagel, E. *Einführung in die Hermeneutik.* Stuttgart: Kohlhammer, 1976.

Humboldt, Wilhelm von. *Gesammelte Schriften.* Edited by A. Leitzmann et al. Academy of Sciences. 17 vols. Berlin: B. Behr, 1903–16. Rpt. Berlin: Walter de Gruyter, 1968.

Humphrey, Laurentius. *De ratione interpretandi libris III.* Basel: n.p., 1559.

Husserl, Edmund. *Cartesian Meditations: An Introduction to Phenomenology.* Translated by Dorion Cairns. The Hague: Nijhoff, 1960.

————. *The Crisis of European Sciences and Transcendental Phenomenology: An Introduction to Phenomenological Philosophy.* Translated and introduced by David Carr. Evanston, Ill.: Northwestern University Press, 1970.

————. *Ideas: General Introduction to Pure Phenomenology.* Translated by W. R. Boyce Gibson. New York: Collier Books, 1962.

————. *Logical Investigations.* 2 vols. Translated by J. N. Findlay (from the second German edition). London: Routledge and Kegan Paul. New York: The Humanities Press, 1976.

————. *The Phenomenology of Internal Time Consciousness.* Edited by Martin Heidegger. Translated by James S. Churchill. Introduction by Calvin O. Schrag. Bloomington: Indiana University Press, 1964.

Hyde, Michael J. "Philosophical Hermeneutics and the Communicative Experience." *Man and World* 13 (1980): 81–98.

Ihde, Don. *Hermeneutic Phenomenology: The Philosophy of Paul Ricoeur.* Evanston, Ill.: Northwestern University Press, 1971.

————— . "Interpreting Hermeneutics." *Man and World* 13 (1980): 325–44.
IJsseling, Samuel. "Hermeneutics and Textuality." *Research in Phenomenology* 9 (1979): 1–16.
Ineichen, Hans. *Erkenntnistheorie und geschichtlichgesellschaftliche Welt: Diltheys Logik der Geisteswissenschaften.* Frankfurt: Klostermann, 1975.
Ingarden, Roman. *The Cognition of the Literary Work of Art.* Translated by Ruth Ann Crowley and Kenneth R. Olson. Evanston, Ill.: Northwestern University Press, 1973.
————— . *The Literary Work of Art. An Investigation on the Borderline of Ontology, Logic, and Theory of Literature. With an Appendix on the Functions of Language in the Theater.* Translated and introduced by George G. Grabowicz. Evanston, Ill.: Northwestern University Press, 1973.
Ingram, David B. *Habermas and the Dialectic of Reason.* New Haven, Conn.: Yale University Press, 1987.
————— . "Hermeneutics and Truth." *Journal of the British Society for Phenomenology* 15 (1984): 62–76.
————— . "The Historical Genesis of the Gadamer-Habermas Controversy." *Auslegung* 10 (1983): 86–151.
Iser, Wolfgang. *The Act of Reading: A Theory of Aesthetic Response.* Baltimore, Md.: Johns Hopkins University Press, 1978.
————— . *The Implied Reader.* Baltimore, Md.: Johns Hopkins University Press, 1974.
Jalbert, John E. "Hermeneutics or Phenomenology: Reflections on Husserl's Historical Meditations as a 'Way' into Transcendental Phenomenology." *Graduate Faculty Philosophy Journal* 8 (1982): 98–132.
Jameson, Fredric. *Marxism and Form: Twentieth-Century Dialectical Theories of Literature.* Princeton, N.J.: Princeton University Press, 1971.
————— . *The Political Unconscious: Narrative as a Socially Symbolic Act.* Ithaca, N.Y.: Cornell University Press, 1981.
————— . *The Prison House of Language: A Critical Account of Structuralism and Russian Formalism.* Princeton, N.J.: Princeton University Press, 1974.
————— . "Figural Relativism, or the Poetics of Historiography." (Review of Hayden White's *Metahistory*) *Diacritics* 6 (Spring 1976): 2–9.
————— . "Ideology, Narrative Analysis, and Popular Culture." *Theory and Society* 4 (1977): 543–59.
————— . "Magical Narratives: Romance as Genre." *New Literary History* 7 (Autumn 1975): 135–63.
————— . "Marxism and Historicism." *New Literary History* 11 (Autumn 1979): 41–73.
————— . "Postmodernism, or the Cultural Logic of Late Capitalism." *New Left Review* 146 (July–August 1984): 53–92.
Japp, Uwe. *Hermeneutik. Der theoretische Diskurs, die Literatur und die Konstruktion ihres Zusammenhanges in den philologischen Wissenschaften.* Munich: Fink Verlag, 1977.
Jauss, Hans Robert. *Aesthetic Experience and Literary Hermeneutics.* Translated by Michael Shaw. Minneapolis: University of Minnesota Press, 1982.

————. *Toward an Aesthetic of Reception.* Translated by Timothy Bahti. Minneapolis: University of Minnesota Press, 1982.

————. "The Limits and Tasks of Literary Hermeneutics." *Diogenes* 17 (1980): 92–119.

Jay, Martin. "Should Intellectual History Take a Linguistic Turn? Reflections on the Habermas-Gadamer Debate." In *Modern European Intellectual History*, edited by Dominick LaCapra and Stephen L. Kaplan. Ithaca, N.Y.: Cornell University Press, 1982, pp. 86–110.

Jeanrond, Werner G. *Text and Interpretation as Categories of Theological Thinking.* Translated by Thomas J. Wilson. New York: Crossroad, 1988.

Johnson, Barbara. *The Critical Difference.* Baltimore, Md.: Johns Hopkins University Press, 1982.

————. *A World of Difference.* Baltimore, Md.: Johns Hopkins University Press, 1987.

Jolles, Andre. *Einfache Formen: Legende, Sage, Mythe, Rätsel, Spruch, Kasus, Memorabile, Märchen, Witz.* Darmstadt: Wissenschaftliche Buchgesellschaft, 1958.

Juhl, P. D. *Interpretation: An Essay in the Philosophy of Literary Criticism.* Princeton, N.J.: Princeton University Press, 1980.

Kainz, Friedrich. *Psychologie der Sprache.* 4 vols. Stuttgart: Ferdinand Enke Verlag, 1940–56.

Kamper, Dietmar. "Hermeneutik-Theorie einer Praxis?" *Zeitschrift für Allgemeine Wissenschaftstheorie* 5 (1974): 39–53.

Kemp, Peter. "Phänomenologie und Hermeneutik in der Philosophie Paul Ricoeurs." *Zeitschrift für Theologie und Kirche* 67: (1970) 335–47.

Kermode, Frank. *The Genesis of Secrecy: On the Interpretation of Narrative.* Cambridge, Mass.: Harvard University Press, 1979.

————. "Institutional Control of Interpretation." *Salmagundi*, no. 43 (Winter 1979): 72–86.

Kimmerle, Heinz. *Philosophie der Geisteswissenschaften als Kritik ihrer Methoden.* The Hague: Nijhoff, 1978.

————. "Die Funktion der Hermeneutik in den positiven Wissenschaften." *Zeitschrift für allgemeine Wissenschaftstheorie* 5 (1974): 54–73.

————. "Hermeneutische Theorie oder ontologische Hermeneutik." *Zeitschrift für Theologie und Kirche* 61 (1962): 114–30.

————. "Metahermeneutik, Application, hermeneutische Sprachbildung." *Zeitschrift für Theologie und Kirche* 63 (1964): 221–35.

Kirkland, Frank M. "Gadamer and Ricoeur: The Paradigm of the Text." *Graduate Faculty Philosophy Journal* 6 (Winter 1977): 131–44.

Kisiel, Theodore. "The Happening of Tradition: The Hermeneutics of Gadamer and Heidegger." *Man and World* 2 (1969): 358–85.

Klassen Grover, Julie Ann. "August Boeckh's *Hermeneutik* and its relation to contemporary scholarship." Ph.D. diss., Stanford University, 1972.

Klein, Jürgen. *Beyond Hermeneutics: Zur Philosophie der Literatur und Geisteswissenschaften.* Essen: Blaue Eule, 1985.

Kockelmans, Joseph J. *Hermeneutic Phenomenology—1988.* Lanham, Md.: University Press of America, 1988.

———. *Martin Heidegger: A First Introduction to His Philosophy.* Pittsburgh, Pa.: Duquesne University Press, 1965.

———. *On Heidegger and Language.* Evanston, Ill.: Northwestern University Press, 1972.

———, editor. *Phenomenology. The Philosophy of Edmund Husserl and Its Interpretation.* Garden City, N.Y.: Anchor Books (Doubleday), 1967.

———. "Destructive Retrieval and Hermeneutic Phenomenology in *Being and Time.*" *Research in Phenomenology* 7 (1977): 106–37.

———. "On Myth and Its Relationship to Hermeneutics." *Cultural Hermeneutics* 1 (April 1973): 47–86.

———. "Toward an Interpretive or Hermeneutic Social Science." *Graduate Faculty Philosophy Journal* 5 (1975): 73–96.

Kortian, Garbis. *Metacritique: The Philosophical Argument of Jürgen Habermas.* Translated by John Raffan. Introduction by Charles Taylor and Alan Montefiore. Cambridge: Cambridge University Press, 1980.

Kristeva, Julia. *Desire In Language: A Semiotic Approach to Literature and Art.* Edited by Leon S. Roudiez. Translated by Thomas Gara, Leon Roudiez, and Alice Jardine. New York: Columbia University Press, 1980.

———. *Powers of Horror: An Essay on Abjection.* Translated by Leon Roudiez. New York: Columbia University Press, 1984.

———. *Revolution in Poetic Language.* Translated by Alice Jardine and Leon Roudiez. New York: Columbia University Press, 1984.

———. *Semeiotikè: Recherches pour une sémanalyse.* Paris: Éditions du Seuil, 1969.

———. *Le Texte du Roman: Approche sémiologique d'une structure discursive transformationnelle.* The Hague: Mouton, 1970.

———. "Women's Time." Translated by Alice Jardine and Harry Blake. *Signs: Journal of Women in Culture and Society* 7, no. 1 (1981): 13–35..

Krüger, Gerhard. *Freiheit und Weltverwaltung: Aufsätze zur Philosophie der Geschichte.* Freiburg and Munich: Alber, 1958.

———. *Grundfragen der Philosophie: Geschichte, Wahrheit, Wissenschaft.* Frankfurt: Klostermann, 1958.

Kuhn, Thomas S. *The Essential Tension: Selected Studies in Scientific Tradition and Change.* Chicago: University of Chicago Press, 1977.

———. *The Structure of Scientific Revolutions.* 2nd ed. Chicago: University of Chicago Press, 1970.

Kunne-Ibsch, Elrud. "Rezeptionsforschung: Konstanten und Varianten eines literaturwissenschaftlichen Konzepts in Theorie und Praxis." *Amsterdamer Beiträge* (1974):1–36.

Kuypers, K. "Hermeneutik und die Interpretation der Logos-Idee." *Revue Internationale de Philosophie* 29 (1970): 52–77.

Labroisse, Gerd. "Überlegungen zu einem Interpretations-Modell." *Amsterdamer Beiträge* (1974): 149–61.

Lacan, Jacques. *Écrits de Jacques Lacan: Le champ freudien*. Paris: Éditions du Seuil, 1967.

———. "The Insistence of the Letter in the Unconscious." *Yale French Studies*, nos. 36–37 (1967): 112–47.

LaCapra, Dominick. *Rethinking Intellectual History: Texts, Contexts, Language*. Ithaca, N.Y.: Cornell University Press, 1983.

Lawson, Hilary. *Reflexivity: The Post-Modern Predicament*. La Salle, Ill.: Open Court Press, 1985.

Leibfried, E. *Kritische Wissenschaft vom Text*. Stuttgart: Metzler, 1970.

Lentricchia, Frank. *After the New Criticism*. Chicago: University of Chicago Press, 1980.

Levi, Albert William. "De interpretatione: Cognition and Context in the History of Ideas." *Critical Inquiry* 3, no.1 (1976): 153–78.

Licher, Edmund. "Kommunikationstheoretische Aspekte der Analyse einiger Gedichte Bertolt Brechts." *Amsterdamer Beiträge* (1974): 163–211.

Linge, David E. "Dilthey and Gadamer: Two Theories of Historical Understanding." *Journal of the American Academy of Religion* 41 (1973): 536–53.

Llewelyn, John. *Beyond Metaphysics? The Hermeneutical Circle in Contemporary Continental Philosophy*. Atlantic-Highlands, N.J.: Humanities Press, 1985.

———. *Derrida on the Threshold of Sense*. New York: St. Martin's Press, 1986.

Lyotard, Jean-François. *The Differend: Phrases In Dispute*. Translated by Georges Van Den Abbeele. Minneapolis: University of Minnesota Press, 1988.

———. *The Postmodern Condition: A Report on Knowledge*. Translated by Geoff Bennington and Brian Massumi. Minneapolis: University of Minnesota Press, 1984.

MacCannell, Dean, and MacCannell, Juliet Flower. *The Time of the Sign: A Semiotic Interpretation of Modern Culture*. Bloomington: Indiana University Press, 1982.

McCarthy, Thomas. *The Critical Theory of Jürgen Habermas*. Cambridge, Mass.: MIT Press, 1978.

———. "On Misunderstanding 'Understanding.' " *Theory and Decision* 3 (June 1973): 351–69.

Macquarrie, John. *An Existentialist Theology. A Comparison of Heidegger and Bultmann*. London: SCM Press, 1955.

Magliola, Robert. *Phenomenology and Literature*. West Lafayette, Ind.: Purdue University Press, 1977.

Makkreel, Rudolf. *Dilthey, Philosopher of the Human Studies*. Princeton, N.J.: Princeton University Press, 1975.

———. "Dilthey and Universal Hermeneutics." In *European Philosophy and the Human and Social Sciences*, edited by Simon Glynn. Hampshire: Gower Press, 1984, pp. 1–19.

———. "Hermeneutics and the Limits of Consciousness." *Nous* 21 (March 1987): 7–18.

———. "Tradition and Orientation in Hermeneutics." *Research in Phenomenology* 16 (1986): 73–85.

Malet, André. *The Thought of Rudolf Bultmann.* Translated by R. Strachan. Preface by Rudolf Bultmann. New York: Doubleday, 1971.

Maraldo, John C. *Der Hermeneutische Zirkel: Untersuchungen zu Schleiermacher, Dilthey und Heidegger.* Freiburg and Munich: Verlag Karl Alber, 1974.

Marassi, Massino. "The Hermeneutics of Rhetoric in Heidegger." Translated by Kiaran O'Malley. *Philosophy and Rhetoric* 19, no. 2 (1986): 79–98.

Marx, Werner. *Heidegger and the Tradition.* Translated by Theodore Kisiel and Murray Greene. Introduced by Theodore Kisiel. Evanston, Ill.: Northwestern University Press, 1972.

Mazzeo, John Anthony. *Varieties of Interpretation.* Notre Dame, Ind.: University of Notre Dame Press, 1978.

Meier, Georg Friedrich. *Versuch einer allgemeinen Auslegungskunst.* (Halle, 1757) Düsseldorf: Stern-Verlag, 1965.

Meinecke, Friedrich. *Historism: The Rise of a New Historical Outlook.* Translated by J. E. Anderson. London: Routledge and Kegan Paul, 1972.

Melville, Stephen W. *Philosophy Beside Itself: On Deconstruction and Modernism.* Minneapolis: University of Minnesota Press, 1986.

Mendelson, Jack. "The Habermas/Gadamer Debate." *New German Critique* 18 (1979): 44–73.

Merleau-Ponty, Maurice. *Phenomenology of Perception.* Translated by Colin Smith. London: Routledge and Kegan Paul, 1962.

——— . *Signs.* Translated and introduced by Richard C. McCleary. Evanston, Ill.: Northwestern University Press, 1964.

——— . "Eye and Mind." Translated by Carleton Dallery. In *The Primacy of Perception and Other Essays*, edited by James M. Edie. Evanston, Ill.: Northwestern University Press, 1964.

Misch, Georg. *Lebensphilosophie und Phänomenologie: Eine Auseinandersetzung der Diltheyschen Richtung mit Heidegger und Husserl.* Leipzig: Teubner, 1931.

Misgeld, Dieter. "Critical Hermeneutics Versus Neo-Parsonianism." *New German Critique* 35 (Spring–Summer 1985): 55–82.

Mohanty, J. N. *Edmund Husserl's Theory of Meaning.* The Hague: Nijhoff, 1964.

Mueller-Vollmer, Kurt. *Towards a Phenomenological Theory of Literature. A Study of Wilhelm Dilthey's Poetik.* The Hague: Mouton, 1963.

——— . "From Poetics to Linguistics: Wilhelm von Humboldt and the Romantic Idea of Language." In *Le Groupe de Coppet. Actes et documents du deuxième Colloque de Coppet, 1974.* Paris and Geneva: Champion and Slatkine, 1977, pp. 195–215.

——— , editor. *The Hermeneutics Reader.* New York: Continuum Books, 1985.

Murphy, John W. "Cultural Manifestations of Postmodernism." *Philosophy Today* 30 (Winter 1986):346–53.

Nancy, Jean-Luc. *Das aufgegebene Sein.* Berlin: Alphäus, 1982.

——— . *Le discours de la syncope. I. Logodaedalus.* Paris: Flammarion, 1976.

——— . *Ego Sum.* Paris: Flammarion, 1979.

——— . *Des lieux divins.* Paris: T.E.R., 1987.

——— . *L'oubli de la philosophie.* Paris: Éditions Galilée, 1986.

―――. *Le partage des voix*. Paris: Éditions Galilée, 1982.

―――. *La remarque spéculative*. Paris: Éditions Galilée, 1973.

―――. "Philosophie und Bildung." In *Wer hat Angst vor des Philosophie?* Paderborn: Schöningh, 1981.

―――. "La thése de Nietzsche sur la téléologie." In *Nietzsche aujourd'hui*, vol. I. Paris: Union Générale d' Éditions, 1973 pp. 57–80.

Nancy, Jean-Luc, and Lacoue-Labarthe, Philippe. *The Literary Absolute: The Theory of Literature in German Romanticism*. Translated by Philip Barnard and Cheryl Lester. Albany: State University of New York Press, 1988.

Nassen, Ulrich, editor. *Studien zur Entwicklung einer materialen Hermeneutik*. Munich: Fink Verlag, 1979.

―――. *Texthermeneutik: Geschichte, Aktualität, Kritik*. Paderborn: Schöningh, 1979.

Natanson, Maurice. *Edmund Husserl. Philosopher of Infinite Tasks*. Evanston, Ill.: Northwestern University Press, 1973.

―――. *Literature, Philosophy, and the Social Sciences: Essays in Existentialism and Phenomenology*. The Hague: Nijhoff, 1962.

Nehamas, Alexander. *Nietzsche: Life as Literature*. Cambridge, Mass.: Harvard University Press, 1985.

Nicholson, Graeme. *Seeing and Reading*. Atlantic Highlands, N.J.: Humanities Press, 1984.

―――. "The Role of Interpretation in Phenomenological Reflection." *Research in Phenomenology* 14 (1984):57–72.

―――. "Transforming What We Know." *Research In Phenomenology* 16 (1986): 57–71.

Nida, Eugene A. *Toward a Science of Translating: With Special Reference to Principles and Procedures Involved in Bible Translating*. Leiden: Brill, 1964.

Niebuhr, Richard R. *Schleiermacher on Christ and Religion: A New Introduction*. New York: Charles Scribner's Sons, 1964.

Nielson, Kai. "Probing Critical Theory." *International Studies in Philosophy* 13 (1981): 81–92.

Nietzsche, Friedrich. *Beyond Good and Evil*. Translated by Walter Kaufmann. New York: Vintage Books, 1966.

―――. *Daybreak*. Translated by R. J. Hollingdale. Cambridge: Cambridge University Press, 1982.

―――. *The Gay Science*. Translated by Walter Kaufmann. New York: Vintage Books, 1974.

―――. *Nietzsche. Werke. Kritische Gesamtausgabe*. Edited by Giorgio Colli and Mazzino Montinari. Berlin: Walter de Gruyter, 1967.

―――. *On The Genealogy of Morals* and *Ecce Homo*. Translated by Walter Kaufmann. New York: Vintage Books, 1969.

―――. *Twilight of the Idols* and *The Anti-christ*. Translated by R. J. Hollingdale. New York: Penguin, 1968.

―――. *The Will to Power*. Edited by Walter Kaufmann. Translated by R. J. Hollingdale and Walter Kaufmann. New York: Vintage Books, 1968.

Noakes, Susan. "Literary Semiotics and Hermeneutics: Towards a Taxonomy of the Interpretant." *American Journal of Semiotics* 3, no. 3 (1985): 109–19.

Noller, Gerhard. *Sein und Existenz: Die Überwindung des Subjekt-Objektschemas in der Philosophie Heideggers und in der Theologie der Entmythologisierung.* Munich: Kaiser, 1962.

O'Hara, Daniel T. *Tragic Knowledge: Yeat's Autobiography and Hermeneutics.* New York: Columbia University Press, 1981.

———, editor. *Why Nietzsche Now?* Bloomington: Indiana University Press, 1985.

Olson, Alan. *Transcendence and Hermeneutics.* Boston: Kluwer, 1979.

O'Neill, John. *Essaying Montaigne: A Study of the Renaissance Institution of Writing and Reading.* Boston: Routledge and Kegan Paul, 1982.

———, editor. *On Critical Theory.* New York: Seabury, 1976.

Ormiston, Gayle L. "Already Not-Yet: Shoreline Fiction Metaphase." In *The Poetry of the Elements: The Sea, Analecta Husserliana,* vol. 19, edited by Anna-Teresa Tymieniecka. Dordrecht: D. Reidel, 1985, pp. 343–51.

———. "Binding Withdrawal." In *Hermeneutics and Deconstruction,* edited by Hugh J. Silverman and Don Ihde. Albany: State University Press of New York, 1985, pp. 247–61.

———. "The Economy of Duplicity: *Différance.*" In *Derrida and Différance,* edited by David Wood and Robert Bernasconi. Evanston, Ill.: Northwestern University Press, 1988, pp. 41–50.

———. "Hermeneutic: A Question of Understanding Sign Iteration, *Et Caetera.*" *Ars Semeiotica* 3, no. 2 (1980): 137–18.

———. " 'I am no-thing'—The Name and Cleft Reference of Wo/Man." *Journal of the British Society for Phenomenology* 18, no. 2 (May 1987): 149–61.

Ormiston, Gayle L., and Schrift, Alan D. editors. *Transforming the Hermeneutic Context: From Nietzsche to Nancy* (Albany: State University of New York Press, 1990).

Orth, Ernest Wolfgang. *Bedeutung, Sinn, Gegenstand. Studien zur Sprachphilosophie Edmund Husserls und Richard Hönigswalds.* Bonn: Bouvier, 1967.

———. "Historical and Systematic Remarks on the Relation between Description and Hermeneutics in Phenomenology: A Critique of the Enlarged Use of Hermeneutics." *Research in Phenomenology* 14 (1984): 1–18.

Page, Carl. "Axiomatics, Hermeneutics, and Practical Rationality." *International Philosophical Quarterly* 27 (March 1987): 81–100.

Palmer, Richard. *Hermeneutics. Interpretation Theory in Schleiermacher, Dilthey, Heidegger, and Gadamer.* Evanston, Ill.: Northwestern University Press, 1969.

———. "Allegorical, Philological and Philosophical Hermeneutics." *Review of the University of Ottawa* 50 (1980): 338–60.

———. "Phenomenology as Foundation for a Post-Modern Philosophy of Literary Interpretation." *Cultural Hermeneutics* 1 (July 1973): 207–22.

Palmer, Richard, and Michelfelder, Diane, editors. *Dialogue and Deconstruction: The Gadamer-Derrida Encounter.* Albany: State University of New York Press, 1989.

Pannenberg, Wolfhart. "Hermeneutic and Universal History." In *Basic Questions in Theology*, vol. 1. Translated by George H. Kehm. Philadelphia: Fortress Press, 1970.

Pavlovic, Karl R. "Science and Autonomy: The Prospects for Hermeneutic Science." *Man and World* 14 (1981): 127–40.

Pepper, Stephen C. *The Basis of Criticism in the Arts*. Cambridge: Harvard University Press, 1956.

Pettit, Philip, editor. *Action and Interpretation: Studies in the Philosophy of the Social Sciences*. Cambridge: Cambridge University Press, 1978.

Phillips, Leslie, and Smith, Joseph G. *Rorschach Interpretation*. New York: Grune and Stratton, 1959.

Plantinga, Theodore. *Historical Understanding in the Thought of Wilhelm Dilthey*. Toronto: University of Toronto Press, 1980.

Pöggeler, Otto. *Martin Heidegger's Path of Thinking*. Translated by Dan Magurshak and Sigmund Barber. Atlantic Highlands, N.J.: Humanities Press, 1987.

———. "Hermeneutik und semantische Phänomenologie." *Philosophische Rundschau* 13 (1965): 1–39.

———. "Hermeneutische Philosophie und Theologie." *Man and World* 7 (1974): 158–176.

Prauss, Gerold. *Erkennen und Handeln in Heidegger's 'Sein und Zeit'*. Freiburg and Munich: Alber, 1977.

Rabinow, Paul, and Sullivan, William M., editors. *Interpretive Social Sciences: A Second Look*. Berkeley: University of California Press, 1987.

Radnitzky, Gerard. *Contemporary Schools of Metascience*. 2 vols. 2nd ed. Göteborg: Akademiförlaget/Gumpert, 1970. 3rd. enlg. ed.; Chicago: Regnery, 1973.

Ramm, Bernard L. *Hermeneutics*. Grand Rapids, Mich.: Baker Book House, 1971.

Rasmussen, David M. *Mythic-Symbolic Language and Philosophical Anthropology: A Constructive Interpretation of the Thought of Paul Ricoeur*. The Hague: Nijhoff, 1971.

———. "Between Autonomy and Sociality." *Cultural Hermeneutics* 1 (April 1973): 3–45.

Raulet, Gerard. "La Fin de la 'Raison dans l'Histoire'." *Dialogue*, 22 (Decembre 1983): 631–46.

Reagan, Charles E. *Studies in the Philosophy of Paul Ricoeur*. Athens: Ohio University Press, 1979.

Reisinger, P. "Über die Zirkelstruktur des Verstehens in der traditionellen Hermeneutik." *Philosophisches Jahrbuch* 81 (1974): 88–104.

Rickman, H. P. *Dilthey Today: A Critical Appraisal of the Contemporary Relevance of His Work*. New York: Greenwood, 1988.

Riedel, Manfred. *Verstehen oder Erklären? Zur Theorie und Geschichte der hermeneutischen Wissenschaften*. Stuttgart: Klett-Cotta, 1978.

Riffaterre, Michael. "Interpretation and Undecidability." *New Literary History* 12 (1981): 227–42.

Robinson, James M., and Cobb, John B. Jr., editors. *The New Hermeneutic*. New York: Harper and Row, 1964.

Rockmore, Tom. "Ideality, Hermeneutics and the Hermeneutics of Idealism." *Idealistic Studies* 12 (1982): 92–102.

Rodi, Frithjof. "Diesseits der Pragmatik: Gedanken zu Einer Funktionsbestimmung der Hermeneutischen Wissenschaften." *Zeitschrift für Allgemeine Wissenschaft* 10 (1979): 288–315.

――――. " 'Erkenntis des Erkannten'—August Boeckhs Grundformel der hermeneutischen Wissenschaften." In *Philologie und Hermeneutik im 19. Jahrhundert. Zur Geschichte und Methodologie des Geisteswissenschaften*, edited by H. Flashar, K. Gründer, and A. Horstmann. Göttingen: Vandenhoeck and Ruprecht, 1979, pp. 68–83.

Rorty, Richard. *Consequences of Pragmatism*. Minneapolis: University of Minnesota Press, 1982.

――――. *Philosophy and the Mirror of Nature*. Princeton, N.J.: Princeton University Press, 1979.

――――. "Deconstruction and Circumvention." *Critical Inquiry* 11 (1984): 1–23.

――――. "Habermas and Lyotard on Post-Modernity." In *Habermas and Modernity*, edited by Richard J. Bernstein. Cambridge, Mass.: MIT Press, 1985, pp. 161–75.

Rosen, Stanley. *Hermeneutics as Politics*. New York: Oxford University Press, 1987.

Rothacker, Erich. *Einleitung in die Geisteswissenschaften*. 2nd ed. Tübingen: J. C. B. Mohr, 1930.

――――. *Logik und Systematik der Geisteswissenschaften*. Bonn: Bouvier, 1948.

Rüsen, Jörn. *Für eine erneuerte Historik. Studien zur Theorie der Wissenschaft*. Stuttgart: Frommann-Holzboog, 1976.

Ryan, Michael. *Marxism and Deconstruction: A Critical Articulation*. Baltimore, Md.: Johns Hopkins University Press, 1982.

Said, Edward W. *The World, the Text, and the Critic*. Cambridge: Harvard University Press, 1983.

Sallis, John. *Delimitations*. Bloomington: Indiana University Press, 1987.

――――, editor. *Deconstruction and Philosophy: The Texts of Jacques Derrida*. Chicago: University of Chicago Press, 1987.

Sandkühler, Hans Jörg. *Praxis und Geschichtsbewusstsein: Studien zur materialistischen Dialektik, Erkenntnistheorie und Hermeneutik*. Frankfurt: Suhrkamp, 1973.

Savile, Anthony. "Historicity and the Hermeneutic Circle." *New Literary History* 10 (Autumn 1978): 49–70.

Schmitt, Richard. *Martin Heidegger on Being Human: An Introduction to "Sein und Zeit."* New York: Random House, 1969.

Schrag, Calvin O. *Communicative Praxis and the Space of Subjectivity*. Bloomington: Indiana University Press, 1986.

――――. *Radical Reflection and the Origin of the Human Sciences*. West Lafayette, Ind.: Purdue University Press, 1980.

Schrift, Alan D. "Between Perspectivism and Philology: Genealogy as Hermeneutic." In *Nietzsche-Studien*, Band 16. Berlin: Walter de Gruyter, 1987, pp. 91–111.

————. "Genealogy and/as Deconstruction: Nietzsche, Derrida and Foucault on Philosophy as Critique." In *Postmodernism and Continental Philosophy*, edited by Hugh J. Silverman and Donn Welton. Albany: State University of New York Press, 1988, pp.193–213.

————. "Language, Metaphor, Rhetoric: Nietzsche's Deconstruction of Epistemology." *Journal of the History of Philosophy* 23, no. 3 (July 1985): 371–95.

————. "Reading, Writing, Text: Nietzsche's Deconstruction of Author-ity." *International Studies in Philosophy* 18, no. 2 (1985): 55–64.

Seebohm, Thomas M. *Zur Kritik der hermeneutischen Vernunft.* Bonn: Bouvier, 1972.

————. "Boeckh and Dilthey: The Development of Methodical Hermeneutics." *Man and World* 17 (1984): 325–46.

————. "The Problem of Hermeneutics in Recent Anglo-American Literature: Part I." *Philosophy and Rhetoric* 10 (1977): 180–98.

Seigfried, Hans. "Phenomenology, Hermeneutics and Poetry." *Journal of the British Society for Phenomenology* 10 (1979): 94–100.

Seung, T. K. *Semiotics and Thematics in Hermeneutics.* New York: Columbia University Press, 1982.

————. *Structuralism and Hermeneutics.* New York: Columbia University Press, 1982.

Shapiro, Gary, and Sica, Alan, editors. *Hermeneutics: Questions and Prospects.* Amherst: University of Massachusetts Press, 1984.

Shapiro, Michael J. *Language and Political Understanding: The Politics of Discursive Practices.* New Haven, Conn.: Yale University Press, 1981.

Silverman, Hugh J. *Inscriptions: Between phenomenology and structuralism.* New York and London: Routledge and Kegan Paul, 1987.

————. "For a Hermeneutic Semiology of the Self." *Philosophy Today* 23 (1979): 199–204.

————. "Phenomenology: From Hermeneutics to Deconstruction." *Research in Phenomenology* 14 (1984): 19–34.

Simmel, Georg. *Vom Wesen der historischen Verstehens.* Berlin: E. S. Mittler, 1918.

Simon-Schaefer, Roland, and Zimmerli, Walter. *Theorie zwischen Kritik und Praxis. Jürgen Habermas und die Frankfurter Schule.* Stuttgart–Bad Cannstatt: Friedrich Frommann Verlag, 1975.

Simpson, Eran, editor. *Antifoundationalism and Practical Reasoning: Conversations Between Hermeneutics and Analysis.* Edmonton: Academic Printing and Publishing, 1987.

Sims, Stuart. "Lyotard and the Politics of Antifoundationalism." *Radical Philosophy* 4 (Autumn 1986): 8–13.

Singleton, Charles, editor. *Interpretation: Theory and Practice.* Baltimore, Md.: Johns Hopkins University Press, 1969.

Smith, P. Christopher. "Gadamer on Language and Method in Hegel's Dialectic." *Graduate Faculty Philosophy Journal* 5 (1975): 53–72.

————. "H.-G. Gadamer's Heideggerian Interpretation of Plato." *Journal of the British Society for Phenomenology* 12 (1981): 211–30.

Sokolowski, Robert. *Husserlian Meditations. How Words Present Things*. Evanston, Ill.: Northwestern University Press, 1974.

Sontag, Susan. *Against Interpretation, and Other Essays*. New York: Farrar, Straus, and Giroux, 1966.

Spanos, William V. *Repetitions: The Postmodern Occasion in Literature and Culture*. Baton Rouge and London: Louisiana State University Press, 1987.

————, editor. *Martin Heidegger and the Question of Literature: Toward a Postmodern Literary Hermeneutics*. Bloomington: Indiana University Press, 1980.

Spieler, Karl-Heinz. *Untersuchungen zu Johann Gustav Droysens "Historik."* Berlin: Duncker und Humbolt, 1970.

Spivak, Gayatri Chakravorty. *In Other Worlds: Essays in Cultural Politics*. New York: Methuen, 1987.

Steiner, George. *After Babel: Aspects of Language and Translation*. New York: Oxford University Press, 1975.

————. *On Difficulty and Other Essays*. New York: Oxford University Press, 1978.

Steinmetz, Horst. "Rezeption und Interpretation. Versuch einer Abgrenzung." *Amsterdamer Beiträge* (1974): 37–81.

Steinthal, Heymann. "Darstellung und Kritik der Boeckschen Enzyklopädie und Methodologie der Philologie." *Zeitschrift für Völkerpsychologie und Sprachwissenschaft* 11 (1880): 303–26.

Störig, Hans Joachim, editor. *Das Problem des Übersetzens*. Darmstadt: Wissenschaftliche Buchgesellschaft, 1963.

Strasser, Stephen. *Phenomenology and the Human Sciences*. Pittsburgh: Duquesne University Press, 1963.

Sullivan, William, and Rabinow, Paul. "The Interpretive Turn: Emergence of an Approach." *Philosophy Today* 23 (1979): 29–40.

Symposium. "Hermeneutics and Critical Theory." *Cultural Hermeneutics* 2 (1975): 307–90.

Symposium. "Hermeneutics, Post-Structuralism, and Objective Interpretation." *Papers on Language and Literature* 17 (1981): 48–87.

Szondi, Peter. *Einführung in die literarische Hermeneutik*. Edited by J. Bollack and H. Stierlin. Frankfurt: Suhrkamp Verlag, 1975.

————. *On Textual Understanding and Other Essays*. Translated by Harvey Mendelsohn. Minneapolis: University of Minnesota Press, 1986.

————. "L'herméneutique de Schleiermacher." *Poétique* 2 (1970):141–55.

————. "Introduction to Literary Hermeneutics." *New Literary History* 10, no. 1 (1978): 17–29.

————. "Über philologische Erkenntnis." In *Schriften*. Vol. 1. Frankfurt: Suhrkamp, 1978.

Thompson, John B. *Critical Hermeneutics: A Study in the Thought of Paul Ricoeur and Jürgen Habermas*. Cambridge: Cambridge University Press, 1981.

Thompson, John B., and Held, David, editors. *Habermas: Critical Debates*. Cambridge, Mass.: MIT Press, 1982.

Tice, Terrence N. *Schleiermarcher Bibliography: With Brief Introductions, Annotations, and Index.* Princeton Pamphlets, No. 12. Princeton, N.J.: Princeton Theological Seminary, 1966.
Todorov, Tzvetan. *The Poetics of Prose.* Translated by Richard Howard. Ithaca, N.Y.: Cornell University Press, 1977.
Tracy, David. *The Analogical Imagination: Christian Theology and the Culture of Pluralism.* New York: Crossroad, 1981.
——— . *Plurality and Ambiguity: Hermeneutics, Religion, and Hope.* New York: Harper and Row, 1987
Turner, Stephen, and Carr, David. "The Process of Criticism in Interpretive Sociology and History." *Human Studies* 1 (1978): 138–52.
Tuttle, Howard Nelson. *Wilhelm Dilthey's Philosophy of Historical Understanding: A Critical Analysis.* Leiden: E. J. Brill, 1969.
Ulmer, Gregory L. *Applied Grammatology: Post(e)–Pedagogy from Jacques Derrida to Joseph Beuys.* Baltimore, Md.: Johns Hopkins University Press, 1985.
Vattimo, Gianni. *The End of Modernity: Nihilism and Hermeneutics in Postmodern Culture.* Translated by Jon R. Snyder. Baltimore, Md.: Johns Hopkins University Press, 1989.
——— . "The End of (Hi)story." *Chicago Review* 35, no. 4 (1987): 20–30.
——— . "Nietzsche and Contemporary Hermeneutics." In *Nietzsche as Affirmative Thinker,* edited by Yirmiyahu Yovel. Dordrecht: Nijhoff, 1986, pp. 58–68.
Velkley, Richard. "Gadamer and Kant: The Critique of Modern Aesthetic Consciousness in *Truth and Method.*" *Interpretation* 9 (1981): 353–64.
Versényi, Laszlo. *Heidegger, Being, and Truth.* New Haven, Conn.: Yale University Press, 1965.
Von Wright, Georg Henrik. *Explanation and Understanding.* Ithaca, N.Y.: Cornell University Press, 1971.
Wach, Joachim. *Das Verstehen: Grundzüge einer Geschichte der hermeneutischen Theorie im 19. Jahrhundert.* 3 vols. Tübingen: J. C. B. Mohr, 1926–33. Vol. 1: *Die grossen Systeme,* 1926. Vol. 2: *Die theologische Hermeneutik von Schleiermacher bis Hoffmann,* 1929. Vol. 3: *Das Verstehen in der Historik von Ranke bis zum Positivismus,* 1933. Reprinted, 1 vol., Hildescheim: Georg Olms, 1965.
Wachterhauser, Brice, editor. *Hermeneutics and Modern Philosophy.* Albany: State University of New York Press, 1986.
Wallulis, Jerald. "Philosophical Hermeneutics and the Conflict of Ontologies." *International Philosophical Quarterly* 24 (1984): 283–302.
Warminski, Andrzej. *Readings in Interpretation: Hölderlin, Hegel, Heidegger.* Minneapolis: University of Minnesota Press, 1987.
Warnach, Viktor, editor. *Hermeneutik als Weg heutiger Wissenschaft.* Munich–Salzburg: Anton Pustet, 1971.
Warnke, Georgia. *Gadamer: Hermeneutics, Tradition and Reason.* Palo Alto, Calif.: Stanford University Press, 1987.
Watson, Stephen. "Jürgen Habermas and Jean-François Lyotard: Post Modernism

and the Crisis of Rationality." *Philosophy and Social Criticism* 10 (Fall 1984): 1–24.

Weber, Max. *Economy and Society: An Outline of Interpretive Sociology.* Edited by G. Roth and C. Wittich. Berkeley: University of California Press, 1978.

Weber, Samuel. *Institution and Interpretation.* Minneapolis: University of Minnesota Press, 1987.

———. *The Legend of Freud.* Minneapolis: University of Minnesota Press, 1982.

Weimar, Klaus. *Historische Einleitung zur literaturwissenschaftlichen Hermeneutik.* Tübingen: J. C. B. Mohr, 1975.

Weinsheimer, Joel C. *Gadamer's Hermeneutics: A Reading of Truth and Method.* New Haven, Conn.: Yale University Press, 1985.

———. " 'London' and the Fundamental Problem of Hermeneutics." *Critical Inquiry* 9 (1982): 303–22.

Wellek, René. "Wilhelm Dilthey." *A History of Modern Criticism. 1750–1950.* Vol. 5. New Haven, Conn.: Yale University Press, 1965, pp. 320–35.

Wellmer, Albrecht. *Critical Theory of Society,* Translated by John Cumming. New York: Herder and Herder, 1971.

———. "On the Dialectic of Modernism and Postmodernism." *Praxis International* 4 (January 1985): 337–62.

West, Philip. "The Redundant Labyrinth." *Salmagundi,* no. 46 (Fall 1979): 58–83.

Westphal, Merold. "Hegel, Pannenburg, and Hermeneutics." *Man and World* 4 (1971): 276–93.

White, Hayden. *Metahistory: The Historical Imagination in Nineteenth-Century Europe.* Baltimore, Md.: Johns Hopkins University Press, 1974.

———. *Tropics of Discourse: Essays in Cultural Criticism.* Baltimore, Md.: Johns Hopkins University Press, 1978.

———. "The Problem of Change in Literary History." *New Literary History* 7 (Autumn 1975): 97–111.

Whorf, Benjamin L. *Language, Thought, and Reality: Selected Writings.* Cambridge, Mass.: Technology Press of MIT, 1956.

Wimsatt, William K., Jr. *The Verbal Icon: Studies in the Meaning of Poetry.* Lexington: University of Kentucky Press, 1954.

Winch, Peter. *The Idea of a Social Science and Its Relation to Philosophy.* London: Routledge and Kegan Paul, 1958.

Wittgenstein, Ludwig. *Philosophical Investigations.* Translated by G. E. M. Anscombe. Oxford: Basil Blackwell, 1958.

Wolf, Friedrich August. *Vorlesung über die Enzyklopädie der Altertumswissenschaft.* Leipzig: Lehnhold, 1831.

Wolff, Christian. *Vernünftige Gedanken. Von den Kräften des menschlichen Verstandes und ihrem richtigen Gebrauche. Gesammelte Werke.* Edited by H. W. Arndt. Hildescheim: Olms, 1965.

Wolff, Janet. *Hermeneutic Philosophy and the Sociology of Art.* London: Routledge and Kegan Paul, 1975.

Wood, Charles Monroe. *Theory and Religious Understanding: A Critique of the Hermeneutics of Joachim Wach.* Missoula, Mont.: Scholars Press, 1975.

Zedler, J. H. "Hermeneutik." *Grosses vollständiges Universallexicon aller Künste und Wissenschaften*. Vol. 12. Halle and Leipzig: J. H. Zedler, 1735, pp.1729–33.

Zimmermann, Jörg. *Wittgensteins sprachphilosophische Hermeneutik*. Frankfurt: Klostermann, 1975.

Zockler, Christofer. *Dilthey und die Hermeneutik*. Stuttgart: Metzler Verlag, 1975.

Contributors

Friedrich Ast (1778–1841), one of the nineteenth century's leading philologists, played a central role in the development of hermeneutic theory and the hermeneutic tradition.

Emilio Betti (1890–1969) was an Italian historian of law. In addition to writing two major methodological treatises on hermeneutics, he founded an Institute for Interpretation Theory in Rome which specialized in juridical hermeneutics.

Wilhelm Dilthey (1833–1911) studied theology at Heidelberg before moving to Berlin where he completed his doctorate in philosophy in 1864. He taught philosophy at Basel, Kiel, and Breslau before returning to Berlin in 1882, where he occupied the Chair, until 1905, once held by Hegel.

Hans-Georg Gadamer (1900–   ) is currently Professor of Philosophy Emeritus at the Universität in Heidelberg where he taught from 1949 until 1968. Prior to his appointment at Heidelberg, he taught at Leipzig and Frankfurt. He has held a long-standing appointment at Boston College. One of the best known students of Heidegger, Gadamer has been a leading proponent of "philosophical hermeneutics" in Europe and the United States. In addition to published works in hermeneutics, Gadamer has published widely on Plato, Kant, Hegel, and Heidegger.

Jürgen Habermas (1929–   ) has been Professor of Philosophy at the Universität in Frankfurt since 1964; he is also Director of the Max Planck Institute for Social Sciences in Starnberg. His early writings drew upon the writings of the American Pragmatists and focused on the critique of ideology. His more recent *Theory of Communicative Action* and discussions of questions regarding modernity and postmodernity have kept him at the forefront of German critical theory.

Martin Heidegger (1889–1976) taught philosophy at Marburg before being appointed in 1928 to the Chair of Philosophy at Freiburg once held by Husserl. Aside from a six year period (1945–51) in which he was suspended from the university by the French military government for his activities during the reign of National Socialism in Germany, he remained in Freiburg until 1967, lecturing and writing on German and Greek philosophy.

Gayle L. Ormiston (1951–) is Associate Professor in the Department of Philosophy and the Institute for Applied Linguistics at Kent State University. His published articles and books span a wide range of interests in contemporary philosophy, especially the relation between questions of postmodernity, narrative and discourse analysis and the study of science and technology.

Paul Ricoeur (1913–) has taught for many years at the Université de Paris X (Nanterre) and at the University of Chicago where he is John Nuveen Professor Emeritus in the Divinity School and the Department of Philosophy. He has published widely on issues related to contemporary French and German philosophy, literary theory, hermeneutics and semiology, and theology. His most recent work is the three-volume *Time and Narrative*.

Friedrich Daniel Ernst Schleiermacher (1768–1834) held the Chair in Protestant Theology at the University of Berlin from 1810 until 1834. Associated with both German Idealist philosophy and Romanticism, Schleiermacher is perhaps is best known for his translations of and commentaries on the dialogues of Plato.

Alan D. Schrift (1955–) teaches at Grinnell College where he is Assistant Professor of Philosophy. His published articles treat issues in contemporary German and French philosophy, especially those of interpretation, authority, and textuality in Nietzsche, Heidegger, Derrida, Foucault, and Sartre. He is completing a book-length manuscript entitled *Nietzsche and the Question of Interpretation: Between Hermeneutics and Deconstruction*.

Index

action, 101
action, communicative, 307, 315, 317
actoris, mens, 291
Adorno, Theodor, 312
alienation, 149, 150
alienation, speechless, 220
allegorias, nomois tes, 106
Althusser, Louis, 313
analogy, 166
analyst, 255
announcement, 3, 5, 74
Anschauen, 119
Anschauungsweise, 64
anticipation, 320
anticipations, hermeneutic, 230, 304
Apel, Karl Otto, 212 n.11, 244 n.31,
  267, 272 n.24, 281, 282, 284, 286,
  291, 312
application, 205, 281, 283, 315
Applikation, 185, 187, 281
appropriation, 122, 220, 327
Aristotle, 1, 2, 6, 8, 9, 10, 12, 27 n.2,
  31 nn.17, 28; 49, 104, 155, 158,
  158 n.3, 199, 274, 275, 293, 326
(arrangement), *Aufstellung,* 75
articulation, 121, 122, 130, 134
  of Being, 135
  assertion, 17, 126, 128, 129, 133,
    136, 153
  and fore-sight, 130
  as the locus of truth, 127
as-structure, 17
  apophantic as, 17, 128, 131
  existential-hermeneutic as, 17, 131
  primordial as, 131
Ast, Friedrich, 10, 11, 12, 18, 25, 159
attitude, subjective, 209

auctoris, mens, 291
Aufhebung, 25, 310
Aufklärung, 301, 302, 303, 305, 332
Auslegung, 16, 66, 86, 87, 94, 97,
  114, 141 n.10, 324
authentic, 118
author, 19, 74, 165
  inner life and outer life, 94
authority, 23, 237, 238, 269, 303, 305

Barden, Garrett, 211
Beautiful, 40, 54
Being, 16, 18, 116
  and language, 207
  as understanding, 17
  Dasein as potentiality-for-Being,
    116
  hermeneutical conditionedness of,
    152
  the as-structure of, 17
  the question of, 129
being, forgetfulness of, 273
belonging, relation of, 299
Betti, Emilio, 11, 18, 19, 20, 211 n.1
  four canons of interpretation, 19
Bewusstsein, wirkungsgeschichtliche,
  21, 155, 185, 207, 301, 305, 308
Bible, 90, 106, 230
Bildung, 55–56
Bleicher, Josef, 270
Bloch, Ernest, 321
Blondel, Eric, 26, 29 n.10, 32 n.23
Boeckh, Philip August, 111, 112, 159
Bultmann, Rudolf, 167, 168, 169, 170,
  171, 172, 176, 177, 178, 194 nn.1–3,
  195 nn.1–13, 195 nn.16–17, 197 n.56
Burke, Edmund, 236

Made in United States
North Haven, CT
21 August 2023

40577272R00217